EARLY WARRIOR

Paul Williamson

A self-published title
Animal Dreaming Publishing
www.animaldreamingpublishing.com

Earth Warrior

A self-published title produced with the help and support of
ANIMAL DREAMING PUBLISHING
PO Box 5203 East Lismore NSW 2480
AUSTRALIA
Phone +61 2 6622 6147
www.AnimalDreamingPublishing.com
www.facebook.com/AnimalDreamingPublishing
Email: publish@animaldreamingpublishing.com

First published 2017
Cover Design Beau Ravn
www.BeauRavn.com

ISBN: 9780995364264

The information in this book is intended for spiritual and emotional guidance only. It is not intended to replace medical advice or treatment.

Designed by Animal Dreaming Publishing
Printed in Australia

In this book, I assume that our Earth is not merely physical matter, but is a living Spiritual being, that supports us, and is deserving of our love and respect. I also presume that, as human beings, we are souls inhabiting a physical body, and when our body dies, then our souls return to the loving Spiritual Realm from where we have come. A further assumption I make, is that there is an underlying reality, which we share, where essentially, we know that all forms of life are lovingly connected, and it is an important purpose in our lives, for us to become increasingly inwardly aware of that. I suggest that all life is sacred, and we need to honour life, in all its forms, with harmony and cooperation, so we can find peace on Earth, and the Spiritual destiny of life on Earth can be fulfilled.

This book is a visionary story of a group of souls that want to help the Earth and the people on the Earth. It is set very slightly in the future, and explores the journey of these souls, both in the Spiritual worlds and on the Earth, as they train and prepare themselves for their mission, to assist the raising of human consciousness. I hope you will enjoy reading this book, and that it may inspire you.

Paul Williamson, December 2016

This book is dedicated to Mother Earth, and all those souls that want to help nourish her and sustain her. A future where we can live together in love and harmony, is possible.

Contents

Prologue

How could I end up like this? I felt so weak and alone. Whenever I struggled to open my eyes, all I could see at first, was that dull, insipid cream-coloured ceiling above me. It just dampened my Spirit. Around me, I could hear machines, and rapid paced footsteps on the hard floor. If I strained my neck, I could just about observe the green leaves of the tree outside the window. This, at least provided some comfort, for I loved trees. On many occasions, I forced my head upwards, to view the tree, even though it caused pain. The tiniest movement took huge effort. I had to face the truth in my worsening situation. My body was dying.

Nurses in the hospital ward were scurrying around, checking monitors, which were attached to my body. My two relatives who sat down nearby, were increasingly nervous looking, and fidgety. I knew that my breathing was becoming more shallow and irregular, and the pains in my chest were like a dull ache that never went away. It felt so long that I had been lying here, hardly able to move, or even talk, and having everything done for me, while feeling physically helpless. What could I do? My body was getting frailer by the day, however much the doctors pumped me up with drugs. A few family members and friends had dutifully come to visit me. But strangely, I felt a sense of detachment. There was hardly anything that I could communicate, to connect with them, and it wasn't as if they could share the experiences that I was having. My life was done, and there wasn't anything, anymore, that I could influence or fix, nothing I could physically do.

For weeks, I had been contemplating the fact that I would die, and I no longer felt afraid of it. Now, it was more like acceptance, or else I felt resignation when I had my attention upon aspects of living that I could no longer enjoy. As I turned my heart to the feelings I held for those I truly loved, I felt sadness at the separation.

Most of those that I truly cared about, had not been present at the hospital. My children were far away in other countries – I did miss them, but I did not want them to see me like this. They had their lives to live. There was also the partner, whom I had loved so dearly. She had passed away many years earlier. I thought of her, and my children often, and it was curious how, almost despite my thoughts and longings, I felt a growing sense of peace and knowing, which took away my anxiety over them. There was nothing more that I could give to any of them; they had to find their own way.

In my latter years, I had not been so social with others, especially after my partner died. Instead, I had focussed upon maintaining a simple life that I lived, and being by myself. It was not that I didn't care about others, I did, but I had sought quietness, for some reason, as I grew old, and I wanted time to contemplate.

There was something that I perceived to be inevitable about my present condition, so there was no point in resisting it, or worrying about things that I would wish to be different. At this moment where I would soon depart from the Earth plane, I felt like I was in my own world, insulated from others, and self-absorbed. But I had faith in the continuation of life after death – I did believe – and so I waited for how that would manifest. I felt that the peace coming over me was a portent of what was to come.

Suddenly, I felt jolted out of my reverie. One of the nurses came in and fiddled around with the machinery attached to my body, adjusting the apparatus to ensure that it functioned correctly. With calm efficiency, she replaced the bag of fluids that were continually injecting nutrients and drugs into my body, keeping me alive. It was quite clinical. She was a woman doing her job. As she went through her procedures checking off the items on her list, there was no point where she looked at me in the eyes – she was making no connection with me, only a little with my relatives, and most of her attention was on the rules she had to follow. If I did not have all this intervention, I would probably be dead by now. Why make the effort?

Once she had finished, I knew that I could relax again, and drift further into my musings. But as I prepared to do that, something remarkable happened. One of my relatives came over to me and brought her chair close, so that she was sitting right next to me. She took my hand very gently and sensitively in hers, and started to talk with me. Her hands were warm, and at first, I was a little startled that she would come so near to me. I could sense tension releasing from my body, as I felt the touch of her hands. It had been a long time since I experienced anyone holding my hand like this. It was beautiful.

Her actions shook my awareness. This was Pia, my niece. She had travelled a long way to see me, and was staying with her mother. I had always been very fond of her and had spent a lot of time with her in her childhood years. She had always been one of those rare people, with whom I could easily be myself. I didn't have to put on any act with her. As I adjusted, I was glad that she was giving me this attention.

I remembered how, when we had big family gatherings, she had always come to be with me, and whatever was going on, we almost always found that we were next to each other. In her youth, I used to tell her stories, as I did with all the young ones around me. But with her, I could tell that she really listened, and took notice of me, more than the others.

Now, she was recounting about some of the times we had been together, times when she had laughed with me, and when I played with her. Pia was speaking with emotion, so warmly and affectionately. It touched me, and I felt like my heart was melting. I wanted to hug her and hold her close, but I was incapable of doing that. My body shuddered a little and that was as much as I could move.

There was a little tear rolling down my cheek, and Pia looked up at me, and smiled a little, and wiped the tear away, very soothingly. She was crying then too. At least she knew that she was reaching me.

For a while, she continued to talk and reminisce, and I loved to hear her speak. Her voice was smooth and caring. She kept going, until finally, she felt that I was becoming tired, and the nurse gestured to her, that I may need a break. I was sorry that she stopped, but she continued to hold my hand.

It was strange, for my body did feel very tired. However, as my body had weakened, I had become aware of a light that helped me to detach from my body, and avoid the pain that I otherwise felt. It was an unusual but peaceful sensation that reassured me, suggesting to me that even in this most appalling physical situation, that I need not be afraid, and that all was well. I could not control these feelings, but it was more complex than this. From this light, a feeling grew in me, gnawed at me, and pulled me. It was as if, within this peace, there was also a whirling of energy that kept returning, repeatedly, with restless and impulsive yearnings. As I listened to what this light wanted to communicate, there was an urge from it, for me to move forward and leave my body soon. Part of me still wanted to stay, so I felt in conflict with this, but the enticement of being able to raise myself out of my body, attracted me and drew me, and when I considered it with any balanced sense, even with Pia's kind touch, there was not much to keep me in my body anymore.

I looked in Pia's eyes and saw the love which was there. It was the first time that she had been able to visit the hospital. I appreciated this, so much. However, even with her presence, and those other family members who came to keep me company, there were long empty hours, when I was alone, and could do nothing except stare at the walls, or sleep.

In these moments, when I had nothing else to do, I would think a lot, not only about my life, but about the topic, which most occupied me, the Earth. During my life, I had never been a very materialistic person, and had lived my life lightly, with not a lot of attachments or accumulated possessions and wealth. My focus had been on helping people's interest in nature, and I had taught horticulture to adults at the local College.

In my later years, I had become increasingly aware of the plight of our planet and the delicate ecosystems that enabled life on our world to flourish. The energy systems of our world were not working so well anymore. People were interfering with them, and too many in our society acted as though our Earth was indestructible, but it wasn't. And I had been watching this, and bearing witness to this and feeling distressed about it.

Although most people did not appear to be bothered by what was going on around them, I felt that the health of our natural world was deteriorating. This concerned me greatly, and I thought about the future of our Earth, often with heavy feelings of foreboding. In my heart, I knew that our Earth was in danger. My response, after retirement from teaching, had been to give a lot of money to environmental charities, and good causes. However, I wondered now, if this gesture had really been sufficient. I tried to search inside myself, if there was anything else I could have done? Now, as my dying breath approached, I began to feel acute unease about this, wondering if I had missed something important.

With the comforting presence of the light around me, these strong feelings of possible regret, were modified and replaced by quiet serenity, instead, but they never completely dissipated. My body had been pumped full of pain killing medicines, and because of that, I was not sure how much this medication may be numbing my awareness. However, with the energy of the light, I had more clarity, not less, so I believed it to have greater influence.

I started to dwell on the light and explore it, and as I did that, then I could increasingly perceive a sense of familiarity, that this was not something external, but my Spiritual awareness, my soul, asserting itself from within me. It felt joyful somehow. This reality agreed with what my faith told me would be so. I kept challenging my thoughts about it, but as time went on, I became convinced the beliefs, which I had about my soul, were true. The desire to merge, and become one with this light, was strengthening, every time that I focussed on it.

My relatives were still there, chatting to each other, about matters in their everyday life. Pia had come with her mother, Delia, my sister. Even though Delia was not nearly as close to me as Pia, I was still happy that she had come. Pia continued to sit quite close to me, and her hand was extended out to mine. Now as her mother was talking, Pia faced more towards her, but every now and again, she would turn back, away from her mother, to look at me, intently. And if I made any slight movements, she would be with me immediately, with her whole attention.

Just then, I felt myself struggling with my breath. Pia must have heard it, for at once, she almost jumped up, as she turned to me. With urgency, she squeezed my hand, and cried a little. It affected her intensely, when she saw that I was in distress, so I tried as much as I could, to quieten myself, to ease her tensions. And gradually I did settle once more. This went on. There was nothing, which I could do, to give her hope, in terms of my physical condition. I wished that I could. Her emotions were very sensitive. I felt her love for me then, much deeper than I had ever realised.

I did not know how much longer they would stay. Delia was looking at her watch, but Pia wanted to continue her vigil. Every expression of her compassion for me, warmed me, and I felt gratitude.

Pia's love prompted me to reflect about my partner, Elspeth. I was reminded of her by Pia's attentiveness, for Elspeth had been good and kind to me too, and we had shared many satisfying years together. I felt the tears welling up inside me once more. It had been hard to watch her go, for when she died, I had sat with her. In her passing, I could almost sense the wafting of Spirit leave her body, in the shudder of her last breath. It was an experience which had helped my faith to develop. And I had missed her terribly, in the years that had followed. Perhaps she would be waiting for me. I did not know quite what to expect. There were many others who I knew, also, that had passed. They may all be there, waiting. I felt very still and comforted as I considered this.

While Pia and her mum talked, I could feel myself drifting into my inner worlds. I did not feel myself much in my body anymore, and I found that I had to pull myself back to remain there. Pia's voice was becoming fainter and I could no longer hear her words clearly. I tried to concentrate, for it felt important to honour her, but I just couldn't do it anymore.

Then, without any warning, I was aware of the two of them standing up, and Pia squeezing my hand once more. Bending over me, she kissed me on the cheek. She didn't want to go, but her mother was not prepared to wait any longer. It was an awkward, lingering moment. Something in me told me that I would not see her again, and I sensed that she knew that too. I felt a burst of sadness with her departing. She looked at me very deeply, and paused defiantly at the door. I wanted to reach out to her. I wished I could. But then, her mother's strident voice pulled at her, and she still hesitated. However, her mother had a strong will, and must have taken her arm. She glanced at me one last time, fiercely holding onto the door, almost with panic in her eyes. Then, as her mother nudged again, on her arm, she sighed, and seemed to surrender, letting go. And so, in the next moment, she was gone.

Vaguely, I could perceive their footsteps as they went along the corridor, becoming fainter and more distant, until there was silence. And after that, apart from the workings of the machines and my rasping breathing, there were no other sounds. However, inside my mind, the energy was stirring. I could feel the excitement of anticipation building, and so many different emotions. Just a little bit longer.

I must have fallen in and out of consciousness, for I had no idea how much time elapsed. Day and night seemed to merge together, and the hospital staff changed over. Nurses came in periodically to check my vital signs, and administer my medication. I just did my best, with whatever they asked, or expected of me. Somehow, I did not feel in discomfort anymore. I guessed that I was continuing to withdraw from my physical body, and now I felt as if I was mostly out of it, without any need to pull back. There must only be a few threads of me remaining connected to my body now. It was a weird but welcoming feeling somehow. The light was beckoning me.

One of the nurses was checking my vital signs, and all at once, she glared at me, and the instruments. She must have noticed, that there had been a change, and my body was calmer and less responsive, more passive, but physically weakening. I could just turn enough, to see on the graph, that my heartbeat was slowing, and dropping in vitality.

I was aware of her agitation. While she rushed off to get help, I was happy inside. There was nothing they could do. I was going now. There would be no one there with me at the point of my death. But I felt content with that. That is how it had to be. With one final gaze, I could see the darkening sky outside, and it invited me to reach out with my Spirit. I knew that I was ready. It was my time. My physical body took that one final rasping breath and then, then I was away.

Part One

SPIRITUAL DEDICATION

JOURNEY TO THE LIGHT

Lifting slowly from that body, it felt such a relief to be finally free, and able to move again. I looked down and I could see the crumpled shell of that old body, wired up and lying on the bed, nurses now rushing in, to adjust their machines, in a futile attempt to bring me back to life. But all was in vain now with their actions, and nothing they could do, would make any difference. At last I felt that I could stretch myself and get out of that restrictive room. My soul wanted to burst free and I rapidly moved away from those staid buildings. It felt good. My awareness was widening. My consciousness was beginning to ascend along that thread of light, on the track that would lead me home.

But then I paused, for there was something important which I still had to do. It felt liberating, that I could direct myself, and I realised that I could propel myself wherever I wanted to go. Now, I deviated from the course my soul had set, for there was someone that I had to see, and in my mind, I set the intention to be in the home where Pia was staying. From this thought, I manifested where I wished to be. Instantly, I was there.

As I looked around, I could see with my Spirit eyes, that Pia was sitting forlornly on the settee, in her mother's lounge room. She was on her own, and her head was down, and she was staring, with her eyes blank. Her thoughts were with me, and I could feel immense sadness, within her energy field. For a moment, I wondered what to do, but then I knew. With my intention, I breathed love into her heart repeatedly, and asked for the love to flow, through me to her. And it did. I kept projecting the healing energy streaming through me, until I knew that she was accepting some of this. Then I spoke to her, with the purpose of reaching her mind, telling her that I was OK, imploring her to be happy. She looked up, and I could see a half smile on her face. I tried to squeeze her hands, as she had squeezed mine, but she did not respond. I am not sure that she could feel it. But the expression on her face told me that she had been affected, by the love I had channelled to her. She was aware of my presence, and I felt very pleased about that. There was a growing peace in the room. For a while, I stayed, and watched over her, and kept projecting love, until finally, her head dropped down again, but this time, it was not despair, but peace she felt. I waited longer, until I could be certain, and she went to sleep.

Now I needed to move on. My soul reassured me, that she would find her way, and I could release her; I did not have to delay my journey anymore.

It felt such a relief to be out of that body, and having completed this task, my speed accelerated, and I travelled rapidly upwards. I felt as if I was leaving the Earth far below me, and moving through realms of space. It was becoming lighter, and the warm feelings of home and well-being, were growing stronger. I needed no comfort from other souls just now, for I felt quite secure in myself. All this journey was somehow very much known to me. I was delighted by the strength of my soul. It led me onwards, with great assurance. The colours of this transition world were marvellous, and the bright passing landscapes, filled my senses with delight. Here in the Spirit World, the wonders and love of creation was undisputed and the reality of what I could perceive, was so much more vibrant and clearer, than on Earth. Part of me wanted to explore and stay with these landscapes and just enjoy them for a while. However, my soul had a purpose and a definite place where it wished for me to travel, and I accepted all these visions and layers of wondrous experience around me, as necessary stages along my way.

On a personal level, I could feel that the vestiges of attachments, longings and remaining thought forms from the physical life where I had just been, were shedding from me and releasing fast. It was not a lot, for I had already been casting away those residues, in the many days before my physical death.

Sometimes, souls would need extensive healing in the transition world, to sort out their confusions, before returning to their Spiritual home. Indeed, there were occasions when I had needed that, but my energy after this incarnation was quite clear. I had confidence in myself. My soul was leading me, and although I still felt a little separate from it, more as two parts rather than one, I trusted that we were combining our energy fields and I could connect increasingly with the thoughts and feelings of my soul, knowing that this was my essential Self.

The further I went on, the lighter the energy became, and my energy field was brightening too. At first, the realm of light around me was almost blinding to my inner sight, until I could adjust to it. The power of love everywhere was profound, but even experiencing that did not deter me. In this realm, there was a sense of acceptance and tranquillity, where souls would naturally blend with each other, while feeling at ease and distinct at the same time. This is what all souls felt. Our free will remained, and our ability to express what mattered to us. However, as light beings, engaging in our various activities, we intermingled together here, with a harmony that for people on Earth, would be very difficult to comprehend.

The energy around me was alive with vivacity, but there was also space in between. There were myriad souls and activity everywhere, and I could sense loving acknowledgment of my presence as I continued to move forward towards my goal.

I approached a familiar place where I knew that some of my soul friends would be gathering. It was here where we had always come to meet, my best and closest soul friends. We knew when we had to be here, and we would be drawn to it like a magnetic pull.

For long ages, this had been our Spiritual home, together as a soul family. We had manifested the details of it, with our shared thoughts. This place was set in restful surroundings, with nature energies, trees and water, full of beauty and love.

But we did not use our home together, so much anymore, for most of us were now more occupied in other realms. However, the group gathered now, for my homecoming to Spirit. I could perceive the presence of some important loved ones, including that soul who had been my partner, Elspeth, in that life. Elspeth's soul was one member of this special group of souls that knew me and loved me. She was among the group, waiting to see me. As I arrived, with my focus and energy, they wanted to acknowledge me, and extend to me, their pleasure, that I was in the Spirit World again. They all seemed to converge upon me, with Elspeth's soul leading them, and it were, as if, we came together and melted, in a wondrous ball of love. It was a most satisfying welcome. We exchanged quite intimate thoughts and feelings, about where our journeys had been, and it was an awe-inspiring feeling, to share with them.

Part of me wanted to stay with them and just enjoy their company and the precious environment. But again, I was drawn by something more urgent in my intentions, and although I did not quite understand yet, for it was the choosing of my soul, I knew that I had to let them go, so I could continue my journey. Only when their greeting was complete, did they accept my wishes, and then released me with love.

I felt gratitude as, slowly, I edged away from the group, and then I was zooming forward. Soon I would be there, where I wanted to be. It was a special chamber, where I was headed, and I was longing to arrive at this destination.

Normally, I would be expected to go through a debriefing process from the life I had just finished, so the various elements of my soul could once more function in unity, and bring the experience of that Earth life more fully into my soul. As I thought about it, the consciousness that I had brought from my physical life was still active, and I could tell that I was not quite integrated, meaning that I was not yet in tune with the full force and awareness of my soul. But my soul felt a compelling urge to resume its work and did not want to delay, and my soul's will, so stridently wanted to go to this place, which I knew so well. Whether it was 'need' or 'ardent desire,' I am not sure, but this was my soul's wish, to do this, before I did anything else. Consequently, I ignored the promptings to undergo a life review, even though I could acknowledge that I should. My soul was impetuous. And so, I went on.

THE EARTH DOME

The dimensions of structures in the Spiritual Realm just opened, altered shape and transformed itself, in one continuous creative motion. There was no beginning or end. The space of this realm was infinite, and yet, there were distinct places, which held their own energy and identity. Now I was starting to tune in more clearly to my soul, and I could start to remember where it was that I was going. It was like I had been in a kind of sleep in relationship with my soul, while I was in that physical body. And yet, in the last stages of my life there, when I was old and had fewer distractions on my time and energy, I had begun to reconnect again. It was no accident that I had become interested in the fate of the Earth in my later years, for this reflected upon what was my strongest passion and interest in the Spiritual world.

From my soul's desires, the place where I projected myself and wanted to be, was a place called the Earth Dome. It was called that, because it was a Spiritual entity, connected with all energy matters concerning the physical Earth, and its well-being. With everything that existed on the Earth, the essence of what was there, these life forms, had a corresponding Spiritual form. Our human perception could hardly conceive of the tremendous radiance, intricacy and love that existed in the Spiritual forms of what we met on Earth. This included the Spiritual form of the Earth itself, which could be experienced in the Earth Dome.

For some considerable while, my soul had been dedicating itself spiritually to working in this place. There were many Spiritual beings here, that were much higher than me, and I was grateful to have a position, which was helping with souls, that passed through the Dome. My job was to offer counselling to them.

Over a long period in my development, I had had an interest in Earth healing, and it was my kind guide, Astoris, who had put me forward to fulfil the placement that I had. The scope of work in the Dome was vast, and there was much that I needed to learn, but I wanted to do my best to serve in this Dome, however humble my input may be. In my heart, I felt a great love for the Earth and wanted so much for this wonderful being to be successfully maintained. Many, many souls were involved in this quest, as a project, especially now, in this crucial phase of evolution for the planet.

While some elements of my soul had been engaged in experiencing an Earth body, other parts of me were in the Spirit Realm, and they could persevere and give attention to my work in the Earth Dome. It was one of those curious facts how, as souls, we were multi-dimensional beings, and threads of our being could be in different places at any given moment. But my soul could not be engaged completely on my Earth Dome work, while part of me was attending to the physical life on Earth that I had. This was frustrating, because I wanted to be involved, and doing my work here with all my energy. I just had had to accept this limitation, for the physical life on Earth was worthwhile too. It was designed to help me to gain further Spiritual maturity. This was important for me to attain, so I could embrace greater degrees of responsibility in the Spirit World.

Now though, I was just relieved to be able to release the limitations of human existence again. I wished that I could be finished with my cycle of lives on Earth, so I could be totally free, and able to fully dedicate my soul to helping with the Earth – I was nearly there. But I had to wait, on the judgment of the Wise Ones, before I could finish.

And as I thought about the Wise Ones, I reflected upon my very own personal guide, Astoris. He was a great Spiritual teacher, and had been with me, caring and loving me for all the long eons of my soul development. Astoris was a wonderful being and I loved him very much. Often, he would be with me in the Earth Dome, but I could not perceive him just now, and so, I was happy to proceed on my own.

In front of me, was the entrance to the Earth Dome. The wall of light that served as an entry point, gave no indication of what lay inside. However, because I had a working position within the Dome, it was possible for me to pass through this wall, as if there were nothing there, but space. I did this. As I entered the outer energy field of the Dome, I could feel both excitement and nervousness.

Now I moved forward, towards the inner sanctum of the Earth Dome. There were advanced Spiritual golden beings here, to meet me and welcome me. These beings were tall and pure in their energy fields. They were the Guardians of the Dome, and I had always found them, to be very respectful towards me, as I imagined they would be, to all the workers in the Dome. They were easily able to read me and suggest where I could best go, to observe and monitor the activities of the Dome, while I became accustomed to the energy again. My soul had left my work, completely, in the Dome, to come and meet me while I made my passing from the physical world. It was good now to return. I was glad to be given this entry, and I did what they told me. By setting the thought intention, I was there where the Guardians had suggested, immediately. Simple!

My Spiritual eyes opened wider. What was before me was greatly inspiring, enthralling and meaningful. Here, there was a huge energetic sphere of the Spiritual form of the Earth, extending in far reaches. in all directions. Even though I had seen this vista many times, it was always new, and my energy body quivered with exhilaration, and I strived to take it all in. It was such an impressive sight – the colours of green and blue especially – the Earth colours – were outstandingly beautiful. And there were light beings moving around, diving in and out, their lights fluctuating with intensity, an active process that seemed never ending, and so fascinating. As my perception became more attuned, I began to distinguish the innumerable souls that were operating and interacting with each other and the Earth being. I could feel the love swell up inside of me, as I connected with this Spiritual essence of the Earth. All my senses were heightened. I loved the Earth so much, and I was not alone. All those numerous souls around me were working fervently to support and assist and merge in their efforts together.

My Spiritual eyes were drawn to the fundamentals and foundations of what was taking place. There were the ancient keepers of the Earth, who were working with composure and assurance, as they always had done, from the very beginning. They were hardly visible to my awareness, but I could sense the reverence, with which they did their work, as I turned towards them. With my inner eyes, I strained to see them, as they ceaselessly worked, to ensure that all the rhythms of life on the planet sustained themselves in harmony, so continuity could be maintained. The Keepers managed the magnetic, electrical, gravitational, and all other subtle fundamental energetic forces, that needed to operate together in equilibrium, and keep the Spiritual and physical Earth functioning. So many different layers of forces all had to be in harmony with each other, and they existed in evolving splendour. They worked, not only for the Earth, but in relation to other worlds, and the greater plan. The work of the Keepers was astounding. I could hardly understand what they did, but could more feel their presence, as a very grounding and reliable power, which operated with huge love and devotion to their task.

From the Keepers, I turned my attention to those high Spiritual beings that enlightened the various kingdoms of life on the planet, the mineral, the plant, the animal and human. Each of these high beings were distinct and had their own note, and pure intention, with so many strata of assisting beings carrying out more intermediate tasks, all with a wonderful sound of joy that emphasised how sublime our Earth really was. These beings were incredible.

Inestimable numbers of beings applied themselves to specialised responsibilities and subsidiary tasks in agreement with other beings, in a multitude of innovative blissful expressions of Spiritual energy, and unfolding creation. It was a privilege to have, even a small role to play, in all these workings, to uphold the vitality and health of the Earth being. And what happened here in the spiritual Earth Dome, did link explicitly with the condition of the physical Earth, and was like an underlying force and living spiritual organism, striving to keep the life energies on the physical Earth alive, in the best way possible.

But all this complex and wondrous Spiritual work, splendid and highly sensitive, as it was, did not ensure that the physical Earth was a healthy and happy place. For this was ultimately going to be determined by the choices of human will on the physical planet itself. And the people of the Earth could decide whether they chose to live in harmony with the loving forces of the Spiritual Realms, or not. Our work in the Earth Dome was like a backdrop to what was happening on the physical planet. There was so much potential for how the Spiritual and physical sides of existence of the Earth, could work together, for the highest good of all, but sadly, this potential was not being utilised, enough.

It was the destiny of the Spiritual and physical Earth, for both these aspects to evolve move ever closer, so that humanity could be guided by Spiritual influences and be given loving stewardship for all the life forms existing on the physical Earth. Then it would be the responsibility for people living on the physical Earth, to care for all life forms on the planet, and to do this with love. Such a responsibility was not a trivial undertaking. The plan had been generated by the High Beings, who gave meaning, to life in our Universe. It was a great opportunity, for people upon the Earth, to evolve, and open their awareness so they could work in close conjunction with those in the Spiritual worlds, so the Spiritual and physical aspect of the Earth could merge as one.

But the people on the Earth, with their free Will, had not been following this plan. The Spiritual awareness of people, except for the few, had not increased, and in many cases, decreased, to levels where communication between the physical and Spiritual Realms had become very faint and uncertain. People had discovered the power to be able to manipulate the physical world to an enormous degree, while closing from the Spiritual awareness needed, to attain a constructive outcome for the use of these capacities.

There was a simple reality, which had become very apparent within the

Spiritual Earth Dome. This was accepted as an accord, by all the main Spiritual planners involved in the Earth Project. A consensus had developed with a clear opinion: Thus, it was postulated, that if more human souls on Earth did not wake up to their soul consciousness, realise the magnitude of the task of caring for the Earth, and start to connect with the Spiritual dimension of reality, committing themselves to this task, then there was every chance, because of the power of human free will, that this whole magnificent creation of the physical Earth being, could be destroyed forever, and its connection with the Spiritual Earth Dome severed. It was hard to imagine, and it made my heart shiver, but it was true.

SOUL ASPIRATIONS

For long millennia, when souls incarnated on Earth, they brought with them, lessons, and challenges, which they wanted to meet and master, so that they could advance as souls in their own development. These challenges would typically revolve around relationships, family, money, overcoming fears, faith, loss, and power, dealing with poverty or wealth, compassion, coping with sexuality issues, and many other learning possibilities. How souls responded to challenging situations on Earth, determined whether that soul would either learn and grow, or not.

In our human life, we were not always aware of the inner perspectives of the dilemmas, which we were facing. With our free will, if we did not tune in correctly, to our best choices, we could easily make mistakes and set ourselves back. And thus, the Earth had really been like a stage or playground, where humans could experiment, explore and express their nature, in many varying ways, while attempting to gain greater soul maturity.

It was tremendously generous of our Mother Earth, to offer herself for us, to use her in this way. And sadly, we humans, had often not been respectful. The allures and attractions of the material Earth, had captivated people's desires, and had drawn humanity to increasingly destructive acts. As our capacities to act, to create and destroy, had evolved, then the very well-being and integrity of our beautiful Earth being had become threatened.

Humanity had reached the stage, where we could no longer use the Earth, merely as a playground, to express ourselves. The truth of our present age, was that collective humanity needed to learn to embrace responsibility for our actions, and become sensitive to the impact of our actions, upon the world around us. It was like a collective soul lesson. And the problem, was that many souls did not appear to be interested to do this – they wanted to continue to play, and do what they wanted, irrespective of the needs of others, and the planet itself. Too many souls on Earth, had not progressed with their maturity, as was needed. Most people did not realise the magnitude of what was happening. This was a tremendously important juncture in human history.

The choice was simple. People on Earth faced a fundamental spiritual dilemma – whether to cooperate with sincerity, and build a respectful life, as one human race, together, or to destroy everything. Both were possible. And there was this enormous struggle, because so much of humanity did not respect loving Spiritual reality and did not want to understand it, or open to it, and many did not even believe that they could do that. Yet, they did not wish for destruction either. There was much confusion and fear that was growing on the planet. People could sense volatility, and the need for change, but they did not know what to do, and how to best react.

It was the time of crossroads where humanity's salvation depended upon the bulk of people acting together, with love and care, for the sake of planetary survival. In previous times, we had been protected from having to consider making this commitment. While the Earth continued to be a playground for humanity, there were many 'free go' areas for individuals and groups, or even nations, to express themselves in all sorts of ways – to fight, to acquire dominance over others, or even to live in peace. But now the starkness of our collective task, was there, for all of us, to either acknowledge, or ignore. With each new generation, people's attitudes were becoming more polarised, and the time of ultimate choice was looming.

RETURNING SOULS

In the Spiritual world, there were now many classes and gatherings to discuss the state of the Earth. Souls were being taught about the crisis that was upon humanity and were encouraged to be mindful of this, while in physical incarnation. Some souls were too young or preoccupied to really comprehend. However, there were huge numbers of souls, who did understand, and were eager to volunteer and help.

Because of this, many souls were now choosing lessons and tasks for their journey into incarnation on Earth, where they would plan to do some service for the Earth, and some component of their purpose for incarnation, would embrace this goal. Being concerned for the needs of the Earth, during a time of challenging change, was also an important growing point for souls.

What we had to aim to do on Earth, was to be like light bearers, with love guiding us, so that the light we generated could be shared, and channelled collectively, together with the love, from other kingdoms of life on our world. This could then meet, with the overall spiritual light of the Earth and merge with that. When enough light was generated, the moment could arise where humanity reached a threshold point, and an explosion of transformation occur. Then, the channels between the Spiritual and physical worlds would open much more fully.

Striving towards this goal was the principal Spiritual force, that motivated all of us in the Earth Dome, to keep going with our efforts.

It was like a strong compelling pull that propelled so many souls associated with the Earth, to wish to be involved with this venture. We could feel so interconnected in the Spiritual Realm, and for those of us, that wanted to serve, the undertaking we all made, was to help bring that consciousness of interconnectedness, into the realm of physical life on the planet, because then, once this happened, we would all know in our hearts, how much we were truly linked together, and that we had to support each other, for everyone's sake. But it was not easy for us to accomplish this.

Thoughts and feelings had their own fields of energy, and on Earth, people would generate and express energy forms, through their attitudes and behaviour. When less clarity and care existed in the thoughts and feeling fields of people, especially on a collective level, like in the stressful rush and bustle of a City, or large aggressive crowds, then this affected the amount and degree of Spiritual light, which could gather in that area. Energy that was more of a lower vibration tended to become, either stagnant or chaotic, and would affect all people and other beings immersed in it. This is turn, would act like a blanket to diminish the shining Earth light, and what people in that vicinity could tap into, with their own inner light. Then, other more gross forms of energy, would assume greater dominance. And the consequence of this, was that people's desires then, would not reach out, but they would focus on self, and they would be less aware of others, and their own essence. The resultant deficiency of love and care increased the possibility of conflict, through people feeling isolated and frustrated.

With well-meaning souls that wanted to serve the Earth, when they came onto the physical plane, conditions were so much harder than on the Spiritual planes. Souls, when they entered a physical body, met all sorts of challenges, including psychological conditioning, trauma, turmoil, pollution and temptations. All this, made it difficult to tune in, and for people to be true to their Spiritual essence. Therefore, it was very testing for souls to be able to fulfil their Spiritual goals. Sometimes, the energy field on the surface of the Earth could be a mesh of confusion, that affected the nervous system of humans, quite negatively.

Fear was the biggest barrier that inhibited souls from constructive action on Earth. What fear did, was to collect in people, like a dense fog, that immobilised them and prevented spiritual truth from being known. It was an energy that turned away from light, and contracted. With all the violence and confusion on Earth, fear occurred to a massive degree.

Consequently, when souls set out with spiritual goals to make a positive difference, there was a lot with which they had to contend. And at the end of their lives, when they went through their transition to the Spiritual Realm, then they would come here, to the Earth Dome, so their work for the Earth, and achievements could be assessed. This could be quite a confronting process for each soul.

For those that had been successful, the energy of their achievements would be absorbed into the energetic matrix of the Spiritual Earth here in the Earth Dome, as light, and this would help evolve, regenerate and sustain our beautiful Earth on both the Spiritual and physical levels

It was difficult when souls failed to complete what they set out to do, for there would be terrible feelings of loss and guilt, about the resultant gaps in the energy matrix of the Earth. It was not an easy thing for souls to accept.

The souls that succeeded with little or none, of what they had promised to do, could not hide from this. For some, it would prompt them to try again with more determination to get it right, and they would go into another physical life with similar goals. Others though, would withdraw, and need to reflect and be counselled, and perhaps choose another way forward.

On the Spiritual planes, for the casual observer, gazing at the Earth Dome, it all appeared to be a wonderful process of love and Spiritual ease, where everything was in order and proceeding beautifully, but that was not the case, really.

COUNSELLING

What I had to do, in the Earth Dome, was to counsel souls, both before and after their physical incarnations, on matters relating to their work in helping the Earth, and assisting in the evolution of human consciousness. With souls that wanted to incorporate work to help the Earth, as an element in their human life plan, then before their physical incarnation commenced, I would be available as one of numerous trained souls, to assist them, in setting out clear purposes, and routes for them to accomplish their goals. I had to be both precise and encouraging with them, and to inspire them, with an experience of the Earth Dome, so they would know the importance of their task.

My personal guide, Astoris, had been coaching me and training me in this work, and he had been pleased with my progress, for I had reached the stage, where I could do my work now, on my own, with very little supervision. Some of the many souls doing similar work to me, preferred to work in teams, while others, like me, favoured an individual one on one approach. There was a great need for helpful counselling to be administered, because so many souls wanted to help with the Earth, and the number of souls involved with this counselling, was growing.

When they returned to the Spiritual world, I would be there to meet the souls I had coached, prior to their incarnations, and I would be waiting in the Earth Dome, to help them reflect upon, and come to terms with, what they had been shown through their Spiritual review, with the Wise Ones. It was important for me to be sensitive in the way that I addressed these souls, and I also needed to trust in my own intuition. This could be very rewarding work, especially when I helped souls to find a measure of peace.

At the outset of my work, I had to discern the mind patterns, and soul character, of the souls with whom I was working. From this, I could devise plans in coordination with their wishes, plans which would suit them, and be hopefully achievable for them, as part of their soul path, in their coming incarnation. It was like the work of a guide which I did for them, but what I did, had a very specific focus, and was not the same degree of responsibility, as with their guide, for I was not overseeing all their soul being. I took the work that I did very seriously. I was also heartened, how, because of the support that I could give, I had developed some fine friendships, with souls that had embarked on Earth healing assignments.

I enjoyed the work, and when a soul returned, having achieved all that he or she set out to do, it felt like an achievement for me too, and I was so glad that my efforts were becoming ever more successful. It was good to be gaining skills.

On the other side, doing my counselling work, I had to cope with the heartbreak when souls returned to the Spirit World, knowing that they had neglected something important, or gone down some track in their lives that had been contrary to the path they had chosen. When souls chose to do Earth service during their incarnation on Earth, and while there, they did not do it, then it was disappointing, not only for the souls concerned, but also for us working in the Earth Dome.

In counselling these souls, I had to put aside my feelings about this, so I could be there for them, and offer helpful advice. This was a process that I found most testing, for, of course, it was the souls who had not succeeded, that needed the most support.

There was a lot to my job, and I wanted to do my best with it, even when part of my soul had to be on Earth. That was why, with the physical life which I had just left, I had chosen that incarnation to be not a particularly demanding life, even though I had some patterns and balancing to do in certain situations, which I had to meet then. But I knew that in choosing such an easy life, most of my soul could remain in the Spiritual Realm, and a lot of my energy would then be present, to continue my counselling work in the Earth Dome. That is what I had done.

I noticed though, that there had been a change in me in relation to the counselling. My passion for the job was dwindling. I no longer felt that I was growing through doing this work. My achievements in helping others was very satisfying to me, and the work occupied me in a very meaningful manner. Also, I felt joy to serve others. However, all of this was still not enough. Despite the enthusiasm that I had had, I did not feel that the counselling work was what I truly wanted to do.

A PERSONAL LONGING

The souls that I helped, were ones that were engaging themselves at doing some Earth healing and transformational work, as a component of their overall life plans for their physical lives. Why could I not be doing that? I missed, that I could not be involved in doing this work on the Earth, helping directly, myself. I was not a soul that was content to stay watching from afar. My soul liked to be active.

And even more, there was something which I had seen, which had inspired me, and I could not stop thinking about it, reflecting, and wishing, that I could be part of that. My guide, Astoris, had shown me, and spoken to me about it. I could remember, when I first became aware of this. It aroused my passion.

Capable souls were being trained, to work in groups, and dedicate themselves to devote, not just some, but all their energies for an incarnation, to help the Earth, and the people on it, to transform. These souls had lives on Earth set out, that were specifically designed to meet this purpose, and this purpose alone. They were souls, who were selected for their strength and commitment, and they possessed character that would not waver in their determination, and they had hearts, which would care, and maintain their compassion.

These were the ones called 'Earth Warriors,' and they were on missions of great importance, to attempt to make a significant difference, to how the process on Earth would unfold. These Earth Warriors carried much of the hopes of the High Beings, who administered the Earth project. What they were endeavouring to do, was necessary and commendable, given how humanity had wavered from the path of its highest potential.

Astoris had told me about the Earth Warriors, and let me see some of them training. I admired these souls, and I felt a burning desire to be one of them, and to do the work that they were doing. I wanted to join with those Earth Warriors and engage in a mission, which would make a difference on Earth. That was my dream, and in my energy system, there was a force stirring in me, and I became tremendously alive when I considered this.

It was one thing, to help other souls in the Spiritual Realm, as a counsellor, and support them while they made their efforts as a small part of their overall plan. But this did not satisfy me. My soul had a long-standing relationship with the Earth, and I wanted so much, for the Earth and humanity to succeed in its transformation. I did not wish to be a passive witness, while others made their efforts. Surely, I could do more.

I had spoken to my beloved guide Astoris many times about this, and he had smiled and listened. His only guidance, was to tell me to trust, and to continue doing the work I was doing, and to put my heart into it, as well as I possibly could. This was so hard for me. I wanted to argue with him, and persuade him, to let me do it, and tell him that I was a suitable candidate, but I couldn't. As a soul, I had to show respect to my guide. If it was right for me, he would tell me.

Astoris did not dismiss my interest though. I was fortunate that special occasions arose, when I could go with him, and observe these Earth Warrior souls, as they prepared for their missions. Even watching from the distance, for I was not allowed to go too close, I found it fascinating, to perceive the intensity of these souls, their contact with each other, and the powerful commitment, which they shared in their group, to the cause that they were pursuing. Astoris made clear to me, that these souls underwent a very rigorous and spiritually demanding training. They had to grow into their tasks, and not all of them could stay the distance, with their training.

My guide explained to me about why these souls worked in groups. He told me that it was generally better for souls to plan a mission together as a group, for combining energies with others could bring strength to a mission, and in places where the Earth vibrations were denser and darker, the members of the group could support each other. Being in dark places on Earth tended to be easier for souls, when they were together, than if they tried to embrace this, on their own. Collective action was so vital in helping the Earth, and helping humanity to grow, also, because at the forefront of the inner learning needed, for the people on Earth, in their development, and the collective consciousness, there was this central theme concerning the reality of interconnectedness.

Seeing these missions preparing, did affect me. I tried to use these occasions positively, in what I had to do. Rather than being disappointed, not to be part of this, I attempted to let my awareness of the Earth Warriors motivate me, so I could continue to improve in my own actions and service.

Astoris knew how much I wanted this. Each time, I went with him, I could feel the desire in me expand further. And he could feel my enthusiasm, for my being was completely transparent to him. But he said nothing, beyond describing their work, and answering questions that I had about it.

While he accompanied me to see these souls working and training, all I could feel was his unconditional love and acceptance of me. Meanwhile, I waited and waited, hoping for an answer to my yearning. And the longer Astoris said nothing to me, the more my desire to train as an Earth Warrior myself, became stronger.

I did not know if anything would ever change, before the Earth transformation process was complete, in whatever way, the outcome of that turned out to be, and if that was the case, then I would just need to accept it. I could not push my wishes onto Astoris, and he was not going to give anything away. I watched and waited, but there was no indication given to me that I could ever be chosen to train as an Earth Warrior. If that was the case, then there was nothing that I could do about it.

Now, as I continued to gaze at the workings of the Earth Dome, I knew that soon, I would have to prepare and continue my counselling work, again, following my life review. Even though, I had felt it so urgent to return to the Earth Dome, after my last incarnation, I could not deny my discontent. I wished for a sign of change, as a progression for my own personal development. It was not easy for me to be patient.

A CLOSER LOOK

Human civilisation on Earth was changing. On a physical level, we could travel around our world with ease. Scientists now knew a lot about how the physical world functioned. In recent times, there had been tremendous advances in technology. Because of this, people could exercise control over elements on the physical Earth, to an unprecedented extent. But what about people's compassion and care for one another and other life forms? This was where the problem lay.

On a Spiritual level, there were high beings, and matrix energies from many other worlds within our Universe and beyond, that were endeavouring to help us, and raise our consciousness so we could grow in awareness for the needs of the whole, and be mindful of the great sacred gift that our Mother Earth shared with us. The main changes we needed to make, were to open our hearts, to consciously shift our focus from being self-centred, to become respectful and considerate towards all life forms, and our place with them. Then, by implication, we needed to learn to be reverential of our world, and its needs, putting that first.

It was clear that we had fallen short of where we needed to be, at this stage as a collective group. The advances in science and technology our scientists had discovered, had not been matched generally, by an increase in wisdom and awareness. The high beings were trying to giving us a boost. And many souls, from many worlds and backgrounds, some with little experience of being on Earth, were being attracted to experience physical life on the Earth now, both to help and because some were interested to gain from this experience.

It was gratifying that so many souls were committing themselves to help our world, and to embrace the aim of bringing new consciousness to Earth. Astoris had told me how even some of the High Wise beings, those higher even than him, were choosing to incarnate, as specialists, with other Earth Warriors, to place in our societies, structures that would help better to support our evolution.

The shift of consciousness was intended to strengthen, on the one hand, our individuality and the acknowledgment within each of us, of our uniqueness. However, more importantly, there was also, a need for us to ground physically, that sense of collective spiritual cooperation, as a natural forming of our life together. This was our task, to choose this, with our wills. Nobody could make us do that. Consequently, even with the influx of all this Spiritual energy, and input from very High Spiritual beings, because we had free will, it was not certain what choices our humanity would make. And the sad fact, was that there were forces on the Earth that were indifferent to this transformation, and even pulling against it.

So many people were still craving power and afraid or unwilling to shift. To those that resisted opening their spiritual consciousness, their wilful resolve to withstand change and defeat forces that challenged them, were getting stronger. Therefore, in the human societies on Earth, there was increased tension, conflict and pressure, where those that stood together with open hearts and a collective intention to manifest what was good, these people were struggling to be heard, and often suppressed, by those that did not want these impulses to be expressed. It was getting dangerous, and even while the awakening process of people was continuing, the resistance of those that did not want to shift, was becoming very reactive, and causing a great deal of damage.

I did not know how this process would advance, but for all of us, as souls, involved in this, there was the feeling, that a huge effort was needed – an effort to help people that were ready for it, to awaken to their true nature, and embrace the shift in consciousness. It could not be forced, but had to be nurtured, gently, with love and healing. We could not aggressively fight the forces opposed to Earth transformation, for this would play into their hands. Instead, we had to encourage those on Earth that had 'awakened,' to be steadfast in their approach to life, living with the principles, which would resonate with the new Earth, and give this energy a chance, to breathe and express itself.

Now, as I opened myself to it, I could perceive how the conditions on Earth were becoming so sluggish, from the resistance to change, which was present. This was affecting everyone's ability to fulfil their Spiritual purpose of Earth service. The opponents of change and transformation, the ones who disregarded care and attention to what was sacred, these elements of humanity were accumulating power, and using the energies coming onto the planet, for their own enhancement, something that ultimately could not bring peace. And this caused instability, because it placed other energies out of alignment and balance.

With damage and degradation to the environment, and the dislocation of human consciousness, the fabric of Spiritual structure of the Earth being, was weakening. The crisis of what was befalling people on Earth, was becoming ever more acute. Even some of those Spiritual Specialists, were failing with the tasks, which they had set themselves, because there was too much chaos on the Earth.

In the Spirit World, we still felt emotion, and at that moment, as I considered this, I felt waves of feeling pass through me, because I wanted our Earth to flourish, and move through this transition successfully, for the good of all. Again, the thoughts passed through me, where I wanted a chance to be there, and do some work for the Earth, myself. It was hard for me just to observe all this from the Spiritual planes, for I felt I had to do something – I felt a mixture of determination and anguished helplessness. Counselling others in the Spiritual planes, while the Earth required souls to be there on the surface of the planet, helping – how could I just stand by with this and watch?

For some moments, I turned inward to reflect and to pray for help, for I had to be selfless in this. In my prayers, I prayed both for opportunities that may exist, where I could help and serve the Earth, for these to come forward. But I extended my prayer. And I also wanted to add my strength to the work of those in the Dome, and support the overall effort.

Slowly I became quiet, as I reached out to the High Ones. As I did this, I felt some peace. I knew that the energy of my prayer was extending out from me, to where it needed to go. Our thoughts and intentions, did that. At least, this was one worthwhile act that I could do.

ASTORIS

As I became very quiet, I suddenly felt an enormous loving embrace from behind me, like a burst of loving energy, which caressed me and reassured me, and it was as if I needed to release my concerns. Perhaps my prayers would be answered. I had not realised how tense I had become within my energy field. As soon as I was touched by this presence, then I knew I had to surrender to it. It was a feeling that was so very recognizable and inwardly I relaxed and accepted what was being given to me.

Immediately, I was lifted out of the Earth Dome, and I was in a very tranquil space, alone with my beloved guide, Astoris. He was the one, who had come to me, and now I smiled inwardly, to be with him, and there was a warm glowing blue light in front of us, and all around us. It was so good to be in Astoris's company again. He was like a wise older brother, and I loved him very much. His energy was vast compared to mine, but also it could be compact when he needed it to be. The colours of his energy field were a dark shade of purple, and I felt so humble to be with him.

He opened his communication channels with me. and what I perceived first, was that he was gently chastising me, questioning why I had not come to see him, before going to the Earth Dome. He was laughing at my impulsiveness and drive.

Astoris must have been listening in to my thoughts, because he wanted to challenge and query my attitudes towards the Earth, and the ambition I had to help. He spoke directly to my mind, and wished to initiate a discussion with me. That is why he had taken me away from the Earth Dome to do this, so we could be in a more neutral space.

'What would it matter if the Earth was destroyed by human abuse?' he asked. 'How would it make any difference?' For a moment, he paused to let me consider this. 'There could be other worlds manifested to take its place. Spirit creation is evolving all the time, growing, expressing, and dying. Love is the only true reality. Why do you need to be so attached to the Earth? You can feel the love here in the Spiritual world. Nothing is ever lost. Could you not let it go?'

I knew that Astoris was testing me, challenging me to search the depths of my motives. Within the atmosphere around me, all I could feel was various shades of love and well-being. In some ways, it was quite soporific, but I did not want to give up my principles, passively. The blue light caused me to reflect, and contemplate, to go inside myself, to my core, and evaluate what I was doing.

'I cannot detach myself to pretend that the Earth is of no consequence,' I answered him. 'My heart is invested with the well-being of the Earth. I am committed to help her. When we feel love, and commit ourselves, then if we retreat from that, we will be dishonouring our intentions. The Earth being has the seeds of potential where it could transform into a place of love and harmony, and all life within it become spiritualised, and blissfully happy. This is a worthy project, and I want to align with that. If I can play a part, towards achieving that goal, and I know within my soul that I have a pure urge to do that, then I must act upon that urge. I cannot disregard the Earth as if she does not matter, just because there are other options. She does matter, and what happens at this crucial juncture, is vital, as to whether this potential transformation will be fulfilled or not. I have had a long association with the Earth, and I do not choose to give up on her now'

'Granted,' Astoris continued. 'This is true. But in your long association with the planet Earth, there have been times before when the Earth faced destructive forces, and you have tried your utmost to defend her. Your tendency has been to be zealous, to the point of obsession, and when destruction has occurred, it has been your pattern, that you have not been able to let go. You have taken it personally, and you have subsequently become bitter or defeated, and given way to dark meanderings, to the cost of your soul, just because you did not get your own way. You know that this has happened many times. How is this process now going to be any different?'

I knew that Astoris was addressing my personal weakness, as was his task, in helping me to grow. Memories of those lives where I had refused to let go, flashed before my consciousness, and I winced as I lived through those processes of destruction in various ages of Earth history and my own reactions to these processes. I could perceive my struggle, and how lost my soul direction had become, on many of those occasions. The light within me, also shone upon other optional paths, where I could have gone more positively, in those past times. What I had needed to do was to be less Ego driven, and prepared to accept help, and allow what had passed, to end gracefully.

In perceiving these inner possibilities, it heartened me, that I could gain those perspectives. I was quite excited by perceiving these alternative possibilities, and I felt lighter by considering these. My consciousness was open to seek more positive approaches now. This was good. However, the more self-pitying reactions still existed in my soul memory, even though I didn't want them. The existence of these implied that there was still a chance that I would repeat those tendencies again.

'In those lives, I tried too much to act alone and do everything by myself,' I reflected to Astoris. 'I over-estimated my own ability and relied too much upon my own will, instead of connecting with the greater good. My way forward is to work within groups and the network of love, to seek and offer support with others rather, than act separately.'

'It is good that you understand,' Astoris retorted. 'But, my soul brother, can you do it?' He was challenging me to be deeply truthful.

'When I met you now, you were on your own. You made no effort to connect with others, except in passing, when you left your body, from your last life. In the last years of your recent Earth life, you retreated to almost be a recluse near the end of that life. All you did when you passed over, was to proceed straight to the Earth Dome without seeking assistance from anyone else, acting on your own. Were you not then, repeating patterns that go back through the eons, those patterns that have limited you?'

My energy turned within, and I reflected upon what Astoris had told me. His words were true, and as much as I wanted to discount what he had concluded, I could not, and I felt shame. I could feel my light shrinking as my thoughts questioned what I had done.

Astoris must have noticed my downcast energy, for he began to laugh, and the lightening of the energy around him, was infectious. I saw a twinkling in his Spirit eyes. He was now encouraging me, to open my perspective wider.

'Come,' he told me. 'I also noticed the care and love you gave to Pia's soul after your passing, and the warm embrace you shared with Elspeth and other members of your soul family. You gave generously to charities in your last years of that life, so you have not been living on an island. Even your interest in connecting with the Earth Dome is motivated by care. I have been teasing you, to encourage you to articulate your sense of self. Do not feel down. On balance, you have been doing well. If you were now in the same state that you had been in those more ancient times, you would not have been able to listen to what I just told you. Your receptivity shows how much you have grown. As you realised, you would not also be able to perceive those other perspectives, if you were still confined by those past experiences. Let us proceed forward now, and find out how you have fared in your last incarnation on Earth. I know you have not regarded this as your priority, but it is important to complete one thing, before moving on to another.

'It is necessary for you to cleanse yourself from your last Earthly life and review what you have gained from that. Your soul is still split and exhibiting facets of the personality you had in that time, including the aloofness that you were living at the end of that life. While you have not integrated that, you are not going to be connecting with anyone very much. By now, it should be clear to you, how we need to go step by step. Do you always try to run before you can walk?'

Astoris could always point out to me, sides of myself, that I did not want to acknowledge, but he was being quite affectionate and light-hearted. I was not a soul that was so inclined to follow rules or procedures, and this was also a weakness that had been to my detriment at times. I smiled at my guide. There was nothing which I could hide from him. With his energy, every facet of my identity was visible to him, more so even, than to myself. I did not mind this, for I trusted him, and this trust helped me to feel freer. It was an enormous privilege to have a guide, so wise and present for me. He did not need to show himself around me most of the time, for I had to learn to manage my direction, and expression of what I was doing, by myself. The fact that he appeared so seldom, was a good sign, that I was improving in my development.

With that thought, I felt more content with myself as we prepared to go for my life review. Together we orientated to this, and in a moment, we were there.

Now I stood before the integration and review chamber. It was like a vast hall of pure light, and when I entered this, I would be able to shed myself of the residues of that previous life so my soul could be fully in union again. Then, when this was completed, I could join Astoris and learn how I could best proceed.

LIFETIME REVIEW AND INTEGRATION

I knew that as a soul, after every life, we would need to go through the experiences of that life, and strip away all the various layers of thoughts, behaviours, and belief systems that we had acquired. This would enable us to gain a sense of deeper truth about what had been presented to us during that incarnation, and how we had utilised our free will, to deal with all those situations. This process involved us being confronted inwardly, with how all our actions had affected others, and, we would be given reflections to help us measure the true nature of our achievements. The life review could be quite gruelling, as we encountered aspects of ourselves that we had not consciously realised, were operating. Usually, souls would have their guides, or other high and wise beings to support them and to counsel them, either during or after these life reviews, for they were the moments when we would learn, if we were growing in our soul maturity, or not. Through this process, we would discover if we had fulfilled our purpose in that lifetime. There was no escape, and no way of glossing over our mistakes or shortcomings, but when we became aware of attainments we had reached without having comprehended it, by remaining true to our life purpose, then this could elicit great joy. We would never know in advance how the life review would turn out to be.

When I was a young soul, I recalled how I felt so nervous and in trepidation before these review experiences. I had liked to consider that I was doing well, and at times, I had been so disenchanted to learn that the opposite was true, or that there had been some essential learning from a life that I had missed. From the outset, I had always been quite an ambitious soul, but that drive had also at times become impetuousness and impatience, which had got me into difficulties. In those early times, I needed much counselling from the Wise Ones to help me, and I did not always listen.

In my formative stages, much of my energy had been caught up with members of my soul group. I pined for them and loved them. I grew with them and sometimes hurt them, or they hurt me, but we always ended up forgiving each other and then being ready for another adventure. They had been at the centre of my world, but now, I did not need them so much anymore. The love we shared would always be there, but through our development, our love had expanded so we had reached the stage to be involved on a larger scale, with projects or service, that would help us evolve further. We still met sometimes, like we had, after I had left my last incarnation, and I could still associate with them whenever we felt the need, but our sense of responsibility had moved beyond our group, and we all accepted that, as we moved on with our own spheres of interest. Not all of us were on that same level of service, and some of us, like me, were still working out some threads of learning on the Earth plane, and so we had to return until we could complete those.

As I considered how I felt, I was quite relaxed about this process now. At my death, I had felt peaceful and I was hopeful that in this review, that all would be well.

Stepping forward, I entered the chamber, with feelings of wonder. The space there, was full of colours and vibration and myriads of sensations. Three high beings were there in the background, watching and observing, making comments when needed. But there was a force directing me into my memories of that lifetime. And at once, the process began. It was like an eternity as feelings, thoughts, and perceptions flowed through my consciousness. Now that it had started, it would not stop until it had finished. I could not halt it, and it was absorbing as an experience, deeply personal, and proceeding to the limits of what I could endure. As it went on, I began to see and feel – all the trends, patterns, deeds and mistakes from different phases of that life. They revealed themselves in rapid succession, sometimes uplifting, sometimes deflating, all adding to an overall synthesis of all that this life had consisted. My feelings were like on a roller coaster, and I became aware of many elements of my interactions with others that I had hidden, and these startled me. Some of these revelations were quite shocking, and I squirmed inwardly at what I had neglected or distorted. The more I experienced of it, the more I could appreciate, outlooks that I had hardly noticed in my conscious mind, during the lifetime itself. I could perceive, both my deficiencies, and my achievements, as a soul in that lifetime, and the breadth and depth of how much I had opened myself to tread truly, and be in harmony with my higher purpose. I could see it all now. There were some moments from the life that revealed themselves, where I felt pride and passion, and could congratulate myself. However, there were others, where I felt, frankly, very disappointed with myself, ashamed of what I had missed or done wrongly. And as the experience continued and unfolded, it was like witnessing an emerging balance sheet that fed into the overall being of my evolving identity as a soul. It was so interesting and engrossing.

In the end, I realised that I had achieved most of what I had set out to do in that lifetime, with a few mistakes that I would need to take forward in some capacity. The life had not been about healing the Earth, even though I had been working with horticulture. My purpose had been more about serving and assisting people, and finding right relationship with people, giving and receiving, as I had done with Pia. This had all been tidying up from the past and preparation for what I needed to do next. When I was so occupied at the end of my life, with thoughts about the Earth and its well-being, this had come from my soul urges as I approached transition, for my soul was very eager to continue my Spiritual work of helping the Earth, and take that to a new stage.

As the process completed itself, the High beings gave a summary to me of their Spiritual judgment concerning my progress. I felt a great feeling of relief, not to be castigated, and to be given support, to continue with my work.

Astoris had waited outside for me while I went through this, rather than being by my side. I was glad to be there with the three High Beings, without Astoris, and stand on my own feet, by myself. As the review ended, and eased into stillness, I could feel my soul being shaking and assimilating, as all the elements of that experience was integrated. I could sense those Higher Beings blessing me with delicate touches while my energy system adjusted. It was only when all this settled that I emerged from the chamber.

Standing beside Astoris, now, I felt elation and a strong feeling of refreshment and wholeness. My being had altered through this process in a miraculous fashion, and I felt fuller, with my energy field now, and stronger. I stared at my friendly guide, and he smiled. It was good to feel his love, and acceptance of me. He waited with me, quietly, until I was more settled and able to be completely alert to him.

SURPRISE

'Well, I suppose now that I must go back now to the Earth Dome, and continue with my counselling?' I put to Astoris wistfully.

'Will you?' he replied. 'And how have you been getting on with that counselling?' Astoris was opening a new line of evaluation. 'Let us go through what you have done.'

Suddenly, my consciousness was inundated with another range of images, feelings and experiences, this time relating to my counselling work in the Earth Dome. I could experience not only my actions, but the thoughts and feelings of those souls, with whom I had interacted. It was like an extension of the review process, that I had just been through. However, this evaluation was concerned with my work on the Spiritual planes. As it proceeded, I could witness the progress and growth in my confidence, and the amount of care that I had given to others. Then this altered, and merged, with memories of my most recent Earth life, where there had been a theme of me needing to selflessly give to others. As this took place, I could discern how well it went together. It was like pieces of a puzzle coming together, and the more I examined it, the more joy I felt in my heart. In assessing this, I could tell, how I had grown, and reached new levels of competence in my ability to help others.

'Are you pleased?' Astoris asked me, when this had finished. And I could feel the swelling pride inside me. I had to admit that I was happy, and I looked across at my guide in anticipation.

'We feel that you are ready for a new stage of your development, 'Astoris put to me. 'What would you like to do?'

I could hardly speak. Astoris knew exactly what I wanted to do. He knew how much I wanted to help the Earth, and go there and attempt to make a difference – he did not need to ask me this. And he was just there, next to me, smiling, while my energy field was full of turbulence, with all my emotion and desires.

Astoris had been aware how much longing I had felt when I saw those Earth Warriors, and this longing was stimulated, as I had watched them train and prepare for their missions. It became clear to me then, that Astoris had, in fact, been lighting that fire in me, deliberately. I gazed back at him with considerable incredulity. There was only one thing in my heart that I truly wished to do, and I did not have to say it, I could not say it. As I paused, I could only hope against hope, that it may come true, that I would be able do that. And Astoris did not disappoint me.

'There is a group that you can join now, a team of souls about to start training, to be Earth Warriors, as a preparation for them to go to the Earth and help her and humanity in this hour of need. Your duties in the Earth Dome have been passed on to others. What is your choice? Will you join in with this?'

I thought that I was bursting. My energy field was radiating in so many directions at once. I did not know how I must have seemed to Astoris.

'Yes,' I cried. 'Yes. Yes. I choose to join.' I gave my Guide a huge energy hug. The emotional energy was pouring from me. 'Thank you for your faith in me.'

'Come then,' he told me. 'We have important work to do. It is time for you to become acquainted with your working group.'

I needed to calm myself for I was very excited, and my energy struggled to contain itself, for the joy I was feeling. This is what I had been awaiting. As I looked over at Astoris's Spiritual eyes, into their depths, they were dancing with playfulness, and I could feel the Spirit of adventure, with what would happen next. He was happy too. But he needed to help steady me, for I could hardly contain myself with my excitement.

For a few moments, Astoris touched me with his energy body, a soothing touch, and this gradually quietened my thoughts and my energy field. I became still to accept this, until finally, I felt tranquil, and was ready to go on.

BRIEFING

Astoris waited a little while longer, checking my aura thoroughly, before he began to brief me. Many thoughts were arising in my mind. I also had doubts. From the beginning, of when I had been aware of those Earth Warriors, while I had been working in the Earth Dome, I had always held a great admiration for these souls doing this work, because I knew that these beings dedicated themselves to lives, where their own personal needs and aspirations were placed completely to one side, while they dedicated themselves utterly, to specific tasks, associated with helping the Earth and the raising of consciousness of the people on the Earth. I considered that these must be incredibly strong souls. Could I do it? Was I capable?

Astoris did his best to reassure me. The other five souls in this working group were also doing this for the first time. They came from diverse backgrounds, but had been selected carefully, so that, as a group, there would be balance, sensitivity, compassion and potency.

Astoris told me to turn inwards to seek the source of my desire to be an Earth Warrior. I did that, and I felt that the line of potential for this went very deep, and I kept following the threads right in to my very core. Astoris helped me. To my astonishment, I realised that the source of my yearnings to be an Earth Warrior, were not recent, but they had been seeded within me, from very ancient times, from my very beginnings as a soul. They were like a potential, and a destiny seed, planted at my conception as a soul, and programd to grow towards fruition. This was incredible. The work that I had been doing in the Earth Dome of counselling souls, and my most recent incarnations had all been there to prepare me for this moment. Astoris told me that he had been waiting and monitoring me to be certain that I was ready. And that the time was right. I was meant to be in this group – I felt that then.

The training that we were to receive would be comprehensive and tough, and would be aimed to be meticulous. We would be preparing, with exercises designed to bond us together as a group, so that we would come to know each other's strengths and weaknesses, intimately, like we were each extensions of our own souls. We would test ourselves, to become clear about what we each wanted to achieve, and all our aspirations, so that when the moment came, we would be ready to incarnate, for our mission. He was confident that I would find the other members of the group interesting, and inspiring to work with. Before he spoke about them though, he wanted to communicate with me about his own role within the group.

My guide, Astoris, held vast wisdom, and his reach extended far beyond mine. I knew that he was involved with many souls, leading and guiding them. It was not just me. So, it was not a surprise, but a delight, when he told me, that he was going to be the main teacher for our entire group, and act as an overseer. Even though he had been involved with the Earth project for a long while, this was the first time, also for him, to be leading such a group, and as such, he would be going through his own learning, as the process unfolded. I felt relieved. Knowing that he would be with me, helped me to feel very safe and secure. However, he also made it clear to me, that he would be treating me equally to all the others, with no special favours.

Astoris told me that there were also higher beings and teachers that were supporting him, for this work that we were doing was important, and needed the highest blessings and supervision to ensure that it had the best chances of success. I need not be concerned about this, for these beings were beyond what I could experience, with my present frequencies of perception. I may, on occasions, gain a few glimpses of them. But mainly, I would sense them as energies of love and peace, and know that they were there for our good, and for the collective good of all. They would help, in their own way, and I could reach inwards to them, through prayer. What I needed to do initially, was to concentrate on my own performance and part in the mission, and do my best.

Soon I would meet them all. But there was still more for me to know. Astoris wanted to inform me that two members of the group, had never even incarnated upon the Earth previously, even though they had experience on planetary bodies of other star systems. They had a special purpose in being in the group, for they brought with them, clarity and pure connection with light, as well as their experience that went beyond the consciousness of humanity on Earth. This was fascinating to me. How would I respond to them? What would they be like?

Astoris explained how humans on Earth were largely closed from their Spiritual faculties, and had become very focussed upon the material world and its manipulation through technology. People were feeling increasingly separate from each other, and this was an illusion that was causing a lot of problems. Souls from other worlds were therefore being called, to attempt to assist waking up people's Spiritual consciousness, so the illusion of separateness could be dispelled.

One of these souls in my working group had gifts that could help channel the Spiritual consciousness of love and connectedness. She would be able to stimulate those energies and the opening of consciousness in others on Earth. Together with the others, I would have to help create the space for her do that.

My wise guide, Astoris gazed over at me. It was not new for souls from other worlds to choose to incarnate on Earth. This had been happening throughout human history. He reminded me that in my soul history from early times, I, too, had lived on other star systems and I carried the seeds of these memories deep within me. The sense of the Earth being my 'home,' was not something that had always been there.

As he said this to me, I suddenly became aware of images and long ago memories of worlds where I had lived, and I could sense the consciousness I had then, and how different this was to my consciousness I experienced on Earth more recently. By sharing this with me, Astoris was preparing me and helping me to extend my perceptual base, so I could embrace these fellow beings in the group, and I felt glad that he was doing this, before I met them.

Part of the transformation of consciousness on our Earth, was not just about helping people to feel interconnected with each other and other realms of life on the planet, but also for our Earth being to open more fully to her interconnectedness with other planetary systems. Therefore, for us to have two members of our group, being souls that were representatives of these other systems was perfect, for what was needed to be done. This was another reason that they would be in the group.

Our Earth could incorporate many wonderful vibrations of energy. She contained within her the potential, to blend these elements together. If souls expressed their energies respectfully and with love, the superb distinctive nurturing brilliant Earth light, could shine through all, and create patterns that would enable living on the Earth for all beings to be a blissful experience. That was the potential.

There was a pause. Astoris had not quite completed what he wanted to say to me. He looked over at me and indicated mischievously, that there was one other revelation which I would not be expecting – waiting for me in the group. This was something that I could manage once I was there. And I had no idea what that he was talking about. What was it? It always unsettled me when Astoris conveyed something like that. But, as I felt my guide's love, I relaxed again.

Astoris quietly asked me if I was ready to join the group now? I nodded, and opened myself to what would be there.

WORKING GROUP

As we went in, I could see, that the colours in the chamber for our working group, were beautiful shades of blue and green, all blending in with one another, and creating subtle vibrations and imbuing the atmosphere with special calm and serenity. These were the Earth colours, in their essential form. And it was fitting that we would gather together, amid their energy. I felt at home, and immediately all traces of nervousness were dispelled.

I could see the light forms of my five new companions and they were placed in a circle with one place remaining, for me. When I slotted into my position, a powerful energy flow began to move between us. Astoris was outside our circle but it was as if he was conducting this energy, with the support of higher beings around us, steadying and nurturing our being together. Those sublime higher spiritual beings were harmonizing our energy, allowing our individual vibrations to find a frequency – the best frequency where we could all meet, so we could communicate and open ourselves to each other. I felt unusual sensations flowing through me, as if I was being analysed and further adjustments being made in my energy field. Because we all chose this, what we experienced took effect by our surrendering to it. The pervading underlying feeling was one of well-being.

After a while, the process settled and it was like my eyes were opening, and my companions' lights were now brighter, and I could see some elements of them clearer, as they could see me. These were to be my five companions. When I counted myself, and with Astoris, that meant that we were seven. The number felt right and balanced. I was open for our training to begin.

Astoris gave us some instructions. Our first task was to have an initial working introduction of ourselves, to each other. This was not something that was casual. What we needed to do was to open and reveal intimate and personal aspects of our soul to the others – including our history, strengths and weaknesses, skills, primary relationships, our affiliations and of course, our inner level of devotion to the Earth. It was almost like the review chamber, because of the intensity of self-examination required. There was very little that we would be able to conceal. When we engaged with this, one at a time, one speaking and the others listening, while we listened, we needed concurrently to explore our relationship with the one that was revealing themselves and how we may be able to combine with them, on many different levels. It was an exhilarating, but also a very demanding process, of personal exploration and self-expression.

There was no chance to pause, hesitate or draw back from this. Astoris was directing, and we had to engage with each other, doing this process, with immediacy. Suddenly, I was immersed in it all – I had to yield to what I was feeling, and my perceptions of the others and what I would choose to give out from myself. Inwardly, I opened to the challenge, to give it my best, for I knew that being with this group was where I wanted to be.

I could only focus my attention fully, on the one that was presenting, and I could feel the different textures of energies that existed in each soul, as we moved around the circle. It was not like we were similar, for there were so many elements coming forth that were new for me to encounter, and I felt my being stretching itself, to embrace them all.

It was interesting for me to meet the two beings, from other star systems. Their energies were very calm and clear, but also extremely contrasting, with one very passive, while the other was active, and they had completely different origins. Their concern with the Earth was from a galactic perspective, for they wanted Earth's part in the galactic plan of evolution to be fulfilled.

When I tuned into their purpose, my usual sphere of perception had to expand significantly to embrace their consciousness. They both had an interest in many star systems in our galaxy that embraced life, not just Earth. The scope of their interests was much wider than mine had been, and there was a great deal that I could learn from them. Where they were vulnerable, was about how they would adjust to Earth conditions. There was a strong basis for their concerns.

The process continued until we reached the others. Even before they spoke and had their turns, I could sense that the other souls in the group all had long lineages of Earthly experience, and had been engaged in previous battles to protect and move Earth evolution forward. As each one took their turn in the centre, I found qualities that I could greatly admire and appreciate. It was a formidable group and I felt privileged to be part of it.

After four of the group had shared about themselves, the focus turned to that soul who was next to me. As I turned to her, I unexpectedly felt very joyful. Why was this? And then I tuned in. I had not realised it, and how, how had I overlooked this? I had not anticipated finding anyone here that I knew. But here was Aurielle, from my original soul group. What was she doing here? We knew each other so well, and had been through so much together. She and I could unite very easily. It was incredible. Aurielle smiled at me with her special gaze. I had not expected this. But when I explored with her, it was clear that her love of Earth was every bit as strong as mine, and she had gifts of healing and channelling, that would be extremely useful. We would be working together, and I had not known. Opening to her was such a delight and so familiar, I would have to be mindful, to have my attention on others as well as her. Now I knew the surprise that Astoris had indicated.

For a few moments, she turned to me privately, and then I could see Pia, my niece from my last incarnation. Pia had been so kind to me in that time before my death. I gazed at her with love, as we acknowledged this connection. How could she have come over so soon? I was concerned. She reassured me. There had been a car accident, she communicated. It had been her time, for she needed to come home to Spirit again. That was a relief to me.

As she then further opened herself, both to me and the others, I could perceive many of the other connections we had shared – so many of them stringed together. We were a good pair. It was so good to have her here. My love for her was very deep and my joy at having her in this circle was tremendous. Listening to her share, I could tell how right it was that she was with us.

Now with her having finished, I could sense the urging of Astoris to bring our attention once more to the circle, so we could continue to build our togetherness. There was only one more soul to open themselves to the group now, and that was me.

As a soul, my tendency had been to be reserved, and conceal a little of what I thought, but here I could not do that, and the word in my mind was 'trust'. I could feel all the facets of my identity being revealed as I opened myself to be observed and studied. At first, even in my Spiritual state, I felt quite vulnerable doing this, but gradually I became accustomed to it, and I could feel the love and care from all the other souls, as they explored my reactions and inclinations. They were so gentle. I had to speak and communicate, and I did that as well as I could. And I felt that they accepted me, and this helped me, on various layers of my being, to be able to accept myself, and acknowledge my place in the group. More and more, a deep serenity descended upon me and I could marvel, at how well, the seven of us could combine. Already, I felt optimistic and in my enthusiasm, I wanted to proceed, as soon as we could. But it was not going to be as easy as that.

Astoris did not take a turn to communicate about himself, but instead, began to outline what was in front of us.

ORIENTATION

Astoris wanted us now to focus upon what we wanted to achieve in relation to the Earth, both individually and collectively as a group, and listen to each other about this. We needed to find clarity of intention. With regards our history and foundations as souls, we needed to work with the qualities, which we all brought to the group, and explore how we could blend those qualities positively, so we could become a unit. We needed to discuss and analyse and dissect our individual attributes in all respects. Then we needed to consider how we wanted to move forward in this project, and particularly, how we felt we could combine with other members of the group. The aim was for this to be an intensive training course, so we could learn, know and care about each other. And we needed to unite about how we could be of service to the Earth.

This kind of process was not completely new to me. I had had some discussions and sessions like this with my soul group in earlier phases of our growth as souls. But the focus was different then, because we already knew each other, and the scope and objective of what we aimed to do then was mainly in working out our patterns with each other, for our own personal growth. It was not for some greater 'good'. What we would be doing together, in this group, would be hugely more expansive.

With agreement from all of us, we continued with this next task, and it filled all the space of our energy systems. Everything else had to be put aside. We were totally occupied with what we had to do, and the processes went on, and on, from one to another. It did not stop, and Astoris was thorough with us, so we needed to go into the minutia of details, learning so much of each other. There was eagerness amongst the members of the group, and urgency. Step by step, this process of familiarisation continued, and I felt wonder as I could sense through layer after layer, the depth and character of my fellow members in our working group. It was a great relief that they also appeared to appreciate me, and my confidence grew.

It was interesting, because there were some characters within the group with whom I related more easily than others. Of course, I naturally blended extremely well with Aurielle. But it was much more, with some of the others where I needed to work, so ultimately, we could all find the keys, and ways how we could relate with everyone. With our two members from other worlds, I found this more difficult at first, because their reactions were different to mine, less emotional, and steadier somehow. Therefore, I gave more attention to them, to learn about them, and to feel comfortable in their presence. They were receptive to me, and gave their best to help me.

Even when we completed this process, we all knew that there would be more that we would need to do around this.

In another exercise, we were presented with the chance to give attention to some other areas of our preparation together. We went to the Earth Dome, and collectively studied conditions of the Earth, and the impact that human activity, was having upon the natural rhythms of life there. It was interesting doing this, with my working group, and I gained many insights I had not considered previously, by listening to their perceptions. And of course, we were now scrutinizing what we may be able to do to help and assist the Earth – much more than pure observation. And that thrilled me. Astoris wanted us to share, with our members from other worlds, what it was like to be human on Earth. There was much for us to tell them. And they could give us an otherworld perspective, on how the evolution of our planet was proceeding. This was an important point of contact where our bonds together could deepen.

With the gap that existed between the potential, Spiritually, of how the Earth was meant to unfold as a living being, and what was taking place, due to the influence of human free will, we considered what we could do to bridge that gap. We began to experiment with ideas of how we could act together to enable the Earth to accelerate in its evolution and the transformation of consciousness on Earth, rather than be held back by those that resisted change. How would we, as a group, deal with this conflict while on Earth? This became one of our main discussion points, and we all had to listen, and learn, and bring out ideas from within us. We had many, many extensive and intensive dialogues about this.

Astoris also wanted us to pray together, and tune in to the higher beings assisting us, and the One Source, who ultimately supported all life. This was a wonderful experience, and brought us together on a Spiritual level. One of our members from other worlds – her Spiritual name was Oiva – was brilliant at channelling. It was what she did on her home planet. And she gave us lessons, about how we could connect with Spiritual inspiration more fully.

While we were at the Earth Dome, we engaged in many meditations together, focussing upon the High Spiritual vision of our Earth's potential, and aligning ourselves with the path that was intended spiritually for our Earth to follow. Astoris wanted the four of us that had had mainly Earth lives, to be well tuned into this potential. Our collective vision needed to be in accord, and for us to be in no doubt, about how we needed to proceed. To assist us with this, we were invited to special lush spaces within the Earth Dome, to study with Advanced Masters. It was marvellous to be with them. Astoris could communicate directly with them, but I could not see them, only sensing their fine and loving presence. While we stayed in these spaces, and linking together spiritually, their quiet thoughts and feelings impinged themselves upon us, and we were given blessings to help us on our path together.

During these sessions, we could envision vibrant nature forces, trees, vegetation, the mineral kingdom, animals and the human kingdom, all interacting with each other in harmony. We could sense the feeling of interconnection so strongly, and we knew that once this was established on Earth, then people would no longer want to deviate away from this. The experience of beauty and love in this vision was enormous, and extended out to other systems of life, on both inner and outer dimensions. Vistas of a positive future for humanity and planet Earth opened to our awareness. We were encouraged to envision this together, so we could see ourselves, as a group, working together with others, with more and more people on Earth moving towards this – and the consciousness of humanity transforming to a state where, what was expressed, was the quality of cooperation, and living together, for the good of all, rather than competition, to exclude one from another.

It was a true and worthwhile vision, and this was what we had to help to deliver. The Higher Masters acted with their energy to imprint this vision firmly through the layers of our souls. It felt like activated seeds, of togetherness, were being planted in us, to complement the individual seeds of potential, that already existed inside each one of us. These collective seeds had the power to grow and be manifested. We had to germinate these seeds, so they would express all their beauty and vitality, and this would be through our mission together on Earth.

There was an enormous amount about the souls of the other members of our group that I learnt. The other two members from Earth had had histories where their souls had been very much absorbed in wars and conflict. Their names were Santi and Amond. They also knew each other, in a similar manner to how Aurielle and I were connected. These were souls, whose path had been to find meaning in conflict and war, overcoming the adrenaline rush of wanting to kill or be dominant, or even self-righteous, and instead, learning about what was sacred and important, and required to be preserved. They both had primary qualities, where they could easily be assertive and their path had been to learn to direct their natures wisely. These two souls were very strong and determined, but they had to open their hearts, so it would not be 'will' but 'love,' that drove them. They had a lot of energy to fight for what was 'good,' but they needed to use a loving energy, to discern what was truly worthwhile, and not to be abrasive with others.

Our two members that had come from other Star systems were on a path of service where they wanted to learn to love and appreciate the Spirit of the Earth, so they could nurture it and bring their sensitive energies to help uplift the Earth. Oiva was one, and the other one was called Deli. They were both very pure of soul. Oiva was naturally that way, from the beautiful Spiritual work that she did on her home world, while Deli had incarnated upon many worlds, gaining much experience and breadth of perspective from doing so. He was going to look after Oiva on Earth. They had no karmic residues from pervious times on Earth, so their efforts would be to work like conductors of more cosmic energy, bringing extra-terrestrial intelligence and sensitivity to support the Spirit of the Earth. They were like ambassadors from worlds beyond, but they also had the ability to help bring humanity back on track.

Aurielle also wanted to be both a channel and conductor. This was a valid aspiration on her part, and of course, she contained within herself very long-standing human experience to ground her. She was one who could interact with people with love, helping them to come together. Aurielle knew the Earth, but she wanted to learn about the cosmic influences that humanity needed to embrace.

This was my task as well, to relate to the people, to be bold, and inspire. I just needed to allow the passion in my heart, to direct me, through all those boundaries that appeared as obstacles within me, so these could be dissolved and I could then be a leader.

Astoris held our Spiritual light and nurtured our togetherness. His presence was one of mystery and multiple dimensions. He was our watcher, encouraging us, while he held the essence of our purpose within his inner soul. It was remarkable that he was also including himself in our group, but he insisted that this was necessary.

OUR FIRST ASSIGNMENT

Thoughts of my previous incarnations on Earth, and even my counselling work in the Earth Dome, faded into the distant past, as I became ever more occupied with the work of our group. We continued our explorations and preparations with numerous activities, for what seemed like long ages. The pace of learning was tremendous, and very compelling. It was such an intense situation to be in. We were all committed to keep going. However, the moment arrived eventually, when Astoris called us together for a meeting. He had an announcement for us.

And Astoris told us that now we had a special assignment to fulfil. This would be a further preparation, and would bring our bonding much closer together. This was a task that would be challenging to us, very challenging.

We must be open to what would follow, and give this experience all that we could, with our hearts and our souls. It was time for us to connect more fully, to the Spirit of the Earth, and to support each other in what we had to do.

I could feel the nervousness and fluttering within my being. What did he have in mind? He led us in a meditation to connect with the Source together, and I could feel such a lot of peace with that. Then he checked with each one of us, that we were willing, and ready, to proceed. I scanned within myself, and the answer felt 'yes,' as it did for all the others. For some moments, we stood in our circle together, and I could feel the love that we were now able to generate through being a group. It was very comforting. But then, Astoris indicated, that we needed to move.

In the next moment, we were all in a chamber that was full of Earth colours and I could sense the brilliant essence of our beautiful planet. We sat together and were instructed to pray to the Spirit of the Earth to help and support us. I could feel that the energy of this was inducing peace to my being, and my consciousness was slowing down. Gradually, without being able to stop it, I was drifting into another dimension. It was some further important step into the unknown, but once more, I chose to welcome this, and surrender to it with an open heart. Once again, the thought of the word, 'trust' rose from within me.

As I looked around, I could perceive the lights of the others with me but we were all drifting downwards, and my awareness of being in the Spiritual world, was somehow fading. At the last moment, I noticed that Astoris was also joining us in our circle, within the chamber. He must be coming with us. That was very comforting.

But the sensations I felt, were disorientating me. Where was it that we going? What were we expected to do? There were energies adjusting in my mind, like I was being programd in some way – so many adjustments, one after the other. This went on, and I could feel complex, troubling emotions.

Soon, I was no longer aware of the Circle, but my own being was descending, as if I was in a tunnel. It was all happening so rapidly, and I could feel the constriction of being pushed into a compressed reality, where the vestiges of my soul had to fit. This was not easy. Did I really want to do this? The sensation in my consciousness was akin to tumbling into another much denser reality. It was just like when I was being prepared to join a foetus, for a human life. And I felt as if I was beginning another life on Earth. That was it. But it did not feel happy, not happy at all.

And as I entered this space, it became darker and darker...

Part 2

BLEAK WORLD

FOOD FOR A BEATING HEART

Once when I was little, I had a dream, a dream that I would always remember, and I have kept it close to my heart, like a treasure.

In the dream, I was outside, watching a twig that extended out of the Earth, near the base of a dead tree. As I watched this twig, it appeared to change. I thought I saw it vibrate, somehow. Then, there was a small bud forming a knob on the twig. And as I watched it, the bud began to expand. It was even starting to change colour as the outer covering peeled away, from being a dull grey to becoming a pale, but then, more vibrant green. I felt enormous happiness, and could hardly contain those feelings. If I kept watching it, I was sure that the bud would soon burst forth into a full expression of life, and leaves. I cupped my hands around the bud, to feel its energy, and I could feel a most scintillating current, that made my hands tingle. This bud was alive. I had never witnessed anything like this – the life force of nature. I knew that the bud was about to burst open. And I could scarcely believe it.

Of course, I couldn't believe it. How could I? Our world did not have any plants growing outside – not one. That was only in the history books, the time before the war. Why torment myself?

And at that moment, I woke up suddenly – I was sweating and trembling all over. Our world wasn't like that, couldn't be like that. I shook my head in denial. But my dream felt real, and the scenes of the dream played repeatedly in my mind. The dream held an experience that captivated me. I could not ever let it go. It was one of the main experiences from my young life, which kept me going.

A WORLD WITHOUT HOPE

I watched and stared through the glass at the hills outside. The sky was blue and the rays from the sun, through the window, were warm. The contour of the land undulated up and down through various escarpments, and I smiled, just a little, at the beauty of these natural forms. There must have been a moderate wind outside, for I could see slight movements in the branches of the trees in the distance. For a few moments, I watched, as the wind gave motion and rhythm to the branches of the trees, moving them in a swirling organic manner. And I imagined how much the trees may like to dance, if they could. Trees were such beautiful and wonderful beings.

But that is when I sighed, and felt a lump in my throat, as tears welled up in my eyes. For there were no leaves on the trees, and there were no birds or signs of animal life, and the soil was bare, without any signs of life. It was only the starkness of a barren landscape that I could see. All of it was empty, and dead. The blue colours of the sky and the browns of the land reflected a vacant space in front of me. I could never quite believe that this was our existence. The trees were not dancing, they were dead, and it was a dead world. But I did not want it to be dead, so I kept on imagining things, straining my vision, and seeking signs of life, any life, to make me feel better. I did not want it the way that it was. And I certainly did not wish to sense that we were so much alone, because I felt incredibly alone. Instinctively, I knew that life should be there, and had to be there. But it wasn't.

No one went outside anymore, even with protective suits, and that felt a great pity, for in many ways, the barrenness of the landscape looked somehow inviting, and I wanted to explore it, and be out there – anything, rather than be trapped inside. But we were told that the land was poisoned. The soil had stopped giving life to the trees, and if we went out there, it would stop giving life to us and we would die too.

I was only a teenage boy, but I felt already quite old. During my short life, besides my studies, I had not yet found any activity to occupy me, which would be worthwhile or stimulating. And I felt lost, without a purpose. I had never been anywhere except this City, where I lived and where I felt imprisoned. The outlaying parts of the City no longer functioned, having been abandoned, by not being secure for life to exist there. Therefore, the only area where we could survive, was the inner walled sections of the City, the safe sanctum, as it was called. This consisted of mainly just the central clusters of high buildings and grounds, which were connected by glass corridors and protected from direct contact with the dangerous and forbidding elements outside. Nothing was left to chance – we were sealed from the world outside of us. The only contact we had with the rest of the world, was through the glass, and even this was monitored and we were told not to touch the glass directly.

Within the complex, we had apartments where we lived and these provided basic living needs – kitchens, bedrooms and living areas – and they were technically efficient. It was the solar power that provided our energy, and the scientists and maintenance personnel did all they could to ensure that we were physically secure, with food, water and shelter. In the respect of material well-being, we were comfortable, with adequate provision to exercise, and enjoy the appliances that technology could provide.

What more would we need? Well, the answer to that was simple, in my mind. Technology did not ensure happiness, and how could we ever be happy, when the world outside the perimeters of our confines was so wasted, and perilous. We needed freedom.

I lived with my parents and my younger brother. They did not provide much company though. When I think of it, they hardly seemed to be alive, most of the time, not even my brother. Conversation was virtually non-existent. No one seemed to do very much. When I looked at my parent's faces, all I could ever see was their deep, deep sadness, and expressions of utter despair – never shifting, never going away.

It stretched all my understanding to speculate how I had been born into such a God-forsaken world, and it took so much effort not to descend into a crevasse of misery, like them. But I knew that if I did that, if I let myself go, there would be no way out, and certainly there was no one that I knew, capable of rescuing me psychologically. Once I gave up, if I did that, I knew that I would not find reason to live again.

At night time, I prayed and I lay awake, pleading with my understanding of God, that there could be some redemption, some sign to give more strength, and reason for living, something better, to be able to dissolve some of this pain.

My parents had known a different world, an Earth with life in it, and they had also borne witness to the terrible process where so much was destroyed. They could not come to terms with it. Nor could they talk about it. And for much of the time, they seemed to be living in a state of inner paralysis, hardly able to engage in any kind of meaningful activity. Each day, they had their minimalist tasks and rhythms that they set for their life, and they repeated most of these things, day in and day out, without variation. They were not prepared to do anything else. By occupying themselves with these tasks, and staring endlessly into their screens, they did not need to think of the horrors that lay within them, did not need to refer to that. And I never really knew what they thought and felt beneath their mindless stares.

They were not the only ones. It was the same everywhere. When I went out of our apartment, I saw other people. No one seemed to smile. People just stared blankly as they went about their everyday life. It was like how I imagined it must have been in one of those old asylums that I had read about. Everyone's mood was affected, because no one was exempt.

I remembered how, when I was little, people had been offered counselling – everyone had to do it, and I had to go through that too – listening to a lady, who repeated over and over, that we had to keep going, so in the future our civilisation could find our way out in the world again, to build a new world. And we needed to be part of that. I heard her words, but I was not convinced that she believed what she was saying. She was just repeating what she had been instructed to say. And in her eyes, I could only see despair. I did not enjoy the sessions. She was not being truthful to her feelings. It was not surprising that her efforts did not endure.

One day, while I was waiting for my weekly session with my mum, suddenly the door opened, and I saw my counsellor, storm out of the room where she worked. She was sobbing. For a moment, she paused, but the tears did not subside, and no-one stood up to help her. Then she went fleeing through the door, out of her office. She did not look back, and all I felt was pity for her. And there were never any more counselling sessions after that. It had seemed pointless really. What hope could the platitudes she repeated give, when we were locked in this cell of isolation within this City?

There was no better life possible, no way out, nothing to aspire to, no actual indications, that it could be any different. And the pervading feeling was so depressed – with the undeniable conclusion, that we were responsible as a race, for largely destroying and wrecking our world, of life, as we knew it. What a sentence of damnation and collective never ending pain, for people to endlessly consider. The counsellors obviously had their own problems, and who would listen to them? Most people did not want to think about their lives at all? No babies were being born anymore.

Essentially, our life in the City, was dying, and soon there would be none of us left.

The suicide rate in our City was very high, and people were not prevented from ending their own life. It was an act of compassion to let people die when there was so little to live for. We had medication that people could use, to make the whole process as easy as possible. Nobody seemed to mind, that others around them were making the choice to end their lives. As time went on, shared living spaces became more and more empty.

In that period when I was little, I did not understand very much – I had longings to be loved, but people did not respond to me, and I didn't know why, for I wanted to play, and no one wished to play with me. In the corridors, I wanted to run, but when I did that, the expressions on people's faces made me feel like I was crazy. I had a couple of tutors to teach me, and the few other children, some rudimentary skills, of being able to read and write. But after a while these stopped too, just like the counselling, because no one had the heart to do it anymore. Consequently, I was left on my own, if I wanted to play, or learn anything.

I tried to engage my brother, but he did not have the fight that I had, and I noticed him becoming ever more listless and living like my parents. I refused to submit to that, but I had to do something with my time. In my imagination, I made up stories of heroes and heroines and tried to keep myself motivated by modelling my behaviour on them. However, the question in my mind kept returning to ask why? I did not want to resign myself. And so, I enquired, and asked members of my family and people I met, if they could tell me anything, anything at all, for me to learn about what had happened. I had to understand why people carried such a lot of guilt. Somehow, I had to know, even if those around me were not interested anymore.

I fantasised about going on journeys and having adventures, as a means of keeping my spirits up. The only place, where I could find solace, was inside myself. After a while, I gave up asking questions from my family, but I was not ready to give up altogether – there had to be another way.

I prayed about this, every night, and kept hoping, seeking those answers. The education I had received had taught me to be able to read and write, but I wanted to learn much more, and at some stage, I realised that the only possibility for me to be able to achieve this, was for me to be able to teach myself.

So, one day, while I was wandering along the corridors, I came across an entry point that I had not noticed before. The door in front of me was closed, but I felt a strange urge to open the door, and enter. Nobody told me that I couldn't go in there, so I did. I looked and explored in wonder.

The place I found was the City library. I discovered later, that the original library existed outside the enclosed perimeters we had now. Fortunately, much of the contents of that, books, computer records, had been transferred across – and this must have happened before the City Walls were sealed.

What I noticed immediately, was that there was not much care evident in this library. A lot of the books had been dumped in piles against the walls of these rooms, and many of them appeared as if they had never been moved. But I wanted to open them, and sift through them. So, I just started looking and reading.

The next day, I came back, and the day after that.

On one occasion, after I had been there a few times, I entered the library, and there was a woman, cleaning there. She was not touching the books, only dusting around the surfaces, and mopping the floor. The woman did not look up, and carried on with what she was doing. At first, I was a bit shy to talk with her, but I finally plucked up the courage. I asked her if I was allowed, if I could be here, in the library. Then she looked up, and seemed to notice me for the first time. She told me, that I could read and study as much as I wanted. Hardly anyone used it. And that was all that she said.

In these rooms, besides the books, there were videos, maps, DVDs, historical records, computers, with vast amounts of information about so many subjects. It was like a huge repository of knowledge. This cleaning woman just popped in every few days or so. She answered my questions when I asked her, and helped me to find sources that interested me. In former times, she had been interested in books, but she did not read anymore. Most of my time in the library, I was there by myself.

This library represented a great opportunity for me. It became a daily habit, to come here, to read and study, for I was very inquisitive. There was a desk where I liked to sit, and do my work. And it wasn't long before I discovered that there were records held in the library about what had happened to our Earth, or at least some aspects of it. Then, I could begin to piece the details together. There were videos, commentaries – recordings held on the computer, for no-one had written about the catastrophe, and the books, all related to times before. But that also interested me. I spent hours going through all this, studying and digesting every piece of information I could, especially about the most recent times before the destruction. It became almost like a fixation to me, and one that captivated my attention.

As time went on, I spent huge slices of time in that library, reading, watching and questioning, until I could make my own analysis of the tragedy that had happened. It was important to me to understand, all that I could, and how such an appalling ordeal had come to pass. It was beyond me just how human beings could have managed this.

When I saw on videos, the lushness of the world that we had, the animal life, the vegetation, the freedom of movement, I really did struggle, to comprehend it all. Only a generation ago, it had been all so different, but the seeds of our self-destruction were already there.

The catastrophe that had befallen our planet, had taken time to unfold, and by some miracle, the Internet had not gone down immediately. I was grateful for this, for it provided the means for me, to see images and read commentaries relating, especially to the early stages, of the collapse of our humanity. Not surprisingly, much less existed in relation to the later stages.

THE EXTINCTION WAR

The cataclysm that destroyed our civilization had been called the Extinction War, and what follows is the understanding I pieced together, of how it all happened, and what took place.

I had been born two years after the so-called Extinction War had finished, so I never saw the beautiful world that existed before it, and all I knew was the aftermath. And my brother had made his appearance two years after me, so he didn't know anything else either. This Extinction War was the most calamitous occurrence that our human world had ever endured. And the continuing shock and trauma of this series of events had just gone on, with no relief, which I could tell, for anybody.

The seeds of the devastation could be traced through all the many civilisations of human history, and was all about the struggle for power. From my studies, I concentrated upon societal and political trends that were apparent from the beginning of the 21st century and how these were formative to what happened later. At the outset of the 21st century, there had been a massive rise of corporate and technological power, to both influence and direct people's lives. Money and greed, dictated the approach of these multinational companies, and governments were swayed by the need to appease corporate entities, lurking in the background. There was much corruption, with many of those companies, offered favours and support in exchange for hidden agendas, which then, shaped government policy.

A chasm began to grow within societies in the world. The wishes and needs of people in the street, came a poor second, in terms of priorities, to these powerful entities. If it wasn't the corporations, it was the governments and the media, exploiting people, and the Earth. Some governments resisted the infiltration of corporate domination, and assumed dictatorial powers, with unethical practices of their own, to subjugate the population around them. Mostly, these governments were overthrown, so they would not block the widening power base of these huge corporate companies. Although there was the appearance of greater cooperation between nations, underlying struggles for ever greater control continued, and in most places, democracy became largely a sham. Only a few beacons of light in the world offered any real alternative.

People made efforts to come together and resist these tendencies of overriding corporate and governmental power. These brave activists campaigned for a more compassionate and caring world. Like green shoots springing up, there were mass demonstrations and uniting of purpose to protect humanity. These actions gave hope and inspiration to many. Grass roots advocates stood up for what they believed in, and there were many that stood with them. At their best, these groups attracted to them, an experience of the collective power of love, which bonded people in these campaigns. But their aspirations were not respected.

Over and over, the voices of these uprisings were cruelly suppressed, often violently. Where the direction of these campaigns was a threat to the Establishment and the powers that had their own vested interests in the background, then the activists were not given the opportunity to express their voice. Laws were enacted, to prohibit them, from standing up for what they believed in. Occasionally progress was made, but so often, it was not. And the motivation of these people, that came so much from the heart, was stripped away through continued suffering, and the walls of resistance that met their pleas.

So many times, these activists were hurt or murdered or bundled into prison or stigmatised until their Spirit was sapped and they could no longer fight anymore. And other people that followed them to stand with them, gradually wilted through repeated threats and torture, and many became too frightened to continue. Some kept up the struggle, but sadly, the noble aspirations of the most caring and humane people, in many cases, collapsed into isolation and resignation, when people became afraid of being hurt, themselves.

The mass media encouraged a consciousness that stagnated with indifference, so people would consider themselves to be dominated by forces far greater than themselves, and thus feel powerless to act. From that base, as had happened many times through history, people became used to accepting things that were not right, and passively submitted to it.

'Development' was hailed as progress, and there were marvellous advances in technology. However, with ever increasing human population, cities were becoming overcrowded and more regulated, and with less and less natural spaces for people to enjoy. Thus, many questions were asked about the merits of where humanity was headed. The quality of life for people, was becoming harder and tougher. People were employed to serve the corporate world, and it was greed that drove developers onwards, the lust to profit from exploiting every resource that could be extracted from our finite Earth, until there was nowhere for it to continue, and the beauty and preciousness of the Earth suffered more and more.

This created unsustainable pressures. And for those that craved power and domination, they were desperate to find continued outlets for proving their superiority and wealth. There was no resting point that was enough, for they always wanted more. And they strove to outdo everyone else, and have exclusive rights, as if they could possess their dominions of power, and defeat any challenges to that.

When these organisations, or national governments, had some resource that was precious to them, and wanted by others, they would do all they could to protect it and guard it. For that, they needed military power to back them up. After efforts were made to try to reduce military capabilities, these began to increase again, more and more. Each bloc of power wanted to have the best weapons, to ensure that they could hold the best resources, at the expense of others. Greed and jealousy, combined with threats and terrorism, made for a very uncertain world.

Scientists investigated the damage being done by carbon emissions and other poisons being utilised, and it became clear that our Earth was losing some of its lustre and capacity to renew itself. Some international agreements were reached, to limit this damage. But these agreements were sabotaged, and undermined, by those interests, which wanted to persist with exploiting the Earth. Then, when the temperatures did start rising more rapidly and conditions deteriorated, the international community was not prepared.

At the same time, there were increasing problems occurring, associated with genetics and the propagation of genetically modified organisms. Governments permitted these experiments, and some of them went wrong, with catastrophic outcomes. There was a pressing need to increase food production – and this provided the companies behind these manipulations, with the excuse to further their experiments. But really, their obsession was about gaining more and more profit and power, by utilizing forces they did not fully understand. They did not care. In some cases, genetic mutations they created resulted in land being wasted and destroyed. Then, drastic action needed to be taken, so unsafe genetically modified organisms could be stopped from spreading through various food chains. A lot was being done without proper testing or evaluation.

Even with the rising population, most people and governments had taken it for granted that there always would be enough, and it was a shock, when the time came, and suddenly, the Earth's resources were over stretched.

One year, there were severe droughts and dire food shortages that created mass suffering, which in turn, bred uncertainty and panic. Tensions were building and building. Groups and nations wanted to look after their own backyard survival, and were not concerned with the needs of the whole. It was a disaster waiting to happen. And when things did snap, the ramifications and impact was greater than anyone could have foreseen.

With chronic overcrowding, widespread poverty, depleted resources, rising temperatures, and overbearing governments and corporations, imposing restricted media access, people felt helpless. They were dealing with forces that did not have their interests at heart. The future was looking less rosy than the past. And leaders of nations, with their military, were looking over their shoulders, wondering what they could seize that would give them some advantage, so that they could maintain their power.

It only needed one slightly unhinged leader as a trigger, to wreck everything. And there was more than one. But it was one who started it all. He was ambitious and reckless, and he believed that he could do anything, and that the people of his country would adore him.

It all happened so suddenly, and was in full flow before anyone could intervene and protest. I still shuddered when I thought about it.

The beginning of it was a dispute around borders, and this quickly escalated, when a group of soldiers were shot by security forces, from the other side. Threats were made. Other countries and then superpower blocks were drawn in, each side blaming the other, but needing the situation to diffuse itself. At this stage, it could have been halted. It only needed one side to back down slightly, and give ground. But it didn't happen. There were provocations on both sides, and warheads were mounted in preparation for possible attack.

This kind of brinkmanship had occurred many, many times before, and always the scenario of what calamitous consequences would occur, had prompted last minute negotiations that averted disaster. And people assumed that it would be like that again. The potential for any other action would be unthinkable. Most people hardly took notice of what was going on, because these cycles of attrition and brinkmanship followed by uneasy truce, had occurred on so many occasions.

But this unhinged leader had other ideas. He got it into his mind, that if he launched enough of his own nuclear missiles, fast enough, before the other side could react, then he could destroy their capability, and win the war. Thus, he would be able to take vast swathes of territory, for his own gain, and be proclaimed as a hero. It was a mad idea. But he was completely power-hungry.

The fact that huge loss of life and devastation could occur did not deter him, for his only concern was to attain victory. He was someone who was conditioned and obsessed by winning, and he did not wish to give way to any feelings of inferiority, or lesser outcomes. Any compromise would be a defeat to him. In this territorial dispute, he was not going to back down. The injustice of what was happening in the world, as he saw it, gave him justification, for what he did next. And no one saw it coming.

One day, without him offering any warning of any kind, he made a decision that changed the course of human civilisation. Using cover of darkness, he initiated the war by launching several nuclear missiles. All at once, a swathe of these missiles was in motion, and there was a point of no return. It was idiocy, with no considered forethought as to what would happen. Whatever goals he had set for himself, in terms of victory, had no chance to succeed, and could never have succeeded. The beliefs that he held, in terms of his own invincibility, were an utter fallacy.

The flight of these missiles, caused automatic triggers of reaction, with the larger Military powers. Now the war could not be stopped, and missiles were launched on all sides. With that initial onslaught, some of the missiles, were blocked by shields. However, there were also missiles that got through, and from a situation of relative normality for people on the ground, in a moment of foolhardy lust for power, suddenly, all was in upheaval, and the resulting destruction was exceedingly massive.

The larger Military powers had many more missile sites than this unhinged leader could take out, and so it was inevitable, that there was retaliation, and then further reprisals began to spread throughout the axes of power in the military regions of influence, across the world. Once this had commenced, it wasn't going to halt. The United Nations sent out a desperate plea for restraint, but the plumes of nuclear fallout were already causing unprecedented annihilation and deaths. Whole cities and regions were being wiped out and destroyed. And the missiles kept on raining through. People wept and gasped and screamed and protested wildly, for the military powers to pause what they were doing, but they wouldn't do it, and maybe they couldn't do it.

Certainly, now, the military had the opportunity to display, and utilise, their best and most potent weapons. Some of these military officers wanted to do that. They even seemed to enjoy war! But doing so, they caused untold misery and dire consequences. Their weapons were not toys.

There was no need for armies in this situation, for it all was being orchestrated by the pressing of a few buttons, and the computerised releasing of forces of mass-destruction that had almost an automatic continuance about it.

As was well known with nuclear bombs, it was not only the immediate destruction of the bombs that provoked obliteration of major cities and their infrastructure, but it was the radioactive fall-out that caused relentless misery, mayhem and huge human loss for anyone that was in its path. The mushrooming of this deadly peril spared no-one whom it hit. The world had never known anything like this. It was like the worst nightmare, that so many doom watchers had forecasted, now coming true, and for the bulk of the humanity, who were not immediately decimated, it was a story of disbelief and complete dismay.

And yet, bad though this was, and extreme in its wake of extermination of societies and communities around the world, it was only the beginning, and the forerunner of a destruction that would be even worse.

If it had only been nuclear war, terrible and shocking though that was, it is possible, just possible, that our human race may have survived, and recovered somewhat. However, there was more, and my body still trembled, about the thought of it.

It did not take long, with all the destruction and elimination of life, that everywhere would soon be in ruin, especially for that nation which had been the protagonist, starting the war. The leader of this country was still alive, protected in the hidden, underground vaults of his military headquarters. He must have been in an extremely vindictive mood, as he surveyed the situation around him. The adrenaline from the loss he was facing must have fuelled insanity in him, even more. And with the fury he felt, and with the powers that he still possessed, he played the last card that he had.

For many years, the military powers had been developing biological weapons, out of sight from people on the streets. These weapons were largely untried and based on genetic manipulation, but potentially, extremely deadly. With all the spy satellites, and surveillance, one side could not develop these, without the other side knowing. There were lots of variants of these created viruses, which were exceedingly threatening to life. No one seriously thought that these viruses, as weapons, would ever be used in war. They were a huge risk, for the unpredictable consequences of releasing these viruses, were unknown and uncontrollable. The results of using them could annihilate humanity. But, even with so much caution and abhorrence from the international community, towards the deliberate dissemination of these types of organisms, on this day, they were unleashed.

There were only three of these biological warheads launched – only three – that was all the warheads, which this leader had left. But it was sufficient. Contained within these warheads, there was an incredibly insidious virus, which had the capacity to sterilise the micro-organisms that were responsible for building life. Thus, when any form of life on our planet, encountered this virus, then it would lose the capacity to have functioning cells, that could reproduce, and it would soon die. This virus was created to multiply and replicate its actions, unceasingly, until there were no more organisms to sterilise. The virus had never been fully tested, to know its lifespan, or how it would be likely to mutate over time, so it was unknown, how far it would continue to propagate.

There were lines of research, that had constructed anti-bodies, which could disable the virus in its conventional form, but no one knew for sure, if these antibodies would be effective in any way, once the virus intermingled with other life forms, and mutated. It was like a death wish, on the part of this leader, to propel this virus into the world. However, in his thought processes, he could not accept the possibility of being defeated, and therefore, it did not matter about anyone else. In whatever way that he could do it, he would keep fighting for his dream of victory, until the end.

This leader had a strategy in his mind. The nuclear war-heads from these missiles were directed to go right in the middle of those zones, which already had high degrees of radioactivity, from the fallout of the nuclear weapons, that had gone before. He supposed that, by aiming the missiles to reach these positions, then, upon impact, the virus would, with high probability, mutate, and subsequently begin to multiply and spread rapidly in a myriad of new forms. In this way, the ability of other nations to counteract the virus would be negated. His country was in ruins. Now he was going to ensure, by the only route that he regarded was still possible, that he would destroy his enemy as well.

And with a huge dose of pathos, it happened just as he hoped. No one could stop this. The three missiles landed in very different locations, two of them in radiation affected areas. Shields had been taken out, so they got through. The third missiles went off-course and landed in the ocean. Nobody seemed to be bothered, but this outcome could not have been worse, for it generated an unbelievably sad result for the oceans and sea life, and another avenue for untold damage and desolation, which otherwise, might, at least for a time, have been spared.

Soon the bunker of this leader was destroyed, in further retaliation, and people warily thought that the wretchedness of the utter destruction, which they had experienced, may have finished. People were in acute shock after the nuclear bomb attacks. Cities had been decimated. Some countries had been spared, but the fallout went everywhere, and so many millions succumbed to radiation sickness and were dying horrible deaths. Law and order had broken down in places, and many societies faced complete chaos and disintegration.

People were coping with the tragedy in so many ways, but with the resilience that people sometimes can express, in times of extreme adversity. At this stage, not all hope was lost. There were groups and societies speaking about resurrection, about the need to abolish weapons of mass-destruction. At this point, a lot of people still thought that they had a world, where they could live, however damaged it may be.

It took a while for the impact of the virus to be even noticed. There was no immediate publicity about it. The first signs appeared when spreading areas of land became like wasteland, where nothing grew anymore, and life simply stopped functioning. It affected plants, trees, animals and humans. There was nothing immune to it. When people went into these areas they soon went through a process of ageing rapidly, and the cells in their bodies would cease to reproduce and renew. Scientists became suspicious, when these 'dead' zones began to extend beyond areas, which were infiltrated by very high radiation levels. And then rumours began to spread, about what this leader had done, and panic ensued. Now that he was dead, it was hard to gain confirmation. For some while, these stories were dismissed, and authorities grappled vainly with their attention, to re-establish fundamental services in areas that could still function, and to help the ill and injured.

People did not want to consider that there could have been any other menace to affect them, besides the nuclear attacks. There was so much overwhelming grief. And people's spirits were not yet defeated. Heroic efforts were made by some, to rescue and help survivors from the nuclear wastelands. People felt the need to construct shelters and outposts, where a few communities could begin to exist again. There was much generosity, and selfless giving. It was just presumed that these increasing areas of lifelessness, might be no more than by-products of excessive radiation infiltration.

As time passed though, concern mounted. These lifeless areas began to spread further and faster, and scientists were at last able to be heard about their fears, and communicate the supposition that something much more sinister was going on. Suddenly people began to take notice, and relay witness accounts about what was happening, and the full horror of this threat started to emerge.

Researchers isolated some versions of the virus but they could do nothing to stop it. They had too little time and resources. Mutated versions of it were multiplying continuously, and the virus did what it had been programd to do – it fed from the cells of different life forms around it, destroying the capability of other cells to reproduce in the process. Only the virus itself kept reproducing and this was the abysmal part. The authorities tried everything they could to contain it and stop it reproducing, but by the time the scientists knew about the problem, it was too late. Too many science faculties had been destroyed, and the virus was spreading everywhere. Surviving people began to panic and there was a growing alarm that life as we knew it on the Earth, could be doomed. Already, the most developed nations of our world, were severely weakened by the impact of the nuclear war. In despair, people in Authority conceded that there were no defences, which they knew, that could stand up against the virus attack.

Some countries had managed to avoid being hit by bombs, and were not severely affected by the worst of the nuclear fallout. I suppose that the country where we lived, was one of those 'luckier' ones, if you could call it that. So, when news came about the virus, our City had a small opening of time, in which to react.

A decision was made, soon after it was clarified about the spread of the virus, that the best chance of survival, which we would have, would be for the City to encase itself, so the virus would not be able to infiltrate. At this stage, there were enough people in the City that were determined to commit themselves to this, that all efforts were made to enact the decision. Consequently, with all skilled people being employed for this task, management, detailed planning, building and construction began. Our workers and engineers engaged tirelessly upon the work of enclosing the central part of the City, encasing the boundaries of our urban area, with thick concrete walls and deep foundations, using reinforced glass to create ceilings, and constructing airtight alleyways, with effective filters, for our water and air supply. Huge enclosed greenhouses were erected for food production, to aid us with our survival. It was a mammoth undertaking that had to be completed in a very limited time space.

For a while, Internet links in other parts of the world remained active, through connection, with the small number of satellite channels, which had been undamaged. And some extremely disturbing images were posted.

There were images from a few of the countries, undamaged by the nuclear attacks. What became immensely upsetting, was the slow systematic manner, in which forests and wildlife and food production areas from these countries, were slowly being rendered lifeless, by the virus. There were enough pictures and accounts that were recorded, to show graphically, the relentless decline that took place. Nobody in these places knew what to do. People could not understand it, or comprehend 'why,' and there were personal accounts of people, who were raging at 'God,' feeling that they had been spiritually abandoned. Their rage did nothing to stop the onslaught.

More and more of the Earth became Death Zones, and it was a hopeless situation to be in. To watch the insidious and inexorable progress of this destruction, was soul-destroying for people's Spirits. Reports from areas, affected by the unfolding catastrophe, showed the wailing and abject despair of people, as they lost all that had been most precious to them.

With the virus approaching, the governing Authorities in our City banned residents from being able to watch any live coverage of what was happening. The Internet was turned off, so people would not feel any more distressed. It was necessary for people to focus on immediate tasks, making progress with those, to keep up morale. There were no further records of what happened, and I could not find out about the final stages of the destruction.

In the last international broadcasts that our City had received, before the Internet was cut, it could be seen how people were retreating into their little pockets of remaining enclaves and trying to find ways how they might be able to survive, in a lingering manner, for a little longer. Hope was sapping from people, as the life died around them, and all that remained was a deep, fruitless sense of helpless despair. It was so sad. And I felt acutely disappointed that the broadcasts did not go on, to find out if any of those people had survived. At least, librarians in our City had preserved the coverage we had, and that made it possible for me to view it.

I wanted to know, if there were any survivors besides us, from other parts of the world. But now, I was not sure if we would ever know.

THE SEEDS OF DESTRUCTION

The research I did in the library enthralled me, but I had no one to share this with. My family were not interested, and people I saw in the corridors and at the markets did not interact with me. Even in the library, the occasional people that visited there, scurried around, locked in their own worlds. Although this disappointed me, it did not discourage me, and I felt a compulsive urge to continue my learning. This was the one activity, that helped to keep me interested in life.

After I had finished learning about the Extinction War, I studied books, video records and commentaries from times before that, for I wanted to learn everything that I could. When I could see scenes of what the Earth was like before the destruction and especially the beauty of nature, I often cried, with a desperate longing for that beauty, to be alive again.

Over time, my interest in understanding the forces behind the cataclysm deepened. The biggest question for me was to answer what went wrong? How could humanity get itself into such a mess that it virtually destroyed itself? How was such a thing possible? I read various social commentators, philosophers, activists and politicians, as I desperately sought to find the truth. Through my reading, there were some underlying messages that became clear to me, and I felt that these pointed to important contributing factors.

On the military level, there appeared to be two main impulses at work. One, more defensive, was the fear of being attacked by another nation or group, and this led to countries making steps to protect their sovereignty. The other force, more aggressive, was the urge to dominate and to demonstrate superiority over others. Both these tendencies fed into each other and created situations where there was a continual spiralling of new and improved weapons, which could generate ever more massive destruction. The rationale, for having these weapons combat ready, was that nations needed powerful 'deterrents' to prevent other nations from contemplating attack. Military chiefs used this as a persuasive argument for continuing the arms race. Ultimately, though, the premise for doing this, proved to be wrong.

The main economic model, had been based around 'growth' and

'development,' where interest groups would compete against each other, and try to outdo each other, to gain the best possible deal. This approach encouraged greed and exploitation rather than cooperation, with companies and governments vying to look after their own interests and gain exclusive rights over products and land. Thus, society was segmented and fragmented, and the ambitious and capable, became richer and more powerful, while the masses became poorer with fewer rights, and suppressed. Rather than cooperating towards the needs of the greater whole, this prevailing model of society fostered attitudes of selfishness and isolationism, and put increasing strain upon the resources of the Earth.

When developers continued to build houses on a finite piece of ground, until conditions became so overcrowded and stressful, and nobody could really breathe and feel a sense of space anymore, then, apart from giving copious profits to the developers, how could such a process be considered 'growth' for all the people concerned? People were told that this was the way the system had to be, and they were ostracised if they resisted being part of it, while those 'in' the system endured increasing stress.

Many people wanted a more humane approach, one that took everyone's needs into account, but the ruling classes fought against it.

My opinion was that it would have been healthier if there had been a sense of working together towards the 'common good,' where cooperation rather than competition was to the fore. Why did people choose this competitive approach? As I thought about this, I considered about the status of men and women in the society then.

Traditionally, women typically, had been the ones nurturing and devoting themselves to the needs of the greater whole, sometimes even sacrificing themselves to encourage the well-being of others. They were the cooperative ones. Men, on the other hand, would reach out and be the protectors and providers, and they also tended to be the fighters. They were the competitive ones. Over many centuries, the balance between male and female had been distorted and unbalanced, with women being suppressed and abused, while the stronger dominating male presences, rejected feminine concerns. This influenced greatly how societies and nations were structured and modelled. Societies then, reflected much more the qualities of the male psyche, rather than the gentler, nurturing feminine psyche or a blending between the two. The values of 'growth,' 'competitiveness' and 'military prowess,' for instance, were archetypal male traits.

Hence, in those end times, rather than having nourishing, embracing communities at the heart of people's existence, where people's collective needs of community were considered, people suffered the lack of this. They felt stifled, acutely alienated and withdrawn from others, even deprived. They lost the ability to be able to trust in anyone, except themselves. When trust was lost, so was care for others. In a society with more respect for feminine qualities of connectedness and working together, I felt that people would have felt better and lived in greater harmony.

The societies where people lived, especially the so-called more 'advanced' countries, where material acquisitions were so highly prized, these had become increasingly remote and disregarding of people's Spirit, despite marvellous technological advances. Many people had to drive themselves to be working, rushing feverishly with the utmost efficiency, so that they could meet some corporate expectation, with the competing marketplace. It was not a way of living that was healthy, and it placed ever more strain upon people, generating anxiety and unhappiness. Corporations and governments wanted control. They were too powerful, and people felt unable to challenge them.

What did it matter, ultimately, who pressed the button, and who ignited the missiles that destroyed our world? If we had lived in a different way, there would have been no button to press. If we had sought to care for each other and our Earth, we could have found a way through, together. How must they feel now, those souls that pressed for greater control and power, greedily and selfishly sapping the Earth of all its abundance and joy, setting up conditions through fear and mistrust where no one could cooperate anymore?

And the last place where one person felt he could take refuge and find his own sense of power in a world, where the overwhelming dominance from governments and corporations was eating away remorselessly at people's sense of identity – this man felt that he had to live out his sense of power, and he wanted to do it, and the way that he found this, was by pressing those buttons, the ones that destroyed everything. By the time that this happened, the obsession with power and influence had gone many times too far.

When I reflected about all this in that library, I often stared outside the window at the rumps and remains of what were once magnificent trees on the hillside. This is what we had become. Humanity had proven itself incapable of managing itself, and our planet. It just filled me with sadness, and I wanted to cry, tears that would never stop.

PLANTS

But I couldn't immerse myself in tears. I had to live; I had to find my way in this City, I had to find a route to a better life.

As a young child, I had the desire to leave the City, and I desperately wanted to go to other places – anywhere. It had taken me a long while to work out why my parents and everyone around me appeared to be so sad and withdrawn. This had confused me, and part of me had felt like, I should be sad too, to be like them. It was only when I had studied the records in the library that I understood. I learnt many things in that library.

When I did my research, I looked up about education for young people, how they used to do it, and I felt dismayed. I had never had those opportunities, like school, or university. All those practices had been abandoned. I felt regret about that.

Now that I knew most of the answers that I had sought about the Extinction War, I needed something else to do. I still wanted to study, but that was not enough for me, on its own. I decided that my next step would be to find work, for I thought that doing that would give me an interest, and I wanted to help with the maintenance of the City.

Maybe it was the dream of the sapling, which I had had as a young child, but there was something about growing plant life, that fascinated me, and I wished to tend to the plants, nurture them and care for them, and learn as much about them as I could.

In our living quarters, we had three plants that were situated by the windows, overlooking the hills. I noticed how, in the afternoon, the leaves of the plants would stretch over and bend themselves towards the sun. In the growing season, I would spend time with them every day, and I regarded them as magical beings, and like companions for me. I enjoyed to touch the leaves, and stems of the plants. Sometimes I would hold my hands near the plants, and imagine that I was sending love to them, like I had seen in my dream. I believed that this was like feeding the spirit of the plants, and they liked it.

One day, while I was at home with my plant friends, a man came by our apartment, to check on our plants. We had workers come to our apartment for various reasons, but there was something about this man that was different. He made eye contact with me, and his eyes were a sparkling blue colour. This was so unusual, as most people, when I saw their eyes, carried such sadness and lifelessness about them, that it made me want to turn away. With this man, it was different, so I gave him my full attention. I noticed how he was genuinely interested in the well-being of the plants. I could tell that in the way that he related to them.

To observe someone else, caring for, and loving plants, as I liked to do, well that was amazing. I had thought that I was the only one bothered to do that. As the man went through his list of tasks, he first came over to our plants to water them and inspect them. Then he had some composted plant food, to give them. When he saw my interest, and how closely I watched him, he showed me the different parts of the plant and told me how much water they needed so they would be healthy. Each plant was different, and only by watching how each one responded, could I ensure that they flourished. They were like children, he told me. When he said that, he smiled, and I could see kindness in his eyes.

Immediately, I felt a bond with this man, and as he was leaving, I wanted to cling onto him and for him to stay. For a moment, he paused, and our eyes met once more. It was strange, but in that instant, I felt closer to him than I had felt with the rest of my family, for the whole of my young life. Suddenly, the loneliness that I carried like heaviness in my heart was gone. And I wondered, in the way that he looked at me, what he felt about me?

But as quickly as those sensitive feelings arose in me, they sank again, as the man quickly strode away, out through our front door, and on towards the next apartment, where he would visit. Would I ever see him again? I hoped so, I really did.

I should have asked him if I could work with him. I wished I had.

Afterwards I went over to the window, and looked outside again, at the dead stumps of trees, I felt stirring in me to discover what made plants live, and what forces could possibly manipulate these beautiful beings, to stop living. I wanted to nurture the plants, and help them to grow. And meeting this man awoke in me the impulse, to act on this. I wished to seek him out. The yearnings in my heart confirmed about the need I had for a change. I wanted to do, what he was doing.

So, the next day, after I had been to the library, I ventured to explore further into the City and go to areas where I had not been before. There was no one to stop me, and no reason that I needed to do the same thing every day. My parents stayed at home. Just because they never varied their routine, did not mean that I had to do the same thing.

As I came across new places in the City, I felt a surge of freedom and expectancy, motivating me. These were not feelings that I had known very much. However, with the meeting of that man, something had woken in me, and I was no longer content just to do the same things all the time. Whatever the conditions were outside the walls of our City, with all the destruction and withdrawal of life energy, this was not sufficient cause for me to die too. I had come into this life for a purpose, and I wanted to learn what that could be.

Over the next days, I went onwards and I began to map the different areas of the City in my mind, as I became more familiar with them. And it didn't take long, after I started doing this, for me to find the expanses of gardens where all the fruits and vegetables were grown. When I first came around the corner, to the entrance of this, I just stared in wonder. Why had I not come here earlier?

During my life, I had never seen more than a few plants growing together, but here, it seemed to be quite a huge expanse of growing plants. This was incredible. As I continued to stare, I realised that these plants must be crops, which had to be grown to supply food to feed the population. I looked around in amazement. What I admired, was how every space was being utilised, even layered to be able to grow as much as was possible. The richness of the aura of the plants, stimulated my senses, and I felt a sudden burst of enthusiasm.

In the background, I noticed that there were spaces that were less developed, and workers were busy planting crops there. It became apparent that this was a project that was still reaching for its potential. I just wanted to watch and learn and take all this in. And I also wanted to get my hands dirty, and join in with all the work. This was a place where I wished to be. Definitely.

I watched for a long time. At first, I was wary and tried to stay in the background. I was not sure that the workers would want me there. However, soon I realised that most of the workers did not even seem to notice me. I wondered if they were going through the motions of existing, not living, like so many other people that I had seen. It was not a happy thought.

I wanted to find the man who had visited our apartment, but I could not see him. At the end of the day, even though I had not connected with anybody, I decided I would come back the next day, and explore further. I felt determined.

The next day, after spending some time at the library, I came there again. Although I loved the plants, and wanted to be involved, the workers in this field did not interact with me, so I just watched. I came many times and they did not stop me, but they did not ask me about what I was doing there either. And I felt uncertain to ask them if I could help. I was unaware at first, that there were more than one garden field in operation. Then, one day, I was around, when I overheard one of the workers talking about the other fields, and it was then that I realised that they existed. So, I resolved right then, that I would visit them too.

A few days later, I discovered the third garden field, and there, digging in the field, with his spade, I saw the man that had visited our apartment. He was busy harvesting buckets of potatoes, and placing them in containers, so they could go to the market place. Immediately that he saw me, he looked up, and stopped what he was doing, and came over to me. I felt that my heart was smiling. I was so glad to see him. And that was the beginning of a new phase in my life.

ADOLFUS

The man shook my hand and introduced himself to me. He told me that his name was Adolfus. Straight away, he invited me to help him. First, I had to put on work clothes, and he was sensitive that I needed to keep my other clothes clean. But then, for the rest of that afternoon, I was shown how to harvest potatoes, and I learnt how to discern which potatoes to pick, and how to arrange them in the containers. It was hard physical work with those potatoes, and by the end of the afternoon, I was tired. The work clothes I had been given were very dirty. But I loved it. And I had to ask Adolfus if I could come and work with him again. And to my delight, he said yes.

And so, wandering down to the gardens of the City to be with Adolfus, every day, I felt happy. Adolfus gave me a tour, of all the gardens, and the rows and rows of vegetables that were planted. There were names for each variety of fruit and vegeatable, and Adolfus knew them all. Meeting him reaffirmed my decision about where I wanted to spend my days, the library and the gardens, both precious in their own ways, and not boring at all. In the gardens, I had human contact, and I could work with the plants. And it was just what I needed.

Adolfus set me tasks to do. At first, these were quite basic, like watering, weeding and picking fruits, but my responsibilities developed as I became more proficient. I was not always able to work directly with him, because he had a multitude of chores that he needed to do, and I became aware, that he was managing the other workers too, and instructing them, as well as doing his own work. But I never felt that he neglected me. He introduced me to the other workers, so I would feel included. And each day I found that I was learning more.

Adolfus was a middle-aged man with long straggly hair and a moustache. His clothes were always rather rough, and he wore thick gardening boots. Whatever his appearance, he was one person in this City I knew, that was alive and working with purpose. So, for me, he was like a beacon of light, and I felt so grateful every time that I could be in his company. At the end of the working day, we had time together, and he told me stories. When he spoke, I could feel my imagination playing and creating patterns inside me, and I listened very intently, to all that he told me.

I followed Adolfus around everywhere, whenever I could. He was the one that I wanted to be with. One of the first things that he did with me, was to give me a simple watering can. This was my watering can, to water the plants. I felt pride, and I was so glad to have it. He taught me that in everything that I did, if I made a mess, then I had to clear up the mess after me and look after what I did. He taught me many lessons, and I respected him. I loved working in the gardens with Adolfus, and he seemed to enjoy me being there.

Sometimes, when he bent down to say something to me, I took liberties and pulled on his moustache. I don't think he liked that so much, because he would then chase me around, and when he caught me, he would have a very mean expression on his face. But then, we would both burst out laughing. We had fun together.

Adolfus had a very beautiful golden Labrador dog whose name was Rusky. I had never seen a living dog. When I first saw Rusky, I felt such joy in my heart. Rusky also liked to follow Adolfus around, and we played games with him, and I loved to stroke his soft fur. Adolfus was much busier than Rusky though, and often when Adolfus was doing his rounds, Rusky would climb up on Adolfus's comfortable chair, and spend several hours sleeping.

I later found out that Adolfus was involved in a breeding program with the dogs, and was actively trying to promote giving families young puppies, as a means of supporting them to have an interest, and more zest for life. Sadly, Adolfus often struggled to find homes for his dogs. Once, I asked my mother if we could have one, but it didn't matter how many times I asked her, she refused.

While I was with Adolfus and Rusky and in the fruit and vegetable fields, I was happy. But it was not so easy for me at the end of the day, when I walked home to my apartment – I just did not want to go there. The corridors were empty. Not many people ventured out, and those that did, always seemed to have their heads down, and I could not help but feel sad, myself, at the loss people felt.

One day, I found the courage to ask Adolfus, if I could work permanently in the gardens, and if I could become his apprentice. By the delight, I saw in Adolfus's eyes, I knew that he was very agreeable, but this was not just a matter between him and I. We would need to approach my parents. Indirectly, I was asking for his assistance to do this. And later, at the end of that day, we went together to my apartment, and spoke to them.

I felt rather nervous, but did not need to be. My parents, in their usual passive state, did not object, but neither did they show great enthusiasm, more apathy. But at least I was informing them of what I was doing, and I felt easier for doing that.

THE SEALING OF THE CITY

Over time, Adolfus and I had many long talks. Sometimes, I arrived back to my apartment quite late. But for me, it was such a relief to find somebody, with whom I could talk. I was glad, for he seemed to welcome conversation with me, as well. He lived on his own with Rusky, and I guessed that he sometimes felt lonely too. Being with him and Rusky felt like having another family – one that was so much more rewarding than my biological family. Adolfus was also my teacher, and there was a lot that I could learn from him.

Adolfus had been very much involved with the sealing of the City, after the initial stages of the Extinction War. It was a harrowing tale, but I wanted to acquire all the details, so I would know the full story, in addition to what I had studied. And I insisted on him telling me, even though he was quite reluctant. In stages, though, he did tell me. And the more he told me about what the people in the City had achieved, the more I realised what a colossal job this must have been, an acute life or death crisis, and a race against time, to ensure the survival for people in the City, against the backdrop of unfathomable cessation of life, and destruction in other parts of the world.

People then, had wanted to believe that humanity could recover, and eventually everything could work out, in a manner that was hopeful. Even with all the devastation, they needed something to cling onto. People knew that the virus would reach us, from reports coming from other parts of the world. Before the Internet was shut down, many people would go online, and seek out news. However, it was evident, the indications of the absolute havoc that was taking place everywhere, without exception. The advance of the virus and its impact was unstoppable. But while it was some distance away, people wondered and prayed earnestly that the virus may weaken or mutate into another less harmful form. By living in hope, it gave people the incentive to work.

While the immediate presence of the virus was still at a distance, people's motivation for protecting the City remained high. Planners, architects, builders, engineers, and scientists all worked together with considered urgency. The Administrators of the City had to draw a line around what parts of the old City could be included, and what had to be left out. Priorities of action were drawn up. The outer structures had to come first, and all the basic support systems that we would need. Teams worked around the clock, and there was no shortage of volunteers to help.

Walls needed constructing, with concrete foundations going deep into the Earth, around every stretch of the perimeter of the new City. There had to be toughened glass, and airlocks and water systems, all sealed in with incredibly precise detail. There could be no mistakes.

The virus could not survive heat, so piping from the nearby dams that supplied water to the City had to be modified so the water would be boiled, distilled and then cooled through various mechanisms before it was let into the City boundaries. Similar techniques of warming and cooling were applied to air that came from outside and this was tightly regulated and filtered to allow air to circulate through to the City without danger to life.

There were so many tasks. One group of people were assigned to construct an organic living sewerage system so our waste could be reusable and provide compost for our plants and vegetables. Other workers had to adapt commercial buildings, so that they could serve as apartments where people could live. All that could be done, was put in motion, to be accomplished.

The efforts to save the City brought the people together, and for a time, gave purpose to everyone, and reason to keep going. The Council Administrators in the City were at the forefront of all the labours, and coordinated all the assembly that took place.

In those times, Adolfus had been a young man in his late 20s. His specified work then, had been to construct gardens and utilise all enclosed spaces that could be used for food production. The Authorities in the City had to plan for what plants, food and minerals would be necessary, as a bare minimum for everyone's nutritional needs. This was an area where Adolfus had expertise, so his input was very much welcomed. Adolfus was also responsible for creating seed banks, and maintaining them. It wasn't easy, and he told me how desperately hard, he had to apply himself in this endeavour.

It seemed like a miracle, that the walls of the new City were sealed just in time. Only two days after the City closed its entrance ways, a man came staggering to our outer walls in a dreadful state of confusion. He was let in, and put in isolation for a period, and fortunately, he recovered. This man had just been exhausted from his plight, and was not infected. But he had seen people in his village begin to be infected by the terrifying onset of the virus. He saw people losing energy, dying in a horrifying manner, plants and animals struggling, and a sense of life collapsing around him. He just ran, and ran, to the only place where he felt he might be safe, and so he came to the City. He was the last person that the Authorities let in.

From then on, the City became like a tomb, completely separated from the outside world, except for the regulated air and water, that was needed to keep life functioning. People could see through the windows, what was going on outside, but they couldn't go there. At first, there was jubilation and celebration. It was a relief that everyone in the City could survive. But it was not long before that feeling began to change.

When people started to witness, through the glass from the City walls, the withering of plants in the landscape nearby, trees losing their foliage and becoming brittle, and even the sight of animals being tormented and dying agonisingly, then the whole experience took on a different complexion. Contact was lost and broken with all other outposts of civilisation, and the reality of utter isolation, and the emotion of what had befallen everyone, began to sink in. Soon, people did not want to be in this crypt that was our City. It was like a burial place in waiting. More and more people became broken and deflated.

For a while, nothing very much happened in the City. People were numb with disbelief, and struggling to come to terms with this new reality and state of being. Their circumstances were so much more constricted than anything that they had known. The ravages of the virus, and its desolation of the landscape outside, became complete, and there were no signs of life anywhere, apart from within the City walls.

Adolfus told me though, that eventually, several expeditions were arranged to travel from the City to discover more fully, the impact of the virus, in other localities. The people going out on these expeditions, were dressed like astronauts in protective clothing, and purified air tanks, to keep them safe from the virus. They set out in sealed vehicles along prearranged routes. Some followed the river to the coast and visited the settlements there. Other teams went inland.

What they found was similarly grim, everywhere. No signs of life remained, and the bodies and bones of people were scattered, wherever they fell. Many of the corpses wore agonised expressions. People in the City anxiously waited for news from these expeditions, and the outcome was extremely discouraging.

As an extension of this investigation, three vehicles set out to go on the very long journey north, to our capital. This was a much riskier undertaking, because of the distance involved, but people felt that they needed to know. If there were any other possible enclave of survivors, then they had to be located.

Because there were no longer the facilities for longer range communication, no contact was possible from these vehicles, with the City. For a long time, people waited, with hope. But none of those vehicles ever returned, and nobody knew what had happened to them.

This then exacerbated people's fears and feelings of isolation. The disappearance of these vehicles, made people increasingly reluctant towards further exploration of this type. The feelings of resignation among the people spread with further dismay.

Scientists did tests, by taking samples from the soil, and from dead plants and animals, in our surroundings. Their findings showed that once the virus had done its work, then it transmuted into a dormant state, but continued to exist. They did further tests by placing food scraps on the ground outside the City walls. The virus became active again and the food quickly deteriorated and became dead matter. There was no lessening of its capacity to destroy organic matter, and the danger for everyone in the city, remained. As much as they tried, the scientists could find no remedy, or means to reverse the harmful effects of the virus. They investigated with many approaches, but there were no reported breakthroughs.

People drew their own conclusions. What the scientific tests emphasised to the people, was that they were alone in the City, with no other existing life anywhere else, and no hope of being safe, to step out of the doors of the City, without protective clothing, because of the continued presence of the virus.

This added to the helpless feelings with regards the convoy, and knocked back any residual feelings of hope that people still had. That is when many people rapidly lost heart and reason to live. Not much more work got done. And the state of people's well-being in the City, declined more and more. There were reports of high levels of mental illness, and people were not coping. Doctors prescribed tranquilizers for many.

And then a landmark decision was reached in the Council, giving people the right to voluntary Euthanasia. For many, this was the best option, although for some, like Adolfus, they did not want to give up. But to keep going, was a struggle, without any obvious reward.

Adolfus told me about all of this, and about his own challenges, in those early years of our confinement. The administration of the gardens and fields were divided up, so the responsibility for it could be shared. Adolfus was nominated for a coordinating leadership role because of his enthusiasm and expertise. But many of the workers that had helped set up the gardens and crop areas, discontinued their labour for the project, and with fewer and fewer workers, it was not possible to give proper attention to all areas of production. Adolfus raised his concerns about the workforce with the Council. However, even though an edict was announced to encourage more volunteers, people could not rouse themselves anymore, and were becoming generally increasingly disinterested in all forms of activity. The only balancing factor was that there were also becoming fewer mouths to feed because of the high suicide rates. The problem of falling numbers of workers occurred in all strata of the community, and it was a dilemma that the authorities did not know how to solve. Adolfus told me that he had to be very strong within himself, and committed, to keep things going.

One of Adolfus's initiatives before the City was sealed, had been to bring in some bee hives so the bees could help pollinate the vegetable plants and fruits. But within a year or two, all but one of these hives had stopped functioning, so some plants needed to be pollinated artificially, and this made the work of the horticulturalists much more demanding.

Also, most people were used to eating meat in their diet, but this just was not possible anymore, and Adolfus had to bear the brunt of many complaints about that.

Then one day, the gardeners suffered a huge shock when it was discovered that many of the plants were dying in one of the fields. When Scientists tested this, it was confirmed that the virus had penetrated this area from underneath the City foundations. Panic ensued, and people fled to their apartments and locked their doors. However, enough volunteers helped, so that this affected field could be closed off in time, and concrete foundations were reinforced around its perimeter to keep the virus at bay.

People needed help to calm down after this. Some people reacted in a hysterical manner, panicking that they would never be safe. But for

Adolfus, it affected him in other ways. Because of this intrusion by the virus, a large section of the agricultural ground was lost and became uninhabitable, like all the other land outside. Adolfus just needed to adjust to this. He was glad that since then, no other virus intrusions had taken place.

FAMILY

I am sure that my mother and father loved me. But they did not show much affection. In my everyday life, I received far more hugs from Adolfus than I ever did from them. Being in our apartment was like being in an atmosphere of continual gloom. My mother cleaned and tidied so everything looked neat, and she cooked meals. My father sat most of the time. He had stopped working, and he spent his time on computer screens playing games and exercising his mind. They hardly ever went out, except if they had to do so. Their only interest appeared to come from their interaction with my young brother, Martin. They enjoyed watching him as he grew and developed.

Once, I started working with Adolfus, they paid very little attention to me. At times, I imagined that I would much prefer living with Adolfus because at least he would notice me.

At times, I made efforts, and tried to help my mother or do something extra, like tidying, which she would appreciate. The most I ever got from her was a small smile, and that was hardly rewarding for what I did. I tried at times to play with my brother, but I could sense that with him being my parent's pride and joy, that my role in his life would be peripheral. It hurt me that I could not relate to them more easily. At times, I felt sorry for them.

Some days, I saw my father staring out of the window at the dead trees and the barren landscape, and there were tears streaming down his cheeks. I wanted to put my arms around him and reassure him, but the only time, I tried to do that, his body felt so stiff and unwelcoming, that I never tried to do it again. With my mother, she also looked very sad, a lot of the time. On a few occasions, I tried to put my hands near my mother, like I did with the plants, so I could direct love towards her, and I could feel the energy pouring through me. But my mother didn't like it, and it disturbed her somehow. She told me to stop. Maybe it stirred in her an awareness of feelings that she tried to block away. Over time, I concluded that she didn't want to feel better. Neither of them did. And I feared for how this would affect my brother as he got older.

At night, I would sometimes lie awake and listen, and all I could hear was the soft breathing of my brother lying in the bed next to me, or the occasional gust of wind outside. On the videos, I had heard the chirping of birds, and I wondered what it must have been like to wake up to the sound of birdsong. How joyous that must have been.

THE TEMPLE

In the middle of our City, there was a religious temple. It was a place where people of all faiths could come to pray and contemplate. It was a round building with a high arched ceiling, and altars inside the building around its circumference. There were some Spiritual symbols painted on the walls and some statues of religious icons, but it was mainly kept simple and plain. Before the War, the site of the Temple had been occupied by a Christian Church, but it had been rebuilt and adapted while the City was being sealed. I occasionally went past it, on my way to the Gardens. I didn't go inside, and it felt barren somehow. Although I could marvel at the physical beauty of the place, when I looked it, I couldn't see any people visiting it.

I remembered, from when I was a little boy, attending the Temple with my parents and brother, at Christmas. During this time, when I was small, the Temple filled with people then, but that did not happen anymore. One memory I had, was of a tall solemn Priest telling the congregation how Christmas was a time of love and giving, and that we should open for the light of Jesus to inspire us. I could not understand what the Priest meant, because, even at Christmas then, people showed very little happiness, and giving, in our community. There was no joy in the Christmas service. People were just too locked, in their own private inner misery. So, it was more a sense of duty and the comfort, of doing something familiar, that brought people to the Temple for this occasion. That was certainly true for my parents.

One Christmas, there was a priest standing on the pulpit, that I had not seen before. He wore impressive robes, and he had longish flowing white hair. His nose was somewhat bent but his eyes were piercing. He spoke with a loud and harsh voice, and he was not gentle like the other priests had been. I did not like it.

He told everyone that the War and the virus and all that had happened, were God's punishment for humanity, for we had been sinners, and we deserved what had happened to us. The only thing we could do was to repent and ask Jesus to take us in his arms.

I looked around, and everyone's head was down. This priest was urging everyone to feel guilty, and I felt like he was encouraging people to give up. I did not agree with this, and wanted to shout out. From deep inside me, I believed that there was a Divine source of love, and we could embrace this, or turn away from it. We had been given the capacity of free will, and this was what caused the problems. It was not any divine source, but us that had brought about this catastrophe. We were responsible collectively for what had happened, but we were also responsible for what we would do about it. I did not want to listen to this defeatist preaching. So, I waited for my moment, and then I stood up, and before my parents could stop me, I ran out of the Temple. I used my free will then, and I am glad that I did.

Some days afterward, I heard news from my parents, that this priest had died, choosing to end his life. He must have felt tormented inside. I was grateful that my parents did not challenge me about me running away. It was one chapter of my life that I was glad to close.

THE GARDENS AND FIELDS

As I continued working in the gardens, I felt a contentment that I had not known in my earlier years.

Adolfus told me another story, and explained how, before the City had been sealed, there had been a heated debate about whether to allow room for some farm animals. One side argued about how that would be very inefficient use of our available plant life and could lead to shortages. Other people were adamant, that we needed to conserve some farming animal population, as an investment to satisfy the requirement, as some saw it, for meat. In the end, one field was allocated for the animals, and some pigs, goats, hens and a couple of cows and a bull lived there. It was not very much, and hardly enough for those that were used to meat diets. Sadly, because of the hopelessness of our situation, there came a time when it was decided that these animal's lives would be sacrificed so the people could have some meat, and the poor animals were slaughtered.

Adolfus told me how, much later, people became so desperate in their craving for meat, that a group of them had approached the Council and demanded that some of the dogs which he had been breeding, be taken and used for human consumption. Adolfus was horrified and he pleaded with the Council about how valuable these animals were as pets for their owners. Bitter arguments ensued. Finally, a few people that owned dogs were granted privileges, in exchange for giving up their dogs for meat. Adolfus told me how much he was against this practice. He continued his breeding program but very carefully interviewed any perspective owner of pups that were born, to be certain that they would care for their pet and not sacrifice it.

When I first heard this, I was shocked, and held tightly onto Rusky, and stared into his adorable eyes. I would never want him to be eaten. The thought of it was appalling.

Adolfus knew a tremendous amount about plants. Not only had he studied conventional courses of horticulture, he had also investigated permaculture, and even visited the indigenous people living further inland. In the months before the virus took hold in our country, he had been out on many expeditions to the hills, and by the coast, collecting seeds for propagation, with a small group of others. Adolfus was successful in establishing a seed bank for the City community, so, as many plants as possible, could survive.

Without this seed bank, I don't know how the City would have managed in terms of food and natural medicines for the sick. Adolfus deserved special thanks for this. But with this and so much else that Adolfus did, he had to find his own strength to do what he knew inside was right, and there was very little encouragement or support around him. I tried to give him praise though, and I know he appreciated this.

Adolfus believed that there could be a future for our world. Despite the utter devastation, the continued active presence of the virus, and the complete loss of life that was self-evident beyond the City walls, Adolfus needed a sense of faith to go on. He could not accept that we would be the only pocket of life that had survived. Surely, the toxicity of the virus would weaken over time, and people's immunity would grow. Adolfus had to hope. It could not all end here. Adolfus had a great enthusiasm for life that never dimmed, and he worked with hope in his heart, every day. And I resonated with his attitude. If only there were more like him.

However, there were very few that shared his optimism. Too many concluded that the period of humanity populating the Earth, was finished. Sooner or later, the people in the city would die, and that there was nothing more that we could do. This was the prevailing thought, and I felt sad, that the views of Adolfus were not mirrored by others.

In the role of being my teacher, Adolfus taught me about growing food forests, and companion planting to nurture the nutrients in the soil. He made sure that we had a good supply of worms and other soil animals to help encourage the soil to renew itself. We had limited resources, and had to be adaptable to ensure the best results we could. He sometimes obtained some quite remarkable results though.

Working groups in the other fields wanted to use synthetic fertilizers that were supposed to yield greater numbers of crops. But Adolfus purported that these synthetic agents were not in harmony with the Earth, and would destroy the natural goodness in the soil. It was an age-old argument between two competing philosophies. However, as the years went by, the fields where Adolfus and his team grew his plants prospered, while the other fields, after promising starts, had diminished markedly in soil vitality, and less and less grew there. More and more of the gardeners turned to Adolfus for advice, and his methods were utilised increasingly by the workers.

Adolfus liked to use every available space for planting, and it was not just for food, but other plants that he wanted to preserve. He would layer plants together, and even use the walls of buildings for nestling plants and giving them the chance to grow. He was a remarkable man, and I felt proud and happy to be with him.

I had my favourite plants in the Nurseries and gardens that I used to nurture and care for very lovingly, and I watched over them every day. It still came to me, the dream of the sapling living outside, from when I was little. Sometimes, I would place my hands over the plants, just like in the dream, and I was very excited when I felt a tingling of energy that seemed to flow through me, to them. I used to pray that the plants would receive all the nourishment that they needed.

Adolfus said many times that I had a healing gift. At the end of the day, when his back was sore, he would let me place my hands over his lower back for a while, and he always smiled, and told me when I finished, that it felt better. I was glad to be able to help him, because he was so important to me, and the plants needed him.

Rusky also mattered to me, and when we finished work, he used to snuggle up next to me, and he often put his paw across my leg, or nuzzled me with his wet nose. He was a lovely dog. One of my jobs was to brush his golden fur, and to give him his dinner each day. Adolfus was careful about what we gave him to eat, for he didn't have any meat either.

As time went on, as well as being with Adolfus and Rusky, I also continued to spend time in the library learning about human history, and when I could, I went on outings to discover more about other parts of the City. Adolfus wanted me to explore because he felt that it was a natural part of being alive to do that, and he could also sense that I was not someone who liked to be restricted.

Adolfus was a great story teller, and he told me tales from his life and the places where he had been. It gave me such warm feelings inside when I heard about how his life had been before the War. I could imagine it all so well. Sometimes it felt like I was being transported into those times, so that they became alive again. And I closed my eyes so I could sense it even more fully. But then, when I opened my eyes again, and looked out of the windows of the City, it was always so disappointing and shocking to be reminded again of what had become of it all.

I tried to persuade my parents and my brother, Martin, to come and visit me and Adolfus, so they could see for themselves the gardens and fields where I worked. I asked them repeatedly, but they stubbornly refused to change their routines. When I pleaded for Martin, at least, to accompany me and go there, they would not let him, and insisted that he stay there with them. With Martin, the sense of duty, and wish to be loyal to my mother and father was always going to be stronger. My poor brother! He did not allow himself to do things for himself. I spoke with Adolfus about this, and he understood very well, my problem.

One day, Adolfus brought Rusky, and came with me to visit my apartment. My parents showed very little reaction. They were polite, and didn't stop Rusky, when he started to sniff around the rooms. However, Martin's eyes lit up, and he certainly enjoyed patting Rusky. And Rusky liked being patted. He always wagged his tail when someone did that. I thought that their hearts might melt, but they made no move to reciprocate and accept Adolfus's friendliness, and his many offers to show them the gardens. As we left the apartment, I saw Martin's eyes drop, when my mother and father made clear, that they wouldn't be making any visits.

I felt acutely disappointed. When I considered my parents, I was not going to be able to change them, no matter how much I wanted it. This distressed me. That night, when I lay in my bed, I felt alone, and tremendously lonely. Even my brother lying beside me, did not make it easier. I did not like living in that apartment, and I did not want to be with my family. They were so different from me. The depressed energy around them did not fit with me, and I wished that I could live somewhere else.

JOYCE

One of the places that interested me in the City, was the old Market Square. It was all covered over now with a roof and plastic ceilings. Adolfus explained to me, how in the times before the War, the Market place had been all open and was the vibrant hub of the community, where thousands of people would go every day. It had been a place, where there were stalls selling food, and all kinds of activities going on. The people loved it. So, when I went there, I had this in my imagination and could envision what it must have been like before. In my mind's eye, I could almost picture the people milling around, and the atmosphere of excitement that must have once pervaded this place.

Now though, it was virtually deserted. Only a few very sturdy stall holders remained, and they seemed to be there more out of habit, than having hope that they could sell their wares.

When I first went there, I was with some of the garden workers, who were taking containers of vegetables. The Square was one of the many collection points for people to obtain food, and this was the main reason that people still would go there.

As I walked on the cobble stones of the old market place, I could feel history underneath my feet. The foundations of this once magnificent City had begun where I stood now. Some of the buildings around the Courtyard were constructed of stone, that were very old.

Sadly, now it appeared not much more than like an empty shell. I stared in silence. It was such an odd mixture, with the structures made of ancient stone being overhung by pylons and artificial coverings of plastics and glass that was necessary to keep out the virus.

Over and over in my mind, I just could not take in the dreadful magnitude of what had befallen humanity, and I was not prepared to accept that life on our planet was just about all over. There had to be a way forward. This place haunted me, for the beauty of the buildings and the picturesque open Square, on one hand, seemed to represent the best of humanity, with what people could make, to nurture a sense of vibrant community together. Concurrent with that, the pylons and plastic roof, reminded me how the Community Spirit of the Market Square, had ultimately been lost and defeated.

One day, I came to the Market Square on my own, for I wanted to perceive more about its history, and take in its atmosphere. With my attention, I surveyed the perimeter of the courtyard, and I noticed the middle-aged lady, who had her table in one corner of the Square. I had seen her before when I was here with the others. She was always seemed to be there. Occasionally, one or two people would visit her stall, but mainly she was on her own. Mostly, she had her head down, or she would be reading a book, so I did not give her any consideration. But today, for some reason, I felt drawn to her, and I tentatively edged my way to where she was sitting. It was strange that I felt so nervous.

As I came closer to her table, I noticed that the cloth over the table was very clean, and she had jewellery and craft items that she was selling. As I looked more closely at them, I marvelled at the exquisiteness and beauty of her work. There was an expression of aliveness in the designs and freshness too. Her jewellery appeared to be all handmade. I glanced up at her in amazement, and she was staring at me with piercing eyes. I asked her, if she made all the items herself, and she nodded. Then she confided to me, that she made something new, every night.

I gasped in wonder. So many people appeared to have given up, barely existing in a form of living 'death'. This was what I had come to expect when I met people. And yet, here was someone, so unexpectedly, who was genuinely alive. This shook me, and something about her, stirred energy inside me. I continued to stare at the jewellery. It felt like the boundaries of my inner expectations, had been shifted, by meeting her.

There was something about her that was unusual. My heart was racing. I felt a knowing that I had been meant to meet her. Her long grey hair was tied at the back, and she wore long ear rings. In fact, she wore lots of jewellery, for she also had on, necklaces, bangles, and rings on her fingers. She wore quite colourful flamboyant clothes too, which contrasted so much, with the dull greys, and pastel coloured clothing worn by others. In her energy, she appeared to me to be like one of those old gypsy-woman fortune tellers, and this was something that attracted me to her.

Why had I not discovered her before?

She asked me to give her my hand, and as I felt her hand in mine, it was warm. For a few minutes, she studied my hand, as if she was reading it. Leaning over towards me, she told me: 'You must not give up. There are good reasons that you are here.'

They were simple words, but they went deep inside me. I knew that I had Adolfus and Rusky, but suddenly, I felt like I may have another friend too. For some moments, I paused, but then, as I released myself from the lady's hand, I felt like laughing inside. It was good. For a while, I stood there feeling slightly uncomfortable, not being quite sure what to say, but before I left that day, our eyes met again, and she smiled. She knew that I would be back.

After that, I returned to visit the lady many times. On the second meeting, we introduced ourselves to each other. She told me that her name was Joyce, and we talked. Over time, she told me where she lived, and about her life. In exchange, I confided in her about my own family, and my work in the gardens. As I came for subsequent visits, she began to show me how to make the jewellery, and to use my creativity to express what I felt inside. Joyce was a remarkable lady, and I came to value her very much.

One day, I persuaded her to come with me to meet Adolfus, at the end of her working day, and she agreed. I waited with her, and when she was ready, I led her there. It was a great pleasure to introduce Adolfus and Joyce to each other. They seemed to be able to relax together. Soon, they talked, and laughed like old friends. It was a good meeting, and the conversation went on until after dark. She liked Rusky too. When it came time for parting, I sensed that she did not want to leave. Somehow, I felt that Joyce belonged with us, and with her being there, our group was much more complete, and balanced. This thought gave me a warm feeling in my heart.

Over the next weeks, Joyce and Adolfus met several times, and became very well acquainted. Most of the time, I was with them when they met and I felt very comfortable with the two of them together. When Joyce came over to visit us, she started helping Adolfus and me, doing jobs in the gardens. She brought some of her equipment with her, to make some jewellery and crafts, and she told us that she would make us each something special, as a gift from her heart.

One day she came to the Gardens, carrying a large object, which was hidden under cloth. This was her gift for me. To receive it, I had to close my eyes and then she placed the object in my hands. I must admit, that I was very curious and excited, and I noticed how heavy the object was. But when I opened my eyes, my heart felt, as if it would burst, for what I held was a wonderful wooden carving. As I looked, I observed that it was the representation of a bird with its wings extended, as if it was about to fly. The energy of it felt so real, so, when I held this bird, it felt as if I was flying too. I could not help it – my emotions welled up, and tears streamed down my cheeks. I had never seen a bird like this, for we had no birds in the City. Probably, there were no birds anywhere. And that was so sad. But holding this wooden bird gave me joy, and hope, somehow, too.

I wondered what type of bird it was, and I searched my mind for names from the video records that I had seen. It was a majestic bird with fierce eyes – the kind of eyes that would search deep into your soul, and look far away, into the distance, when needs be. I marvelled at how sensitively the eyes had been made. And the talons – they were strong, and I could feel that their grip would have enormous power. The wings were only half open, and when they were extended, I sensed that they would be incredibly wide. And then I remembered the name. It came to me in a flash. This was the model of an eagle.

I must have looked down then, just considering, how I could be worthy of such a gift? But Joyce noticed, and she lifted my chin, and made me look at her in her eyes. At that moment, I saw such steely determination and softness, at the same time. She told me that this bird carving, was made for me, as a gift of vision and strength. The eagle radiated both those qualities, and whatever happened, the memory of this creature, needed to stay in the memory of humanity. She wanted me to embrace strength and vision in my life too.

For me, the eagle was already extremely precious, and I wanted to touch it and feel every crevice of its body. Somehow, I loved birds, and holding this, increased the desire in me, to find one that was still alive.

I asked Joyce if she had ever seen one, and she told me that she had. There had been many that lived on the hills before the War. They were great predators, with a strong affinity to the land, and Earth. Adolfus interjected, and shared how once, when he had been out climbing, he had discovered on a ledge, an eagle's nest, with three large eggs in it. He had not approached it, out of respect, for their life together. As I listened, my heart was pounding with excitement, but as I looked in the eyes of Joyce and Adolfus, I also saw their regret.

That evening, I placed the bird wood carving next to my bedside, so it was looking at me, and every morning when I awoke, it would be there to greet me. My parents did not even ask about it. But I expected that. I felt that Joyce must have great faith in me. However, I also felt awe for her creativity, and her ability to sense, and express the Spirit of the eagle. In my heart, I felt huge warmth towards her.

It was just a pity that I could not confide in my family, like I could with Joyce and Adolfus. But I knew that each day when I woke up, I had a choice, and could go in one of two ways. I could choose the path of 'deadness,' routines and wishing not to be here, and this seemed to be what my parents portrayed, in the way that they lived. Or I could choose the path of aliveness, and building towards some form of future. That is what I felt, being with Adolfus and Joyce. This was a daily confrontation I had with myself, but only one of those choices was worthwhile to me, and I never deviated from it. When I went to the gardens each day, I was singing.

BREAKING POINT FOR THE CITY

On the day of my eighteenth birthday, an announcement was made, of a proposed public meeting, for all residents of the city. The notice which went with this announcement, informed us all, starkly, that only about thirty percent of our population, which had been, remained. Numbers were continuing to drop. It was about five years since anyone had had a child, because no-one wanted to bring a little one into such a despairing and dying world. If the present death rate continued, then, in a few short years, there would be only a small number of people left. It was possible, that we were the last vestiges of people surviving on the planet. If that was the case, then soon all human life on Earth would be gone.

The question on the agenda of the meeting was what we wanted to do about it? Was there any positive action that we could take, which would make any difference?

A few determined administrators remained on the Council, and they were the ones who organised it. I was eager to attend, and when I talked with Adolfus and Joyce, they also wanted to come.

I tried to persuade my parents to attend, but they were pessimistic, and did not believe that anything good could come out of it. They refused to come. I also talked to my brother, separately, and while he listened politely, when it came to his decision, he told me that he needed to stay and look after our parents. At least, he retorted, that he would like to know the outcome of it. I just sighed.

Over the next days, I spoke to as many people as I could, to attempt to inspire people to come along. Several announcements were directed by the internal PA system, into every home, to inform people. Real efforts were being made.

The night of the meeting came. We were among the first ones to arrive. As we sat in our seats, I kept turning to the entrance, willing for more people to come. I was hoping that the hall would be full. But it wasn't. In fact, there were less than fifty people, forty-eight in fact, and I felt quite disenchanted. The start of the meeting was delayed in the hope that more people would arrive. No one else came. It was an awkward hush, while we waited, but then eventually, the meeting began anyway.

There were a panel of seven at the front of the Hall. Three of them were administrators, and the other four were scientists and engineers. An older man in the middle was their spokesperson. His name was Philip, and after introducing his colleagues, he spoke gravely to us, outlining our current situation. It was put to us that we needed to act. Whatever the risks, if we did not seek the means to expand our lives again, then before long, our City would no longer be viable. We had to discover if there were any other pockets of life existing, and if so, how had they survived? In addition, we needed to check on the virus, and do tests to discover if the land further away from our City was any more hospitable, so we had more options of where we could live. If possible, we had to explore and ascertain what had happened to that expedition that went to the provincial Capital.

As a first step, the administrators called for volunteers, to help the remaining Scientists and engineers, so research about the concentration of virus presence, could be done, in outside areas. People were hesitant. There was not a lot of enthusiasm. Both Adolfus and I offered to volunteer, but we were refused, me because I was too young, and Adolfus, because his skills were too vital for the City, for him to be put in any danger. I was disappointed.

It was so frustrating. I passionately wanted to help, and the explorer inside me was crying out to do something. Inside, I felt impatient and wished to be involved. It irritated me that I was not allowed to participate. But there was nothing I could do to make them change their minds. I thought about it, and as I turned it over inside me, I felt the inner urging, telling me to let it go, and so I did that, and accepted that I had been refused. If I had to wait for another opportunity, then I would. I felt calmer after that.

The Committee struggled to find enough volunteers. However, eventually, teams were assembled and given tasks.

Over the next weeks, volunteers were trained and work began. In the first stage, under the supervision of Scientists, groups went outside and tested the soil, taking samplings from material that had once been organic matter. They travelled to many different sites to gain a cross-section of places to ascertain the concentration of the virus, and whether it still had the potential to destroy life. Of importance, was the question of how much the virus still existed in its dormant phase, and how much mutation had occurred, which may have reduced the virus to be less of a threat?

When all these findings were tabulated, and compared with previous testing, carried out in the early years after the War, it was confirmed, that the concentrations of the deadly virus, had indeed lessened. The degrees of concentration also varied between areas. This was encouraging. But the levels were still not safe, and we had to test, on current levels, how the virus would respond if organic matter was in its vicinity.

When a well-watered pot plant, was placed outside the walls of the City, it survived for two days or so, before shrivelling and dying. This was much longer than the survival rates in those first years. We had to feel heartened by that. However, it still was not enough for anyone to venture out, without protective clothing. Similar experiments were carried out in areas where the virus concentration was lowest, but none of the plants could sustain their life. What that meant, was that if we went outside, we might not be affected quite so quickly by the virus, as at the beginning, but we would still die.

Going further with the second stage, expeditions were then organised to scour the countryside for any signs of life. The findings from this, confirmed what had been found previously. Along the coast road, in and around the various townships, there were skeletal bodies lying untended on the streets, scenes of distressing misery, and past suffering, from those that died there, but no life anywhere. The plants were all dead, and there were no hints of animals living. Much of what was seen, was videoed, so it could be studied further in the City. Later, when these studies were made public, there was nothing hopeful to be seen.

People wanted to set up another expedition to go to the Capital, but this was not so easy. The infrastructure for communication over long distances, just was not working anymore. Satellites had been destroyed in the war, and the national communication network with no one to maintain it, had broken down long ago. However, it was not deemed satisfactory, for another expedition to go along that route, without people in the City being able to monitor it. Some line of communication would have to be established. The engineers on the panel wanted to consider the viability of a relay operation.

The panel hesitated about approving this new expedition, but were willing to consent to planning it. The idea was for a group of volunteers to travel in a convoy, far along the coast. Engineers worked with the communication equipment we had, to attempt to improve its performance. They constructed a series of transmitters and receivers, which could be employed by vehicles in the convoy, as they strung out, along the coastal road. With the number of vehicles that they had, it was calculated that, to keep the communication channels open between the Convoy and the City, that they could reach, almost to the outskirts of the Capital, but not quite to its Centre, before the limit was reached. They just did not quite have enough equipment, to make the whole distance. The last two vehicles with the expedition would need to go on alone, to complete the journey.

There was a lot of debate and strategy meetings, to decide what to do, but people now wanted this expedition to proceed, and so, eventually, it did.

On the day, that the convoy left, people watched through their windows. There was no rousing send off, just a silent vigil. I knew, that the outcome of this undertaking, would mean a lot to people.

Regular reports came in over the City loudspeakers about the progress of the expedition, while the vehicles spread out along the long coastal road. So far, they had not found any signs of life. We all waited, until it was finally confirmed, that the limits of communication had been reached. Now, the last two vehicles would continue in tandem, and out of communication range, to venture through, into the heart of the Capital.

This is where we all held our breath, with a mixture of hope and anxiety. To allow all of us left in the City, to witness the unfolding of this journey, there was a public screen set up, where we could observe, with a video camera from the furthest point of contact, pointing in the direction, where those two leading vehicles, had last been seen. A small crowd gathered to bear witness to what was taking place. Adolfus, Joyce and I were among them. It was an eerie feeling, staring, and being captivated, by the emptiness of the landscape, on this screen. My stomach felt knotted with fear. I could see that Adolfus's knuckles were white, as he clutched the chair in front of him. We all felt the tension.

We watched and waited. The clock on the wall showed, that we had gone beyond the point which had been agreed for them to return. More time was given for them to appear. There was anxious conversation between the Expedition members, and the administration in the City. The expedition members remaining, became concerned about the air supplies they still had. But they could not abandon their friends. Surely not? I strained my eyes on the screen, wanting so much to see some slight indication of their presence. However, there was no movement, no objects, nothing.

Further time elapsed. There was then discussion whether those in the most forward vehicle that remained, should follow them to try and help. After much discussion, the decision was made, that this was not deemed safe, or offering a realistic chance of rescue. For long ages, the forward vehicles remained stationary, while their ability to stay there diminished. The night fell, and then the new day came. Still, there was no news. More waiting, until finally, there was the order from the City Authorities, and we could all hear it, the order which we dreaded, and nobody wanted. The mission was told to abort.

The two vehicles that entered the provincial Capital never did return. The population was devastated. Did this imply that some unfriendly survivors did exist there, or that there was some other unexplained risk? Nobody knew, but with the disappearance of those vehicles, adding to what had happened with the first expedition, the remaining hopes of the people in the City also went with them. In due course, the other vehicles in that relay team returned. The Expedition members were very despondent and upset.

After that, the leaders of the Council in the City had no answers anymore, about what they would do next. People slunk away, feeling disillusioned and despairing. It was a terrible disappointment, and it was no surprise, that following on from all this, there was another rise in applications for voluntary Euthanasia, and more shut up, empty apartments that I noticed on my way to the gardens and fields.

A CITY DYING

For the next few weeks, Adolfus, Joyce and I were all deeply upset, and quiet. However, one evening, we had a conversation, and Adolfus asked us how we felt about it. We all vowed to keep going, and I was so glad that we could say that to each other. But not everyone had the same resolve.

One of the workers that had been with Adolfus since the beginning, came one day, and said his goodbyes to Adolfus and told him that he just had had enough. Adolfus would have to do without him.

I was with Adolfus, when this worker spoke about this. His name was Ramos, and he was a single man. He could not see any point in continuing. Although he was talking with Adolfus, I spoke up and tried to argue with him, and tell him that his work was important. But he didn't want to listen. The more he shook his head, the louder I argued for him to stay. In the end, Adolfus gently signalled for me to stop, and looked affirmatively at his co-worker in resigned understanding, and let him go. The numbers of workers throughout the City was thinning by the day.

Efforts were made by the Authorities to try to encourage people to stay alive. If the levels of viral activity were dropping, then there was a future for people to be able to live outside the City. This existed, and we needed people to be around for that. But the death rate in the City indicated that, by the time the land was safe enough for us to venture out, the chances were high, that there would be none of us left.

We had a sperm bank in the hospital, to help with pregnancies, but this had not been utilised for a long time, for there was no one wanting to carry a child, either through artificial conception, or by more natural means. I hoped that this sperm bank could still be useful in the future, but I was not sure. With there being so few younger people, how could the propagation of our race, succeed?

At night time, I would speak silently with my carved bird, as if we could have conversations. With him, I could pretend that there was the potential of a solution for the people of the City. Of course, there was none really. But I was not going to give up, even if things got very hard. My will and my subconscious held different emotions though. Sometimes in the night, I would wake up with a start and I would be shaking with fear.

RUSKY

One morning I woke up with a different form of dream, one that felt true, and saw the vision of Adolfus's face in front of me. At first, I did not even know that it was a dream. He was pleading with me to help him, and I wanted to rush forward to do so. But as I moved towards him, however close I got to him, he appeared just out of my reach. Suddenly, I felt a huge outpouring of love for Adolfus. I opened my eyes with a start, and was shaking.

That day, I knew that a crisis was coming to test my good friend. I just hoped that I would be able to offer some support.

For some months, Adolfus's beloved dog, Rusky had been becoming thinner and eating less. The times that he slept were more extended, and his ability to go on long walks had decreased. He was an old dog by now, but he still wagged his tail and was very affectionate. Through the years that I had known him, he had been such a wonderful faithful companion to Adolfus, and I could sense the deep love between them. I loved Rusky too, and his presence had made such a difference to me.

About a week after my dream, we had a shock one morning, when Rusky refused to get up and do the rounds with us. He wanted only to stay on his mat outside the main garden area, and sleep. Adolfus tried anxiously to rouse him, but he wouldn't budge. We were all worried. I could see panic in Adolfus's eyes. Joyce was regularly with us in the mornings now, and she suggested that I go and do the rounds with her, and that Adolfus could stay with his dog, but Adolfus felt compelled to adhere to his normal routine. That morning, as we watered and tended to the plants, not a word was said, but there were plenty of feelings going on underneath. Throughout the following days, Rusky became more listless and his eyes were glazed. He was getting weaker.

I tried to give Rusky some healing with my hands, and I felt a lot of energy channelling through, and this seemed to brighten Rusky up for a while, and he even tried to stand up. But, as we watched him, he didn't have the strength anymore, so he would flop back down onto the mat again. Adolfus was anxious and fearful. Joyce had some plant remedies that she had prepared and brought one morning, and we tried that too. She placed some drops of these into Rusky's mouth, and indeed they also made a difference. And for a few days, Rusky found some energy again. But, as with the healing, it did not last, and soon, we exhausted all the possibilities of what we could do to help him.

One evening when I went home, I told my parents and brother, Martin, about Rusky, but they seemed so disinterested and dismissive, I decided not to bother any more with them. Why did they not care? That night I cried myself to sleep, and asked myself the unthinkable – what would happen if Rusky died? I didn't want to think about it, but as I asked the question, my heart became tight, and I could think only of Adolfus and how he could possibly cope with this loss.

For the next few days, Adolfus and I stayed with Rusky by the gardens and did the bare minimum with our work. Joyce came to join us for much of the day, and went out, doing the rounds for us. Because Rusky could not get up anymore, at night time, Adolfus slept at the Garden shed with him. We both knew without speaking, that the time was approaching, but we could not bear to admit it. There was so much sorrow around our garden shed, and I did not know what to do. My fear was that it would get worse.

Then one morning, while I was watering the plants, Adolfus quietly called Joyce and me over to him. Rusky had stopped breathing. Frantically, I went over to him to shake him, and tried desperately to resuscitate him. But it was no use. Adolfus just stood forlornly by, watching, with tears streaming down his cheeks. Rusky was dead. Joyce tried to put her arm around Adolfus, but he didn't want it. We wrapped Rusky gently in his blanket and sat by him.

For days, Adolfus was inconsolable. He lost all interest in his work. Neither Joyce or I could do anything to motivate him, and we had to do the garden work ourselves. For the first two days, Adolfus did nothing else except sitting there staring into space. He was lost in his own worlds.

It was a loss for me too, for I had loved Rusky dearly, but I had to give my attention to Adolfus, for I did not want him to give up his Will to live. I asked my parents if I could go and stay with Adolfus for a few days, and I was grateful that they did not object. It was vital for Adolfus to have company during this time, and I was happy that Joyce was also mostly around. I must admit that I felt very worried, and I was not certain, whether, Adolfus would go the same way as Ramos. And if he didn't want to live, where would that leave me?

Joyce's rhythm was such that she was there to help us in the mornings and then later in the day, she would go on to her market stall. However, with this crisis, her time with us had been extending longer and longer, and she was returning to be with us for a while at the end of the day too. I missed her when she was gone, and wanted her to be with us all the time.

One afternoon, I felt a longing to see Joyce and so I left the gardens and went to visit her at her stall. I had to be with her. As soon as she saw me, she advanced towards me. There were tears in her eyes. She gave me a warm hug, and then leaned back, looking deeply in my eyes. Her warmth moved me. I could not find any words, and just moved forward, burying my face on her shoulder with floods of tears. For a few moments, I felt embarrassed, but as she stroked my hair gently, I knew that I could trust her. I could not stay long, because I didn't want to leave Adolfus by himself, but those few moments were very precious.

The next day, Joyce appeared at the gardens and announced that she had packed up her stall for good. From now on, she wanted to offer her services full-time to help in the gardens and fields, and to be with us. I was overjoyed, and even Adolfus looked up and gave a half smile.

Following on from that, Joyce and I continued to be the ones that kept things going with the plants and crops. As much as we tried to get Adolfus involved, he only made a few token efforts of contributions. At least that gave us some encouragement. Adolfus watched Joyce, and I was glad that his eyes at least, were showing some interest. It was good having her with us full-time.

One afternoon, Joyce sat down with Adolfus and asked him very gently if he wanted to talk. Adolfus showed no movement, but Joyce was patient and she waited for him. From the distance, I stared and was hardly breathing as I strained to view what would happen. After a few minutes, Adolfus leaned his head over and placed it on Joyce's shoulder, and began to sob. She put her arm around him to comfort him, and he let her do it this time. And he cried for a long time. Joyce smiled at me, as she gently reassured him, and he could start releasing layers of grief that he had been holding inside.

Later that night, we talked about Rusky, all three of us, and we shared stories about all that we loved about him. We stayed together until late in the night, and then finally left together. Joyce came with us to Adolfus's apartment, where she said 'goodnight' to us both, while I remained with Adolfus. I stayed awake, until I could hear Adolfus gently snoring. That night I started to feel happier again.

In the morning, we did a ceremony of thanksgiving for Rusky, and we placed his remains in with the compost for the plants. The nutrients from his body, as they decomposed, would enrich the soil and provide goodness for the plants. It was the best way how Rusky could continue to support the work that we were doing and for us to feel him with us.

About a week after this, we heard news that one of Rusky's offspring had given birth to a litter of pups. I tried to persuade Adolfus to come and see them. There was something inside that told me that this was important, and Joyce had a twinkle in her eye. At first Adolfus was resistant. He felt that seeing the pups would just remind him of the pain he felt over Rusky. But we implored Adolfus not to hide away – that seeing Rusky's grandchildren may be positive. And at last, he agreed to a brief visit. So, we went to see the litter, at the end of our working day.

There were three adorable pups, and they all looked like a young version of Rusky. It was so good to see them. And they were running around getting up to all kinds of mischief. They loved to be cuddled, and I felt such a lot of joy to be with them. But there was one of them that seemed to be very much drawn to Adolfus. He came up to Adolfus, and was sniffing at his leg and biting at his trouser leg. At first Adolfus tried to dismiss him, but he kept returning, and wagging his tail, and he wanted Adolfus to pat him. There was something about the way he moved and positioned his head that was familiar, and I noticed how Adolfus could not take his eyes off him.

We stayed there for a long time, much longer than I had anticipated. But this pup would not leave Adolfus alone, and gradually Adolfus was starting to open to him. Joyce and I stood and smiled at one another.

Then Joyce turned and told Adolfus that he had found the new Rusky, and Adolfus looked up, and there were tears of joy in his eyes. That evening, when we left, there were four of us, not three, and Adolfus had a new dog. We smiled at each other.

In the weeks that followed, I wondered if the Spirit of Rusky had moved into the body of this pup – they were so much alike, and the sense of recognition was very strong. It did not come as any surprise to me, when Adolfus named him 'Rusky,' just as he had called his ancestor that had left us. It was a fantastic declaration to me, that life could go on in a good and loving manner, and that is what we had to aspire to achieve.

RESTLESS LONGINGS

Over the next period, I continued to work with Adolfus and Joyce in the fields and gardens and I took on more responsibility for the administration of it all. I enjoyed the companionship of Adolfus, Joyce and young Rusky, very much. We all had a lot of fun together.

Even though I was old enough to have my own apartment now, I continued to live where I had done. I felt protective of my family. While my parents and Martin, continued to potter around, and carry on with their routines, and I had an outlet with my work in the gardens, then I felt comfortable, and could cope with the stark conditions that we faced.

But every time that I glanced around and noticed another empty apartment, or a decrease in the amount of produce needed to feed the inhabitants of the City, it occurred to me, how our community was continuing to slowly die. Our situation was like a seeping wound that just would not heal. People refused to step outside the City, and no more tests were done. After that last fateful expedition, no-one wanted to expose themselves to the dangers of the hostile world outside our walls. And nobody talked about it. Watching people wander around, there was a depressed energy, even worse than before, that made me so glad that I had my friends.

Even though I was comfortable, I was not satisfied to be in the City, and I did not want to resign myself to the life here. More and more, I wished to leave. These thoughts, I carried inside me privately, and I yearned to find a way how I could do that. Adolfus and Joyce, now, seemed more content with the life that they had, and their bond was becoming stronger. They had similar thoughts to each other, and wanted to support each other. I was glad that they were content, but I was not.

Adolfus had travelled extensively when he was younger. He knew the country around our City very well. If there was any chance that anyone had survived the virus, he would know where to look. And yet he had said nothing of this to the Authorities, ahead of the expeditions setting off from the City, nothing at all. It was odd. I wanted to test him, and get him to tell me about the communities he had visited. I felt uneasy and restless, wondering if there may be anything, anything at all, that he was withholding, and could be useful.

Hence, from then on, I started initiating conversations with Adolfus about his earlier life outside the City. He tried to change the subject, but I persevered, and kept asking him questions. Was there any chance that there could be other settlements with survivors? I was insistent, and had to obtain some answers.

I did not understand Adolfus's reluctance to engage with me? He appeared resistant to my probing, and he became irritable as I asked questions. But I was not going to stop. Somehow, I had to know. As I pressed him, I could tell that he was becoming emotionally affected. There was something here that he did not want to talk about. He also seemed torn about it. On a few occasions, he almost appeared ready to disclose something, and then he retreated again. It was very frustrating.

One morning, I felt very determined, and put my questions to him again. Adolfus frowned at me, and resolved with me that at the end of that working day, we would sit down and talk, and he would share with me what he knew. I had to accept that, and for the rest of the day, I waited impatiently, while Adolfus was very silent, often staring into space. Joyce picked up on it and asked him what disturbed him? But Adolfus said nothing.

Finally, we sat down. It was beginning to get dark, and Rusky lay by our feet. Joyce had asked if she could stay as well, for we could all sense that there was something important for Adolfus to say. And Adolfus agreed to proceed.

As I looked at my guardian and friend, I noticed lines in his face from all the feeling and effort that he had put into his life. He had an open face, and I had always known that I could trust him. But there were also signs that he was becoming worn out and tired. I didn't want to see that. With Joyce's presence, I hoped that their relationship would preserve him for a long time to come.

Joyce made some herb tea for us, and then Adolfus began to share. His voice quivered, and filled up with emotion, and even though he gave us a few glances, he stared downwards as he spoke. Once he started, we both listened intently.

'In my early days before the War, I travelled and met some wonderful people that had a deep love and affinity with the Earth. These people taught me a lot about plants and about methods that I use now, to nourish and nurture the plants. Some of these were indigenous people, people whose ancestors had lived on this land for thousands of years. They had ancient knowledge of the land. In their consciousness, they belonged with the land and felt connected to it, as if they were part of it. Meeting these people touched my soul and I believed in the strength of these people.' He paused for a moment.

'I am sorry that I have not told you about these people before, because their existence is important. But my time with these people is wrapped up with events in my life that are still very painful for me. For a long time, I have not wanted to think about it and have tried to protect myself.' Adolfus was trembling and there were tears in his eyes. But then, there was also anger rising in him, and defiance.

'If any people on our world could survive the onslaught of the virus, then they could. I experienced that they were people, greatly sensitive and attuned to their environment, much different to us. In our High-Tech City life, such people had been under-valued and unappreciated. That is a shame, and we could not be proud of that. Neglecting the wisdom of these people was one of the reasons that our world ended up the way it did.'

He stopped then and looked up at us, taking a deep breath in the process, before saying more. 'One community I visited, was situated up in the hills, to the north. I spent a considerable time there. There were a mix of people living there, with some indigenous people and others of more Western heritage. But they preferred a simple way of living, close to the Earth and to each other. They did not agree with the High-Tech City life, and regarded this as alien to them, and deadening to their senses. They were like the old-style hippies from our former times. However, they had genuine regard for the values that they lived, and as people, they were happy together.'

I found myself very much enthralled by what Adolfus was telling us. He went on. 'I felt inspired by these people, not only by what they knew, concerning plants, but by how they lived. And I wanted to join with them. For many months, I did that, and I felt a peace that I had never felt in my life.'

The emotions were rising in Adolfus, as he paused, and hesitated again, and then swallowed deeply. I opened my hands to direct energy towards him, and asked inwardly that he could find courage. He couldn't look at us at all now, but he was breathing in deeply, to steady himself, and to speak the words he needed to say.

'There was a young woman in this community, and her name was Mary. I fell in love with her.' Tears rolled down his cheeks. This was very painful for him. Joyce gently placed her hand on his knee to offer support and to urge him to continue. 'I lived with Mary in her wood built house, and we were very happy together.'

'But I could not stay, because I had a duty to return to the City with my research findings. I felt a responsibility, and had to leave. It was desperately hard to separate myself from her to do this, and I resolved to return as soon as I could.' Adolfus shook his head with regret.

'And it was shortly after I returned to the City, that the war struck. The viciousness and overwhelming destruction of the war resulted in panic and shock within the City. I felt torn. I pleaded with the authorities of the City that I could return to the Community where Mary was staying. But those Authorities were unbending in their resolve to me, and insisted that I had to stay. I was needed to administer the food production for the City. They knew and I knew, that without my skills, that they would not manage. So, I had to decide whether to act for the well-being of all the people in the City and their survival, or for my own personal happiness. I could not do both. It was such a hard decision.

'With the relentless encroachment of the virus, as I continued to work on supporting the City, it reached a point where I did not have a choice anymore. I had lost contact with Mary. The Community where she lived had their own struggles, and she was committed to stay and help there, where she lived. But in my heart, I wanted nothing more than to be with her, and I did not know how I could do it.

'There were times when I was involved in all the preparations for sealing the City, when I felt very tempted to leave, and return to the Community in the hills. But I was committed too, and my work with the seed banks and preparing agricultural beds, was part of an immense effort to save people, and I felt that I could not forego that.

'When the virus killed the trees and all the plants outside, it was like, my heart inside breaking into many pieces, for I could not bear the thought that Mary's community and the beautiful trees around that, would be dying too. I just had to hide my feelings and be strong, to keep going, and do my work each day. There was not a day that passed when I did not think of Mary and pray for her.'

For some moments, he was silent, reflecting with the pain he felt. Then he looked at me, down at little Rusky and over to Joyce, and he started to sob. We put our arms around him, and his body was warm with the emotion. We held him for a long time, until finally, he looked up at us, and gave a half smile. Then he continued.

'There were many times when I wondered if the Community and Mary in some way had managed to survive. But I stopped myself from ever asking that an expedition be organised, because I could not face that people from the City would go there, and then discover that it had all been destroyed – like everything else.' Adolfus sighed again.

'Sometimes I hear Mary's voice talking to me in my mind, with her sweet and caring voice, and she encourages me. However, because of this, I have also assumed that she must not have survived and is now in the Spirit World.'

At this juncture, Adolfus stopped and more tears rolled down his cheeks. It was tremendously brave of him to share all this, when he had kept it all inside himself for so long. And I felt greatly moved by the story of this Community, but also stirred by it, for it opened a possibility for me that, until now, I had not known existed. The three of us hugged each other with love and appreciation, and we felt very close to each other and bonded through the openness of Adolfus's sharing.

However, that night, I tossed and turned in my bed. I could only sleep fitfully. Something was working in me, and I had unsettling dreams, dreams with vivid images that I could only vaguely remember afterwards. But there must have been something significant going on. In the morning, I somehow felt different, like a seed was germinating within me.

A FLICKER

Over the next weeks, I continued to have restless nights. At times, in the mornings, I felt wrung out from emotional release of dreams I could not quite reach. I did not quite know what it was all about. Then one night, I had a particularly strong dream that I did remember clearly.

In the dream, I was sitting on a hillside overlooking this beautiful valley. As I looked down into the valley, I could notice a thick undergrowth of trees, with birdsong and people moving about. There was a community of wooden huts near the base of the valley with a lush and winding river winding its way through the magnificent landscape. I felt startled with the scene I saw, and I was shaking with disbelief. The beauty of it was extremely real and I wanted to breathe it into all my senses.

Suddenly though, it all changed. There was a shudder in the tranquillity of this community, and it felt like an enveloping energy of malice rapidly invading the space. It was the virus; I knew it was the virus. I could feel this force choking and suffocating the life forms there. People were screaming and the lifeblood of the place was being destroyed. I desperately wanted to help, but I could not move, and was frozen to a spot, removed from it all. Soon it was nearly all gone – trees dead, an eerie silence, and desolation everywhere. Horrifying. All that remained was a small fire that flickered mournfully. At that, I woke up with a start, and I was shaking and drenching wet with perspiration.

Over that day, I turned this dream over and over in my mind. Was my dream a true vision? It did not feel like an ordinary dream. I felt greatly disturbed by it, and I kept coming back to one detail that puzzled me. Why should there be a fire remaining after the virus ravaged the community? What could this mean? Did that mean that some of that community had survived?

Later that day, I shared my dream with Adolfus and gave a thorough description of what I had seen of the Community. Adolfus was astonished because the details that I described, matched exactly with what he remembered of the beautiful community where he had lived, and been with Mary. We were both perplexed, excited and alarmed at the same time. Adolfus became upset. He did not like to consider that Mary and the other people of the Community could have suffered. I sensed that Adolfus would not have been able to cope with me sharing about the agonised expressions I saw on people's faces there – so I had kept that bit from him.

I had to go there. There wasn't any question or doubt. I had to do it. I just needed to go and find out. It was as though the dream held a deep calling for me to rise out of my routines, and move, and I could not refuse. Several times, I spoke with Adolfus about it, but he was not keen. He was concerned for my safety, especially after what had happened to those members of the expedition with the provincial Capital. Adolfus tried to dissuade me, and I guessed that the underlying reason was that he did not want to lose me. What chance was there that anyone in the Community could have survived?

I could not accept his concerns, so I persisted and argued with him, and I could feel that I was becoming more adamant. Adolfus wanted me to give up on the idea, so he tried another tack, and he put to me about my parents and brother – that if I went, what reason would they have to continue to live? They were quite close to the edge already. I reflected on it. His argument might be true, but I was not going to listen to that. My reply was to counter that if someone did not make the effort, we would all be dead soon anyway.

Eventually, Adolfus relented, and said that he would come with me. We would need protective clothing and supply cases that would keep the virus from infecting us. He wanted us to proceed respectfully, so we went to the Council to put forward our proposal.

Adolfus was passionate in presenting our request. I was surprised. But the Council Authorities rejected our pleas. They only had a limited number of the protected clothing outfits and supply kits. They did not have the capacity to obtain the materials to be able to make more. If there were to be any more expeditions, the priority for the City Authorities was for them to be able to make another attempt to reach the Provincial capital and investigate conditions there. This is what they regarded as the best hope of finding other survivors. They could not afford to lose any more equipment with our expedition, and they considered that the exploration that Adolfus and I wanted to make would carry a lot of risk, because it went inland, and the terrain was less hospitable.

I could understand the logic of this, and I argued my reservations about their outlook. Who would be available to make that third trip to the provincial Capital? There were less and less people left. The thread of hope in the City community now was so thin, that any more mishaps would destroy, utterly, what slender longings for life remained. When would they ever go? They were blocked in their attitudes and fixed in their ideas. It was frustrating, for they were not open, and not prepared to listen.

Adollfus made an appeal to the Head Body of the Council. I went with him, when he met with them and put forward my proposal, once more, to them. Adollfus had approached the Council many times with matters of concern, and usually they were very agreeable and sympathetic with all that he wanted to do. But on this occasion, they challenged him because of the conflict that this posed with their own priorities. They asked me to explain my reasons for wanting to do this. I could only repeat what Adolfus had told me about the existence of the Community prior to the war, and that this was an area that had not been checked. Bravely, I then also expressed to them about my dream and the meaning I had given it.

The Council Head Body were not convinced. Dreams meant little to them. They were administrators with practical minds, and could only rebuke the foolishness of what I was suggesting. I thought then about how dreams did matter and should be considered. There had to be more to our lives than practical decisions.

Before they finished, the Council Body also made clear that they could not afford for Adolfus to leave the City. His work in the Gardens was vital. They would not allow it.

When I walked out of the Council Chamber that night, I felt downhearted. Adolfus suggested that I may just need to be patient, wait until the time was right, and ask again. But I feared that the time would never be right with them. And I wasn't going to be deterred. I knew that this was something that I had to do. Adolfus had reached his limit of how far he was willing to support me with this. If anyone was going to go out and visit this Community, it might have to be me, and I may have to do it on my own.

Over the next days and weeks, I questioned Adolfus about the current levels of virus activity outside the City. Was it still dangerous and lethal? Could it be possible to go outside now without protective clothing? Adolfus became exasperated with me. He did not know, for the Scientists had not yet done extensive further testing. The regular monitoring, which they did just outside the City walls, showed that the levels were still dropping. But they were not yet safe. And from the more far-reaching testing carried out previously, the level of virus activity was variable. For anyone going out there, the places where the virus was more concentrated would be invisible. There were no instruments which we had, that could measure those levels immediately. Therefore, it was not safe.

I did not let go, and I persisted with my questions, until one day, Adolfus broke down in front of me and beseeched me not to go. I looked in his eyes and saw the sadness there. There was such a lot of loss in his eyes, and he did not want me to add to it. But there was loss everywhere. In this City, the energy was dying. I did not want to die without making this effort.

I held his gaze, and he embraced me, wishing that I would understand.

I did not say anything. At that point, I decided that I would be quiet and not trouble Adolfus anymore. That day, I found a project in the garden where I could be on my own, thinking. If I was going to do this, I would need to organise it carefully.

CONSIDERATIONS

What Adolfus had expressed about my family had struck a difficult chord inside me. Although, they did not engage with me very much, I did love my parents and my brother, Martin, and I wanted them to survive. My parents did not appear to value me very much. However, I knew that I still mattered to them. If I went away to search for this community, then they would feel that I was abandoning them. I did not want to give them another reason to give up on life, or even to die. If I left them and something happened to them, how could I cope with that without feeling guilty or responsible? It was a big dilemma for me.

Perhaps, out of a sense of that impending guilt, I started making efforts with them again. When I came home from my work in the gardens and fields, I tried to speak more with Martin and my parents, and build up my rapport with them. I felt that my best chance of finding peace with them would be if I could reach the point of being able to share my plans of leaving with them and to discuss it.

But try as I did, they were not interested in anything outside their daily routines. It was as if I was hitting a brick wall. One day, my father shouted at me, and forbid me to talk about this Community. He didn't want to hear about it. My mother, also, did her usual thing, and busied herself with household chores and didn't want to know. It took a lot of effort for me to continue to be with them. I did not share their reality, and they didn't want to share mine.

My last hope was to speak with my brother, Martin, about it. One night, I dared to do that, and I even shared about my dream. For some moments, I could tell that he was considering what I was saying. But then, it was like a curtain coming down inside him. He reacted derisively.

'They could not have survived. No one did.'

And that was his way of dismissing the conversation, and stopping me in my tracks. I felt completely deflated. After that, he did not want to talk about it anymore, and I didn't either. And I was left to dwell on my thoughts by myself.

I did a lot of thinking, and I concluded firstly, that I could not change people that did not want to change. In addition, I could not allow myself to sacrifice myself to them, to join in their ways, when they were not my own.

What could I do about the urges in me to leave the City and go to that Community? At night time, I lay awake tossing the different arguments around in my mind. If I waited, how long would I have to wait? The Council was only interested in one possible expedition, to the provincial capital, and fixed in their attitudes. Meanwhile, the population of the City continued to dwindle, and the place felt ever more like a tomb that no one would ever leave. And there was also no guarantee that the Council would even agree to a trip into the hills to explore about the Community, whatever happened. My family had emotional needs, even though they expressed these very little, but I was not responsible for their lack of interest in life.

Until now, I had been acting as positively as I could, participating with Adolfus and more latterly Joyce, to help manage the plants and agriculture. We had enjoyed so many human interactions that were completely worthwhile. But all this was no longer enough for me. With the lifeblood of the City dying and there being so few young people living, what was there to hope for? I could understand why people were lining up for voluntary euthanasia.

If I did not make this trip, then I would be sabotaging what I really wanted, and going against myself. When I used my imagination to project myself forward, into my future – considering that I made the choice to stay in the City – then it was clear that I would gradually lose the Will to live, and become depressed. There would be nothing to drive me on, in the City. Sooner or later, I would become like the other members of my family, even if I tried to fight against it. When I listened within myself, my deeper self was at peace with the thought of me going. This gave me confidence that it was right.

From the time when I was very little, I had had a knowing instinct inside of me that I could rely on. When I was in doubt, this knowing would guide me, and I could ask it questions if I was struggling in some way. It was very helpful for me to have this faculty, especially with me being so different from the other members of my family. It was that knowing which had guided me to seek out Adolfus and Joyce, and to study about the Earth history. When I listened to this inner aspect of me, I was happy and strong.

My mind, on the other hand, was full of fears. There were so many reasons for saying 'no'. I could not anticipate the outcome, what would happen in the City, with my family and with Adolfus and Joyce? Certainly, I could not predict if I would survive outside the City, whether I would die from the virus, whether my supplies would last, and if there would be any sign of life outside the City. It might all end up being a huge disappointment. The possible uncertainties and concerns stacked up, and as soon as my thoughts buzzed around these, I felt very anxious and restless. The only way I could counter this was to be still, and to listen inwardly.

And then, each time that I did this, as I considered what was my inner truth, not only did I feel peace about going, I also felt joy, and even excitement. The time to do this was now, not postponing it. I had delayed making my decision about this, only because I had to work it out, with all the different parts of me. What gave me the impulse to do this – the strongest reasons – to leave the City, and go on this journey, was the dream that I had, and my faith. The decision was made.

Now I could go into action. The next day I would make my preparations for leaving, by gathering food and water. With clothing, I could do nothing to insulate myself against the virus, so I would wear clothes that suited me, and take one spare change of clothing with me. I planned to write two letters, one to deposit with my family and the other with Adolfus and Joyce. These letters would inform them what I was doing, and I also wanted to urge them to keep going, and stay alive while I was away.

I was uncertain if I could face them directly with this. The emotions I felt, and they would feel, about this journey, were very strong. For the start of my journey, I wanted to feel peaceful, with my resolve clear. After one day of preparations, the following morning, after that, at dawn, I would leave.

A LEAP OF FAITH

During my day of preparations, I spoke with Adolfus about the virus – again, and while I tried to avoid arousing his suspicions, I sought to gain as much information as I could, so I would know how I could best protect myself while I was on my journey.

Adollfus might have guessed my motives, but he willing to share what he knew. He considered that it would be madness to go outside the boundaries of the City without a protective suit. Even though the latest scientific measurements had shown that the levels of viral activity outside the City gates had reduced beyond 'low' to even 'negligible' in some places, that did not mean that it may not multiply again if there were living organic matter in its presence. The research showed that the virus was now increasingly mutating into harmless forms and posed much less of a threat. But the danger remained, and there were pockets where the virus concentration was still high. Adolfus leaned over to me, looking tellingly into my eyes, to emphasise, that when a person was infected by the virus, there was no cure. Once the virus had taken hold, its impact would be inevitably fatal.

I asked Adolfus what symptoms, a person could expect if they became infected by the virus. Adolfus was incredulous to be even asked such a question. He turned to me again, and with a very stern look in his eyes, he accused me of being grossly foolish for considering going out there. But he told me that with the virus breaking down the cell's capacity to renew itself, the first sign would be tiredness that would progressively increase, followed by break down of functions in the body. Once this all started, symptoms would just become worse.

When I asked for Adolfus's advice about how a person would best avoid the virus when they were outside the City, he laughed at me and told me that the best remedy was simply not to go. He looked at my downcast expression and then sighed. After a long pause, he offered me advice, suggesting that the best places to be, would be in the open, and to avoid going near dead organic matter like trees or bodies, just to stay away from those.

Adolfus must have realised what I was planning, and was resigned that he could not stop me. I could appreciate, with the love that he felt for me, that he would still answer my questions. I guess that he knew that it was better for me to have this information than not, whatever I would do.

With Adolfus being so forthcoming, I decided, bravely, to ask him for directions about how I would get to the Community and any hazards with the terrain. As I put this to him, he gave me a half smile, and then answered. He did not draw a map, but gave me landmarks that I would encounter to direct me. These, he described in detail, until I understood and he was sure that I would adhere to them.

One of the main problems with the notion of visiting the land where this Community had been situated, was that it was positioned in quite a remote place, where there were no sealed roads, and it was out of range of the City's remaining communication facilities.

Vehicles for driving in the outside terrain were locked away. Nobody had use for them anymore, even though a small number of them had been saved for the occasional expedition. But I had no clearance to use those; I did not have any experience of driving anyway. So, this meant that I would have to walk. According to what Adolfus calculated, he estimated that it would take me four days full walking to get there, and involve strenuous climbing to traverse the hills. He pointedly remarked that a person would need to be very fit to make that journey, even under normal circumstances. When he made the trip in his younger days, he had a four-wheel drive vehicle. Now it would be much more difficult because of all the debris.

As I put together what Adolfus told me, I discerned that from the moment I left the City gates, I would be completely on my own, with no support, and there was so much that could go wrong. Should I go? The part of me that craved to feel safe was screaming for me to back down, but the knowing in me still told me, that I had to do it.

In my mind, I travelled through the route I would take, and how I would get out. There were only a few points of entry in and out of the City. All doorways had been sealed long ago. But these entry points were not heavily monitored now, because nobody dared to use them. One of these access ways had a relatively easy mechanism to manage, for I had been there to study it. There were two doors to pass through, with a transition corridor in between, that was made so people could pass. The airlock, nowadays, was only spasmodically guarded. I considered, that if I proceeded with care, then I could get through those doors, before any alarm was raised from the monitors.

That afternoon, I gave both Joyce and Adolfus a tight hug each. Adolfus looked at me very uncertainly, and there were tears in his eyes. They knew what I was doing, even if we did not speak about it directly. They knew. I put the letter I had written on the table, and asked them only to open it in the morning.

I wasn't going to say anything, but then I decided that I had to be brave. Because they were my closest friends, I decided to acknowledge what I was doing. Looking at them in their eyes, I quietly announced my intentions, and pleaded with them both to wait for my return. Adolfus replied that they would. I could sense the sadness that he was feeling. He did not know if I would survive. Neither of them did.

At that point, I could not stop the welling up of emotion in me. I did not want to be engulfed by those feelings, so, before I could change my mind, I forced myself to react, and with an empty feeling in my stomach, I turned, stepped away from them, and without looking back, left them.

ZELDA

It was early morning now. I had my supplies, and I had placed the letter for my family on the dining room table. Now I was preparing to leave. They were all still sleeping.

The one problem that I had, was with my wooden bird. I was so attached to him, as if he was a living friend. He had been an enduring comfort to have with me for such a long time. I so much wanted to take him with me, but part of me reasoned that if I left him in my room, then he could act as a protector for my family in my absence. So, when I woke up, I prayed with my bird and asked that he would help to keep my family safe. I felt very sad to leave him, and my hands were wanting to pick him up and carry him, but I knew that I had to be strong, and my bird had a job to do. But it was very hard leaving that room. It felt like leaving a part of me behind. With my last glance, my bird seemed to be looking down at me from the bookshelf and I gave thanks for what a precious companion he had been.

I breathed deeply, as I closed the door quietly and strode along the corridors. The first rays of the sun were just starting to break over the horizon, and outside, it looked like the start of a beautiful day. I had to focus on the beauty rather than the bleakness.

I reflected how, during the night, I had had more dreams – going through doors to scenes of terror. I know that these were my fears expressing themselves, but I had to counter this somehow. Hence, in the middle of the night, I had spoken to myself, telling myself to be peaceful and strong, and I affirmed this, like a mantra, repeatedly. Then, after a long while, I had finally slept, and I slept deeply, so when I awoke, my knowing was clear again, and I knew that it was the right time to go.

Because I was so much in my thoughts, I hardly was aware of where I was going, with all the corridors. It was programd in my mind. I just passed around the final corner to reach the entrance way, when I saw a girl, hunched up and sitting on the ground there. She was crouched right next to the airlock, so I couldn't help but notice her. What was she doing here? As I looked closer, I observed that she was sobbing quietly to herself, with tears streaming down the side of her face. Nobody else was around. I felt perplexed.

As I listened, I could hear her irregular breathing and her distress. It was so early in the morning for her to be in this corridor on her own? And where were her parents? I had never seen her before. She must only be about fourteen years old.

I was torn about what to do. Part of me wanted to stop and comfort her, and find out what she needed, but the other part of me was focussed on getting through that entrance way before guards came on duty. What was the matter with her? Why could I just not go?

I bent down to her, and then, without warning, she reached out, put her arms around my neck, and clung on to me. She was holding me tightly, tighter than I would have wished. Soon, I tried to free myself from her, but she was not going to let go, so I sat down, and she buried her head in my shoulder, and cried. We stayed like this, longer and longer. Inside, I could feel my anxiety rising. This was not in the plan. I could not allow anything to stop me. My mind was seeking for an escape from her. But in my heart, I wanted to help her; I did not want to see this child suffer.

My inner knowing was quiet. This was a struggle between my will and my heart. Although my mind was racing, wanting to proceed, and go on, my heart was feeling warm and compassionate. I had to take notice of my heart. With that girl clinging to me, I could not rush, and I would have to be patient with her. I took some more deep breaths to steady myself, and then resolved to surrender to being with her. That felt better.

Slowly, she relaxed. She seemed to respond to the warmth of my body. I sat with her, stroking her hair, and quietly paced my breathing with her. She continued to cry, but gradually, the tension in her began to subside, until finally, she released me somewhat, and I could wipe her tears. Then she glanced up, and I saw her deep blue eyes. She was not afraid to look at me, and I waited while she continued to try and compose herself.

She had taken her hands from around my neck now, but I kept physical contact with my arm around her shoulder, just being with her. I wondered if it might help to ask her questions. I remembered how Adolfus had been with me, when I first came to work with him – so shy and unsure of myself with others. He was patient then, and I had to be tolerant and accepting of this girl, and give her space, for she was still choked up with emotion.

The first question I asked was about her parents. It may not have been the best move on my part, as she burst into tears again. It was very raw, and my question certainly was a trigger for her. She tried to tell me, but I could hardly understand the words with all the emotion, so I had to get her to speak clearer, and to focus on her breathing. Until she was steadier.

'They're dead,' she kept on saying over and over. 'My mummy and Daddy are dead'. The distress in her was huge, but I felt that she had to tell me the whole story, so I persevered gently with questions. She wanted me to know. Finally, I could piece it together.

Two nights ago, her parents had gone to the hospital to undergo voluntary Euthanasia. They had wanted her to go with them, but she had overheard them talking about it a few days earlier, and when the time had come, she had run away because she did not want to die. She did not want to leave them but she could not save them. She could only save herself. The last contact she had had with them was with her father. He was beckoning her to get into their town vehicle with them, and go to the hospital. She couldn't do it. He had a strange far away expression in his eyes, as if he was in a daze. Her father did not even seem to care about her any more. Again, she started to sob.

I felt so sorry for this girl. In my feelings of despair for her, I hugged her tightly, and she accepted my concern for her. She told me that her name was Zelda. She was only a girl, one of the few girls we had left in the City. For this to happen to her felt so tragic. And at the same time, her plight brought to the surface all my fears and anxieties concerning my parents and brother. I could not save them from their choices either, but even so, I loved them and wished for them to be safe. Soon, I was trembling with Zelda, and we were both holding each other for comfort.

In my mind, I was trying to work out what to do with her, for she would have nowhere to go. I felt that the best place to take her would be for her to be with Adolfus and Joyce, but I didn't want to see them now, because if I did, I may decide not to leave any more. Perhaps I could give her directions? I still did not know what she was doing here? Why was she positioned at this entrance point, of all places?

After a while, Zelda looked up at me with her big blue eyes, and she noticed my confusion. 'I am feeling better now.' She told me.

'You need to be with people that can look after you,' I implored to her.

She looked up at me and I was taken aback for she smiled. And she answered in a matter a fact voice, 'I want to be with you.'

I pulled away from her and did not know how to react. She could not be with me. I was leaving the City, and her life would be in jeopardy. There was no way I could have her with me. I could not accept that responsibility. She sat quietly, and continued to look at me. Her eyes were insistent and she repeated her wish. 'I want to be with you.' This time she spoke with even more certainty and assurance, and I could feel my chest churning with emotions. I decided that I had to be truthful with her.

'I cannot look after you because I am leaving the City, and it would be too dangerous.' I hoped that this would persuade her to pursue other possibilities. But her response alarmed me.

'I know that you are leaving the City,' she spoke calmly. 'That is why I am here. I have been waiting for you. I have known that I would go with you and I knew you would find me. The only thing I didn't know is whether you would disregard me or want to care for me.'

What was she saying? 'How do you know about me?' I reacted, and my thoughts were spinning with confusion and wonder.

'I have an inner voice that tells me things,' she confided in me. 'I listen to this voice, and it tells me what to do. With the help of my inner voice, I knew how to avoid going with my parents to my death. Whenever I have followed my inner voice, things have worked out for me.'

As I listened to her, I understood what she was saying.

She continued. 'You need to take me with you. Otherwise, you will not survive. You have a choice. I have been told that I cannot make you'.

I had never met anyone like Zelda. In what she conveyed to me, she appeared so inwardly clear, and yet she was only a child, and a very bereft chid at that. Her words and manner, as she described about her inner knowing, was extremely calming to me, and in my heart, even though what she suggested seemed quite crazy and irresponsible, there was something about it that held truth for me. I asked her how it felt to meet me. She answered.

'As soon as I saw you, I knew that you were the one I needed to meet. I had seen you in my dream.' It was astonishing.

In that moment, I decided that I would accept her guidance and open myself to her companionship. She had nothing to lose anymore, and in some mysterious way, it felt right for her to be with me.

We needed to get organised and fetch some supplies for her. She told me that her apartment was close by, so we could obtain what she needed from there. Then we smiled at each other and were ready to move.

Just a little later, we went through the airlock, closed the door to the City behind us, and we were on our way.

THE COASTAL ROAD

There was something strangely and wonderfully freeing about being able to leave the boundaries of the City. I had been within its confines all my life, and never known anything different. Now I could breathe the air around me, and part of me felt like a child again. The ground under my feet was hard and crunchy, with small stones scattered around. At first, I trod quite gingerly, suspicious, because of the fear, that the virus may travel from the ground and infect me. But the ground felt quite normal and supportive. Nothing happened to me. Gradually, I gained confidence. It felt good to be doing this.

I looked back at the City walls, and there were a couple of people looking down at us from the window of their apartment. It must have been quite a surprise, and astonishing for them to notice that we were outside, and without safety suits. They continued to stare at us quite passively. I decided to acknowledge them, so I grinned upwards and waved at them. Their reaction dismayed me, for they promptly turned away and disappeared. It was sad that they wouldn't wave back.

What we were doing went beyond what they, in their world, felt possible. But that was their sense of reality, and not mine. I felt joy in my heart that we were undergoing this journey. It did not matter if no one else had attempted our journey. For me, it was a case of being true to myself, and that felt liberating! I hoped that the authorities in the City would not interfere with what we were doing. It seemed unlikely that anyone would dare to come after us.

My thoughts turned to Adolfus and Joyce. They would be arriving at the gardens and fields around about now and would have read my letter. At least I knew that they had each other now. And of course, they had Rusky. I knew that they would be worried about me, but, as well as telling them, I had urged them very strongly in my letter for them not to give up. Perhaps they would think that I was foolish and that I was doomed. They knew they could not stop me and I wished for them to believe that I could succeed. I hoped so much that they would understand and accept.

It did not take long for my mood to change, and for the euphoria of being free, that I felt initially, to abate. We passed all the disused buildings in the outer suburbs of the City, walking on the main road. Many of the houses were crumbling now, and they were completely vacant. There was a feeling around them, of death, and I did not like it. Soon we were away from the buildings of the suburbs. For me, it felt a sigh of relief. I was glad to be away from these remnants of civilisation, and out into the open countryside, but there was no comfort here either. Now I could witness the dead remains of all the trees and bushes. It was incredibly isolating, and no easier than observing all this through the windows of the City.

Zelda was next to me, and for some of the time, I held her hand. Every now and again, though, she would go running off to look at some object in the landscape. She seemed happy enough now, and it was comforting for me not to be on my own. We made an agreement that we were not going to touch anything if we could help it, and we would stay in the open spaces. I remembered the details of directions that I had received from Adolfus, of where I would need to travel to find the Community. In my mind, I was confident that I could trace the route he had told me about, and I was determined that we would do it.

After a while, we lost sight of the City as we ventured on, heading towards the sea, where we would meet the coastal road. Despite my assessment that no one would come after us, I still felt quite watchful and cautious, and kept looking back, straining my ears for any signs of vehicles. But, with no indications of that, we proceeded and made quite rapid progress.

From what Adolfus told me, I anticipated that we would pass one of the townships soon after we reached the sea. As I looked around now, the landscape was bare, with clumps of tree stumps, the only sign of the residues of organic life, anywhere to be seen. It felt extremely unnatural, and at intervals, when she was next to me, I was glad to feel the physical touch of Zelda's hand. As time went on, I valued her company more and more.

During my earlier studies and more recently, I had seen videos of the ocean, so I knew a little what it would be like, and when I saw the blue haze in the distance, I realised that this must be it. As we got closer, I listened, and could hear the roar of the waves, with the ebbing and flowing of the tide. I had never heard anything like it, and my whole feeling of it was breath-taking. It was marvellous to sense the power of nature within the sea, and so sad that I had to remind myself of its true reality – that the ocean was as empty and devoid of life as the land, and with unknown toxicity.

When we came over the sand dune and saw the ocean directly for the first time, I just had to sit down to watch, so I could take it all in. I gaped at the waves with wonder, and I had to be strong and disciplined to keep my shoes on, and not to place myself in the water. For Zelda, I imagine, it was even harder, and she ran along the sand near the edge of the water line, watching the froth and movement of the salt water, and she came perilously close to getting herself wet. This was so precious, and yet, it was such a tragedy not able to enjoy it. We were deprived, and my heart was pained by what we had lost, and again, I could not comprehend it.

For a while, we stayed there by the sea side, breathing in the damp air, and I could easily have chosen to rest there, but our journey had barely begun, and we had to advance further.

We were now on the coastal road. From our first encounter with the sea, the road went slightly inland as it followed a track towards the first township. Zelda was reluctant to leave the ocean, but I was firm with her, and she eventually came with me. I was dreading what we would find in the town.

I had never seen a dead body before, and I knew we were going to encounter lots of these on our journey. I told Zelda to stay close by me, and she quietly did as I asked.

When we entered the town, I could see decaying skeletons strewn out in the streets and alleyways. Some of them still had patches of flesh on them. No one had been able to do anything to bury them. Most of these were human, but there were also the remains of domestic animals. In my mind, I could imagine the suffering that these people and animals must have gone through, and it both hurt me and repulsed me at the same time. How would they have been able to understand why this was happening to them? It was such a traumatic means to die. Appalling!

I did not want to linger here too long. Zelda walked next to me. I did not have to remind her to stay away from the bodies. She had no desire to go near them. It was strange with her; for I was not sure if she stayed close to have support for her own feelings, or because she wanted to protect me.

The buildings were quite intact. Some had been affected by the weather and crumbling, but many looked as if they could still be functional, and it was so odd that nobody was alive here at all. We could hear the treading of our footsteps and our breathing. Apart from the distant roar of the waves of the sea, there was one continuing silence.

Somehow, I could still feel the atmosphere of the settlement as it had been, and I imagined how it might have been when the people were still alive. It was as if their energy imprints were around, for I could also inwardly hear the echoes of the people's screams as they lay dying. The psychic residues of all that had happened, was still pervasive, and I felt such relief to be able to move beyond this township, and reach the open spaces again.

I did not feel at ease with myself. Walking in this deathly environment was unsettling, wherever we went, and it felt eerie to be treading on such a desolate landscape. I had seen pictures and videos of this coastal area, not just the settlements, but the natural environments – as it used to be. Once this area had been a vibrant and beautiful setting with lush green vegetation, bird and animal life – an ecosystem that had been alive and plentiful. There were even specific trees that I had seen in photographs, some of them, centuries old, and very precious. I sought a few of these out, and when we found them, my heart contracted as I could witness only the bare shell of them that remained.

At this point, I began to speculate if we had been infected to any degree by the virus, and how it may affect us, if we had. I glanced across at Zelda, and she still appeared to have energy and curiosity to explore the various settings of our journey. We had already gone quite a distance, and made considerable progress. It seemed remarkable, and I began to speculate if the virus had now diluted sufficiently, so we would be able to function, and not be incapacitated by it. We had to hope for that. It would be a great boon for us, if true. It was a huge relief to me, that thus far, my body felt in good health, and we were walking steadfastly.

If only that had continued. As we trudged further along the coastal road, I began to feel tired. Zelda was her usual self, walking and skipping along beside me – she did not say much, but seemed content. I wondered if my tiredness could be explained as an emotional reaction to all that I had seen. However, as I walked on, the fatigue I felt became more pronounced, and my limbs ached. I started to feel worried. The symptoms I was experiencing were exactly those that were the early stages of infection by the virus. I tried to push that thought away, and make myself keep going. If I had caught the virus, there would be no hope for us.

I checked in with Zelda and asked how she was doing, and she smiled back at me, in a comfortable fashion. Perhaps it was just my fears. I wanted to hide my symptoms, so we would keep going. And we did that. I took step by step, and repeated inside myself, that I was well and able – that we were going to make it, to reach our goal. I resolved that through the force of my will, I could counteract any infection that was there.

Doubts began to gnaw at me. It would be a miserable mistake if it all ended now. What if I did die now? What would I have gained? I couldn't shake this fear out of me. And thinking this started to weaken me further. The effort of walking on, occupied all my physical attention.

I started to wander in my mind, and remind myself of what I had left behind. I thought of Adolfus and Joyce, and how much despair they would feel if I never returned; it may destroy them. And what about my family – if they decided to end their lives – I would feel that it was my fault. It was too late to turn back. What if I had the virus? They wouldn't be able to help me, and it would just make the situation worse, if I tried to return.

Although it was flat ground, I found each step increasingly arduous. We may have travelled a considerable distance but there was still much more walking to do. We had three more days to walk, per Adolfus's calculations. And with the barren isolation of all that was around us, there was no adult that I could turn to. The only company I had was a fourteen-year-old girl, who had just lost both her parents – I should be looking after her, rather than expecting her to help me. Inwardly I began to panic, and my head went down as I concentrated to step on further – I had to keep going.

As the sun dropped lower towards the horizon, I struggled even more. It was only my sheer determination that kept me upright. My legs felt heavy and aching. My breathing was becoming laboured, and I had less and less energy. I could really feel myself fading. All I wanted to do was to lie down and sleep. All afternoon, I had been trying to ignore these feelings, but I could not do it anymore. I motioned to Zelda if we could take a break and sit down for a while. We did so, and I was so glad to stop.

Zelda looked over at me with a concerned expression. 'Are you OK?' she asked. And I shook my head. There were tears rolling down my cheeks, as I felt so disappointed with myself.

'I knew that this would happen,' Zelda confided. 'I was told what to do, and you need to let me help you.' My thoughts were spinning. Who was this girl? Could she really help me? 'Who told you?' I asked. And she replied that it was her inner voice. At this stage, I felt I had no choice but to submit to what she was guided to do. At least I was not on my own. I don't know how I would have coped with that.

'Let me help you into a sitting position,' she spoke tenderly. She moved behind me and placed her arms around my chest and pulled me up. I tried my best to help her. There was a large smooth stone nearby, and she directed me, if I could move, to sit on that. With all the force that I could muster, I did what she told me.

She spoke to me. 'What I can do is to channel energy to you to replenish you, and reactivate your cells, so you will feel better. Sleep will help you too. And I may need to keep doing this at intervals until we reach where we are going.'

Zelda addressed me, speaking like a mature adult, but I perceived that she was acting as a channel, and relaying what she was being told inwardly. Her inner faculty of 'knowing' was much more fully developed than mine, but my own inner knowing was willing to trust her, and she emphasised that this was important too.

'You must imagine the healing energy travelling right through your body,' she told me gently. 'That is how you can assist the process and we can work together. I have been doing this for myself all day, to keep me going'

Then she placed her hands around my head, and I could feel tremendous heat and tingling coming from her hands. I did what she requested, and imagined this spreading through my body. And it was like a soothing liquid that alleviated the physical pain I felt. It also relaxed me so I felt a sense of well-being and peace. She moved her hands to my shoulders and chest, and then my feet. Each position where she placed her hands, I felt the heat, and I knew that it was doing me so much good. This was like the healing that I had sometimes channelled with Adolfus, and the plants, only I felt that this was much more powerful.

When she finished, all I wanted to do was to close my eyes and sleep. But she insisted that we drink and eat first, and lay out the simple bedding that we had brought. Zelda told me that although it had the capacity to affect her, she was immune to the deadly impact of the virus. Zelda conveyed simply that it was not her path to die from that infection. What a remarkable girl!

After my meal, I felt more awake and I sat with Zelda while we watched the stars. They were so bright in the evening sky, and I loved gazing at them, as they twinkled and shone their light. We engaged in conversation about the journey, and I asked her to tell me more about herself. I was interested in the gifts that she had, and asked her about those. Her simple reply was that she was born with them. She had come to help the Earth, and her meeting with me had been planned beforehand.

I had a lot of further questions. However, in the peace of the evening, I felt drowsier now. That brief burst of energy had gone. All that I wanted to do, was to relax. It was a huge relief to be alive, and to have received that help from Zelda. I could sense that all the tension which I had accumulated in the lead up to this journey, was releasing too. At last, I felt able to let that go. As I sat back, under the stars, I enjoyed how different it felt to be without those tensions. And I smiled at Zelda. I was so glad she was with me.

JOURNEY TO THE HILLS

I must have slept deeply, for I had no memory of stirring in the night. The warm sun was already beating down when I opened my eyes, and Zelda was sitting on a rock nearby, gazing towards the sea. To my surprise, I felt refreshed, and because I felt energy within me. I wanted to get moving and make progress on our journey.

As we sat and had some food and drink before setting off, I thanked Zelda for her healing, and she smiled at me. During the coming day, we would need to walk a somewhat further along the coastal road, before turning inland. I remembered from the maps, the landmarks I needed to watch out for.

While we walked, I asked Zelda about her early life. She told me that she was an only child, and while she was growing up, she had no other children to play with. The main person with whom she had contact, was her mother, but her mother did not engage with Zelda – a bit like my family, with me – so Zelda had been left very much on her own. Consequently, she had spent a lot of time in silence, with her own inner worlds, but this is also where she found her strength. She felt that she was guided by voices within her, and they helped her. These were beneficent voices, and I did not sense that she was mentally ill. Rather, she was attuned to some inner Spiritual sources that helped give integration and purpose to her life. From my own curiosity, I enquired about what her voices had told her regarding the Community where we were going, but she did not have an answer to that. All that she knew was that we needed to go there.

Zelda was quite playful and liked to throw stones. Sometimes she raced me along certain sections of the landscape, just to let out her energy. Being with her, it was easier to withstand the passage through the barren environment around us. Her presence lifted my mood, and I was glad that we were on the move again.

However, as we went through the afternoon, I again became tired as I had the previous day, and when the sun went down, Zelda offered to do more healing with me. I accepted this, for I knew how much it helped me. It became part of our daily routine – and I was very appreciative, for I knew that without it, I would not have been able to go on.

By now, we had turned away from the sea and were climbing through the hills. This was more laborious, for before the virus infiltration, there had been quite a dense tree cover here. The trunks of the trees remained and branches of varying sizes were scattered over the ground, and we had to climb over them. The wood was all brittle and dead, and the smaller branches crunched under our feet as we stepped on them. I kept wanting to see creatures scurrying around. But there were none. Now that we were away from the sea, the silence of the land was even more pronounced.

As we went along, I was less certain about the direction that we should be going, for I no longer had recognizable landmarks to guide me. I relied now on the position of the sun, and guess work. Again, Zelda came to my rescue, and there were occasions when she remarked to me, that it would be better if we went another way from where I was leading her, and she would show me which way would be most helpful for us to traverse. I trusted her, and followed her suggestions, without question. Going further inland, the altitude was higher, and the air had a wonderful crisp and fresh feeling about it; the temperature was cooler.

On the fourth day, I could sense that we were getting close. Adolfus had told me that the Community was near, and to the left-hand side, of the highest peak in the range. And I was sure that I could see that peak in the distance.

Zelda was agreeable for us to go there. However, it took a good while for us to ascend it, and I needed a couple of doses of healing to make it. When we reached the top though, the view was spectacular, but still very sad. On one side, far away over the hills, we could observe the sea, while on the other side, it looked like a huge expanse of desert, with flat terrain, stones and sand covering the ground. Once, this view would have been very beautiful, for it was the vegetation and animals that had brought beauty to the Earth. Without that, it was extremely bare. I felt very emotional and tears rolled down my cheeks. Zelda grasped my hand.

I asked Zelda to show me where she thought the Community was situated, and she pointed towards a range of hills and valleys over and to the side of us. Those hills appeared no different from the other lifeless ones around us – nothing to encourage me or give hope. After all this effort, what if there was nothing there, if all those people had died? What if all that we could find would be a few skeletons and empty buildings like we had witnessed on the coast?

I could understand now why people did not venture out from the City. There was nothing to reward our souls being out here. Human beings needed other life forms to interact with, to give purpose to our existence. We were not made to live in isolation. This went against the longings in our hearts, and if our hearts were not happy, then we could not survive for long.

At that moment, I felt again, very grateful to have come across Zelda. Besides her ability to help me deal with the virus, I don't know how I would have managed without her. In all my enthusiasm, I had not been prepared for what this expedition would entail. It was miraculous to be still alive.

That night, we camped on the mountain side in a clearing. The next morning was the fifth morning, and we were ready for the final stage of our exploration. Zelda seemed quite excited, and was jumping around much more than she had at other times. I tried to calm her, for I did not want to allow my hopes to rise, and I could feel the anxiety in my stomach indicating fear that I would be disappointed.

We had travelled a long distance now, and used up most of our supplies. If the Community had been decimated by the virus, as my rational mind told me, was most likely, I didn't know what we would do. Soon would be the moment of truth.

COMMUNITY

In the morning, we walked towards the hills that Zelda had indicated. After we stopped for some lunch, Zelda was eager to tell me that over the top of the next hill in front of us, was the valley where she felt that the Community was situated. My heart was racing as we climbed up that hill, and then when we reached the top, I gazed down with a mixture of hope and dread. At first, I could see nothing, just more lifeless landscape, with the rubble of dead trees, everywhere I looked. There wouldn't be any community. How could there be? I was ready to sit down, so we could consider our options. But, as I faltered, Zelda was straining her eyes, looking downwards. Suddenly, she started screaming at me and dragging on my arm to look. I tried to focus on what she was seeing. Where was it? And she was trying to point with her arm to show me. I wiped my eyes so that I could see better. Then, as I looked at the valley in front of us, I became aware of what was making her so excited.

Right down near the base of this particular valley, the undulating land forked, and the left fork disappeared behind the rise of the hill. But protruding from that left-hand fork, there were some trees. However, they were not dead trees. They had leaves on them. And the leaves were green. For a moment, I stopped breathing. I could hardly believe it. Were my eyes deceiving me? Was I just seeing what I wanted to see? Zelda was in no doubt.

For some moments, I just stared and tried to take it in. It was only the edges of a few trees that we could see. However, the green of their leaves was astonishing to behold, and so different from the other entire environment around us. How could such a thing be possible?

Zelda and I looked across at each other. Then, in a few moments, we were running. I hardly knew how I was managing it, but I was going so fast down that hill. With all my haste, I slipped and slid down the embankment several times. However, it did not stop me. And Zelda – when she slipped, she laughed and got up again as quickly as she could. Nothing would stop her. We were both so keen to reach the trees. As we went lower, I became more aware of how the division of the valley to the left appeared to widen out, and the few trees that we saw initially had many companions.

They were young trees, but they seemed to nestle together very happily. I strained to be able to obtain a fuller view, and was impatient to know what would await us, when we turned into that valley, and we reached the base of the hill.

Zelda was racing ahead of me. Her nimble legs propelled her swiftly forward, and as she reached the opening to the valley, I was still clambering down the slope behind her. She stopped and was gazing in amazement. Soon I reached her, and I halted too. For I heard a sound, like a squawking – and it was so strange – only slightly familiar – for it was a sound that indicated life, animal life. My eyes were drawn to the trees in front of me, and there was a flash of colour. Then all at once, this went into the sky, and was moving about. My mind was struggling to comprehend this. However, as I reflected, I remembered the videos that I had seen, historical videos from the library in the City – and I realised that for the first time in my life, I was seeing a bird, an actual living bird. And it was flying.

I cannot begin to tell the joy I felt in my heart at that moment. It was as though my whole concept of life had suddenly been transformed and new possibilities opened inside me.

As I stood with Zelda, the sight of the valley in front of us was incredibly amazing. There was a nursery of young trees, thick like a carpet, and extending right down the valley and up the slopes of the hills on either side. There was a path winding its way through these trees. The trees were full of rich shades of green foliage, and it wasn't only one bird, but flocks of them, with their chirping voices that enlivened the atmosphere around us. As I listened to all the birds, and the gentle breeze blowing through the leaves of the trees, my ears tingled with the sounds, and I felt a sense of health and vitality that had been missing from my experience, for all my life. Even the gardens and fields that I had cultivated with Adolfus, were not like this. I searched with my vision to see if there were any eagles, like my wooden bird, but I could see none, but this did not discourage my high spirits.

Further along, we could perceive what could be, the outline of wooden huts with smoke rising upwards. This must be the Community, and there had to be people alive here. I swallowed with incredulity. After all the challenges of the journey, the outcome had been worthwhile. I affirmed that I could trust my inner knowing. It had told me the right thing to do!

Zelda and I wandered slowly along the path. I touched the living soil beneath me, the bark of the trees, and the leaves. These were all new sensations. We were not locked in the City; we were out in the open. Why did the virus not impact on these living organisms? I would have to find out. As I walked on this pathway, I felt a great love for the Earth and all that it provided. There was something about this virus that felt as if it did not belong to our Earth. And I wanted to defeat it, so that it would no longer destroy all that was precious in our world. Perhaps I was picking up on the thoughts of the people living here. Soon I would meet them. What would they think about us, and how would they react to our arrival? The smoke from the fire was much closer now, and I could smell it in the distance as the wind wisped towards us.

When we moved around the next corner, the line of trees ended and we were in a clearing, with huts in front of us, and a warm fire was burning in the middle of the clearing. People were milling about, and they seemed busy with their various tasks. There were also children, that were playing and laughing. I swallowed to take this in. This was another new experience for me.

One boy was sitting by the fireside and throwing sticks into the fire, watching them catch alight. This boy must have been about the same age as Zelda. After nodding to me in acknowledgment, she went over to him and sat beside him, and he seemed to accept her presence with him, as if they already knew each other.

Outside one of the huts, there was a man with a chisel, working with wood, and he appeared to be making some form of sculpture. He was a tall man, middle-aged, with long flowing grey hair, falling down his back. He wore loose fitting casual clothes, as did the other people around the Community. There was a small group now, that had noticed us and were standing back, taking in our arrival, but smiling too. These were happy people. The man stood up, and came over to me, and welcomed me. He told me that his name was Linton. I asked him in astonishment, why he was not surprised to see me, and he answered with a sense of mystery, that we had been expected. I did not understand that.

Linton had a hut ready for Zelda and I, and, as I went inside the hut, I was struck by its basic simplicity. The hut had a floor made of compacted earth, with two beds and hardly any furniture apart from cupboards for our clothes and a mirror on a table. Out the back was a composted toilet. Zelda came in with me, and our host invited us to rest and make ourselves at home. He informed us that we would soon eat around the fire, and could talk then.

At that moment, I did feel tired, and greatly relieved, and decided that I would have a rest. The tiredness this time, was more natural, and my inner senses told me that while I was here, I would not need Zelda's healing help any more.

EXPLANATIONS

Zelda nudged me to wake me up, and told me that we had been called to eat. I must have been sleeping very deeply. Slowly, I motioned myself to get up. I felt quite shy as we ventured out to the fireplace. There was a gathering of people there, and a buzz of contented conversation. The people here did not treat each other like strangers, but were interacting with each other. Many of them were talking and laughing. I already knew that life here would be very different from the City.

We sat on tree stumps and were given a bowl each, to eat from. Then we were invited to help ourselves from a big pot of vegetable broth. They had waited for us, to start. Before we ate, there was a meditation, and Linton spoke, giving thanks for the food, and invoking cleansing for the food so that it would be healthy for us. There were around thirty people altogether, and half of them were children. Zelda appeared to be already making friends with them, and she sat with the boy that had been playing with the fire, earlier.

It was a time for me to ask questions. First, I spoke to the group and spoke out my gratitude to everyone for welcoming us, and they all seemed pleased. But then I turned my attention to Linton. He was sitting quietly, next to me, and appeared to be waiting for me to speak first. I had to restrain myself, and work out what I was going to say.

My first question was to ask Linton about the existence of the Community and how they could have possibly survived. Linton had the air of being the leader of the Community, and there were others now tuning in and listening to what he would tell me.

Linton began, and spoke solemnly. 'At the time of the War and the onset of the virus, we were a community of over two hundred people. Many travelled great distances to be with us, because we explored Spiritual forms of growing plants, working with the soil, and living with each other in harmony. We were a very peaceful, happy family of souls seeking to be close to nature and to each other. Some of us were inspired by the 'hippy' generations from many years earlier, while others came from various Spiritual traditions that were important to them. What united us was an ideal of living simply, and in natural harmony with our environment, and opening to the Spiritual energies that underlined our existence.

'The way we chose to live contrasted sharply with the cold clinical high-tech world of the cities, where most people resided, and the tendency that people in these places had, to manipulate elements to gain dominance and mastery. We did not want to have power over the natural world to further our own ends. What we aimed to do, was to work cooperatively with the forces of Nature, for the good of all.

'In our Community, we felt that the task of humanity was to be guardians of our world, to nurture and look after all life forms on our planet, and to ensure that all the many strata of life were protected and nourished and able to thrive together. This outlook contrasted very dramatically with the aims and intentions of nations in other parts of the world. We wanted to exist as a model to inspire others with our example.

'The virus that caused such hideous ruin is not a natural organism. It was formed through genetic manipulation by the military. For many years, they had been carrying out biological experiments to create organisms that could be utilised in warfare, to weaken the other side. However, with all their spies and invasive surveillance technology, what one side achieved, the other side could copy.

'Because this virus was not natural to the Earth, but made through genetic manipulation, it was not easy to find a natural Earthly cure. The Military were concerned with defending their territory and outwitting the other side, but viruses did not recognise state borders or any kind of restriction. Once this virus had been released, and started to multiply and interact with other microbe organisms to prevent their reproductive capacity, there was nothing to halt its advance. Scientists did not have the time or ability to find any form of counter to inhibit the onset of this killer, especially with so much of the civilisation on our Earth already destroyed by the nuclear war.

'We know now that it was not the wish of the Spirit of the Earth for this destruction to happen, and all the devastation that ensued stemmed completely from the actions of people, and people have been responsible for this.

'With our community, we utilised the tools that we could. Of course, we did not want to die. As a means of defence, we did not have vast amounts of concrete or glass to encase ourselves away from the reach of the virus – as I understand you have done with your City. Our Community was in the open, and freely interacting with all the elements of life around us. So, we did what we do best; we meditated, we asked for Spiritual protection and we cared for all the life forms in our care, to the very best of our ability.'

He paused gravely. 'And it wasn't enough. We did slow it down – our prayers, meditation and rituals did have an impact. But the landscape around us died, and more and more of us became infected. Our land stopped producing, and I must say, that I really did fear that all would be lost. But it wasn't.

'We had some indigenous tribal members amongst us, and they helped. It was essential for us, not only to ask for inner Spiritual help, but to connect with the Spiritual being of the Earth itself. If the Earth did not want us all to die, then we had to call on it to help save us, and show us how we could preserve ourselves. Our indigenous friends shared with us, all their secrets, and we worked with them, trying all the energetic magic that they knew, desperately struggling to put up some energetic walls to keep the virus out. And for a while, these efforts did appear to stall the progress of the virus. We did Spiritual rituals with them to protect our space, and create lines of energy, where we determined, that the virus would not cross. The virus was repelled by these energy lines, but only by us applying a continual effort.

'But this constant exertion needed, to keep the virus out, took an enormous toll on our indigenous friends. They could not sustain it indefinitely, and they had to be on alert and keep working to keep up these energy lines. Even with some of us helping them, there were hardly enough of them to do it. Gradually, they weakened. Then, a couple of them succumbed, and became infected with the virus. When they died, much of the sap of hope within us went with them. The only response we could make, was to bring the lines of protective energy closer to us, sacrificing more of our land, so we could hopefully survive a little longer.

'One day the remnant group of us that remained sat around the fire; we meditated and called on the Spirit of the Earth. These were fraught times, but we had to stay true to our Spiritual principles. And one of our members went very, very deep into trance. She went so deep, that when the rest of us had finished, we could not rouse her at all. The knowing in me told me that she was safe, so we helped her to lie down and covered her in a blanket. We watched her closely. Then, after a while, she shivered and there was some alteration in her energy, as if she was being taken over in some way. Then she cleared her throat and made a noise with her voice, a noise much deeper and more guttural than her normal voice. And she started to speak. It was not her that was speaking – a Spiritual force was speaking through her. She was channelling the energy of the Earth Spirit. It was quite extraordinary. And we listened to everything that she channelled to us. The words she spoke gave us hope – the Earth Spirit wanted us to live.

'There was an amazing feeling of peace about us that night. From that first experience, this woman member of our group became our Oracle, and what she channelled, formed the basis of what we needed to do to save our Community. It worked.

'We were told by the Earth Spirit that there were specific practices that we had to do regularly if we were to survive. These were exercises to assist our inner development, to help us attune to the energies from the Earth Spirit. When we acted together, we would be able to resist the influences of the virus through the strength of what we would be doing. The power of the Earth Spirit could help us to push back the area that the virus controlled so we could have more land in which we could live. But we were needed as instruments to facilitate that.

'The processes that we had to do were quite simple and consisted of visualisations, energy work and attuning together so that all that we did was in the name of the Earth Spirit and was expressing the Will of our Mother Earth. We could accept this easily, for it embraced our philosophy. However, the practices we were being asked to do added discipline, and the channelling of the Oracle gave us Spiritual strength. We were being asked to utterly surrender ourselves in service to the Earth, so that this became our first and only priority as a matter of course, to ensure the expression and continuation of life on our world.

'From then on, we did as we were told. It took a while for all of us to open our inner perception to direct connection with the Earth Spirit, and while we were in that transition phase, we continued to suffer deaths and further degrading of our resources. Eventually though, there reached a point where the energy we were generating was sufficient to counteract the virus, and when we knew that we had achieved this, we celebrated. Once we passed that threshold, we knew that the sphere of activity in our Community could expand again – and that is what we have been working to build upon. We continue with the practices we were given then – to this day, and will maintain these and expand on them into our future. It is our hope and wish that we can assist the restoration of life on our planet.'

Linton stopped there, and looked across at me. I sighed and leaned back. There was such a lot for me to take in. I wanted to ask him if he could share more about the specifics of the practices, but he responded that in the morning, we could join with everyone, when the Oracle would channel, and that we could learn then – by direct experience, how to open ourselves to living in harmony with the Earth Spirit.

THE ORACLE

When I woke up in the morning, I was excited. I had been told that the meditation with the Oracle, would take place in the largest, wooden, round hut in the centre of the Community. This was the Sanctuary. There were cushions around the circumference of the perimeter of the room and in the centre of it, there was a large brown blanket. Here is where the Oracle would lie. The Sanctuary filled up and Zelda sat next to her new friend.

I found a cushion near to the entrance way, and watched as people murmured in low voices. There was an atmosphere of reverence and respect in this space. Linton came in and sat next to me, and he suggested to me that in the meditation, that I follow my instinct, and to be open to blend with the energy of the group. By doing this, I would feel in harmony with everyone, and be assisting the process.

Suddenly, there was a hushed silence and the Oracle entered. She was a tall well-built woman, middle-aged with tanned skin. Her hair was long and black, and flowed down her back, almost to her waist. Without a word, she lay down on the blanket and closed her eyes. As I gazed at her, she was very still, and the only movement I could discern, was the slow gentle rise and fall of her chest, with the rhythm of her breathing. I felt transfixed by her, but then I forced myself to look away, and noticed that everyone else had closed their eyes, and they were joining with her – even Zelda. All at once, I knew I had to do the same.

Following Linton's advice, I uttered a prayer to myself and asked to be in harmony with the others and the Earth Spirit. Then I felt my consciousness becoming much quieter and sinking downwards. As I did this, I could feel that something was opening inside me, and I could sense myself joining with the others, in some form of group consciousness. Next, I felt a strange sensation of surrendering myself and opening collectively with the others, to the presence of a being, that was vast, rising from beneath me. The force of this being, was greater, spiritually, than anything that I had experienced previously. I continued to travel down, joined with the others, and I felt as if we were on a voyage deep into the bowels of the Earth. The experience was warm, welcoming and alive and I wanted to be there.

Then, as we went further I sensed that this being that I had sensed, had brightness about it, and a joyful, living, creative presence. I was privileged to be part of this. The being had to be the Earth Spirit, and I realised immediately, that whatever ravages this virus had brought to the surface of our world, on a deeper level, the Spirit of the Earth was alive and well. And as we tapped into this energy, I felt a tremendous surge of hope and optimism. In my heart, there was joy to relate to this. It was the Oracle that had facilitated this. She was the instrument by which we could tap into this marvellous resource.

And now thoughts impressed themselves on my mind, as members of the group communicated with the Earth Spirit, and responses were forthcoming. Shared exchanges of thoughts were occurring on a deep inner level. It was not so much words, but a knowing that I could hardly articulate. There was willingness and group receptivity to these impressions. It was like we had become one mind, together.

Then the Earth Spirit gave us a vision, where collectively, we were being taken upwards and could perceive images of the community, but it was not in its physical form. It was like a map of consciousness, with tracks of Spirit energy spreading around the various landmarks of the Community. With this, we could see where the energy was strong, where it was weaker, and where it needed to extend itself. And I could feel members of the group applying themselves to focus on the weaker areas and what they would need to do to strengthen these places. It was a very practical meditation where guidance was being imparted for those that were ready to hear, and act in accordance with the Earth Spirit's Will.

With these exchanges, I could not grasp all the details. My consciousness was not as open or as developed as some of the others that were here. But suddenly, just as I had begun to retreat a little bit, I sensed that there was a question from the Earth Spirit directed specifically to me. I was being asked what it was that I wanted to do. In response, I sent out the thought that I wanted to learn like the others.

At once, I felt a whoosh of energy. This affirmed to me an agreement being made with the Earth Spirit. I felt exhilaration because of this, and I received a further message, that there was one in the Community who was ready to teach me. With this person, my own consciousness would develop. I would be guided to this person and she would help me!

The energy shifted away from me, and I felt a peculiar sensation. It was as though we were now collectively focussing outwards to the land and landscape around us. Energetically, I could perceive the stands of organism that was the deadly virus. It was like a crab with claws that wanted to grasp and swallow all living vitality around it. I did not like it. We could see how colour lost its essence when it neared the virus, becoming dull, before losing its vitality altogether. But when there was no further life for it to feed on, the virus acquired a dormant form that was like a massive cloud of grey. It was still dangerous.

The pure energy of the Earth Spirit could not be drawn into this grey, but was stronger than it and it could repel it. So, with our minds, we acted together, as one mind, with the Earth Spirit, to fend off the virus and its reach – pushing it back. We all did this together, and imagined it receding. And it did withdraw, so that there was more land exposed that was free from the virus, and this land could now be enriched and enlivened by the powers of the Earth Spirit.

This was a process, inwardly, where, in conjunction with the Earth Spirit, the Community members were clearing the land throughout this valley of any infiltration by the virus. The inner experiences correlated and connected to outer reality. This inner energy practice was a tool that that the Community used, with the power of the Earth Spirit, so that we could start to claim back areas of land on our Earth, for life.

I could conceive now how this was an exacting process, that needed to be repeated every day, in a struggle for ascendency. At least this was something that helped, and I could feel the effort that was involved. On some level, it tired me, because it was a struggle.

The meditation continued, and I became aware that I was somewhere deep in the Earth, and could not feel my body anymore. I felt very light. It was an amazing experience, and replenishing to my energy system.

This had all been such a lot for me – and I sensed that with my first experience of it, that my ability to sustain what we were doing was nearing its end. As I could sense that my concentration was starting to weaken, I became aware that I was lifting again, and, with a further whoosh of energy, I was in my body once more. Then I could feel the cushion under me, and the presence of the other bodies around me. As I opened my eyes, the group were all humming sounds together, and I sensed that this was another expression and shared connection to bring forth the presence of our Earth Spirit. I felt very happy. In that moment, I knew to some extent, how these people had survived, and how their Community had dedicated itself to move forward. I was blessed. And when I looked around the circle at all the members of the Community present, I felt as if I was among kindred Spirits. I did want to learn from them all, and be part of what they were doing, as much as I could.

KENDREN

For a while, I sat on my cushion in the Sanctuary, watching, while people filed out to begin their daily chores. There was one young woman on the opposite side of the Circle. She was a similar age to me, and had wavy brown hair. What I noticed most with her face, was her twinkling eyes. While the others moved about, she remained sitting, and she was looking over, as if she was studying me. I felt slightly embarrassed to be the focus of her attention, but she did not turn away. Eventually, I made the move to stand up, and that was the signal for her to come over to me and introduce herself.

She told me that her name was Kendren. Linton had informed her that she was to be assigned to the job of helping me with my orientation. She had to explain about the tasks of the Community, and what I could do to contribute. Kendren's demeanour was quite serious, but I liked being with someone similar in age to me. There was something about her that felt familiar. And my heart was warm with anticipation.

We went to the vegetable gardens, which were situated at the back of the huts, further down into the valley. I could see rows full of very healthy vegetables, many varieties, and nearly all of them exposed to the outside air. Beyond the field of vegetables, were orchards of fruit trees, and I could see groups of people tending to them. It was a very peaceful scene and I felt very much at home. Kendren could see my delight, and she smiled.

'We have more than enough food now,' she spoke, 'but it wasn't always the case.' She pointed to a row of onions where we would be working today. There was a wooden seat nearby and she motioned for me to go with her there first, so we could talk.

'It is quite miraculous to meet you,' she spoke, 'and you are the first two people from anywhere outside our Community that I have seen. I have been told that I must teach you, as if you know nothing, so you can learn things that are obvious to us. The world where you have come from is what we call the 'old world,' and our ways are very different to yours.

'Every day when we meditate and tune in with the Oracle, to the Earth Spirit, we are tuning in to the Spiritual being at the source of the material world that we live in, and this helps us to become sensitive to the Spirit that exists within life forms, rather than perceiving only the physical aspect. We feel the joy of the Earth Spirit and choose to be devoted to that. When we work in the gardens, say, with the onions, as we will do today, we open our perception to the Spirit of the onions and we see that Spirit as light and love, with a quality that corresponds with the being of the onion. And we nurture that light and the physical onion, by opening our hearts to love that and care for the onion. By doing that, the Spirit light of the onion radiates stronger and the physical form of the onion grows healthily. If there is a problem with the onions, we ask them what they need, and we listen inwardly for what they tell us.'

'Do you really see the Spirit of the onions?' I interrupted.

'Yes, I do.' She replied, looking over at me. 'And you can learn to do that too. Every time you meditate with us, your senses will open a little more.'

I could feel that my hands were tingling. It was fascinating how my body was responding to her words. When I asked Kendren about that, she laughed, and told me that I had the hands of a healer.

'We have to give concentrated individual attention to all these plants in turn. Otherwise they might not survive in the conditions that still exist.' She went on. 'It is not only the plants that have a Spirit light. Be still for a moment and focus on the ground beneath you.' I did as she directed, and could feel a subtle vibration, that was somehow very comforting.

'What you feel is the Spirit of the Earth. As you become more inwardly aware, you will feel that with increasing vibrancy.' She smiled at me. 'There is a fabric of energy from the Earth Spirit that extends around all the areas of our Community. We are in the process of enlivening this. Our aim is to help all the Earth to be fertile again. We believe that we can do this.

'The fabric of the skin of the Earth was severely weakened and damaged through the war, and particularly with the virus taking away life, but even before then too. In the way how society was set up in the old world, lots of damage was being done. We are basically acting as channels, working with the Earth Spirit to nurture this fabric every day, so it can very gradually repair itself, grow stronger and establish itself again. It has not always been an easy process, but we are making steady strides now.'

'How has it not been easy?' I asked.

'Well the beginning was very difficult,' she spoke, and her head went down. Her voice suddenly became less steady. 'When the virus came, it decimated our crops – everything really, and many people died. Even when the Oracle started channelling, this did not save us immediately. It was a very challenging situation for us in many, many ways. We faced a desperate struggle to save as many plant and animal species as we could, but also keep ourselves alive. As our inner faculties improved, we could work more effectively, but there were many uncertain times when we did not know if we would make it through or not.'

'Were you alive then?' I asked hesitantly.

Kendren slowly looked up at me and there were tears in her eyes. 'I was born six months after the war, just as the virus started attacking life forms around us most fiercely. Those were such distressing times, but I do have small memory flashes of that period, even though I was so young. The virus attacked plants, animals and people and more and more of us died because of that. Because so much of our resources were destroyed, we had very little to eat, and some of our community died purely from starvation, and because they could not fight anymore. We had some food in storage, and thankfully we had seed banks that we could draw on later. For anyone that was weak, the Community had no means to support them enough then, even though people cared.' She paused for a moment, and I could sense the emotion welling up inside of her. There was something important that she wanted to tell me. And it was not easy for her.

'My mother was one of those weak ones, and she died not long after she had me.' Kendren could hardly manage to speak the words. Her body was shaking, and I raised my arm to put around her.

'How did she die?' I asked feebly. Kendren continued to look down.

'She just bled when she had me, and it undermined her strength so that she could not withstand the virus. Even though she kept on working, and she had lots of healing, in the end, it was not enough. Her ashes are here in the garden. I always think of her when I am working, and I feel that spiritually, she is here with me, giving me courage and commitment to go on.'

'What about your father?' I persevered.

'I never knew my father,' she replied. 'He was a visitor to the Community and stayed for a while, but then left. I understand that he was planning to return to be with my mother, but then the war came, and contact was lost. He was almost certainly killed.

'I was looked after as a Community baby, and always have felt that the community is my family. When I was little, they used to place me in my crib, next to the Oracle when she was meditating. Apparently, I was always very still then, even if I was awake, and I used to like the energy of the Oracle very much, and would sometimes make soft little noises when the Oracle spoke. I still like the energy of the Oracle today, and I find it very easy to meditate.'

'What about you? What about your life?' She wanted to know about me too, and not just have the attention on her. She had a curiosity to know about my life in the City. So, I shared with her about this. We must have talked for hours, and we were so absorbed in each other's stories. The gong went for us to have lunch together, and we had not got any work done that morning. Kendren sighed and shrugged her shoulders. I was very glad to have made a new friend!

A NEW WAY OF LIFE

That afternoon, we did work in the garden. We still talked, but while we talked, we worked. I told Kendren about the methods I had learnt from Adolfus, about helping the plants. Kendren found this very interesting, as some of these ideas were new to her. She told me how a lot of the knowledge that they had had about plants, had been lost at the time of the destruction, and they relied almost solely on the guidance they received and their intuition.

In turn, she began to teach me how I could open my awareness to experience the Spiritual essence of the plants and the fabric of energy travelling along the ground around us. Kendren told me that people also had energy fields and she could see them with her inner eyes. I asked her if she could see my energy field, and she told me she could. Kendren told me that my energy field was bright and filled with blues and greens. She smiled, and added that when we were talking, there were shades of pink that came out from my heart.

At that, I turned away for a moment, for I felt quite embarrassed. When I asked about what that pink meant, she spoke coyly, and suggested that it was a sign that I liked being with her. And of course, that was true.

When we finished doing the physical work, Kendren showed me some practices to help me open my inner sight. She encouraged me and was very patient. I found it fascinating.

By the end of the day, I was tired from working, but also, I had a lot to absorb from my interactions with Kendren. I wandered to the fireplace and found Zelda there with her friend, throwing sticks into the fire. They had been given the job of looking after the fire, and appeared to be pleased doing that. She seemed contented.

I was amazed how happy I felt being in the Community, and how eager I was to learn. For a few moments, my thoughts drifted back to the City, and I wondered about Adolfus, Joyce and Rusky, and how they were coping without me. I wished I could communicate with them, so I sent out a thought and prayer to them that they would know I was alive and well. Then my mind turned to my family, and I suddenly felt a knot in my stomach, and I felt afraid, so I tuned into my wooden eagle and asked him to help them. It was as much as I could do. I must have appeared preoccupied, for Kendren commented upon it, and I tried to shake myself out of it.

Over the following days, I settled, and became accustomed to my new routines. Daily life in the Community was very simple, and had specific rhythms to guide us. To start, we always had the meditation with the Oracle in the mornings. I continued to work in the gardens and orchards with Kendren and we formed a good team. When we had meals, the members of the Community all came together around the fire, and I started to get to know people and what they were like. Before we ate, there was always a short meditation, asking the Earth Spirit for the food to be blessed so that it would nourish us. It was a meaningful blessing and we held hands together in silence. This blessing was designed for us to link together so we could invoke Spiritual sustenance and healing for the essence of the food we ate, to ensure that it would not be contaminated. Kendren told me that, as we attuned in meditation, the energy field which connected with our food, became light and dancing with energy. She could see it, as could others, and when this occurred, the Elders of the Community could signify that it was safe for us to eat.

For me, my learning was to open to the Spiritual dimension of reality, to know that this existed, and to learn to cooperate and be aware of it in all my interactions. Life in the City had given no consideration of this, and the belief system of nearly all the people was that the material reality was all that existed. When people chose voluntary Euthanasia, they did so to find peace, rather than in expectation of having any survival after death. Even Adolfus was uncertain whether any divine forces existed. What was most important to him had been his companionship with Rusky and me, and more latterly, Joyce. This is what gave meaning to his life, rather than any faith.

It was very refreshing for me to be able to embrace a more Spiritual outlook. As a child, I had always felt the powers of healing energies that could express themselves through my hands. And in the way, I had met Adolfus, Joyce and Zelda, I just sensed that there was some greater power at work. With this openness to Spiritual forces, I felt much more at home in the Community than I had done in the City. I had a passion to acquire and develop my own inner capacities.

In the mornings, I looked forward to the Community meditations with the Oracle. Each time I did this, my level of meditation seemed to deepen, but the content of what I experienced, also changed and covered different topics. Always though, I could feel the warm comforting presence of the Earth Spirit, and the distinctive guttural tones of that inner guidance from the Oracle. The guidance was consistent, and imparted knowing, vision and direction to help all of us, and align us all together in harmony.

I asked Kendren why the meditations were always different, and she replied that our existence was in a state of continual evolution, and so no experience repeated itself. If we tried to hold on to experiences that we had had previously, then this would block the flow of energy bringing what was new, into our awareness. Also, she commented how each person would also have their own individual experience within the meditation, even though we were choosing to link collectively. We were all unique beings, and the divine presence of the Earth Spirit would channel distinctly through each one of us. However, by being linked together, the sum of what we experienced was in collective harmony and would be the best foundation for our Community to move forward. For the well-being of the Community, our choice to serve the Earth Spirit and work for the survival of life on Earth – this was sacrosanct.

I was amazed sometimes at the wisdom that Kendren could express, and at times, it was like she was a gifted Channel herself. She told me that in her own meditations she had been told that she was being prepared so that she could become a Channel like our Oracle – that this was her destiny.

It was such a matter of fact manner, in which Kendren told me this. Therefore, I guessed that this knowledge was something that she accepted, without doubt.

For me, Kendren was a young woman with many aspects. It was interesting to me how the Spiritual side of her nature combined with her more hidden, vulnerable side. Working beside me in the gardens, seemed to ground her, and it had the same effect upon me.

BLESSINGS

Soon, it felt very natural, living as part of the Community, and going with its flow. Although I shared a hut with Zelda, I hardly saw her during the day, but she seemed to be happy enough, and exploring her own worlds. She was also helping with planting, but her big love was the animals, giving healing to them and nurturing them so that their numbers could grow.

In the evenings, when sitting around the fire, I often noticed Linton looking at me, and smiling. He was like the father to the Community. His eyes would be watching everybody, and with his hat and long grey locks of hair, he was a very distinctive presence. Linton appeared to be well respected by all.

Over time, I opened to him more and more, and we had many talks about our lives, and the work of the Community.

I wondered about the Oracle and what she was like as a person, for she rarely appeared at the fireplace. Linton took her food. She must be quite reclusive, and to me, she was a person of mystery.

Some mornings now, Kendren would not be with me working, and would instead be with the Oracle, receiving individual training. Kendren rarely spoke about these trainings, except to affirm that the Oracle was a good teacher, and working very closely with Spirit. I noticed how happy and centred Kendren would be after these training sessions. They were good for her.

I missed Kendren when she was not with me, but it gave me the opportunity to get to know some of the other residents, and to explore. And I welcomed this. People living in the Community certainly did originate from a variety of different places, some of them even from other countries. It still astonished me how open all these people were to talk with me – so different from the City.

Although there was still a pervading sadness about all that had happened in our world, I felt that people here in the Community were enthusiastic and committed to their work. And they had one quality that had been sorely missed for me, when living in the City – and that was the quality of hope.

One evening, I was sitting next to Linton on one side of me, and Zelda on the other. Zelda had with her, a small furry animal that she was nursing, and she appeared to be giving it healing. Zelda was very contented doing this. As I watched Zelda with her furry friend, this was a stimulus for me to ask Linton how the animals had survived from the virus, as animals were wild and unable to be controlled. Linton looked up at me with a quizzical expression, and proceeded to tell me in more depth and detail, the story of the onset of the virus to the Community and the place of the animals in this.

'In the period, immediately following the War, we counted our blessings for we believed that we had largely escaped from the huge catastrophic ravages that had destroyed many areas of the planet. We had not been carrying nuclear weapons like some other countries, and so, we had been spared involvement.

'In our Community, we did not have advanced technological resources, so in that 'in between' period, after the nuclear attacks, and before the direct onset of the virus, we had to rely mainly on word of mouth to learn what was going on in the world. There were travellers that were still reaching us by foot. For a while, there were also aircraft that still flew around. From both these sources, we started to receive reports of the lethal virus, and this made us confused and very anxious. The verbal relayed information that people shared, was terrifying.

'Soon the planes stopped, and this was a clear signal to us that the overall situation was worsening. We knew that we needed to prepare to defend and protect ourselves. So, while you in the City were constructing glass buildings and sealed passageways with airlocks and filters for the water and air supply, we were attempting to summon Spiritual protection for the area around where we lived.

'Refugees, fleeing from the coastal regions, came streaming into the hills and sought safety with us. Numbers in our Community swelled beyond our capacity. The tales of annihilation people told us, put us in a state of high alert. When we did group meditations, many of us had visions of a horrifying darkness encroaching across the whole Earth. Most doubted that we could survive. We did not have the Oracle awakened at that stage, so we relied on the shamans in our midst to help us.

'There was a group within the Community that coordinated our response. I was one of them, and Kendren's mother, was another. Kendren's mother was a very powerful shaman, and she gave every ounce of her strength to do what she could, to protect us. We managed to set up a collection of energy points around the valley, and we linked them together spiritually with the assistance of the Earth Spirit. We did not have the depth of connection with the Earth Spirit then that we have today, but we reached for it through our rituals – even then, and used every resource that we could.

'We had scouts that told us how plants were dying off at an alarming rate in the land closer to the sea, and it was not long before our valley was under threat too. We always aspired to treat all forms of life in our vicinity with the most natural and uplifting ingredients to make it stronger, spiritually. It was our belief that the poisonous fertilizers and genetically modified crops, widespread in other parts of our land, only served to weaken the resistance to any form of disease, including the onslaught of the virus, for there was little Spiritual strength in these artificial ingredients.

'With our rituals and Spiritual ceremonies, we certainly felt that we managed to slow down the spread of the virus in our area, but we failed in stopping it. People working on the perimeters of our energy lines, started suffering from exhaustion, some died, and the quantity of healthy plant life at the edges of our land, diminished. What were we going to do? We brought our defences into a tighter core and released some of our outlying areas, but it still did not hold. Each day, we were losing ground, and our population were becoming sick.

'Those of us that remained held a desperate meeting, and we meditated to plea with the Earth Spirit for help. On that day, our Oracle connected with the Earth Spirit for the first time, and she spoke instructions that we all needed to follow. Our Shamans were asked to locate the tracks of Spiritual light surrounding our main encampment and including a small amount of bush land for the wildlife, and we were to meditate and call the wildlife into this area for the sake of their survival. Those of us attuned to the animal worlds helped with this. And it was remarkable for us how animals then did come into this place – even the birds came. It was as though they knew instinctively not to go out of this safety zone, and we invited them to live with us, and tried to care for them. It was quite crowded then, for all of us – human and animal, to live in such an overall small space comfortably. And sadly, we suffered more losses, and the amount of vegetation and food supplies we had left, reached critical levels. Our commitment though, was to preserve every life, human, animal and plant, as much as we possibly could.

'From that day, onwards, we spoke to the Earth Spirit through the Oracle and followed the instruction given, and this marked the first steps of finding our own strength to withstand the virus, and so we would not perish. The crisis remained with us for a long time, but our defence held, and some of our animal friends also survived and we have been nurturing their viability since then.'

I did not fully understand all that Linton was telling me, particularly about the lines of energy and how these would keep out the virus. However, afterwards, when I thought about it, I came to appreciate that the Earth Spirit was a supreme creative force, and even though people had the capacity to destroy, or unleash forces that could destroy, at least on a physical level, the Earth Spirit also had its resources to be able to continue its innovative mission. It was on the inner, subtler realms where the virus could have less impact, for it was an invention that consisted merely of the human genetic manipulation of a physical organism. While it could physically stop cells from reproducing, it could not destroy Spirit or human souls.

I speculated whether the uncaring violent power of human beings could destroy all life on Earth, or if the Earth Spirit would always have the means to deal with people's ways? As I sat in stillness considering this, the thought impinged upon me, that indeed, people could destroy the Earth – utterly.

That is why our efforts were so important in the Community now.

INNER DEVELOPMENT

Every morning, when I attended the meditation with the Oracle, I would go on inner journeys into the realms of the inner Earth. The closer I felt that I approached to the Earth Spirit, the more the light and love for the Earth, I started to feel. Deep inside, I was growing to feel increasingly connected and inwardly attuned to the Earth. At times, I could see visions of the areas of land within the Community. This land appeared lit up with light and with growing aliveness. With my thoughts in the meditation, I was urging the living vitality of the Community to become stronger and bigger. Doing this, I felt my heart expanding, and it was as though I was making a positive inner contribution – working with the visions presented to me by the Earth Spirit. This was something that we were all doing together. It was marvellous to share such dedication.

Just as Kendren had predicted, these meditation experiences did influence how I interacted with the plants, when I was working with them. The tingling vibration of the Earth Spirit, under my feet was getting stronger. I did not want to wear shoes anymore. This feeling was like electricity, running up through my feet, and travelling right through my body. It was a very comforting and pleasurable sensation – very alive. And I also felt energy coming from my hands, whenever I touched one of the plants or trees, and I felt such a lot of love in my heart, for all the life forms around me.

When I walked around, I began to be able to discern subtle differences with the degree of Earth Spirit energy, depending on where I stood. I realised then that there were places of power where the Earth vibration was very active, and other places where it was more blocked. As I thought about it, I could now understand what the shamans living here, had been doing, when they were setting energetic boundaries to attempt to protect the Community in those early days – those times when the virus was at its worst.

In my daily meditation with the Oracle, I set my intention with my love for the Earth, and added my voice and call with the others, for the energy of the Earth Spirit to assert itself from the heart of the Community, and widen its channel to heal further areas of the outer world. I believed that the inner work we did, had a direct influence upon the physical world around us. It was good to be part of this.

One morning, while Kendren was busy with the Oracle, I walked up the hills to the side of the Community, only as far as the living boundary, but I wanted to gain an overview of the Community land. I found a place that I liked, and stayed there for a while, breathing in the beauty of what I saw. Then I noticed, next to me, that there was an old dead stump from one of the trees that had lost its life to the virus. And next to this stump was a seedling, with a new young tree beginning its life. This was amazing. My hands were tingling with energy, so I directed this energy to the baby tree, and I sensed that it was quivering with appreciation. Then I remembered my dream from when I was very little – the dream that had helped so much to sustain me with hope and determination, during my young life – and this was the dream coming true. Shivers went up and down my spine. Wonderful. I was in the place where I needed to be.

Later that day, I shared with Kendren the story of my dream, and she was so happy, that she gave me a big hug. She wanted to know if I had always known how to heal? I shared with her, that from an early age, I had wanted to help the plants, and also, people by placing my hands near to them, and imagining the healing rays reaching them. I told her how I had been able to help Rusky in the time before he died.

Kendren asked me to reflect on this and how I channelled that energy, and I was aware that it was not from the Earth and Earth Spirit where I had drawn this energy to heal, but from above, and then through my heart. She then taught me that we could channel universal energy from the Spiritual planes beyond the Earth to help life around us, as well as from the Earth Spirit. They were two different sources of Spiritual energy, but linked together. Kendren explained, that, although our bodies were drawn from the substance and Spirit of the Earth, our soul came from the Universal Spirit above. This was the place that our souls regarded as home. And so, when we channelled healing energy from the Universal Spiritual sources, this would also be feeding the Earth Spirit and giving it sustenance. By doing this, we would be giving back energy to the Earth Spirit to help balance all the wonderful nurturing life we received from it. I felt very happy knowing this, and it gave me more options about how I could apply Spiritual practice into my daily working life.

Each day from my meditations with the Oracle, and from my work in the gardens, I sensed that there was more progress made with my inner connection. I felt Spiritual meaning and a deeper dimension of fulfilment to my work with plants than I had ever had, while I was working with Adolfus in the City. This did not denigrate what I had done with Adolfus, and how much our work there had ensured that life in the City could carry on. In that moment, I hoped that I could meet Adolfus again, and share with him what I had learnt. I felt some tears in my eyes – I missed him.

One day, Linton took me on a tour around the Community, and he showed me the extent of how small the area of fertile land had been at the beginning, when their situation had been direst. Then, we walked to the edges of the land where the Community now worked, and around this circumference, going past the seedling that I now regularly visited. The change and transformation in the landscape was immense. The people of the community had made tremendous advancement. I could see the satisfaction in Linton's eyes. But before I could feel too gratified, Linton then turned around and I moved my eyes with his, and we gazed outwards at the wasteland beyond. There, we could both perceive what a mighty task still lay ahead.

The next morning at the meditation, I had a vision where I was deep inside the Earth, and then I could somehow see the Community on the surface of the Earth and it was like a beacon of light in between vast areas of darkness. The line of energy from the core of the Earth Spirit to the surface and the Community was firm and sure. But there were other lines too. For a few moments, I struggled to understand what this meant, but then, as they started to reveal themselves, more clearly, I realised to my astonishment, that we were not the only survivors and communities left on this Earth. There must be other groups like us. That is what this vision was indicating. Wow. Could that be real? I knew that I could trust in visions that came to me in these meditations. If there were others still alive like ourselves, then this would be an incredible situation for us to savour, and something very much to celebrate. Had others seen this too?

Later, I dared to speak with Kendren and told her what I had experienced. Kendren smiled. She was glad that I was beginning to envision more of what she had known for a long time.

CLOSER

As time went on, I spent more and more time with Kendren. Prior to my arrival, there had been no one of her age in the Community. Without her mother or father, even though she had been accepted into the Community wholeheartedly, she missed them, and there was an emptiness that she had felt. Apart from my brother, I also had been deprived of interactions with others of my own age. We had both known loneliness. So, it was a comfort, and a new, but welcome experience, for both of us to be able to be together.

For me, it felt very natural being with her; we talked easily and could have fun together; we were both dedicated to the well-being of our plant friends; we had shared Spiritual interests; we worked together well. In the morning, when I saw her for the first time in the day, my heart felt warm. I noticed how she smiled when she saw me. Our feelings for each other were growing.

By now, we knew nearly all the details of each other's past, and it was precious to be able to trust her, and know that she trusted me. I felt accepted by her, and we enjoyed each other's company immensely.

In our free time, we liked to explore. One favourite place where we regularly went, was up on the ridge where we could gaze down from the top of the valley and view all the land of the Community. It was here that the little sapling of my dream was growing, and we sat on the tree stump next to it. This was a place of hope for us. Linton had pointed out the vast amount of work that we still needed to do, in combating the virus and returning the Earth to its vitality, and we both wanted to help in the transformation of the land.

We spoke about our longings to travel and explore. Kendren was fascinated by what I had learnt from the videos in the City. She wanted to know all about the former life in our world, and the various places that used to exist. Her curiosity and thirst for knowledge was as keen as mine, and it was a delight for me that she was interested.

Kendren lived in a hut with an older woman, whose name was Jenna. Jenna was kind to Kendren and had been like a doting grandparent to her, but they did not talk very much together anymore, and Kendren had felt rather confined living with her. More and more, Kendren would spend the evenings with me. I invited her to visit the hut, which I shared with Zelda, and soon this became part of our daily rhythm.

The three of us got on very well, and Zelda's teenage friend, Christoph, used to join us often as well. We would play games and had a lot of fun together – it was such a change for me also, to be with a group of young people. We felt like we were all discovering parts of ourselves that we had not had the chance to live before. It was very precious. My feelings of fondness towards Kendren were deepening with every passing day.

One evening, when Christoph had gone back to his hut, and Zelda was sleeping, Kendren asked if she could stay. I felt shocked and surprised at first, because I had not expected it. However, I also felt warmth in my body, and my heart was racing. Yes, I wanted her to stay, and for us to be close.

For a while we talked and then she took the lead and asked if we could lie down together. We did this, and I don't know why I felt so nervous. With a mixture of embarrassment and pleasure, we put our arms around each other, and we kissed. It was quite a beautiful feeling, and so we did it again, and again. Our noses got in the way of each other and we broke off laughing. Eventually we relaxed. For both of us, on this night, it was enough that we kissed and lay together. I felt very happy.

The night was a special time for me. Usually, I stayed awake when I went to bed, for I liked to listen to what was going on outside. There were a couple of owls that lived in the Community – Zelda liked them very much, and in the night, we could hear them hooting. They never went far away – for obvious reasons. As well as the owls, there were also sounds of insects adding to the music of the night. Their presence was close, and their music only seemed to come alive at night. But beyond that, and the sound of crackling of the community fire, with occasional voices, there was silence.

On this night, though, there was a new sound, and I could also hear Kendren's breathing next to me, as well as Zelda, as she lay in her bed on the other side of the cabin. At one point, I sat up in the bed and gazed outside the window. I could observe the enchanting moon, casting its light on the encampment. It was wonderful to see. Kendren stirred, and soon she was sitting up next to me. We both listened to the nature and watched the heavenly sky outside. The whole atmosphere of the environment, was fascinating and compelling.

It was such a contrast – the life within the Community, buzzing with vitality, while outside of the perimeter of this, there was stark deadness and desolation. Kendren could sense this too. She was an empath. Often, what I would be feeling, she would feel, and vice versa. That was very beautiful – how connected we could be.

In this moment, perhaps triggered by our thoughts concerning the Earth, I felt extremely sad, and tears came to my eyes. As I glanced across at Kendren, she was crying too. There was grief that all of us felt within us, about what had happened to our world, and sometimes, almost inexplicably, this grief would want to express itself. I had seen it also in others, including Adolfus and Joyce. Even in this beautiful Community, it was present, and something that everyone understood and shared. Now it was my turn to feel it. Kendren put her arms around me to comfort me, and I relaxed again.

I wanted to discuss further with Kendren about the vision that I had been given during the Oracle meditation – the one I had revealing other pockets of life and survivors in various parts of the world. Kendren smiled at me, and told me that she also found that to be very reassuring. The Earth Spirit was priming us and supporting us all to believe that we were not alone. Perhaps the Earth Spirit wanted us to go out and connect with some of those groups. We looked up at each other. That would be a wonderful thing to do. Kendren smiled at me, and I knew then that she shared a similar desire.

We talked about the specifics of what we had seen inwardly, but neither of us had enough detailed information to know precisely where these groups would be located. I decided that I would confide with Linton about this, and ask if he had any knowledge of these other groups in the world.

After a while, we settled down again in the bed. Her body was very warm and we fitted together very well. It was so easy to be with her, as if we belonged together, and I felt a great sense of peace.

I must have gone to sleep, for the next moment, there was light streaming through the window and the sun was letting us know that the new day was upon us. My movements must have wakened Kendren, for suddenly she was stretching beside me and we hugged. She had a big smile on her face, and she told me that she had really enjoyed her night. And I had enjoyed it too.

Kendren asked if she could move in with me permanently. Without hesitation, I agreed. She wanted to go and tell Jenna. In the days that followed, Kendren brought her belongings over to my hut and we set up house together. So, from then on, we slept together every night. Another older woman in the Community moved in to be with Jenna. In the meantime, Zelda had an invitation to go and stay at Christof's hut. They had a spare bed there, and she was delighted to do that.

In the weeks that followed, the bond that Kendren and I shared became ever more intimate. We became even more familiar with each other's habits and our patterns of everyday life. It felt very easy to share a room and bed with her, and somehow, our lives felt much more complete. We did not talk about it very much; it became a 'fact' that we both acknowledged without words. In my heart, I felt a quiet joy. Our rapport increased. One evening, after we had been sitting by the community fireplace, she reached for my hand so we could watch the sunset together. Moments like these brought tremendous happiness to me.

TALKING WITH LINTON

Often, in the evenings, we would find ourselves at the fireplace, talking with Linton. I felt very drawn to him, for he had such a lot of knowledge. We talked about many things. I asked about the existence of people and groups in other parts of the world, and he confirmed that he, too, had had visions of this, and had consulted with the Oracle about these. She had suggested that when the time was right, contact between at least some of these communities and survivors would happen. This felt very exciting to me.

At the back of my mind, there was one topic, that I dearly wanted to explore with Linton, and that was about Kendren's father and mother, and their relationship. Kendren had told me all that she knew, and it was very little. She became emotional whenever I mentioned it. Even so, I asked Kendren if I could raise this with Linton, for he would know a lot more about this. Kendren looked at me with an uncertain expression, but she agreed for me to make this initiative.

There were some things, that I felt, I had to know, and it was not just for my sake. Whenever I thought about Kendren's origins, it stirred something within me, and I became unsettled – it was not just to do with Kendren. This was because of the stories that I had heard from Adolfus, and his visits to the community. Who could the woman be that Adolfus loved? I needed to clarify about the identity of Kendren's father and how Adolfus was involved in the Community. Was Kendren linked to this in some way?

One evening, we were with Linton and feeding the fire with small twigs. I dared to begin a conversation about this. Linton stared at me, and the touch of Kendren's hand on my knee suddenly tightened. The atmosphere between us suddenly became very intense.

Linton then gave me a strange smile, and he replied to indicate that he had been waiting for this. Slowly Linton positioned himself more comfortably and openly so he could address his words to both of us. Kendren nestled in close to me, so she could feel more secure. We both listened expectantly while Linton shared the story.

'Kendren's father had been a scientist, very interested in plants. With the signs of imminent war, he had taken it on himself to build up seed collections of plants and trees so that whatever happened, important species of plants could be preserved. He travelled around and worked tirelessly to generate banks of seeds and he also constructed nurseries. Kendren's mother was also devoted to plants and so they worked together. Soon they fell in love and wanted to create a home together.

'It was just before the war when they parted. One night I remember being with them. They were watching an eclipse of the moon and there was a strange light in the sky. I looked at them both, and there was a disturbed energy between them, as if they knew somehow, that something was not right. It was very sad, the next morning when Kendren's father left. He insisted on going alone, because he felt it was his duty. He had to go and do more foraging for seeds from other areas, and then go on, to the location of the central seed bank that he had been developing, and complete his work on that. He pledged to her that he would return. Neither of them knew that she was pregnant.

'Of course, their wishes to be together did not eventuate, because of the War. They lost contact. And then, from the war, there was the growing terror of the insidious virus. Kendren's mother was desperate, and wanted to go after him, and several times, I needed to restrain her. She kept going to the ridge, somehow hoping, that she would see him in the distance, walking towards her. But he never came.

When the virus took hold of the life in the land, her desire and grief almost became like madness, and she could not accept that he would not be there. She never let him go, but she channelled the love she felt for him into desperate attempts to save the community. And she gave more of herself to this than she was capable.

'She did not want to give birth on her own, without him by her side. We had mid-wives, but the process of the birth was more difficult than anticipated. Kendren's mother did not rest as she should have done. After her daughter's birth, although she was weakened by blood loss, she insisted on continuing her work, and she never stopped trying, and putting every ounce of her energy working with the others to keep the influence of the virus at bay. There was not a day when she did not go up onto the ridge to look for him, vainly hoping that he would come, that she could just see him again.'

Kendren's face was against my shoulder and it was wet from her tears. She could not stop herself from weeping at this tragic story. Kendren had always assumed that her father had died, and her mother had died while waiting for him. Now she didn't know anymore, if he had died. The recalling of her mother's devotion to her father was tremendously emotional for her.

Suddenly, the tension was mounting inside me. I asked Linton more about the identity of Kendren's father – about his appearance, his voice, his habits and other characteristics. Next, I urged Linton to confirm the place where the central seed bank was being established. With each answer, I became more certain. All the details matched up. I could see that Linton was gazing at me with wonder in his eyes. There was something more that I had to enquire about. The atmosphere between the three of us had become very quiet, and full of expectancy.

'What were their names – Kendren's parents?' I spoke softly to Linton. Linton caught the gaze of my eyes and looked deep into me.

'You know their names,' he shared with me. And through the glistening tears from my eyes and his, a warm flow of energy flowed through my body. The realisation made me feel exhilarated. I took Kendren's two hands and held her closer to me, so I could address her directly.

'Your mother's name was Mary, Kendren, and your father is Adolfus,' I exclaimed to her. 'Your father is alive!'

CONSULTING WITH THE ORACLE

Suddenly, so much made sense and I felt very happy. The attraction I had felt to Kendren had roots that went far beyond what I had assumed. I looked over at my friend. Kendren was ecstatic, and could not keep still. She hugged me and Linton. So much was processing through her. She needed to move, so I suggested going on a walk. Kendren wanted me with her so we could talk. We must have just forgotten about Linton at that point, for we were in a world of our own – laughing, sighing. I stood up, and we went off into the night. One of the owls was hooting in the distance.

We didn't sleep that night. The realisations we had been given, precipitated long talks between us, as we both scrambled to comprehend the full ramifications of it all. Instead of going to our beds, we stayed out, and went up to the ridge, and the old tree stump, where we always liked to be. Kendren wanted to know everything about Adolfus, and I had to repeat information I had already given to her. I described again how we had met, and important interactions we had had. Now, it was not merely the case of Adolfus being an important friend of mine – he had a whole new meaning for Kendren. She kept on shaking her head and hugging me. With each conversation, she felt a stronger desire to go and see him, for now, Kendren wanted to meet her father. We both wished for this, and although she felt nervous, the fact of how kind and loving Adolfus had been to me for all those years, gave her confidence. In some ways, I had been like the replacement child for what Adolfus missed. Kendren felt sad about this, for her own sake, but also glad, for she could appreciate what a positive difference his presence had been for me.

In the days that followed, the topic of Adolfus came up frequently in our conversations, as Kendren continued to work everything out in her mind. There was nothing that we could do immediately, about her wish to meet him. We returned to our normal working patterns, but neither of us felt settled. It was as if some big change was brewing, and we hardly knew how it would manifest.

One morning when at the meditation with the Oracle, I had the most amazingly beautiful vision. I saw that I was going together with Kendren, up the hills and away from the Community, walking a long, long distance, striding along, with calm and confidence. When we found shelter, and sat down together, we linked with the Earth Spirit, and gradually, around us, in the midst of all the barren land, there was an abundance of plants and life that began to burst forth from the ground. Tears flowed from my eyes as I was given this, for I could hardly believe it. Why would I be given such a vision? And then, when I saw Kendren and shared it with her, before I could finish, she interrupted me, telling me how the vision ended.

How amazing! She had been given the same vision as me. From this inner world, it felt as though the knowledge of what we had to do, as the next step in our lives, was being revealed to us. Then the tears flowed from both of us. Kendren held my hands tightly and we stood up. The energy she conveyed was one of resolve and determination.

Later that day we told Linton about our inner experiences, and he put to us that we needed to have a talk with the Oracle. Linton had a strange expression on his face, as if – once again – our coming forth with this, was something that he had expected.

For some reason, I felt quite nervous to meet the Oracle. I did not know her as a person. Although Kendren spoke glowingly about her as a teacher from her own interactions, there was something about her that made me feel uneasy. I had never spoken to her or even had eye contact. After the morning meditations, she would retreat to her own quarters; a simple dome-like construction made of wood, and would not be seen again. To me, the Oracle felt very remote and unfathomable. Her actions had saved and resuscitated the Community and her service to the Earth Spirit and the Community was sacrosanct, but I had no idea what she was like as a person.

I felt quite reassured that Kendren chose to hold my hand as we entered the Oracle's dwelling place. Linton had come with us to announce our arrival, but then he left us so that we were alone with her. For a moment, I gazed around the interior of her dwelling hut. There were a few simple mats to cover the floor and cushions, where people could sit, but other than that, and some symbols drawn on the wall, there were no furnishings. It was an astonishingly simple setting. The Oracle was clearly not a person to have possessions. As I took in the energy of the room, I could feel vibration under my bare feet. My awareness of this had been growing anyway, but here, it was particularly strong, and that energy was indicative of the presence of the Earth Spirit.

The Oracle had a youthful appearance, and it was hard to tell her age. She wore a simple purple gown, but combined with her flowing loose black wavy hair and her fluid movements, the sight of her was quite captivating. Strangely though, it was the energy of calm emanating from her that affected me most. She motioned us to sit in front of her, on the cushions. And we did this. She looked up at us. When her eyes met mine, I could discern her depth, and there was no wavering in her gaze.

Linton had told me about the rhythms of the Oracle's life. Basically, she did the public Channelling, private meditations and had audience with members of the Community whom she trained. Most of her time was in solitude. Her service to the Community and her dedication to Spirit, were steadfast, but she had devoted herself to this at great cost, for her personal life as a woman, and member of the Community, was virtually non-existent. I marvelled at this, and her commitment. I did not know if I would ever be able to live a life quite like she did or if it was my path. People were important for me, and I wanted to live in the world, not apart from it. Perhaps that is why I felt uneasy – she was so different, and I could not identify with her lifestyle.

Kendren told the Oracle about the vision that we had both been given, and the Oracle smiled and looked back at us. She asked us to tell her, each in turn, what we felt that this vision was calling from us? Kendren replied that she felt that it indicated that we both needed to go out into the world together and find a place from where we could help to regenerate the life of the Earth. I had to agree with my companion and her interpretation. But the Oracle wanted more.

'For you to do this, would not be an easy undertaking,' she spoke. 'You, Kendren, would need to be in a location where you could open up the channels to the Earth Spirit, both for yourself and others. In your vision, you did not see the people around you, but there would be people there. Your path is not just one of being in isolation from other human beings. She told me that my role would be to both protect and support Kendren in her endeavours, and be a stable and reliable connecting force with people that were there. You would both need to commit yourselves to each other, the needs of the Earth Spirit, the Community around you, and your service. This would have to come first, before any personal desires on your part. Could you do it?'

Suddenly, I shuddered and started shaking. I did not want to become a recluse. Too much of my life had been spent in isolation, and I did not like it, and I still felt the fear of it working through my energy system. The Oracle must have noticed my reaction, for she reached out her hand to touch my shoulder.

She went on, speaking with a low and gentle voice, reassuring me. 'You do not have to live like me. If you choose this path with Kendren, you will be together and will not feel alone. You will not have to divorce yourself from people or your worldly activities. In fact, you may be able to inspire others through your own actions and way of relating together.

There is an ancient spiritual tradition coming from people of the Earth, from long ago, where then, some students of the Earth Spirit would work, not singly, but in pairs. This way, they could complement each other's energies and accomplish Spiritual goals through their connection, and the field of energy that they could establish from their togetherness. This can work very well, and spiritually there is the openness where you could embrace this together. Do you want to do it?'

Kendren and I looked at each other, and I could feel the love in her eyes. In my heart, I felt both joy and relief. Inside, I felt a huge urge to make a difference and to help the Earth, and the thought of doing this with Kendren delighted me. We hugged, and I knew that she felt similarly.

'Please join me with meditation,' the Oracle implored. So, we sat together with her, and she asked us to imagine a triangle of energy where we opened our hearts to blend and join together while also strengthening and embracing the Spirit of the Earth. As I went with this, I lost all sense of the dwelling place where I was sitting and I was fully absorbed with an inner world where I felt intense love and the vibrancy of life that the Earth Spirit brought forth. I could perceive the Oracle with us, but gradually her energy seemed to surrender itself utterly, to become one with the Earth. I could hear her voice like a whisper, communicating for us to follow her. I was entering a space that I could not consciously retain.

Suddenly I was jolted by the Oracle, whose hand was pressing on my shoulder. As I gradually stirred, I noticed that Kendren too was slowly coming around from what must have been a very deep place for her too.

Around the perimeter of the room there were stones laid out, and the Oracle asked us each to choose one.

I knew which one I wanted, and chose the turquoise stone, which resonated with my heart. The colours felt just right for me. And while I wondered at this, Kendren chose a beautiful pink rose quartz. The Oracle then brought out a cloth and wrapped this around our adjoining arms so that we were bound together, while still holding our stones. These stones would be for us, gifts from the mineral kingdom to help us on our personal journey of activating our service with the Earth Spirit.

Before she proceeded, she checked with us and looked in our eyes. Then she asked us, in turn, if we were sure that we wanted to do this? I answered that I did, as did Kendren. I had never felt so certain about anything in my life.

The Oracle asked us to recite and vow our allegiance to the Earth Spirit and our commitment to work for the rest of our days on Earth. This was not like a normal marriage, but a joint commitment of service to the Earth – to put that first before all else. In my heart, it felt right. Then the Oracle uttered some sounds in a language that I did not understand, but I felt the deep resonance of it vibrating through my body. I felt tremendous peace and joy. Just then, all I wanted to do was to get out there into the world, with Kendren, and start.

For some moments, we stood in silence while the energy settled. The Oracle assured us that we would know, when the time was right, to branch out with our work, and where it is that we would need to go. She beseeched us to trust, and allow the process from what we had just done, to unfold.

Slowly she loosened the cloth that had bound us and freed our arms from it, and I looked lovingly at the beautiful Turquoise stone that I carried in my hand. I moved the stone into my other hand so I could hold the hand of Kendren, and she did the same with her stone. We were ready to go outside.

TRANSITION

Over the next weeks, both Kendren and I were quite silent, as we went about our daily tasks. She was preoccupied with her thoughts and I was with mine. By forcing myself to do my work in the gardens and concentrating on that each day, I found that this helped me to ground myself, so my thoughts did not stray too much into uncertain areas. I did not see Kendren in the mornings, as she continued with her training from the Oracle. When she emerged from these sessions, she had a radiance and serenity about her that helped me feel calm.

As time went on, I found that my thoughts were moving in one direction, and they would not deviate. There was a place where I wanted to go with Kendren. I had to speak of it to her. One evening, I could not contain myself any longer. Inside, I was bursting. I had to know what Kendren was thinking. She smiled at me when I started. I was all over the place. Then she laughed.

We found that our thoughts were aligned – almost identical. It had come to me for us to go and do our work together in the City. We had both had the same idea. Kendren wanted to meet her father, and I wanted to see Adolfus. However, there was another strong pull for me, because I was concerned about my family. It felt such a long time since I had been away, and although I rejoiced that I had discovered both strength and purpose here in the Community, I was fearful for how they would be faring.

The City was slowly dying, and my departure would have surely weakened the resolve of my family and friends to go on. I did not know how they would have reacted – even though I made Adolfus and Joyce promise to wait for me, I did not know how strong they would have been. And I was even less certain with my parents and brother, Martin.

As I considered these thoughts, I could feel a cold sweat making my clothes feel clammy and sticky. I was anxious about all of them. For some time, I had been able to place thoughts of them to one side, while I had enjoyed being in the Community. But now, since that talk with the Oracle, I could no longer ignore their plight. Something had shifted inside me.

If Kendren and I had work to do in the world, then, for myself, this was where we had to start. I could not dismiss the feeling of responsibility that I felt towards my loved ones there, and I had to check that they were all living, and functioning. Maybe now, we might be able to help them.

For Kendren, when, over so many years, she had assumed that her father was dead, and now to ascertain that he could be alive, then she had to find him. She needed to meet him and hear his story, and she felt very open to spend time with him. Her sense of identity depended on it, and she would not be able to forgive herself, if she did not make the effort.

That evening, we talked continuously, late into the night. From sharing our feelings, and listening to each other, the resolve in us rapidly firmed, that we needed to go to the City. We both felt peace about this. If this was to be the initial destination for our work together, then it was a choice that we could both make, without question. We had to work out how we would get there.

I had the thought ask Zelda, if she would accompany us. But she seemed so settled in the community now, and so independent, that I was not sure that she would want to come. It may be just the two of us that would go there. We would have to survive that journey, but if we could do that, then this would surely give some hope to the people of the City.

The next day, we spoke to Linton, and he agreed in the truth of what we had decided. He supported us that we could trust our longings and instincts to do this. Linton suggested that if residents of the City were still alive, then we could help rejuvenate the place. Later, it may be possible to start some form of exchange program with the Community, to help each other. His thoughts and wishes were very positive.

We went and saw the Oracle too. Linton came with us. I wanted to ask her, with her visionary eyes, if she knew about the well-being of my family and friends. However, her deep still eyes, gave nothing of this, away, and I knew that she would not tell me. I had to trust. It would be necessary for us to be open with our courage to face whatever was there, without knowing what to expect beforehand. We would both have our challenges, and could support each other. However, I still felt a knot of fear in my stomach, even with these positive affirmations.

The Oracle led us in a brief meditation and offered us a blessing from the Earth Spirit. She reminded us that with the stones that she had given us, that if we were ever fearful or uncertain, that we should touch our stones and that this would help steady us so that we could find our way forward. It was not automatic that our vision would be fulfilled. This would only happen through daily diligence, and the utmost of dedication, sometimes through extremely trying circumstances. She endeavoured to soften this, by affirming that the Earth Spirit had chosen us to undertake this work, and must therefore regard us as being capable of succeeding. We needed to trust our capability too.

As we left the Oracle's dwelling place on this day, I looked back and saw Linton and the Oracle standing together. And for the first time, I sensed that they were also a pair, engaged in their own form of joint Spiritual commitment. Inwardly I smiled and was grateful.

JOURNEY

In the days leading up to it, I became very emotional at the thought of leaving the Community. This had been such an important place of 'home' to me, even after such a relatively short space of time. I had felt safe in the Community and able to be myself. The ideals of this place were what I also believed. And I did not know how we would cope when we left this wonderful sanctuary. Nearly all my life, I had lived on edge, and now in the Community, I had been able to relax and feel at ease. How could I consider leaving?

For Kendren, it must have been equally testing, if not more so. This was the only place she had known, and she had always felt nurtured and supported by others here. Now she would need to look after herself, and for companionship, she would be reliant upon me. Kendren did not know how Adolfus would react to her. There would be new opportunities, with people in the City, but we both knew that this may not be easy. So much there needed to be transformed. It needed a lot of trust, for us to go there, with so much uncertainties ahead.

The day arrived, and we had our provisions, our stones, some clothes, food and water with us. We stood at the entrance to the Community. Zelda had come and given us each a hug. Her eyes were joyful, and I took this as a good sign. Her decision had been, unhesitatingly, to stay. She said to me that I did not need her anymore, and that I should have faith. Zelda was wise beyond her years.

She was not the only one, there. People came to wave us off, and to wish us success. There was a long line of them. Kendren gave a special hug to Jenna. And there were others that wanted to honour her – they knew her from her whole lifetime of experience.

We lingered for a long time. But finally, I turned around and saw

Linton's smile, as he stood there with his arms extending around Zelda's shoulders. He waved goodbye. It was time for us to move, so we started towards the bare hills in front of us.

Kendren and I had resolved that once we left the Community, we would not look back, but go forward towards our destination. Now though, as we walked on, it was not so easy. As our path took us beyond the sounds of the voices and wildlife of the community, I felt emptiness inside me. The landscape in front of us was unyielding, dead and decayed. I gasped as I realised the extent of our task.

We both held hands tightly, as we clambered up the slope. I stopped for a moment to tune in. In vain, I attempted to feel the vibration of the Earth Spirit beneath my feet, but it was so faint, I felt almost lost without it. As soon as I held hands with Kendren again, it appeared to be little stronger, but I could hardly believe the difference. We were very much on our own. I could only console myself by remembering how Zelda and I made the trip here in the months previously. If we managed then, surely Kendren and I could make the return journey now.

I did not know how much the residues of the virus would affect me this time, and indeed how Kendren would cope with it, but we strode forward purposefully. Our route was the reverse of the way I had come. We would have to climb through the mountains and hills and head to the coast first, and then we could find our way south.

For the first few hours, the two of us hardly spoke, and we could hear the puffing of each of us breathing, and the squelch of our boots as we trod on the wasted soil and ground under our feet. It was so silent – no birds, no children, no rustle of leaves. It left me once more, with a feeling of acute sadness in my heart, and that all too familiar heavy feeling of grief for all that we had lost.

When we sat down for a break and to drink, Kendren told me that she was shocked, and there were tears coming down her cheeks. She had not comprehended that it would be like this. Kendren wanted to be held, and while I did this, I could feel how much that she was shaking. All our talks had only partially prepared her. She was glad that we were together. It took a while for her to settle.

I was impatient to make progress, but the walking became more difficult as we went further – trudging over the hills. The sun was beating down, and sapping my energy. But it was the lack of feeling of the vibration of the Earth Spirit beneath my feet that disturbed me. I could feel a thick layer of inertness in the soil, and this was impenetrable. Without having the support of the Earth Spirit, I worried that the virus could attack me once more, and dissipate my life forces. With this thought, I started to feel increasingly tired. I also felt despair.

If I could only feel the vibration of the Earth Spirit more strongly, I knew that I would feel better. I wondered what it would be like for Kendren. She had grown up accustomed to that support? How would she be managing, inwardly? She would be feeling that something vital to her, was missing.

Neither of us felt like talking; we just went on, stepping through the remains of dead forests, tracing pathways up and down forlorn and empty hills. It was around mid-afternoon when we had our next break. We still had some considerable distance to go before we would be within sight of the sea. But we were both ready to stop for a while. Kendren motioned to a clearing in the shade where we could rest, and we both half collapsed onto the ground, and were panting for breath. I felt very weak, and looking at Kendren, I could tell that she was faring not much better. Should we turn back? Was it just too difficult for us to reach the City?

We had water that the Oracle had prepared for us – water that had been especially blessed. Drinking this revived us. Kendren came over closer to me so we could talk. She looked vulnerable, so I put my arm around her, and then she expressed what she had been feeling.

'I never thought it would be as tough as this,' she admitted. 'I miss the Community so much, and we have been away for less than a day. I cannot believe how lifeless the Earth is here. Nothing is breathing in the soil – it has no joy. To think that all the Earth was once as it is in our Community, and now look and feel what it has become; it is like we are outcast on the desolate remains of our own world. How can I forgive those elements of humanity that have done this? Our Earth has been nearly all destroyed. I realised this mentally before we began our journey, but walking in this, I can experience it, and it is dreadful, utterly dreadful. While I lived in the Community, it was like being in a bubble. But I am out of that bubble now. I cannot draw on any physical or energetic sustenance out here. There is nothing. And it is so sad. I just want to cry and scream and change it into something better. I am angry, and so disappointed.'

I felt what she was saying, and there was nothing I could say to comfort her. Being in the Community had been like living in a kind of paradise temporarily, but now, we had thrust ourselves back into the starkness of the reality of a world that did not support life anymore. And it was terrifying and seemingly without hope.

'I need to do something and try to connect with the Earth Spirit,' she told me, and making herself comfortable, she closed her eyes in meditation. I stayed very still so that I would not disturb her. After a while, my eyes closed too. I wanted to follow Kendren. And I found myself going down and travelling inwards until, to my surprise, as I relaxed, I could feel familiar threads of that warm comforting vibration of the living Earth. Then, I knew that I was with the Earth Spirit and that Kendren was with me. Sensing this was tremendously comforting.

When we returned from the meditation, I felt much better and more peaceful. I turned and gazed into Kendren's eyes, and I saw that tranquillity in her being that I loved. She smiled at me and stroked my arm in appreciation for my company. Then she told me to lie back and I felt her gentle hands on my shoulders as she channelled some refreshing healing for me. It helped a great deal. So later, I did the same for her. We had not made a lot of progress, but we had gone far enough for today. Looking around I gathered a pile of dead wood to make a fire, and we set up our camp for the evening.

In the night time, we were again feeling devastated by the emptiness of what was around us. There were no birds, no sounds of nature, just the sounds of our breathing and the shuffling of our bodies as we adjusted ourselves. It felt very lonely. We were not meant to be on our own, living on this Earth. With the plants, animals and other humans, we were a community of life. That is what we needed – what we all needed. And we had to find harmony, based on mutual respect and support for each other – not separation or destruction. We needed to find a new way to live together on Earth. If we were to be given another chance, we could not repeat the same mistakes.

The night air was cool, and we snuggled close under our sleeping bags to keep warm and for comfort. I was not awake for long, and I had no awareness of any dreams, or any movements from Kendren. When I opened my eyes, I was surprised to see the sun.

Once we were up and ready to move with the new day, we were more prepared for what lay in front of us. With determination, we moved ahead at a steady pace and with less desperation.

We reached the point in our journey where we were by the ocean. The sea was a sight that Kendren had never seen before, and for her, it was spectacular. She ran along the sand, and then looked at me with an expression of mischief and a great sense of adventure. I could not stop her, for she wanted to go into the water. Momentarily, I froze with fear, but then I saw how uninhibited she was, jumping around without her clothes, getting joyfully wet. I could not stop myself from joining her. The immediate feeling of coldness was replaced by exhilaration, as I accustomed myself to the sensations of the moving water. Soon, we were wading in amongst the waves. I had never experienced anything like it. We knew that there were risks with the virus but I had great fun with her in the water that day, and the feeling of the ocean water against my skin was immensely pleasurable. We splashed and dived into the waves, and enjoyed every moment, even when the waves dumped us. It was the first time for either of us to be in the sea. Kendren seemed to be at home in the water – like one of those fish that I had seen in the historical videos.

I wondered what had happened to all the dolphins. I remembered seeing magnificent films of them – and the whales. They looked so majestic, the way they could jump out of the water. Sadly, I shook my head. I guessed that they would all be dead now, all gone, like all the other life in the sea – all killed by the virus, apart from the water itself, which continued to bellow against the shore – another sad moment of reflection.

Afterwards, when we lay on the sand, drying ourselves, I could feel that creeping weakness again, indicating the presence of the virus. I couldn't help it and must have swallowed some salt water. Looking across at Kendren, her eyes were also now looking quite drained. It was disconcerting how quickly our Spirits could change, and our physical being be weakened by this. I had to open my trust again that we could counter the effects of the virus.

We both nodded, and made the effort to close our eyes and meditate, so we could seek the remedy of life and vitality from the Earth Spirit, and then channel healing to each other. It took longer for us to get there today, but eventually we managed it. For a long while, we sat quietly, with a mixture of different thoughts and feelings flowing through us. For me, the great experience of enjoying the sea together for the first time, had been compromised by knowledge of the reality that our oceans had become dead worlds.

That afternoon we sat there on the sand. Neither of us wanted to go further. The healing restored our energy so we could feel more peaceful. When the sun sank over the horizon, the evening sky was spectacular. What a beautiful world we could have, if we looked after it.

Another night's sleep, and we were ready to continue our walking. Now we journeyed south, along the coastal road, getting ever closer to where we wanted to be. When we passed the first of the forsaken villages, I wanted to shield Kendren from seeing the evidence of skeletons of humans and other animal remains – the residues of what had been once thriving communities. But she saw them. How could I stop her? And she gasped when she became aware of them. Seeing this, was a very cruel reminder of what the Extinction War had produced – and the clear message that the pursuit of power by human beings, only ever resulted in destruction. The devastation that we witnessed could hardly have been any worse. Much as she was affected by this though, it did not deter her. Kendren kept moving forward and I walked with her. Neither of us wanted to stop now.

I started recognizing certain landmarks that told me that we were approaching nearer to the City, and I could feel tightness in my stomach, of fear, as I did not know what we would meet me there.

That night, the stars were twinkling in the night sky and the crescent moon dipped close to the horizon. Kendren and I talked for a long time about Adolfus and the conditions of life in the City. She was talking fast, and I could tell that this was a sign of her anxiety and nervousness. I tried to explain to her in more detail, about the layout of the City, the system of government, the housing blocks, and how people existed in there. But I was still not sure that she grasped it all.

Kendren was used to being around people that lived with joy, hope and purpose – while all I had ever experienced in the City, besides when I was with Adolfus, Joyce and Rusky, was sadness and despair. I spoke to her about how I had needed to protect herself when people continued to look down, and explain that this was not personal, but was more a sign of how people were feeling inside.

I did not feel happy to bring her here. But I suppose, we had a job to do and people to see. As I considered it, the whole vision of helping to bring new life to our world, was so much easier to embrace while we were still in the Community, with the Oracle and Linton. Here, I felt exposed and vulnerable – we both did. Each day, as we walked, we were struggling to survive. The confidence that we had both felt before we left the Community, felt a long way away.

That night, as Kendren lay close to me, I sensed that she was seeking reassurance and comfort to allay her fears – it was good that we could support each other. We had one more full day's walking to do, and after our next sleep, we would hopefully be on the last stretch before we reached our destination.

RETURNING TO THE CITY

It felt very strange and unnerving as we first caught sight of the outskirts of the City. For me, the environment was both familiar, and uninviting. What awaited us within these walls? Kendren held my hand tightly. Both of us were nervous and anxious.

As we approached the entrance airlock at the City's gates, we gazed in through the glass, straining our eyes to notice any sign of habitation within the city buildings. We could see none, and this only increased our sense of fear and apprehension.

Before I opened the outer door to the City, we looked at each other in acknowledgment. We had done well to get this far. Now we had to go in. Kendren lifted her hands, so we could open the airlock together.

I was relieved to find that the airlock was operating normally with automatic control. We stepped forward and waited patiently while the air cleansing process proceeded. Finally, the inner door opened. Nobody was about. We turned to each other and I breathed a sigh of relief. At least, we had made it inside.

Kendren was looking for me to lead and show her the way. We had agreed to go to the gardens and hopefully see Adolfus first. That had to be our first calling point. For Kendren, the possibility of meeting the father she had never seen was a very emotional prospect and a thin line of silent tears was slowly streaming down her face. She clasped her arms tightly around mine. I had never known her to be so tense. I could feel the emotion within my body as well, like a curled-up spring, that was ready to burst open.

We had to walk down one of the main thoroughfares, but there was still no one about. This was unusual, and I could not understand it. My biggest dread was that there had been some form of mass suicide from the remaining residents in the time since Zelda and I had left. This did not seem beyond what was possible, and I just wished that the pervading feeling of hopelessness in the city had not extended that far.

Then, around the next corner, there was a man scurrying along. His head was down in typical fashion. Although, we tried to attract his attention, he was not interested, and just went faster towards wherever he was going. But this proved that people were still alive in the City, and part of me wanted to jump with joy and celebration. However, he was the only one we saw. I felt perturbed by that. To me, this was an indication that activity within the public areas of the City was very much diminished from what I remembered. What did this mean for the survival of those here that we loved?

We kept walking along the corridors until we reached the entrance to the gardens. At this juncture, Kendren let go of my hand. She looked in my eyes and told me that she had to face this meeting by standing in her own energy. I understood and respected this.

When we opened the doorway, I half expected all the gardens to be lying dead and disused, but they weren't. The beds were not as big – some sections were not being used any more, but those that were being utilised, were flourishing. It was all green, and the plants were standing lush and healthy with sprinklers watering them. At the back of these garden beds, I could see people picking vegetables – just a few, but it was enough to give me hope. I looked at Kendren, and could see the wonder and appreciation in her eyes. Now there was some vibration in my feet. The Earth Spirit was here. Kendren looked over at me and smiled. She took off her shoes.

To find Adolfus, the most likely place to find him, would be at the far end of the gardens. That was where he, Joyce and Rusky gathered for their time together. As we stepped along the edges of the vegetation, I could feel nervous perspiration escaping through my skin. I just prayed that this would all go well. Kendren was alongside of me. She seemed a little more relaxed without her shoes on.

It was not long. And I could hardly believe it when we came to the edges of the potting shed, and there was that familiar open basket with the blanket inside it. Lying on that basket there was a dog sleeping – a dog that had to be wonderful Rusky. And there, sitting next to the basket, there were two people that I loved so much. I could hear their voices, and they were talking contently.

It all happened so quickly – Joyce saw us first, and she urgently tugged at Adolfus's arm; they got up immediately, and came running. There was an explosion of emotion and joy. Rusky woke up of course, and his tail was wagging, he was barking, and I had never seen a dog so excited. But then, after the initial hugs and tears, and well-wishing, I stepped back, and Kendren was there standing alone. She was eyeing her father, and he saw her. I could see the puzzled astonishment in his eyes and demeanour. For a few moments, they just stared at each other, and then I just had to tell Adolfus – tell him that he had a daughter, and this was her. Perhaps I didn't need to tell him. They knew. He knew. But my saying this was the catalyst for them to move. I had never seen two people so enraptured. They embraced and held each other. It was like a timeless moment of bliss. I gazed in Joyce's eyes and could see the happiness there too.

That afternoon was a blur of conversation, an abundance of hugs and joyful reunion. I was so glad that they had waited. Joyce told me that they had had faith in me. They had prayed for my survival, and their faith told them that I would do what I had promised, and return. And then they were determined to keep their part of the bargain as well.

We were right about the population. In the months since I left, there had been a big increase in assisted deaths. The Council had stopped meeting, and some of its leading members had also chosen to finish their lives. It was a signal to most people, that the City was doomed, and there was no point to carry on. The maintenance of the City was now left to the few. Adolfus and Joyce had tried to rally people, but only a small number were interested. The gardens were one of the only focuses of concerted activity that remained functioning, and even with that, despite the best efforts of Adolfus and Joyce, more than half of the garden beds had now been abandoned too. Why grow fruit and vegetables when there were not the people to eat the food? It had been a very difficult time. Adolfus found that those with pets were more likely to wish to continue their lives, for they had a form of life where they could express their love, and be loved as well. Hence, he had persevered with his dog breeding program.

I asked about explorations outside the City, and only one expedition had taken place. Vehicles had been sent a little way along the coast roads in both directions – to places that had already been explored, but no sign of life had been found. It was a token effort. The conclusion reached was that there was no other life besides that in the City, and this conclusion only made people's despair worse.

When I found the courage, I asked Joyce about my parents and brother. She looked down, and for some moments did not speak. She told me how, for many weeks, she and Adolfus had made personal trips, to visit them and to bring food, so they would have what they needed to survive, but also to offer personal contact and encouragement. My parents had asked a couple of times if there was any news about me. But they only did it in a half-interested fashion. In general, they had seemed blank and uninterested in life – as they had been. Joyce told how it was an effort for her and Adolfus, to engage in any form of conversation with them, but they tried. Gradually, my parents had become further withdrawn, and they hardly gave any acknowledgment when food was brought.

Joyce spoke of the one day when they visited, and the door was locked, and they were unable to enter. This had only been ten days earlier. She and Adolfus had knocked loudly, but heard no noise inside, and eventually had to leave. Since then, they had visited twice and got a similar response. They had had no contact with my family since that time, and they did not know what had happened.

A shiver of fear shook me. At that moment, I knew that I had to go, immediately. I just hoped that I was not too late. Inside I felt acutely responsible. Suddenly, I was overwhelmed by emotion, and I was struggling to breathe steadily. I could not stay any longer. Kendren was happily sharing with Adolfus, I had to go, so I rose to my feet, and ran. Joyce half shouted out at me, but nothing would stop me. What could I do? My mind was in overdrive. I did not go in the direction of my family's flat, but towards the Central Precinct, where I could get a master key. At least I had the foresight then to think!

The authorities did not easily give me the key. I had to persuade them. They wanted to know where I had been, but I had no patience to tell them the details of my story. What could I tell them? I offered an excuse, lied, and said that I had been staying with Adolfus. Finally, they accepted what I said, and I grabbed the key they gave me with frantic desperation.

In those next moments, I rushed with all my might, to get to that flat, moving faster than I had ever run – as if it would really make any difference. The number of corridors I had to go along seemed endless, but I knew the way and I would get there. Finally, I turned a corner and reached the block of apartments where my family lived.

By now, I was puffing and tired. One part of me wanted to burst in, but the other part hesitated, as I began to consider what I may find. I reached their apartment. Putting my ear to the door, I listened to hear if there were any sounds, any signs of life. Maybe they had just been resting when Joyce and Adolfus came to visit. They may have merely not wanted any visitors, wishing to be by themselves. It wasn't as if they needed food from my friends. They could have easily gone to the storage rooms to obtain their own food. Why could they not be alive? I knew that I was trying to convince myself of their well-being, so I could hide from the sickening dread that I was feeling.

I wanted so much to be able to see them alive. They were my family – I had grown up with them. I shouted out through the door, for them to speak, and tell me they were alright. Memories flooded into me of times we had been together. I wanted to remember happy times, but I struggled to find any. Maybe those memories were there but I just could not recall them. What I did recollect, was visions of all three of them, staring into space together, in their lounge room, hardly moving, hardly hearing a word that I would say. I felt so disappointed, and I still wished that it could have been different.

I strained to listen from inside the flat. But there were no sounds of life. The only noise I could hear was from the air filter systems disseminating clean air to the corridors around these apartments.

Now I had to do it – I had to enter and discover what was there. Slowly, I turned the key. I hesitated, longer, longer, debating with myself, if I had the courage. I had to do it, and so, I did. I pushed the door open, just a little. Immediately, I felt pushed back, and I staggered. I cannot begin to tell my horror. It was the smell that alerted me – the overwhelming stench of decaying flesh. And I knew, straight away, then. But I had to see. Turning away for a moment, I took a deep breath with air from outside the flat, and then went in the main room. They were sitting there in their arm chairs, all three of them – their bodies – with an opened bottle of tablets next to my father and half emptied glasses of water. They must have made a pact. And they were all dead – they must be long dead. I did not want to touch their bodies. They looked horrible – empty shells. I stared at them, each in turn, and my body started shaking.

And suddenly I could not stand to be there anymore. I had to leave. This chapter of my life was over, well over, and it had finished in a way that could not have been worse for me to withstand. More than pity, I felt acute frustration with my parents and brother. Why could they have not wished more to live? Life was worth living, it had to be, even in these most devastating conditions. We had to make the effort. I could not understand that they would not do so. And I knew that I could not have done anything to save them, I could not rescue them. My brother, Martin, had been so loyal to my parents. He had sacrificed himself. But Martin had shown no inclination to rise above them. I gave him so many chances. And I did not have the power to make them change. It seemed such a waste. In my anger, I wanted to bash at the walls and furniture, and tear it all to pieces. But this was just an expression of my sense of futility, at not being able to obtain what I wanted. It was their will, not mine. And now, I would have to find my way on in life without them. I screamed for a few moments; I had to get that energy out of my system.

It was demoralizing. But suddenly, I remembered something, something important. I could not understand why I had not thought of this earlier. In haste, I scrambled into my bedroom. That is where I left my bird, my dear wooden eagle. I hoped he had not been taken, or be gone. And I was panicking. As I looked inside, my gaze went straight to the top of the chest where I hoped he would be. And he was still staring down, where I had placed him. Nobody had moved him. Oh my bird – I felt so sorry for him, having to be here while all this happened. I know I had asked him to watch over them, but he couldn't do anything, and it was so sad, that he had to be here, while they died.

I clutched at my bird as if he was alive, and held him, like I would a loved one, and only then did I cry. All the feelings I wanted to share with my family now, could only be expressed with my wonderful wooden bird. He did not let me down, or abandon me. He did not give up. I carried him gently and tenderly out of the house, caressing him and comforting him, and without looking back, I closed the door.

I don't know how I managed to walk back to the gardens that day. I do not remember it. My emotions were all over the place. But in my sobbing, when I reached the potting shed, there were three other people and a dog there, ready to meet me, and offer me the warmth of their love, and wipe away my tears. I put my bird down next to the basket where Rusky lay. He would be safe now.

We had all known loss in our lives – tremendous loss. But this was the worst that I had faced. I felt like my foundations were knocked out from under me. However, at that moment, Kendren put her hands around me, and I felt the healing from them, and it gave me the beginnings of peace. As I became quieter, I could sense the love with me, supporting me, and that love was just what I needed. My three friends here offered support that was stronger and more present than anything that my family had ever been willing or able to give me. The burden of growing up with my family had been a huge struggle for me, and it had not been easy to contend with their apathy and disillusionment. I could go on. It was just that I needed some time to realise it.

For many hours, I just sat there silently in my own thoughts, not knowing what to say, and the others were quiet with me.

HONOURING THE DEAD

That night when we were in the room that had been offered to us, Kendren climbed into bed beside me and held me. 'I know what it is like to lose your family,' she told me. 'Even though you wanted from them more than they could give, you cannot help loving them. It is how we are made as humans. I am so appreciative now to have met my father, and must thank you for what you have done for me to help me. I will always be interested in you and listen to you. You must not feel that you are on your own.'

Kendren's words must have helped to release something inside me, and I cried many tears that night. In the hours after I found their bodies, I felt much guilt for leaving my parents, and had wondered, if I had stayed, if they would still be alive. But I had to go. I had to make that journey. Knowing that without me, Kendren would not have made her journey to come and meet her father, I knew that going to the Community had been right and needed. I could not doubt that.

Kendren told me that she and her father, Adolfus, had talked, and with my permission, they would prepare a cremation service for my parents and brother. Joyce wanted to help too. It was a good idea. I agreed. For a few days before then, I could rest and recuperate. I felt immensely grateful and I did not want to resist.

The day came. I put on my best clothes, and then we went together. Kendren, Adolfus and Joyce led me to the room where the service would be held. Rusky was not going to be left behind, and he also accompanied us, sniffing and wagging his tail happily, all the way.

For a long time, there had been no funeral services in the City, even though there was a room at the crematorium for this purpose. Bodies had just been delivered to the furnaces and burnt. People had not wanted to acknowledge their feelings.

So, having this cremation was a special occasion. Much effort had been made to prepare the room and to enliven it with flowers and decoration. I felt a warm glow around me as we entered.

We had to wait for people to arrive, and I was surprised that around thirty people attended. Kendren and Adolfus had been busy inviting people, giving the ceremony as much energy as they could. It was the first gathering in the City for a long time, where I had seen so many people together. My heart was glad.

Kendren was going to conduct the Ceremony and I sat at the front with Joyce and Rusky. When we started, after opening prayers, Adolfus stepped forward and gave some warm appreciations for my parents and brother. He could describe many of their characteristics and habits. Among the items, which he mentioned, he spoke of my father's utter dedication to his computer and my mother's obsession for their house to be clean. He made it sound funny. But then, he finally spoke, about how proud they must be, to have had a son who had done so much to help the people of our City. I could not believe that he would say that, and the tears rolled down my cheeks.

Next, Kendren led a meditation for us to join and send our love, not only to my parents and Martin, but to all those that had surrendered their lives here in the City, that they may rise up to the light of the Spirit World, and be received in love, and be healed of all that they had been through.

For a moment, I felt moved to look up, and there above me, I sensed the presence of my mother and father standing together, with Martin in front of them. They were smiling. In that instant, I knew I didn't need to worry anymore, and I could feel myself relaxing. Just as quickly as the images had come, they faded again. But I felt, with all the members of the congregation, that we were acting together for good.

After the Service, Kendren asked if everyone could stay for a few minutes while she gave an address. People were willing to do this, and they all waited expectantly. Kendren spoke loudly and clearly, and projected her voice to all the corners of the room. She wanted to introduce herself.

'My name is Kendren, and I am the daughter of Adolfus. I want you to know, that all my life, I have lived in a Community, over four days walk away from here. My Community has survived all the years that you have survived – in fact, we have grown, in size and population. So, I want to tell you this. There is other life besides what is in the City. I can testify to that. My presence is here to give you hope – the knowledge that we can build our lives again on this world, and all is not lost. I want to share with you all over the coming time, how our community has survived, and show you all how your city, too, can not only survive, but expand again. Not all is lost. We can rebuild our world, and give it better foundations. It is time for you in the City to stop dying and to start to live. Join us so we can work together. Let us live, and find happiness again.'

It was a short speech, but had people spellbound. She had passion in her voice. I was so proud of Kendren. Suddenly, after a long silence, people started clapping. I had never heard anything like it. I felt so proud of Kendren.

Afterwards, we went to the reception room and ate together. There was not the atmosphere of silence and withdrawal, that had been so prevalent with other meetings in the City. Today, there was a buzz about the place, and people were excited. They were talking about Kendren's speech, and wanting to meet her. To me, this did not feel disrespectful. I felt so glad that this day had happened.

I sat quietly at a table with Adolfus, Kendren and Joyce, and listened while the others talked. They all seemed quite familiar with each other now. At first, they spoke about my family to comfort me, and I appreciated this. They tried to be sensitive to me, but they were very enthusiastic about plans they were developing, and being with each other. I wanted to be part of it.

Kendren and Adolfus did the rounds, to visit other tables of people. They spent considerable time at each table, and there was much that they needed to convey. When they finally returned to our table, I felt relieved, and it was good to have them back.

There was an atmosphere of quiet contentment among us. The initial exchanges between father and daughter had been done days earlier, and now there was acceptance and growing love within the group of us. There was a kind of familiarity between Kendren and Adolfus, and, somehow, they both seemed to be more complete now. It was astonishing, but just as it should be.

And as we sat and ate together, Adolfus looked up. He had an announcement he wanted to make. Now that he knew that it still existed, Adolfus resolved that he should visit the Community again. He wanted to exchange more seeds and possibilities for propagating life. The hope of life growing again on our world inspired him, and it was not only him, but all of us. The excited conversation started to raise in volume again, and as it did so, I could feel myself feeling tired and sleepy, slouching increasingly, little by little, on the chair where I sat. I could feel myself drifting.

In the next moment, I opened my eyes, and the sun, streaming through the nearby window, and onto my face, was low on the horizon, and there was a blanket over me. Rusky was sleeping next to me, and I had my wooden bird wrapped up, under my arm. The others were there, sitting around, and smiling at me. When I stretched to wake myself up, Kendren told me that it was time for us to go, and so we did.

A NEW BEGINNING FOR THE CITY

Over the coming days and weeks, a lot of plans were made. My own energy began to recover again. The enthusiasm between us was infectious. We did meditations together to attune to the Earth Spirit, and did visualisations to bring the awareness of these sensitive vibrations, into the gardens of the City. The vibrations from the Earth Spirit needed much strengthening, and with our efforts, the channels were slowly opening. Joyce and Adolfus took to these meditations very easily, and soon were delving inwards to fantastic experiences. They both had latent Spiritual sides to their natures, and had spent much of their lives yearning to express this. So now, with connecting to the energy of the Earth Spirit, they felt that their desires were being fulfilled.

Being together with Joyce, Adolfus and Kendren felt like being in my true family. We cared for one another and took an interest in each other's well-being. As a group, we were bonding together. I could sense that the growing love and affection between Kendren and Adolfus was blossoming with ease. It felt so good to be part of this, and I noticed how the traumatic memory of what had happened to my blood family receded with every passing day. I had to look forward, not back. I still cried sometimes when I thought of them, but I did all I could to concentrate on the project of nurturing the Spiritual energy in the City.

There was a seed of action and creativity that was germinating in this City with us, and it wanted to be fully expressed, with my companions and I being at the core. The four of us were good together, and that was not to forget Rusky the dog, who was our honorary fifth member. He was certainly not going to be left out. I could tell that my confidence and energy was rising again.

It was not long before we were reaching out to other people. We needed to inform people about our work – and break through the shells of indifference that so many people carried. It was necessary to talk with people about life on the planet expanding, and about the Earth Spirit. We had to be patient, and gradually build up a sense of positive purpose for people to explore. Over the next weeks, we composed and prepared a leaflet that we could give out to people. We knocked on the doors of houses, and gave out our leaflets at the food pick up points. So many people turned away at first, but we did not give up.

We had big plans. What we needed was to manifest a venue for larger group meditations, so there would be the potential for all the people of the City to be involved. We thought that one of the abandoned garden areas would be perfect as a beginning, for where this could be placed. Adolfus had a couple of builder friends, willing to help us, and offer advice. This would be our first sanctuary in the City.

To build such a meditation room, was a big undertaking, and it needed to be planned and constructed well. The vision we had, was to make it into a dome structure with wood and stone, even bringing some of that from outside the City perimeters so we would have sufficient of what we needed. The builders we consulted were rather anxious about this, but Kendren and I explained to them how it could be safe. We didn't need to be so afraid of the virus anymore, and we could learn to deal with it, in the way that Kendren, Zelda and I had managed. Then, within the City boundaries, we could activate energy lines that were there, like the Community had done. After some further frank discussions, it was agreed.

Building that dome together felt very good. For many weeks, we devoted ourselves to that task, and from advice that we were given, we could form the structure and complete it. I was surprised how many people helped us. Some of the gardeners also gave time to assist us with the physical lifting, and putting materials in place. Other builders came along and offered their strength and their skills. There was something in this cooperation that seemed different, fresh and even alive. I was hopeful. Joyce and Kendren prepared drinks and snacks for the workers so they would feel part of a group.

Once the foundations were laid, and the outline structure put together, it was soon done. People came to look and ask what we had constructed. We were so happy when we could be inside this Dome. At the beginning, this would be Kendren's space, primarily, and she wanted to spend a lot of time here conducting rituals and building the connection with the energies of the Earth Spirit so it could become a truly Sacred space. She had been taught how to do all of this by the Oracle in the Community.

One night, the four of us and Rusky met in the Sanctuary to do a meditation. Kendren invited us, and she wanted to do a meditation, where we could link with the Community, with the Oracle and Linton, and offer gratitude for their help, and then form an energy bond of love, that could grow and strengthen between our two Centres. When I closed my eyes, I saw the images of Linton and the Oracle, smiling at us. I sensed that they were with us, in Spirit, and that there was a cooperation of love, with them.

Soon our new Sanctuary would become a public domain, and we planned to utilise the Dome to function like the Meditation space in the Community had done. I joined Kendren in the Dome sometimes, and I could feel the energies of the Earth Spirit getting stronger.

Word spread among the people of the City. The news of another living Community and the journey that Kendren and I had made – this is something that wakened people up – not all of them. But a growing number of them wanted to be involved.

We called a meeting, for an initial community wide meditation, with a discussion to follow, about how we could join, and together, work out our future. Kendren was going to channel the Earth Spirit and become the Oracle for the City, and I had to help her. This was such an important moment in the formation of our goals, and I was nervous, even after all the invitations that we had issued, wondering if anyone would come.

The night of the meditation arrived. We waited with burgeoning excitement for the first people to join us. One by one, people did come to the Dome, and entered. Adolfus and I welcomed them and showed them where they could sit. With each new person arriving, our joy increased. Some came with friends and family, and were people that I knew. Others must have heard about it by word of mouth. People were murmuring and talking in the Dome. There was genuine interest. I counted just before we were due to start. The Dome was not full up, but with the fifty or so people that were there, it was a beginning, and more than I had expected.

There was a hush as we opened proceedings. Adolfus came forward and welcomed everybody, and spoke how what we would be doing this evening, and how this could be an important step to future survival of humanity on Earth. When he had finished, Kendren and I stepped into the centre of the Circle. We told the tale of the journeys that we had made, and the wondrous story of survival, which the Community had endured. People wanted to know how this had happened, so we answered questions, and shared it in detail. We told about the Oracle and Linton, and the supremely courageous efforts that the people in the Community had made – not only for themselves, but in recognition of all elements of life in our world, the human, animal, plant and mineral.

There were gasps in the audience as we continued, with people releasing sighs of disbelief, as they processed the imparting of what we had experienced. Many times, people made interruptions with questions they had. All of them wanted to assimilate and comprehend what we said.

Adolfus stood with us and confided about the wonderful feeling of joy that he had felt in meeting his daughter for the first time. He confirmed his conviction, of the truth, in what we put forward, and told his own story of his association with the Community. People were in awe, and some were shaking their heads.

Kendren then suggested that we move on to the meditation. While everyone watched, Kendren went to lie on the blanket in the middle of the room. Now she was ready to go into deep meditation.

People had to experience the Earth Spirit, and know its vibration through direct participation in it. This would be the best proof for people. Today, Kendren would channel, and voice the words of the Earth Spirit in public for the first time. She had done her own preparation for this event, and as I gazed across at her, I saw that she was calm, and her energy was serene. She was ready to do this, and there was an excitement and anticipation in the room as we prepared. So much had happened, so quickly, since we arrived in the City, and now this was the culmination and what could be a new dawn.

All those in the room became very quiet as Kendren closed her eyes. I urged the gathering present, to close their eyes in solidarity, and prepare to meditate with her. They all did this. There were long moments of silence, while we waited, but then Kendren cleared her throat and started to breathe more deeply, and I knew it was coming.

People were linking inwardly together; I could feel it. When Kendren spoke, her voice was much deeper and more solemn than how she normally spoke. She was really channelling and giving herself over to this. The words bellowed from her mouth, and projected itself through the Dome. The vibrations of those tones affected everyone there. First the tones were in rhythm, like chanting, and then, slowly, it changed, and she could speak and say some simple words of welcome. It was not her saying this, for she was now channelling the Earth Spirit. The atmosphere in the room was electric. Inside I was smiling.

To have something like this in the City and help people to begin to rise out of that morass of hopelessness and despair, this made life feel worthwhile. And the aspiration of healing and restoration of life on our planet, I believed, this was possible, and on track. I knew that Kendren's channelling would help. People would listen to her, and what the Earth Spirit spoke through her, and this would transform people's values and give them a purpose to live.

Kendren had been a faithful student to the Oracle, and what she was doing now represented a brilliant step forward. And I wanted to help and support that. There was a sense of unity in the room, and people were attentive. There was always going to be more work to be done, that would extend way beyond my time. But we were entering a period of reconstruction, and that had to be good. The happy feeling I experienced was immense.

COMPLETION

The meditation continued. I could feel myself now going deeper down, going into my own inner worlds, and the journey was taking me inwards to a place that was both familiar and new. For this was the beginning of a new project. And there was a new Earth that we could help to form. It was time for people to help build the Spiritual Earth and stop destroying it. We had to know that the Earth was not a place for us to use but a place for us to protect. If we wanted our Earth to breathe and support us, then we needed to work for that, and place the needs of the Earth alongside our personal needs so that one did not dominate the other. We were a living partnership, and it was our choice whether we would abide by this or not.

Through the war, we had seen the result of people carelessly abusing powers for their own interest, and the destruction this could bring. We must never allow that consciousness to rule over humanity again. Next time, there may not be any way out, or any redemption for physical life on the Earth. And that would be an extreme tragedy, for our planet was supremely precious. We had to rebuild and create conditions where souls could once more live, and this time, it had to be in harmony, and we would always have to remind ourselves and remember the huge and catastrophic losses we had had.

I drifted further and further within, until I felt very peaceful and relaxed. It was like an ending now as well as a beginning. It was a strange feeling of completion that I had not expected. And I felt as though I no longer needed to be attached to it all anymore. With this thought, a change occurred.

All at once, it was becoming lighter and lighter, and it was as though I was being taken upwards. Surely this was the opposite direction from where I needed to go? Did I need to correct this? At first, I did not understand, for it felt as though I was being extracted from that world where I had been so involved. That was not what I wanted. How could I be leaving? But I was not there anymore with my consciousness, and my soul was lifting.

Even the Dome and gathering were getting further and further away, as if they did not exist anymore. It was all over somehow, and I was still getting lighter and rising upwards. Where were the people that had come to the meeting? What would happen to everybody? Was this happening to them too? I wanted to go back. But I couldn't, and I had to accept what was occurring. Some part of me wanted to fight against this – I had work to do there. But as I thought that, I heard a voice from above me telling me to let it go.

Then, it was as if some aspect of my consciousness woke up. I knew I was returning home – my home in the Spiritual world – and that some experiment had just ended. However, I was in conflict, and a part of me did not want to acknowledge this transition. The promise of creating something good had been so alive just there at the end. I wanted to be with that, and join in.

However, much as I may have wished otherwise, it was over, and now I was in a chamber, a Spiritual chamber with other beings around me, and I was slowly orientating myself, and I was reconvening with my working group in the Spiritual world.

Part 3

JOURNEYING
TO NEW
REALMS

A SHARED PROJECTION

I was still fighting it, for I didn't want to be in the Spirit World again; I wanted to be back on the Earth, assisting the reconstruction. I felt so happy there, and we were making progress, helping our world to build again. Why did I have to leave just at this point? It didn't seem fair. I struggled with the sensations that brought me more and more into the light. However, the pull of the Spiritual world felt so enticing – so pure and loving. I knew that I had to let go. Yet, as with so many other occasions, my will was reluctant to acquiesce. Increasingly, I could feel the tranquillity of the Spiritual world enveloping me with love, and my perspective was changing as I became more removed from that involving experience. I felt sad to leave what we had just had.

Increasingly, I could feel that profound sense of belonging, and being in my Spiritual home. I became aware of my soul eyes, and they wanted to open. So I stopped longing to go back, and focussed upon being present. My inner eyes were ready, and when I opened them, I was sitting in the Circle of light, with my Earth mission Spiritual working group. Those six other souls were all there with me. They seemed as if they had been on a journey, just like I had, and I could tell that they were also adjusting, while my guide and teacher, Astoris was outside the circle with his huge and expansive energy, supporting our togetherness.

He asked us all to look at each other. Suddenly, I could feel emotion rising in me. As I concentrated, I began to recognise, members of our working group had been involved in that life. One by one, their identities became apparent to me. They were all there. When I looked around, in the light of my soul friend, Aurielle, I could see the face of Kendren, with Santi there was Adolfus, and Amond had Joyce's features. Turning to our two members who were with us from other worlds, I could see Linton's face with Deli and the Oiya expressed the energy of the Oracle. My spiritual perception became more focussed, and thoughts came into my mind. I realised that, as a group, we had been learning together in that life, putting our energies into joint action, finding out how we all acted and reacted in challenging situations, and building the love between us. That is what it had been about! I smiled.

Then, when I brought my attention to our teacher, Astoris, to my great surprise, I saw the face of Zelda. He had been there with us too – all the souls in our group for our Earth project, all sharing a life together on that bleak world. So many thoughts and emotional adjustments streamed through me. I began to consider how we had fitted together, the part that we had all played, and the individual relationships that we had shared. It felt so right, somehow, but I was full of questions. I turned my awareness towards Astoris, for I was searching for further explanations.

There were memories and experiences of that lifetime that were rushing through my consciousness. It had been a very emotional experience. How could it be that we had all done that? And what of the other people that featured in that life? I wondered about some of the other significant characters, such as my parents there, and Kendren's mother. There had been lots of souls involved, even though, in the dramas we faced, the other members of the group, were the central ones.

I waited. It was as though Astoris was giving space for all of us to begin the assimilation of our experiences, before he gave his input. We all had our own perceptions and feelings about what we had been through. It had been a positive endeavour, in very challenging circumstances.

Finally, Astoris brought us together. I could recognise his strong thoughts in my Spiritual mind, as he addressed all of us. We gave him our full attention.

In answer to my unspoken question, Astoris relayed that there were some souls from outside our circle, which had featured and interacted with us in the life.

'Those souls were from other groups, and were using the shared experience of living jointly in that world, for their own learning. However, what they did was of secondary importance where you are concerned. Your joint experiences had been a constructed reality, set up as a Spiritual preparation for what you will need to do together on Earth in your mission.

'Higher Spiritual beings had created this world for you, making it as real and Earth-like as possible Some of the characters you encountered in that experience, were not even souls on their learning path, but energy constructions from Spirit to fill out the connections and relationships that you would have. It was intended to feel completely real to you, and was created as a testing space for you, for your souls working together.'

Now I felt confused. I thought that I had been on Earth, and that I had lived a substantial, meaningful life. With all my senses, I had been living it, as if it was real. What was this all about? I had put so much effort into it all. My emotions were reacting, feeling shocked and disappointed. Was it all for nothing? For me, it was not just about my interactions with those other characters – I wanted to make a positive difference to that world.

I could feel Astoris trying to reassure us. 'It was meaningful,' he conveyed to us, emphasizing those thoughts. 'The shared experience you had, facilitated Spiritual growth for all of you. Also, throughout what you lived, you were attuning to the Spirit of the Earth and its needs. And, as I have suggested, most of all, you were attuning to each other.'

Slowly, I came out of myself-absorbed reflection and began to bring my awareness to the others around me. I wondered what they were feeling. How were they reacting? Did they feel similarly to me?

It was quite incredible to observe everyone now, in their light bodies. I could tell now, by tuning into their energy fields, that the others were feeling various degrees of bewilderment, just like me. While I opened my perception to the others in the Circle, Astoris continued to communicate with us.

Our guide could relate to more than one of us, individually, at a time. And that is what he did. He was communicating with each one of us to address our concerns, at times relating with us collectively, as a group, but then switching into individual needs, and answering those, doing all of this simultaneously. He was endeavouring to address our needs, while also waiting for us, collectively, to relax further. He was a very impressive and expansive teacher.

The questions kept bubbling up for me. Why had we lifted out of the experience before the end of our lives? I felt a little cheated by that. It had been such a demanding and ultimately satisfying experience, and I had felt that I was not ready to leave at the end. Again, Astoris was aware of my thoughts, and he opened this up, telling me and everyone, that, at the point when we were brought back to the Spiritual world, the learning and bonding we needed to accomplish as a group, was complete, and there was no more that we needed to do.

The questions kept bubbling up from inside me. If this was not a real life we had been through, then what was it? I had to somehow understand all of this, and I could perceive the rapidly changing states of emotional and mental reactions processing through my own soul, and I assumed, the souls of my friends. How was it that we could be withdrawn from this experience in mid-life? I had never known this to happen. What was going on? The puzzlement I felt was communicated around the group, and we looked to our teacher to help.

Astoris conveyed an energy that was very still. He was doing this deliberately, and gradually I found myself modelling him; the others did this too. This is what he wanted – so he could have our attention, in a deeper and more focussed capacity. As we all became quieter, peace embraced us. The chaotic flickers of turmoil and questioning that we had all been expressing, since we first arrived here, were slowly transforming into energy fields, that were flowing and more receptive.

Astoris was watching us and smiling. When the moment was right, he moved from outside and placed himself in our circle and at the centre of our attention. In the space that he now occupied, he paused, until he was sure that we were fully with him. However, then, he did not hesitate from being direct and forthright, and what he shared confirmed the initial impressions that we had had and what he had already imparted.

'What you experienced together was a collective projection of being on Earth. It was not a real life, because you did not share it with all the other souls that inhabit the Earth. This was shared only with the small group of you present, plus the few others that I mentioned. You were placed in a mental world, where we structured numerous elements within your shared experience to make it as much Earth-like as we could. It was the maximum level of Earth reality that we could attain for you. We set this up for you so it would test your soul qualities to their utmost capacity. The purpose of it was to help bond you, and get you used to working together under Earth-like conditions.'

'Why did you not tell us in advance?' Santi asked. For a moment, our teacher paused, and he again gathered us all in his awareness. In so doing, I felt like his Spiritual eyes were staring right through me. Indeed, his eyes were penetrating into everyone else as well. Astoris continued.

'For the experience to be most effective, it was necessary for you to approach it, as if it was real, and in a state where you felt that you were totally involved, and living it. And if you knew that it was only some form of rehearsal, how would you have taken it seriously? We could not inform you in advance. Does that make it clearer?'

He stopped now for a while, for us to take in what he had told us. In the space that followed, I began to have many more reflections about what we'd been through. I thought about the fate of our beloved Earth and how much, Earth and humanity, had suffered in the experience of that life, and it made me wonder if this was a likely scenario of what may happen to our real Earth?

Astoris heard my thoughts and answered to all of us.

'What you experienced is just one of copious possibilities for the future of the Earth. So much is in the balance right now on Earth, and it depends on so many choices, and collective decisions, as to what will take place. That is why, every moment, and every action, of every soul, that is on the Earth, is like a foundation for the future – and will alter what is possible. And depending on how conscious and awake the people on your world become, this will affect how much you can work together, with compassion, as interconnected beings, to transform your lives together there, and generate a much more spiritualised form of life on Earth – a form of living that has its basis in peace. And it is also possible that people will not reach this point. Your goal – the goal of your group, is to assist with the transformation of consciousness, especially working directly with humans, on the planet Earth, so they can become more mindful of generating peace and harmony, rather than endless destruction. The world that you have just experienced, is an example of what humanity could manifest, if they don't transform.

'Consider what you have been through, and the appalling waste of that destructiveness, which human beings can bring on to each other, when their hearts are not open. We could have picked even worse scenarios for you to live through, for there are dire possibilities of what you could do to your world.

'You have an important mission in front of you as a group, and choices that you must make now, as a collective group. Consider this. There are a lot of young souls on the Earth just now, souls that are at the beginning stages of learning, and those souls are being buffeted by all that is going on around them, but they don't have a lot of awareness. In addition to that, there are also many experienced souls on Earth – souls that have the potential to sense much more, about what is going on. But conditions on Earth are not easy for people. And many people are lost to their souls, and are not motivated to do anything. They do not believe that they have the power to make any difference. A lot of them just close their eyes to what is going on around them. Those that lead, are caught up in the materialistic world, and engaged in power struggles to gain an advantage over others. This is terrible, and is exactly what will bring on tragedy, unless more souls become involved, with bringing on the transformation of human consciousness.

'You are approaching a critical point on Earth, where as a collective consciousness, together, your actions and intentions could take planet Earth one way or the other. The possibility of complete destruction on the earth, is real, as is the potential for human beings to walk the pathway of their redemption.

'I know which way all of you want the evolution of the Earth and its inhabitants, to go. It is not necessary to convince you. And it is true, that you would not be here, only that you all love the Earth, very dearly. This love can be your driving force, for you are needed so you can be teachers to help others learn and to wake up. You are needed to educate, and most of all, to help people find peace. It is not all down to you, and so many others are being called upon to help make that crucial difference – if they can. But, as you have experienced on that bleak world just now, whatever happens, and however humanity reacts to its challenges, you can always adapt, and help in the best way that you can. The secret is to be open with your heart, and remain true to your path.'

Again, as Astoris paused, further memories of the experience where I had just been, traversed my mind. Living in that bleak world, had been such a very moving and poignant experience. The abysmal sense of futility for humankind's failure to preserve the beautiful world we had, was balanced by the efforts that our collective group were making, towards the end of the life, to repair and create something better. If I hadn't been motivated to help the Earth and its people before this life experience, I certainly felt that commitment now.

Astoris went on. 'There is much fear pervading planet Earth just now. Fear creates feelings of separateness in people – separateness not just from each other, but separateness from the Spirit of the Earth, and separateness from the soul. And this illusion of separateness will ultimately lead to the planet's ruin unless it is healed with love, and people's awareness opened. The avenue of Spiritual potential that is now available for the Earth, will then be closed. There is no longer the option of delay. For those that do manage to awaken, they will be able to take this forward, either on Earth, or if the Earth is destroyed, then on other worlds. In such a case, the others who stay closed, may need to wait and find other opportunities.

'If much of the Earth is destroyed or damaged, you will all feel that – not only you here, that care, but all of humanity. For you all have hearts, as human beings – and although many people are what we might call, "skilful," at being able to hide what they feel in their hearts, it is not possible to hide forever. And the tremendous loss of the beautiful life on Earth – the wondrous world that you have had, and the even more precious life that exists in potential, for how you could live in the future, which is humanity's dream – the loss of this, will be acutely felt by all, if you do not manage it.

'We on the Spiritual side are trying to help, as you know. And it can be frustrating for us, because as much as we are eager for you souls on Earth to do well, and establish the manifestation of a positive vision in your life together, living in a happy world, we cannot do this for you. We see the potential vision of what you are reaching for, and we know that you are truly aspiring to manifest this, from deep in your hearts. And we almost despair, when so many people ignore that. We wish to be close to you, but it is your life, not ours. And this is your test as a collective humanity, and how high you are willing to reach towards living your ultimate dream, on Earth.

'As individual souls, choosing this mission to help the Earth, you will have your tests too. We know that your work is occurring more, in a voluntary capacity, because of your love for the Earth, and you have largely worked through many of the issues that others on Earth are grappling with. However, you still need to feel as those others feel. When you are on that Earth, you are members of humanity, and not aloof from that, in any capacity. You will be subject to the same conditioning, and all the limiting beliefs that will be around you. Somehow, you will need to rise above that, by connecting with your souls, so you can live freely, and attuned to what you are meant to do.

'With our latest assessment, the balance of well-being on the Earth, is not tilting towards the fulfilment of our aims and heart wishes. It is more going the other direction towards a possible scenario that could be like your bleak world. This is just how it is, at this moment, from our observations of the Earth Being.'

For a while, we were there in a space of silence. It felt quite daunting, the task to be able to help humanity on Earth. However, it also stimulated my own feelings of determination, and as a group, we were attuned to these feelings collectively.

It was good to listen to Astoris speak and communicate so clearly to us. I could feel his underlying passion for our aims and objectives. I remembered when I visited the Earth Dome after the conclusion of my last Earthly life before the Bleak world, and I recalled how desperate I had been, wanting to be in a position to be able to act, and be part of a working group. Now that was happening, and I was training to be an Earth Warrior. I was fulfilling my dream, and felt very happy about it, but I would be even more pleased, if I could help the Earth.

I thought about my relationship with Astoris, and felt so grateful for his support. I was in a unique position where he was concerned, for he had been acting as my personal guide for long ages. Now, for the first time, our work was becoming linked together in this project. He was my teacher and also my colleague in this venture. I felt huge respect for him.

The speech that Astoris had given about Earth conditions had been forthright and uncompromising. Yet the feeling in the atmosphere infusing our group, was all love and compassion – so typical of the Spiritual Realm. It made me realise that even though there was a desperate struggle in process around matters concerning the Earth, on a deeper inner level, it was as though nothing could go wrong, and all outcomes could be accommodated.

GROUP LIFE REVIEW

It was not long before we were involved in the next stage of our training. We would have to review our lives in the bleak world. This would be another process in our circle, where we could explore our individual learning from that life experience, share with each other, and give feedback where appropriate. Again, we would each take a turn to step into the centre of our Circle, and with the one in the Centre, we could then exchange our thoughts and feelings.

Oiya was the first one to step forward. She had been the Oracle in that life, and, as she began to share, she related from the contrasting perspectives of her Spiritual form as Oiva, and then, what she learnt from being the Oracle, the woman she had been then. There were many similarities. As she opened herself up, she first, told us more about her life on her home planet.

The race of beings of which she was a member, existed on a planet, where she engaged in disciplined meditative practices. She had acquired skills to be able to attune with deep feeling and clarity, to the consciousness of the planetary body where she lived. In addition, she could transmit energy to other planetary bodies throughout the galaxy. Her sensitivity enabled her to be aware of the matrix of loving connections that linked various star systems together, in unfolding patterns of evolution, and, as an important component of her work, she could channel love and other helpful impulses to that grid.

She told us how the Earth was important in this, and had its own position relative to the other star systems, and that her concern for Earth is what brought had her here to be with us – so she could help us to awaken our own sensitivities to that dimension of connection.

Much of the work that she had done on her own planet had been in solitude, and she felt comfortable with being physically on her own, and this was how she preferred to be. In some ways, for her, it felt quite strange to be part of a group, rather than on her own. She had to make efforts to be present with us, and not withdraw. Her people did not mix very much with each other, but gained sustenance from their energy interactions with the very beautiful energies of planetary bodies and star systems.

In her life as the Oracle, the work of channelling the Earth Spirit had been easy and also satisfying. It felt good for her to become familiar with the specific frequencies of our Earth being, and gain knowledge of it, so she could listen and respond to what Mother Earth wanted to communicate, and to express this to others through the channelling. As the Oracle, she held the space for others to strengthen their relationship with the Earth Spirit. This was a very valuable service.

Oiva found that the vibration of the Earth Spirit was quite different from the vibration of the Spiritual being of her home planet – for it was richer and more varied, with a deeper timbre. But it was also less developed. However, she had grown to enjoy the Earth Spirit energy, and love it somehow.

She gravitated easily to Deli, who had been Linton in that life. The two of them had formed a strong partnership, and they had a common link with the fact that their souls had both come to be on that representation of the Earth, from other worlds.

Because of the awareness that she had, from her history of living on her home planet, then tapping into the Spiritual energies of the Earth Spirit, sensing the energy lines, and being aware of Spirit in all life forms – this was like second nature to her. It was a capacity that people on Earth had largely lost.

Just then, Astoris interrupted Oiva, and stepped forward. He gave us a vision where we could see, how, in earlier times, there had been societies on Earth where sensitivity to the Spiritual energies of all life forms, had been acknowledged and felt. Sadly, these groups had been overpowered by people more interested in exploiting all the elements around them for their own advantage. Now, people needed to reconnect with those sensitivities and let them grow, so Spiritual awareness rather than materialistic desires, could form the base for our societies on Earth.

Oiva was someone who could open to this awareness, and be a leader. She was like a beacon of light, where people could learn from her, to access the pure consciousness of Spirit. She had a very important role in our group.

Now Oiva continued with us. She shared how, from her life experience in the bleak world, what was more difficult for her, had been the task of forming a relationship with other people and being somewhat human. Forming that bond of trust with Linton, had been an essential component of her inner plan for that experience. From their shared non-human backgrounds, this gave them a link and a capacity to empathise with each other. She had been given signals for them to recognise each other, and she managed to open up to him. He then, had made efforts to understand her, and give her the space she needed to channel the Earth Spirit, and for this to guide everyone. The Spiritual practices introduced to the Community, and how the Community eventually flourished as a result of these practices, beating back the threat of the virus in the process – this was a triumph of the cooperation that the two of them were able to attain, helping to bring out the best in each of them. Their efforts brought a new way of thinking to the Community, and an outlook that was an excellent model for how human society could function in a potent and harmonious new form.

It was in training Kendren though, that Oiva made her greatest strides forward. For Kendren was human, and, she had a strongly human soul background. Oiva told us that she had to learn how to relate to Kendren as a human, and discover how her consciousness worked, so she could teach her, and help her to develop gifts of channelling. This was all new to Oiva, for human consciousness had faculties to it, which she had never previously encountered, especially around areas of vulnerability. Oiva was used to being very steady and steadfast, but humans tended to fluctuate a lot in their energy systems, both in their thoughts and feelings. Kendren was a lot steadier than most, and this helped. Over time, she came to enjoy assisting her student to learn. She enjoyed their interactions. Kendren appreciated her teacher as well. They were able to gain from each other.

Oiva was happy with what she had achieved as the Oracle in that experience, and she felt that she was able to do what she had set out to do. When she had finished, we channelled love to her, and I could welcome further understanding of her nature and the part she played with us all.

Our other non-Earth soul, Deli, was the next one to step forward. He communicated to us how he came from a very different soul background from Oiva. Deli had previously been through many diverse lives, on dissimilar systems – very different experiences. This included lives, of a type, that were peaceful, and passive, incarnations where he and his fellow beings, had functioned together, with a collective consciousness base, lives where he had very little self-awareness, but where a great deal of cooperation existed. To complement this, he had also experienced lives that were almost the opposite in nature, lives where he had been strongly individualistic, and where he had incarnated as someone, at the forefront of exploring new frontiers, and motivating himself, from his own sense of initiative, and acting alone. In this life as Linton, he had sought to bring these characteristics together.

As leader and manager of the Community in the mountains, he had expressed a lot of strength to help the people there to find harmony and a positive vision, encouraging them to cooperate together. He was used to working with energies, and was able to utilise his skills to help the defence of the Community from the virus. With the Oracle, he had to be very sensitive to her. He spoke up for her special position, and ensured that she would be safe, and respected, so she could serve the Community to the full. He told us, how, as a soul, he was most comfortable being somewhat reserved, and not too involved with others – maintaining his independence. But here, he had to be both available and friendly, so people could feel resonance with him, while inwardly, there was a part of him that wanted to withdraw from the others, like the Oracle.

He managed to support many of the Community members, including Kendren and myself, and he also maintained an awareness of the needs of the whole. It was a big learning for him to combine these skills, and he equipped himself very well. He adapted to the human form of being Linton, and I sensed that, with Deli, that this ability to adapt to very different circumstances, was one of his strengths that he had developed as a soul.

When he had finished conveying this, Deli hesitated. He seemed unsure about something, and although I sensed that there was more that he could have communicated, he stopped himself from doing so, and Astoris did not challenge him.

At this point, we completed with Deli, and then we moved on, to continue our process. Gradually, we worked further through the group.

With Santi and Amond, as Adolfus and Joyce, here were two souls that already knew each other very well. They had both lived many lives as warriors together. However, in this situation, it was more the fight for survival, and the fight to protect an ideal, and a shared determination for there to be continued life for the City community. These were the factors that drove them on. They were both able to utilise their warrior instincts in a most positive manner. What was important was their resolve to keep going, and not give up, and their wish to help others to keep going, too. They managed this by keeping the love in their hearts open, even throughout the most trying of circumstances.

For Amond, she lived most of her life, as Joyce, on her own, and it was a huge effort for her to maintain her integrity, and to practice each day, to express her creativity with her jewellery. When so much was slowly dying around her, this is what she felt that she had to do, to maintain her life, and to preserve what was best, within her heart. When she could finally be with others, and form her friendship with Adolfus, this was a great relief for her.

Once Joyce and Adolfus met, and they started working together, they naturally became closer to each other, for they could anticipate each other and be aware of each other's thoughts, quite simply – and this capability developed, the longer they were together. They both felt satisfied with the contributions that they had made, and I smiled, as I listened to their reflections, and I could appreciate, on a personal note, how much they both helped me, in all our encounters together, there.

Now there was a pause, and we could observe the emotion rising in Santi's energy field. He wanted to express to us, how much, as Adolfus, his dog, Rusky, had given love and sustenance to him. We could feel his gratitude, and how much it meant to him. And then, all at once, we all saw the Spirit of Rusky, with us, in the Circle, with Santi, still with so much affection. It was like he was bounding around joyfully, and so happy to see us. Santi gave Rusky a huge, warm, energetic hug. And it reminded us all, of the preciousness of the link that we shared with the animal kingdom, and our connection with that. It was beautiful to share.

For his part, Santi also shared, how, as Adolfus, he had known love, with Mary, and loss, with his separation from her, and then finding love again, with the very moving surprise of meeting his daughter, Kendren, at the end of the life.

Mary's soul was someone that Santi had met many times previously during their lives on Earth, and the scenario was therapeutic for them to meet again, in the way that they did. Adolfus had demonstrated leadership within his position in the City. He also expressed a lot of love, by opening his heart to support all those around him. These were characteristics and strengths in Santi's soul, and he was glad to have utilised those gifts, so constructively. Santi wanted to say more, but he looked across at Aurielle, (Kendren from the Bleak world), and she nodded to him. It was her turn to step forward now.

As she transferred herself to the centre, I could feel my heart reaching out to Aurielle, wanting to give her encouragement.

Aurielle had her own challenges living her life as Kendren, for it was not easy in her situation. From losing her mother so early in her life, and living without her father, she had to cope on her own. The only family she had, was the family of the Community. But she embraced this, and chose happiness and openness of heart, rather than isolation. This was her test. Her developing connection with the Earth Spirit also helped to sustain her, and she felt how much she grew through the experience. She definitely had choices in that life, and with no particular person to guide her, she had to find strength inside her, to make a positive decision, and join in fully with the life of the Community. Ultimately, she faced a test of trust, which occurred through meeting my soul, and the friendship that resulted between us, as through this, for the first time in her life, she had the opportunity to open up deeply and share love with another human being, rather than live purely within herself – and she managed this, to her great joy. She had to consider if she could allow forgiveness around her father's absence, and the decision, of whether she could find the additional trust to open up to him, and meet him, or not. It made such a difference for her to say 'yes' to this challenge. She felt that as a result of this experience, that she could deal with any conditions more bravely now.

I felt proud of her as she told us this, for I knew how far she had come, through all the turnings of her soul history. A lot of the time, in her various incarnations, I had been with her, and we had been learning together. And it was amazing now, to witness her as a mature soul.

Aurielle went on further, to describe the dynamics she felt as she opened up to specific contacts with the other people and how it felt to be Kendren. She was happy now, as we completed with her.

I was the last one to be called, and I felt peace as I stepped forward. In my own case, I realised what a struggle the whole life had been, and what a relief I had felt, by the end of it, when I could finally reach a point, where I believed that my actions could make a positive difference. For me, I was a soul, who needed to act, to feel a sense of purpose and achievement. It was not easy then, when so many around me were giving up, and I wanted something different. I had to be strong to stay positive.

As I went into the experience more deeply, I became aware how a crucial moment in the life for me was when I met Zelda. She was someone that needed my help, and what I didn't realise at first, was that she was actually someone that I needed, to help me. Now, I could have pushed on to begin my journey outside the City, and ignored her. This would have been me pushing on with my will – a pattern from my past, where the zealousness to act alone and do what I wanted, without due consideration of others, had often got me into trouble. But here, with my heart opened, I did stop, and help her, and then Zelda's support for me turned out to be invaluable, for me to be able to complete the journey to the Community. The test for me had been about attuning my Will to the Collective needs, and not reacting to circumstances, where I would isolate myself and act alone. For a moment, I glanced across at Astoris, and he smiled knowingly.

It was no accident, that I had been given that test with Zelda, at that moment. It had been the primary action of Astoris in that life, for him to be embodied as Zelda, and provide me with that opportunity of service, to support me through a character weakness, so I could find my strength. I could feel the peace and relief as I shared this.

With the love bonds I had formed with other members of the group, I knew that in this experience, I had succeeded, and the enthusiasm I had expressed, and my willingness to explore, and extend boundaries, had been a catalyst for bringing the life together, for all of us.

At this point I finished, and we completed our feedback process. There was much more that we wished to share with each other, and after the formality of our sharing in the Circle, we broke into smaller groups where we could pursue this further.

As we all considered the intertwining of our various relationships, which we had shared during that 'lifetime,' I could notice the extent of loving interweaving that had occurred, and how much growth and actual love, we had been able to express to each other, to help each other to fulfil the paths, we had chosen to live. In my heart, I knew that we were much closer as a group now, and each one of us had come through this test on a personal front – with flying colours!

TWO DIFFERENT SOCIETIES

After this, we had a short break from our working group, and I was glad to spend some time with Aurielle during this space.

However, it was not long before Astoris called us together again, for there were further teachings waiting for us, with our training, now.

Astoris asked us to open our perception to how society on Earth was structured, and the relationship between how Cities and communities functioned, and the drives and beliefs of the people living there. He wanted to talk of these matters with us.

'The beliefs that people hold on Earth, is fundamental to the kind of life, which they create there. For instance, if people are not open to Spiritual realities, if they do not sense the living Spirit within animals, plants, trees, and, of course, the mineral kingdom, then all these marvellous spiritual beings are not valued and they become no more than commodities. They can be used and exploited to fit in with people's designs. People then, have no respect for anything, except other human beings, and even that, in many cases, is quite limited.

'By not honouring sufficiently, the sacredness of the animals, the plants, the minerals, and even the Earth itself, people have degraded what is most precious around them. By closing themselves down from the awareness of spiritual realities around them, without even knowing that they are doing it, people then feel isolated and separate from their world. The more that people desecrate their world, the more self-absorbed they become, until eventually, people become closed, also, from each other. And as much as people try to take comfort in materialistic luxury and greed, they will never be satisfied by that. We can see that this is what is happening on the Earth, and it all originates from the beliefs people hold, and how they choose to conduct themselves.

'With the competitive urges in people, to prove that they are stronger, or better, this stems from the urge to survive, with the added ingredient of a misplaced arrogant sense of superiority – the desire to conquer. It does not make sense. We do not conquer our friends, we support them, and they then support us. If people keep fighting to prove they are better, then sooner or later, there will be no one left. The urge to dominate and to compete, are instincts that have outlived their usefulness on Earth. People need to learn to rise above their instincts, and live according to their wisdom and intelligence – and learn to cooperate. There is nothing to be gained by wiping out the whole planet.

'In your bleak world, there were two societies, where you associated. One was the City, where people had no belief in the sacredness of living beings, apart from human beings. Here, technology and science were valued and revered by the people, as the means for their lives to be preserved. Meanwhile, the other society, in complete contrast, was the Community in the mountains, where faith and openness to the Earth Spirit was central to their lives, and the use of science and technology, in a conventional sense, played a very small part. Notice how both of these societies coped with the infiltration of the virus.

'People in the City initially worked together to close off from the virus, so it could not attack them. They used their technology to insulate themselves from the outside world, and through their dedicated work, they were successful in keeping the virus out. But once, they saw the life around them dead and dying, they began to feel cut off and increasingly isolated. People became very depressed. Without faith, they had nothing to live for, so more and more of them took the route of killing themselves. The whole place was dying. Science and technology here, could give people a comfortable standard of living, but on its own, it could not bring happiness to people.

'In the City, it was people, like the two of you, acting as Adolfus and Joyce, people with some compassion – you were the ones that kept the place going. As Adolfus, you cared for the plants and nurtured them – you did not just regard them as a commodity. For you, the plants were living beings, and sacred, and this made a huge difference. Even with animals, you established the dog breeding program – an outlet to honour and value animals too. People with dogs in the City felt less isolated. Because of your positive outlooks, your caring, and the value you placed on all life, the two of you, as Adolfus and Joyce survived, while others around you, did not.

'By contrast, for those living in the Community situated in the hills, faith featured as an extremely important feature of everyone's life there. Their settlement was in a very exposed position. The only means that they had, to protect themselves from the virus, was to connect with the Earth Spirit, and inner forces that could help them. Collectively they drew upon this, in a desperate attempt to overcome the threat, with which they were confronted. When they aligned themselves with Spirit, Spirit could work with them, and they were able to start to turn their situation around. Their disciplined and cooperative actions made all the difference.

'The people of the Community had an open outlook, and sensed a loving connection to all life. From this base, they found purpose, unity and hope. They were happy people that enjoyed being together. Their approach to life was completely different from those in the City. In the City, people retreated, while in the Community, people expanded, and reached out. They worked with the plants, the animals and the Earth Spirit rather than feeling disconnected from that.

'However, from the perspective of the consciousness of people in the City, when the two of you travelled from the Community to the City – bringing your Spiritual practices with you – people in the City were willing to listen, and change to a more Spiritual outlook. In one way, this happened because they were inspired by the thought of other life existing in the world. However, more than that, they were willing to open up, because a spiritual outlook was what they truly wanted.

'On the Earth today, there are people with faith, people who believe in the interconnectedness of all life, and honour the sacredness of the Earth. These people clash with those that are not open to these beliefs. It is an ongoing power struggle that will determine which way the prevailing thought forms of humanity will unfold. This world of struggle is what you are preparing to enter, when you go on your mission.

'You have heard this before, but there is a certain threshold of consciousness that humanity must cross, if it going to be able to achieve its spiritual potential. If this threshold is reached, and enough people do open their awareness to the Spiritual realities, so people on the Earth can understand, then there will be a huge transformation in the way people live on Earth. The societies of the future will be very different from what they have been more recently. You need to be open for this, as you prepare for your mission together. It is part of your work, to help lay positive foundations for the future, that could exist.'

At this point, Astoris stopped speaking. We were all in silence, as our guide and teacher finished his speech. None of us could deny the truth of what he was saying. It made us all very thoughtful as we completed our meeting together. There were many questions in our minds – questions, that for now, were unspoken. We needed to contemplate on what had been presented to us, take it all into ourselves, and decide later, what we would do about it.

THE GALACTIC DOME

Later, after a period of reflection, we were called together again. A new phase of our training was to begin. We were going on an adventure together – travelling to a place with which I was familiar from stories that I had heard. But I had never been there. We were going to visit the Galactic Dome.

The Galactic Dome was like the Earth Dome, but hugely vaster in size and scope. Within the Galactic Dome, there was the spiritual consciousness connecting with all the worlds and beings, that inhabited the whole Galaxy in which we lived.

The prospect of visiting the Galactic Dome was very exciting for me. I knew of it from my time in the Earth Dome. When I considered the dimensions of it though, I felt in awe. In the Spiritual worlds, so much was possible, and I never ceased to be amazed. Going to the Galactic Dome, I would need to stretch my awareness in ways I had never done before. It was remarkable to be given the opportunity to explore this realm. I turned my attention to my teacher.

Astoris was speaking to us through our minds, telling us about what we would soon be experiencing. We had to trust in him, and let him guide us. Astoris was urging us to open our perspective. He wanted to give a focus for what we would be doing.

'The Earth is a living being, but as a planetary body and as a member of a star system, it is only one of a myriad of living planetary beings. Every star system and planetary body is unique, and all have precious qualities to add to the whole. And most importantly, all are linked – in a matrix of love, majesty and purpose. Many of the planets have vital forces that can support physical organisms to be alive, and for other forms of energetic life to exist. And the stars, themselves, radiate higher frequencies of light, heat and creative force. All of the star systems, and their planets, are in a continuing state of evolution and unfolding expression, not just physically, but spiritually too.

'Your Earth was just one of so many planetary beings. It has its place, and from the all-embracing love of the immensely encompassing Galactic Being, what happens now on the Earth, matters. And this is because the consciousness of the Earth Being now has the potential to break through into a new octave of Spiritual consciousness that will impact everywhere in the galaxy. Nothing happens in isolation. For those high beings of creation, love and light, their impulse clearly wants the Earth being to succeed in its transformation. The note of this desire resonates throughout our Universe.

'For so long, the consciousness of humanity has been restricted and narrow, encrusting a sense of Ego and individuality in a densely formed physical world. Your Ego has been a marvellous gift to cherish, for it has encouraged the faculty of free will to develop and the capacity for people to make choices. But a by-product of this process has been for humans, and especially males, to feed a sense of self-importance and self-centredness, that ultimately has become very destructive. It has fostered a tendency towards greed, and an urge for acquisitions and dominance.

'Human beings live in a system where they need to give and receive, with love. Many people have lost sight of that. Instead, they use other life forms around them to feed their sense of Self, to inflate themselves and grow more powerful. This is not in harmony with Universal principles, and it is not conducive to a spiritual way forward, for humans to expand themselves in this way. The perception that people have acquired, that they are the only ones that matter, is an illusion, and has become very addictive.

'Humans need to awaken, not only to the spiritual interconnectedness that exists with each other, but also the many layers of interconnectedness that occurs with other life forms on the planet – and even more, with the sense of shared aliveness with all the other worlds and Beings of creation. That is what we are going to explore now.

'This is a big step, for people to realise, that they are not the only living beings in the Universe, and that there are other layers of consciousness, including Spiritual consciousness. When people can acknowledge this, it will revolutionise thinking and people's outlook on the Earth.

'If people can embrace this, then it will bring about a quality of humility and openness that will invite a marvellous light of truth and well-being to become apparent to people. Humanity will then be engaged in a process of liberation, and the Earth could henceforth become a joyous place for all to live there and experience the abundance of what 'is'.

'It will not all happen instantly. A lot of work will be involved. As people embrace this new consciousness as their goal, all those in the Spirit Worlds will then be able to help manifest this reality, and then this will bring humanity into harmony with other elements of existence, both with other physical worlds, within the Galaxy and beyond where life exists, but also with the Spiritual worlds of love and creation.

'Most people do not realise how, from long ages of history, human civilisation has been seeded by the consciousness and physical infiltration of beings from other worlds. Most of these beings have been trying to help. We need to honour that humanity on Earth has had associations with many other influences. There is much more to your existence than you have realised. So you can learn about this, is one of the reasons that you are coming with me now, to visit the Galactic Dome.

'With the growing Earth population, many souls whose heritage has been from living conscious lives on other worlds, are now coming to Earth to gain experience, and in some cases, to help with the Earth transformation. It is like a massive soul migration to Earth from many different places. And somehow, it is a soul task for humanity to make our planet a happy home to all. This level of population cannot sustain itself, and it is one of the tasks of leaders on Earth, to work out how to manage it, and how to bring vastly different communities together. It is all part of the challenge of the transformation occurring.

'Within your working group, there are two members with no previous experience of being on Earth, but they each have specific gifts that they are bringing to help humanity. This is not abnormal, and the human race has much to learn from others. The lessons of tolerance and opening to true understanding, are key fundamentals that humanity has to develop more fully.'

Astoris paused, and we turned our attention to our two soul friends, Oiya and Deli. They were both excited about going to the Galactic Dome, for they knew about this Dome already, and they wanted to show us their own planetary systems, and how these were linked to Earth. Oiva appeared very eager, Deli less so.

As I gazed around in our Circle now, I could tell that we were all ready and we awaited Astoris to give the lead. Next, we linked, and set a united intention.

All at once, we were there, and the Galactic Dome was in front of us. It was a huge living organism of colour, light and energy. I could feel the vitality of it everywhere, with movement and vibrations linking one part to another. It was enormous. Like the Earth Dome, this was a Spiritual representation of Galactic life that connected to physical form. Just gazing at it from our vantage point, I felt overwhelmed. The intricacy of it was profound. I hardly knew where to turn with my attention. However, by remembering what I had to do with the Earth Dome, I knew that by concentrating on specific places, I could bring aspects of that form into greater focus. But where would be the best places to experience? I felt as a complete novice.

There was an unending richness of love pervading the space around us. This love was like a shifting tapestry flowing about the space. It felt a privilege to be here

OIVA'S WORLD

Astoris wanted to help us to orientate. He recognised, that for most of us, the experience of the Galactic Dome was completely unfamiliar, and we were floundering to know what to do. Our Guide motioned us to come closer together, and he placed Oiva in our centre. Astoris instructed us to concentrate on her, and so we did that. As we tuned in to Oiva, we were then able to see through her Spiritual eyes. We were going to embark on a journey together, with her guiding us. As we put our attention with her, she channelled her perception to us, and we entered this with our own minds. Quite suddenly, then, it was like worlds were passing by us, one after the other, in rapid succession, and we were travelling through space. Our awareness was as one being. So many different worlds were there, and with Oiva's consciousness, we experienced threads of connection between each one.

Soon, in front of us, there was an enormous rich blue white star, which, as we approached it, became like a sun. The love emitting from this giant celestial being encompassed fine bright vibrations, of compassion and warmth, which I had never felt before, and I experienced myself drawing this into myself, with amazement. As we slowed down, we could see that there were several planetary bodies some distance from this central star. And we were travelling to one of those, a planet that was exceedingly beautiful. The excitement in Oiva's being was palpable. For this was her home planet.

Slowly we descended to the surface. I was astonished, with the sublime variety of colour, and particularly, I was struck by the vibration of blues and greens, from land and seas, which appeared to emanate such peace and tranquillity. As we came closer, I could distinguish wonderful expanses of water, and strange looking vegetation. There were hills, and some mountains. All the forms of nature on the planet appeared so pure and untouched. Just being near this living vegetation was extremely nurturing, and made me feel happy. And when I looked up, the sky appeared orange from the thick atmosphere, and there were piercing rays of warmth, stemming from the central star high overhead. The disc of this star was smaller than our sun on Earth, not because the light from it was weaker than our sun – more the contrary, but it was to do with distance, for we were further away. The rays from this star were very potent, and the vegetation on Oiva's planet had adapted, and appeared to be delightfully healthy.

Oiva adjusted her vision, so we could see with her, more finely. As we shifted our awareness, in unity with her perception, we could begin to sense some of the life forms on this planet, with their individual beauty. Oiva took us on an extended tour, which was quite captivating. We wanted Oiva to show us her people. And so, she did.

We went to an area that was more sheltered from the central star. The ambience here was very tranquil. At first, it was as though there was nothing, and I had to open my inner awareness more creatively. Only slowly did I start to notice her fellow beings, for they were hardly physical – rather, they were translucent and tall, and there was a great aura of equanimity that emanated from them. I could not see many of them, and they all seemed to have their own space. In some gaps between the vegetation, there were stone surfaces where I could see members of her race, sitting in silence. Oiva gave simple acknowledgment to some that we saw, and they looked up at us calmly, and with compassion. All of them were studiously occupied, with their inner tasks and commitment. Their energy systems were very composed and still, and this showed a great deal of spiritual advancement. Outwardly, their existences seemed very simple, and physically, their movements were slow and deliberate.

I could perceive a deep and reverent cooperation between the members of Oiva's people. Here was a species of living beings that cared very much for all that was around them, and beyond. The planet where they lived, and its life forms, were flourishing, with a radiance, which was little different from what we would find in our Spiritual planes – the physical environment was pristine in its expression. Oiva was beaming with her energy, and she was so happy to show us. If only our human civilisation could aspire to generate a way of living somewhat like this!

There was something more that she wanted to show us, and her being was almost quivering with anticipation, as we travelled low over beautiful terrain, and the scenery rolled along gentle undulations, until, at the end of this, the land rose till we reached a ledge, and the splendour of the vegetation was exquisite. We were standing then, on the ground there, and we noticed, in front of us, almost hidden by the lush vegetation, that there was a small cave. Oiva led us in, and there was a comfortable space inside. Here, the natural light was dim, but energetically, the atmosphere was very beautiful, and there was a peacefulness that emanated from this place. Oiva was utterly thrilled to inform us that this was her home. We were welcome to enter there, with her. She told us, that while she was away with us, her people were caring for her home, but it would always be waiting there, when she returned.

It was strange to visit Oiva's dwelling place, for it was not like a home, in any sense, like what I had observed on Earth, for there were no furnishings or amenities, just natural stone and vegetation. On Oiva's world, there appeared to be no animals, just an abundance of plant life, that nestled harmoniously amongst the race of beings, like Oiva, that lived and did their work there. Her people did appear to live in a very solitary fashion – alone, but never lonely. Here, Oiva appeared to be so completely relaxed, as someone would, when they were at home. It was a privilege and remarkable to be here with her. For a while, we all stood there, silently marvelling at it.

We joined with Oiva and she led us in a meditation so that we could gain more of an overview of her world, and she showed us where many of her friends lived. There was one cluster of her race that lived together in a small central community. They were like coordinators for the functioning of their civilisation. The beings on this world strove to be in complete harmony. My heart felt expanded, and I felt great love on this world.

Oiva encouraged us to explore with our own consciousness. Her people knew that we were here and they welcomed us, so we all then ventured outside. I did not go far, but just marvelled with the marvellous nature. After a while, Oiva called us back, for she knew that we needed to move on. Gently, she passed over to Astoris again, so we could follow his directions.

For some further moments, we continued to draw energy from Oiva's home, and the wider world of her home planet into our awareness. But then, we were lifting again. Astoris wanted us to envision a higher perspective. And, as we journeyed above the planet and nearer again to the central star, we could observe threads of golden spiritual energy that extended from this uplifting star system to places far away, in a myriad of different directions. These were threads of service and loving support, being offered to other planetary bodies and star systems that needed it. Basically, Oiva's people were involved in administering these streams of energy, and sending them out, as an act of service, and for the betterment of all beings in our Galaxy, and the wider Universe. Oiva confirmed, that a large part of her work, had been to help vitalise and enliven these threads, moulding them into specific energy forms, that would be of most benefit to those receiving this input.

Now it was through Astoris's eyes that we saw, and we followed one of those threads, as it steadily continued its path to another planet, far away. We could feel that rushing sensation of vast distance being traversed, exceedingly rapidly, as we tracked this thread of immensely powerful, loving energy, closer and closer to the planet, to where it had set its course.

Then we could see it, and this was another quite outstandingly beautiful sphere of a world, that was also filled with blues and greens. Although I felt happy to come to this planet, I did not want to draw too close, for I knew that if I did, the comparison with Oiva's home world would make me sad.

For here was the Earth. And the star system associated with Oiva's home world was sending continuing bursts of loving supportive energy to the Earth, in an endeavour to help our home planet, as it grappled with the potential transformation which it was going through. Oiva had been dedicated to helping to channel these threads of energy to Earth and other systems for long ages. With the critical phase that the Earth was passing through, she had reached a point where she wanted to help in this work more directly, and therefore had responded to the calling given by Astoris, for her to join our mission. I felt immense gratitude, and was so glad that Oiva was with us, and I could feel the others acknowledging her presence equally.

The extent of our Galaxy and the wider Universe was all so massive; I could scarcely begin to comprehend it. However, I felt safe in Astoris's care. He had much knowledge of Oiva's world. But that was not all!

I could sense that he was gradually directing our exploration within this Galactic Dome, to particular systems of reality, that were relevant to us. He was doing this quite precisely, and in a progression to help us learn more widely, and understand strands of what was unfolding with our prescient Galaxy being. It was as though I was a beginner student again, for all that I observed was so new and inviting. I felt like a child with big eyes of wonder.

A DEAD WORLD

Next it was Deli's turn, and to my surprise, I could observe disquiet in his energy as he moved into the centre of our group. His energy was fluctuating for some moments, so he stood still until it settled. He shared with us, that although he had lived on several planetary systems, and been somewhat of a planetary explorer, there was one important place where he had lived, at the beginning of his evolution. This place had felt like his home, and the experience of being there had affected him drastically, and had shaped many of the incarnations that he had had since then. It was with a little trepidation, that he wanted us to visit this place with him, and to experience it, as it existed now. He was not happy about it, but he felt that he had to show us. So, we turned our attention to him, and he channelled his awareness to us. We were travelling again.

Although in the Spiritual worlds, we could be anywhere instantaneously via the intention of our thought, for this journey through space to Deli's home world, Astoris and Deli were drawing it out. By doing this, we could gain a further overview, and appreciation of the enormity and multi-layered existence of our Galactic being. But it wasn't just that. Astoris informed us, that we would need to adjust our thoughts and emotions, to what was coming to us – it may upset us.

I felt puzzled by this, but I let it go, in trust. As we travelled through the vast reaches of space, I continued to be impressed by the intricacy of what we saw, and its aliveness. I could not imagine anything that would be too challenging.

However, the closer we came to the situation of Deli's home world, the tenser I felt inside. There was something about this, which was not going to be easy. Deli could not hide his emotions from us, and the feeling of this world was altogether different, from what Oiva presented. I was not sure that I would like it.

There was an enormous, expansive orange sun at the heart of the star system of his home planet, but the energy of this sun, was not happy. Circling this diffuse globe of light, we could see several planets. It was not obvious which of the planets would be Deli's home world, for none of them were shining brightly,with Spirit light. In fact, they all appeared particularly inert and uninviting.

We came to the surface of one of those worlds. It was bare, rocky and fractured. There appeared to be no life and there was no atmosphere. It was not really a place that I wanted to visit. I noticed that Deli was shaking, and my own energy system was reacting too.

We stood together on the surface while Deli steadied himself. This was quite an ordeal for him, and we were all sending him energy, to support him. Could this be the place where he had once lived? We looked over at him, and he confirmed that this was so. He paused for a while longer, and then began to speak.

'This planet once hosted a great and thriving civilisation,' he started. 'It was my home for many of my early incarnations.' He paused, and he was gulping with emotion. Astoris stepped into the centre to be with him. Deli continued. 'There was much trade here, and intellectual activity. With technological advances, our people were on the verge of space travel. But it was when we became more technologically adept, that our lives began to deteriorate.

'People here were a little taller than humans on Earth, and we had a marvellous sensuous brown complexion, which was very beautiful to behold. The dwelling places where we lived, were formed by using and manipulating the natural lush vegetation on the planet. There were abundant resources. Many of characteristics shared by our people were like those of humans on Earth. We had thought processes, emotions, free will. It was possible for us to make sounds to express our emotion but we mainly communicated through our minds. There was so much opportunity here, for everyone.

'Like humans, we possessed strong desires, and with some of our inhabitants, these desires were quite untamed, and became exaggerated with the abundance of our conditions. Tendencies grew, where people wanted to take more, for themselves, and with technological advances, different factions of our people grouped together, and rather than cooperating, they developed threatening instruments, to be able to acquire more of the wealth of the land for themselves, and leaving little for others. From a society where we naturally shared, a propensity grew, for these groups to be increasingly aggressive, and covetous.

'In some ways, we were like how the Earth is now, and in other ways we were different. For, on our planet, we had not known wars, and from our earliest times, we had existed in harmony. It had been such a pleasant place to live. However, with technological advances and an increasing population, testing the capacity of our resources, all of this began to change. In the beginning, we had been nature loving, and the energies of the natural world generated an atmosphere of peace for us. But, with all this technology, we became more centred in our minds, and increasingly removed from the spiritual influences of the land, and its beautiful vegetation.

'We could feel that things were not right, and there were protests. Swathes of our wonderful land was being desecrated by technological experiments, by those that wished to increase their personal power. We did not want this. But our leaders did not listen. They wanted more resources and riches, and exploited a lot of what was good in our world to feed their ambitions. Tension and conflict grew, and there was fear among our population, about the possibility of war.

'For a while, this was averted. Nobody wanted the terrible consequences of war. We were a world where people had been happy, where there had been enough for all, and it was innate in us, that this is how we wanted things to be. We set up administrative structures, for groups to talk and work out their differences. A world body was set up, to oversee how resources were used, and to ensure that distribution of goods and services were done fairly. But the leaders of the factions did not like this, and they felt that the world body diminished their power. Hence, they resisted it. Another development was that borders were set up between different areas of our land, separating our people from each other. This was quite alien to us, because freedom of movement was so intrinsic to us, but the trends towards exclusion grew more stringent, until our people were increasingly restricted about where they could travel.

'Under the cover of this political settlement, some of those new nation states secretly developed sophisticated weapons to uphold their own interests and borders, and to claim more than that which they were entitled to have. There were riots in some of the other communities when people found out about this. Many in our society were afraid. What little trust remained towards the leadership of these nation states, was fractured more and more. For the first time in our history, we had crime with people taking from each other, and this generated further isolation and uncertainty. The tensions in our society rose to higher and higher levels.

'In my last incarnation here, I was a diplomat, and I was one of those that desperately scurried between various interest groups, to attempt, with all my might, to rebuild bridges of cooperation and trust, and attempt to balance out all the distortions that were emerging.

'One of the faction leaders decided that he should be the leader of the world body, for he wanted absolute power over everyone. The other leaders were aghast and furious, and were determined for this not to happen. These were the conditions that precipitated the war, for neither side would let go. This time, there was no yielding, and threats and fiery rhetoric brought the different sides very close to the edge. For a while, the arguments went on, while people on the street looked on in horror. There were some ugly provocations.

'One day, six protesters tried to cross a border into the land where this factional leader lived, and they were killed. This could have been the final catalyst, and it seemed that our people were beginning to hate each other. Defences in all the nation states were put on high alert, and it seemed that there was very little room for manoeuvre. The opposing factions both decided that the only way that they could resolve the situation was to wipe out and destroy the power base of the other side. So, they set out to do that. And that was how the war started.

'We only had one planetary war, but it was enough. 'The military had aircraft, nuclear type weapons and laser weapons. Once started, the war did not stop, and vast tracts of land and cities were annihilated. Many people died, and much of what was most precious in our communities were destroyed. But it was the laser weapons that precipitated the worst catastrophe. Somehow, these weapons managed to create a fissure that disturbed the atmosphere that wrapped itself around our world, and the air started to dissipate from our planet's surface. When they realised what was happening, our remaining scientists were absolutely frantic to try and stop this. But it was too late.

'As the atmosphere escaped into space, life in all its forms began to die. It took a little time, but it was an inexorable process. We all needed air to survive. Some groups of people attempted to maintain pockets of air for themselves, but they had very little time, and could not sustain it. Many of us were witnesses, as the final vestiges of life on our precious world ebbed away. And all was lost. The Spirit being of our world could not function anymore, and despite some lingering struggles, life on our world died.

'Unlike the bleak Earth world life, which we have just shared together, there was no happy ending – no chance of any reconstruction. It was all gone, and could not be built again.

'I remember my final afternoon there, with the flashing lights in the sky, and the ground rumbling under my feet, people rushing here and there. It was utter chaos. When I looked up, the sky was a strange colour and it was as if the vitality of our atmosphere was being drained away. I was straining to breathe, and I felt complete despair. In that moment, I lay down to die – I just gave up, for I could not cope with it any more.

'I was just one of many millions of people that died in that war. And as a soul, I felt a sense of failure and loss that I carried with me for many, many lifetimes after this event. Many, many rimes, I searched in myself if I could have done more – and I accept now, that I did all that I could.

'It was an unfathomable tragedy for all those souls, with whom I lived on our world. I guess that our leaders completely underestimated what could happen because of the war, and using all their destructive weapons. There was not enough reverence for the Spirit of our land. Conditions on our world had been too good for too long, and people took it for granted, that they would always have what they wanted. In the end, the consciousness of our people became caught up in the Self, and we forgot about the needs of the whole. I still find it hard to believe that this occurred.

'I have lived on many worlds since this one and I have seen how worlds can pass through this phase of possible self-destruction to glorious cooperation and peace. And I have also witnessed other worlds destroying themselves, like on my home world. We have the Earth now, at this crossroads. I would like humanity to succeed, but it may not. This world, where we are standing now, was my first world, and as such, because it died, it will always be like a scar on my soul, and I will continue to remember what happened. No amount of healing can change that.'

There was silence in our group. I felt enormous sympathy for Deli, and admired his courage for sharing this with us. What Deli experienced, living and dying while his world also died around him, is what I feared for our Earth.

As I turned to Deli, I could think of no experience, that could be as devastating or utterly defeating as this. I wanted to shout out to the people on this world that were responsible for the war, and castigate them for their folly, but I remained quiet, as did all of us.

Astoris stood very close to Deli and comforted him, for he was shivering with his energy field, and needed support. Because we had been standing together, we had been able to collectively shield each other from feeling the energy of being on this dead world, but now Astoris wanted us to step out on our own and explore being on this world, in our own individual space, and to learn what it was like.

Here was a planet now, where nearly all Spiritual energy had been withdrawn. It existed in isolation. As Spiritual beings, we were used to being in an environment where we were supported by Spiritual energy all around us, with a wonderful presence of love, permeating every thought, feeling and emotion that engaged us. Here, that was to all degrees that I could perceive, absent. The contrast between what we experienced on Oiva's world, and now this, was stark and extremely uncomfortable. I could only venture away from our group with small steps, and I wanted to flinch and turn back.

'Breathe into your own strength,' Astoris put to us. He was watching us, and monitoring how we would cope. I was so used to a flow of energy passing from outside me to inside me, flowing back and forth. On this world, there was nothing I could take from outside me. I could only draw from what was inside me. It felt so desolate, and the lack of vitality distressed me. This reminded me of being outside the City, while I was on the Bleak world, but what I experienced now, was worse. I had to bring my attention completely into my own centre, and be with that, and only then, could I focus a little more on what was around me.

The others did not appear to be moving any more confidently than me. I noticed Oiva just standing still, as if in prayer, and that was probably what she was doing. In our Spirit forms, we could connect with the psychic residues that still lingered, and although these people did not speak like humans, I could sense the memories of their screams, and tortuous anguish – their last gasps in a world that died. It was a horrible, agonising emotion – the fear as well. My strongest reaction, was just in considering all that potential, going to waste and ruin. It was an appalling calamity.

There were no obvious physical traces any more, of the great civilisation that lived here – just lifeless boulders and craters and a black colourless sky, and stars that twinkled far away. I felt uneasy to be too long here, and was so relieved when Astoris suggested that we come together again and depart.

As I stood there, with the others, I was very grateful to feel the life energy of my fellow group members once more. We hugged each other energetically in gratitude, and then quickly rose away from the planet. Astoris told us to be very gentle with ourselves, while we worked through our feelings, of what we had just witnessed.

LIBERATION OR RUIN?

I had a vague sense of us travelling very fast, but I must have lost consciousness while my inner being digested what we had experienced. It was safe to surrender to this, for I knew that Astoris would look after us. But when I opened my Spiritual eyes again, we were in a very different location, for we were gathered together in a chamber, adjacent to the Galactic Dome, and Astoris was showing us a map on a gigantic screen. He wanted us all to be present, and checked with everyone before he commenced. This map was a multi-dimensional representation of our galaxy.

As I opened my perception to it, I could see a myriad of sparkling points of light designating the innumerable living worlds in our galaxy. I could not begin to count the number of such worlds that were there. I marvelled at this, but Astoris had a very specific reason for showing us this map.

From being mesmerised by the vitality of all those living worlds, Astoris now placed these in the background, for he wanted to bring to our attention, another aspect of our Galactic being. What he was doing, was to mark out and highlight the planets that were now dead – ones like Deli's world, casualties of the self-destructive impulses of the civilisations that lived there. These were signified like black dots in amongst the representation of all the worlds, in front of us. I was surprised, because there were not just an isolated few worlds here and there, like this, but there were lots of black dots. The more I looked, the more I saw. And as I started to take this in, there were too many for me to count, and I began to feel both despair and fear.

I didn't want to see this, and I could feel my energy system churning with anxiety. What if Earth was to end up like one of those black dots? It would be such a waste. We just could not let that happen.

Astoris made sure that we were all with him, and he then emphasised, that with all these worlds which were dead that in none of these cases, was any external agency involved. The reasons for their self-destruction were solely due to conflicts that had occurred purely between members of the races of beings that lived there.

'In your physical Universe, numerous life forms have been created by the loving God-force. Some exist in a form of collective consciousness. Others have been granted more independence. Each has been given its own unique features and modes of expression, all contributing to the whole. Some have had the appearances that have been human-like while others have had attributes that could not be more different.

'One branch of divine creation has been of beings that have been given self-conscious intelligence, with the capacity of free will, combined with the ability to connect with the underlying Spiritual love that guides everything. These beings have been seeded with potential to be able to learn and master conditions around them, and to be able to manipulate the environment of their world, to obtain what they want. Humans are one such race that has been given these gifts, and the civilisation on Deli's planet was another.

'At a certain point in the evolution of beings like this, they are given the collective ability to be able to determine their own destiny. On the planets where they live, they can learn to cooperate together and humbly find their place in the greater scheme of existence. And with this, they can co-create with Spirit, beautiful structures of love and healing such as what has happened on Oiva's planet. Or else, they can become so attached to their controlling faculties of free will and limited intelligence, and build this up to such an extent, manipulating all around them, as they proceed, that they eventually revolt against each other, in that quest for ever greater power. Then the outcome of this pattern is self-destruction.

'Beings with free will always have the capacity to connect with their inner Spiritual sources. But when they choose to close off from this, perhaps because they are lured by the lust for power, then they tend to become selfish and concerned only with their own wants. They will also lose perspective and not appreciate the needs of others. By Spiritual law, the needs of all beings are important and sacred. When souls begin to close their perception to this, they will feel empty and life will lose meaning. In their lust for power, they will take from others to fill the emptiness, but this will not satisfy them. So, they will take more, thinking that this may fulfil them. But it won't. And this can easily cause tension with those that feel not respected. Then a spiral of struggle is generated and will not stop, until either there is war, or the pattern can be turned around.

'Now the people on Earth are fast reaching that position where they face this crucial choice. Humanity has developed sufficiently where it could wilfully decimate all that is precious, and all that you love in your world, and render the Earth to be a dead world, like the one we have just seen. Alternatively, there is also the possibility, with an awakening of consciousness, that people could come together and genuinely work in harmony to co-create a better world – putting the needs of the whole first, and opening to appreciate the sacredness of all life and to honour that together, seeking guidance to be able to do that well. Then, people on Earth could feel great joy, in being guardians and stewards of the beautiful life on your planet, rather than being the architects of its ruin.

'Life on Earth is multi-layered, with far greater complexity than what existed on Deli's world, and there is also more at stake. Dealing with wars has been an ongoing aspect of human history, and this has brought with it, many opportunities for human beings to learn, about what utter devastation war can bring. I must say that planet Earth has the potential to be a leading light within the galaxy. There are some very precious elements of existence on Earth, many of which are hardly even known by humans on the planet until now. But these potentials can only be realised, if the right choices are made now.

'Certainly, at this stage, a lot more people need to wake up in their consciousness, to their purpose, and a true sense of who they are. Dominating self-centred individuals and corporations are already causing substantial damage to the fabric of the Earth and are weakening the resolve of those that would want spiritual liberation for your world. But you know that it can still be turned around, and there will be great celebrations in the Spiritual world if you can all manage that.

'If the Earth is to succumb to collapse of its life forces, there will be two factors. It will be because of the actions of individuals, that have been able to disregard the needs of others, and, more importantly, because not enough people have been willing to assert their true place on Earth, and defend the rights of all your life forms there to exist and flourish. For the Earth to transform into the potential love and peaceful co-existence, that it could express, this will not come about, due to any one person or even small group of people leading over the rest of you; it must come from the good efforts from masses of you, together.

'This should give you some indications of what you what you need to do when you embark on your mission to the Earth, and how you must relate to others that you meet there. It will not be easy, and you cannot anticipate how others will react to you. If you stay true to your hearts and your link to Spirit, then hopefully you will make good progress. You can then be a model to others'.

Santi had a question, which he addressed. 'Is it inevitable that beings which have the faculty of free will, have to reach this stage of evolution, that they will either transform spiritually or destroy themselves? Could there not be the situation where some beings on a world are willing to open up spiritually and others are not, and that it stays like that?'

Astoris responded. 'The collective process involved, with how beings of free will manage their own sense of power, has been known to be very prolonged. But once a certain stage of evolution has been reached, with the races that share life on a given planet, then the struggles around the use of Will is an issue that will cause tension until there is a resolution. We are not speaking here, about an individual soul on its spiritual path, but of the spiritual path of a race of beings, and the the relationship that they share, with the planetary being where that race lives. You must become aware, that, as souls, when you live in a physical world, you have a responsibility, not only to your own individual soul, but you must learn, to share responsibility, also for the well-being of the collective race, of which you are part, and in addition, the preservation of the world where you live.

There will come a point when this must be addressed, decisively, by the race of beings concerned, or else, that race simply will not advance spiritually any further.

'In the earlier stages of your human evolution on Earth, you instinctively would look after yourself, your family and your clan or community. That is where your concerns would lie. As time went on, this developed so your concern would include your nation or group of nations. Now, it has reached the stage where this is not enough – it is now about how concerned you can be for all of humanity and all life forms within the Earth. Many people on Earth have not embraced this yet, and they continue to be occupied with smaller, more immediate concerns. But forces are pushing more and more of you to be open to the needs of the whole. The test is about how you manage this, and if you can manage it. You have the tools, and you have the capacity. Can you open your hearts and choose to do this positively? For it is with open hearts that you will succeed with this. It is about caring for the Earth and each other, together, and not laying waste to everything.

'If you look at what is happening on your Earth just now, there are forces and energies giving people the opportunity to awaken spiritually and to act with a greater sense of responsibility. People now can open to a sense of the sacredness of all life. There are networks of communication now that spread right across your globe suggesting this. What are you going to do with that?

'There has been much exploration of different forms of society on Earth. As I have shown you, in former times, there have been pockets of societies that have been in harmony with the Spirit of the Earth – peaceful societies that functioned well, but they have only been able to function that way in isolation. Because there have been more aggressive self-seeking groups and nations elsewhere on the planet, these peace-loving groups have not lasted, and have been invariably taken over and their values suppressed. But today in your world, it is different, for it is ultimately about survival, not just for a few of you as individuals, but for the whole planet. Now, there is still diversity, but you exist as one group, one world, and you must decide what you do, collectively.

'Nothing happens in isolation on your world anymore. The awareness is growing for your people about, how what happens in one part of your globe, affects the rest of the world. Anything that happens anywhere in your world, is interlinked. This occurs in so many avenues of your lives together, and an appreciation of this is increasing, with the new impulses of consciousness that are being given to you. There are tests for you about letting down barriers that separate you from each other, and you are being challenged to create more open and tolerant and accepting societies, choosing pathways of health and environmentally friendly lifestyles. Do you listen to these impulses, or ignore them? The pressure is growing. The only way that you can really ignore these, is by putting up greater barriers. The effect of doing this, is to breed hate, and lack of tolerance. Where will that lead? These are all signs, and part of the process you are engaged in.

'If enough people welcome these new energies, there will be that threshold to be reached, where there is a revolution of consciousness and a new equilibrium will be embraced. You can see in your world, the well-being that people feel, when they choose to come together in unity to affirm some cause, which they know is good. There are more and more causes, and reasons for people to come together. However, the opposition is intense, and anyone with vested interests of power does not want to give those up. So, there is a lot of confusion, and struggling for positions. This is the beginning. If the threshold is reached and the revolution of consciousness occurs, it is likely, for all intents and purposes, to be irreversible, for you will not want to go back to the old ways. Your outlook then will be so much more harmonious and peaceful and you will have succeeded in ways that not so many civilisations have. It will be a great sense of achievement for all of you. But you must get there first, and that is by no means something you can take for granted.

A BIGGER PICTURE

'Let's step back for a moment, and you can look through my eyes. There is something I want to show you.'

At the invitation of Astoris, we did that then. We came together as a group and Astoris told us to set our intention, to merge into his being. This was not something that we had done before with my teacher, to such an extent. I felt a little uncertain. However, we were told to proceed. We had to open our awareness, so that our perception could blend with him and expand. For some moments, then, we would be able to embrace his consciousness, and learn through identifying with his being.

Astoris guided us to make this transition. It was only by invitation that we could do this. As I entered him, I could feel myself expanding enormously. It was like nothing I had ever experienced. I was awe-struck at the wonderful outlook that he shared with us all. The qualities of love and awareness that he expressed, was huge. He asked us to focus on what we sensed to be around us.

From how I functioned in the Spiritual world, I had a certain range of perception with which I was familiar. I could experience the energy of love and thought projection, and the endless unlimited divine creative life flow, which brought joy to my heart. I knew that fundamentally all was well and I had nothing to fear. When I had moved from my limited human consciousness into the Spirit World, it was like moving from a small room, and stepping out into the open skies.

However, now as I looked through the eyes of Astoris, it was as though my awareness was opening into many further beautiful dimensions of reality, that I had not known was there.

I was looking at my own energy form, and the energy form of our working group, experiencing them with greater clarity, and with more detail and perspective than I had ever seen. It was quite marvellous to behold. I could view weaknesses, strengths and potentials, all there, and how the members of the group blended together. And then beyond this, there were star systems and planets and the Galactic being, all shining and swirling with their own energy forms. We focussed once more on the dead planet of Deli's home world and I did not experience it anymore as being quite dead, for there were some small vestiges of Spiritual energy there – some underlying force that enabled this world to continue to exist, but it was so sluggish now, and hardly moving anymore. I felt compassion for Deli.

But then, it all began to dissolve. And what were distinct forms of being, began to merge, and what was individual energy became incandescent light. And all was one, and nothing was separate from anything else, anymore. There was one light and one love and one voice, that was all. The feeling was incredible. We were experiencing the underlying 'God' consciousness directly. Every existence was an expression of this 'God' force and that which was emitted from this 'God' force, was evolving beauty and love, which was so splendid and uplifting and inspiring – an expression that was like a mirror, so that the formless could be formed, and the unknowing could know this 'God'. And all was One. It was like the ultimate mystical vision. We marvelled in this and I felt utter contentment in my soul.

Slowly this altered, and I could see the Galactic being, and how it was linked to other Galactic beings, and other Universes, and a multitude of unseen, hidden dimensions of being that were becoming manifest – all on their own journey of perfection, and unfolding majesty. And I could see the members of our group, all of us, including myself, on a loving unfolding path, stretching towards blissful infinity and self-knowing. It was all there, waiting to be lived – all that love in potential.

And even the Earth with its beauty and vibrancy standing at its crossroads – it was held within bedrock of love, whatever happened. It mattered profoundly, and yet, the Divine plan would adjust, whatever the path that people ultimately chose to live.

But then, as wonderful as this opening of perception was – sharing this together as a group – it began to close again. Astoris gently told us that we would be withdrawing from him now, and he held us, as the bliss of the vision through his consciousness, gradually receded, and we found ourselves drawn once more, into our normal, individual Spiritual consciousness. I did not want to let it go – I wanted more, but it could not be. He was outside us once more, and beaming love to us. It was almost painful to be within the limits of my own outlook again.

DELI'S PLACE WITH US

Within a moment, we were at our meeting place again, and our group was in its Circle, with Astoris positioned around us. Visiting the Galactic Dome and gaining the deeper perspective through Astoris's eyes had certainly given us all a lot to think about. I felt in my heart, adamant, that I wanted to do all that I could with our mission, so the consciousness of humanity and the Earth itself, could move higher. As I reflected, I kept thinking about that map with all those dead planets, and I remembered what it was like on Deli's home world. That was not the way that I wanted our precious Earth to go.

When I glanced around the circle, the spirit lights of the others were in a state of processing, just like with me. For a while, we stayed there together in silence, and I could feel the nurturing love of Astoris supporting us. Then, only when our energy systems had all settled, Deli moved into the centre of our circle, to address us. Deli spoke.

'I have known since my own home planet was destroyed, that my own redemption and path of healing would lead me eventually, to a situation which would offer me the chance to help very directly with people living on a planet similar to mine – a world where people there, would have the chance to open themselves beyond their egos, and make that transformational transition into a spiritualised cooperative existence – a potential that the people on my home world did not reach. I have wanted this so much with my desires.

'When my world collapsed, my heart was empty and barren, like the physical landscape on my home world. The thought of war, was like horror inside me, that over many, many lives, just would not heal. I have never wanted to see that kind of destruction again. For long ages, I had to work with feelings of guilt – torturing myself that I may have contributed to that calamity – searching in myself for answers I could never find. I punished myself in so many incarnations, staying aloof from others, witnessing other planetary situations, but never becoming involved, until, through prolonged prayer and contemplation, I finally learnt to be able to love myself again.

'This was a crucial moment for me, for then, I could, at last, look forward, rather than back. My own reactions during all those lives, had been to seek to be with souls, that I had not met previously, for I did not want to be reminded of the catastrophe of my home planet being destroyed, by being with others that had shared it with me. So, for a long period, I became a very lonely soul, feeling like an outcast, until I found my way forward.'

I was glad that Deli had the courage to share this with us, for when we had been introducing our history to each other, he had focussed on his later times, after this calamity, and he had hidden the truth of what had happened to his home world. Now, as he told us this, it was like waves of relief unburdening from him, and liberating him, to join more fully with our group. It made so much sense now, the reason that he was with us. We all took turns to embrace him, and then we gave him a group spiritual hug of joy.

There was still more that Deli wished to say to us.

'When it was brought to my attention about the possibility for this mission, I wanted so much to join, for it seemed the perfect opportunity for me to fulfil my goal and heal from my past, so I would be ready to make that Spiritual transition, myself. The conditions on Earth have many resonances with what I faced on my home planet, and at times, as we have been considering conditions on Earth, it has caused shivers of fear to flow through me.

'I cannot take for granted that we will succeed this time, for, as Astoris has pointed out, the Earth people may destroy themselves, and my misery then could be compounded – I face that risk. But I am willing for the challenge, and will do all that I can do, so that whatever does happen, I can feel peace with myself.

'The experience as Linton has given me good preparation, for I know that when I come to Earth, I must focus on healing and bringing people together, from the very beginning, if I am to do my best for everyone.

'I have found in myself, because of the 'life' we shared on the devastated bleak Earth world, that my love for the Earth is growing, even though I have never lived there. It is as though, the love I felt for my home planet and my wishes for it, is translating itself into similar feelings for the Earth.'

SOUL LEARNINGS

At this juncture, Astoris suggested that we pause, and for us to go somewhere to relax more fully, and share more. Deli's story was triggering responses in all of us and these would need expression. We let our guide lead, and soon we were in a landscape with beautiful trees and a flowing stream of water nearby. I was entranced by this. The sounds of water cascaded rhythmically over stones while birds and other animals, scurried playfully around us, and there was the fresh scent of flowers and moist bark on the ground. It was like being on Earth – our Earth at its best. There were stones placed next to each other in a circle where we could sit together, near the water. This whole place was immensely soothing with the gentle nature around us.

And so, the space was opened, for processes that were coming to the surface, with members of the group, and needing expression. This was a necessary sharing, and important for our bonding.

As I opened my senses to the others in the circle, I noticed a dullness and agitation emerging through Santi's energy field. I could tell that Armond, next to him, was attempting to comfort him, as she knew what was in his mind. For Santi, Deli's recounting of his trials had stimulated soul memories in him – and they were not pleasant ones. He wanted to speak to us all.

'In my younger days on Earth as a soul,' he started, 'I had a great lust for power. On many occasions, I felt exhilarated when I could prove my strength over others, and win battles. It was like a feeling of intoxication, to have others bow down to me, and do my bidding. Then I could sense an emotion of 'greatness' and invincibility. I became so attached to the sensation of power, that I sought for it in every situation, and fed on it, to the exclusion of all else. It was not a happy position for those around me, for, in my pursuit of power, I became quite blind to my loved ones, and cared only for my own glory. In my zealousness, I took on leadership, and was responsible for many deaths, and the annihilation of numerous towns and cities, and there was even one civilisation where my actions drove the forces, which led to the downfall of this once valued society. Many times, Armond was my partner, and sometimes my enemy. We went through this together, but my lust was greater.'

Santi paused for some moments, and I noticed how Armond had moved closer to her loved one. He continued. 'My guides in Spirit worked desperately with me, to attempt to turn these tendencies around, so I could balance them out. Subsequently, I went through numerous lives, where I suffered at the hands of others, so I could learn by being on the receiving end of someone else's power over me. I did not like it, but it did not stop me. My hatred for those that did this to me, spilled out into further lives of mindless violence. It was only after I had been the cause of some particularly horrendous destruction, of people, and their homes, and I was forced to spend three lives afterwards in that same land largely on my own, in a state of poverty and despair, that I began to realise what I had done, and vowed not to do it again. That was just the beginning of my healing.

'It took me many lives to renounce the longing for power for its own sake, and to find more constructive modes of living. I still fought in battles, but now they were battles in the pursuit of righteousness. I had to learn by helping to build up societies and strive to help people live in harmony with each other rather than selfishly destroying what was precious to others. Slowly, step by step, I did learn, and Armond travelled with me on this journey. We always remained close in Spirit. During my recovering restitution phase, I began to appreciate the gifts and bounty of the Earth, and take joy and pleasure from that. This opened me, in an entirely different, and more satisfying way, and my dedication to the Earth has continued to grow, until I have been able to come to be here, with you, to support this group as we try to help the Earth.

'I was fortunate not to lose my planetary home, as you did Deli. For many lives, I did not care, and it still upsets me, that I could have been like that.'

Santi was now releasing emotion, and Armond held him lovingly. For a while, we sat in silence together, allowing the calming energies of the beautiful nature setting, where we sat, to bring healing. A squirrel came bounding down from a nearby tree, and scurried around, until it stood right next to Santi, its whiskers twitching. For a moment, the squirrel seemed to look up at Santi, quite unafraid, and curious. Then, in a moment, it turned, and bounded off again. We all smiled.

Astoris had words and thoughts to impart to us to supplement Santi's account of himself. 'Many of you on Earth have succumbed to the lure and temptations or pursuing power for its own sake. For you to be able to deal with this force, is a necessary stage in your maturing process as souls – souls with free will and self-awareness. You are learning what it is like to control energies around you, and to experiment with that. Because you have free will, you can do what you like. Ultimately, you learn to bring the tendencies of taking and giving, into balance, in harmony with Spirit – not because you must do that, but because, as a mature soul, you will recognise that this is the path of joy, and what you want to choose.

'To get caught up in the pursuit of power for oneself at the expense of everything else, is like an empty shell, that can only bring an exaggerated sense of isolated and lonely individualism. It is intoxicating, as you say, Santi. Nothing of substance can be gained from it – only the lesson about how meaningless it is.

'Yet, on Earth, similar mistakes continue to be made. What people need to comprehend is that when you cooperate and work together, this can also engender feelings of satisfaction, and that shared activity, when it is conducted with care and love, does have inner substance and can bring fulfilment to the soul. People may fear, that when they surrender themselves to work with others cooperatively, that they will lose their sense of individuality so they are merely part of a collective, but this is not so. When you link lovingly with other people and life forms, this enhances your sense of uniqueness and individuality, and you will be aware how you have a definite place, how the contribution that you make, cannot be made in quite the same way as you do it, by any other being. You can then celebrate your individuality and it will be appreciated by others. Therefore, you are happy, and you raise the levels of love for all.

'As I have suggested earlier, the test for you on Earth now, is not just how you handle this soul test individually, but how you are prepared to work with power, collectively, as humanity. It is a necessary growth in maturity, that you need, if you are to survive as a species. And the prevailing consciousness on your world needs to shift from a state where one individual, group or nation is pitting itself against the others, to one where you consciously choose to work together for the highest good – and that you can do that with honesty and sincerity.

'Whatever energies, we, in the Spiritual Realms may be directing, to try and help you, ultimately, it will be your own free will decisions that will govern how your Earth will be. If you listen to us, the streams of Spiritual energy in our realm will open in your physical world and bring about a tremendous transformation. The choice is yours. If you shut us down, you will place yourselves, very much, on your own.'

I could now see, as I looked across at Santi and Armond, that their lights had brightened again. They brought with them a tremendous 'fighting spirit,' which they had gained during their soul learning. This 'fighting spirit' had strength and determination within it. These attributes were qualities that we needed in our group, for our mission, and this was one of the main reasons, that they had been chosen to be with us.

Santi reemphasised to us all then, how much the experience of being Adolfus, had encouraged his determination to help others, for him to never give up, and not to act alone. Through his soul learning, over the many lives that he had lived, Santi had become a great humanitarian.

For some moments, we were now in silence. Our discussion was ready to take on another turn. The next one who wanted to speak was Aurielle. As she placed herself in the centre of our circle, all our attention was upon her. She began.

'My challenge as a soul has been very different to yours, Santi. From the beginning of my incarnations, I have been sensitive, and always felt a great communion with other life forms, and with the Earth. It has given me joy, to dance and interact with other life forms, to share my love and be happy through togetherness. I have had the capacity to channel delicate and beautiful energies, to enhance the ambience of any environment where I was present. The essence of my creativity, has been the expression of oneness and a strong devotional nature.

'But I have been hurt many times, and suppressed, and others around me have wanted to use my gifts for their own pleasure and enhancement. The pain of this has tested me greatly, for I have felt that others wanted to possess me, and I could not be myself. When I have been in the presence of others going through suffering, this has also affected me, for I had empathy, and it was like, I was suffering with them. At times, I felt that I could not cope with any more. On occasions, I reacted to this with rage, and wanted to hurt back, anyone that hurt me. There were lives where I completely lost myself in violence. However, often, my reaction was the opposite to this, and I retreated and hid myself, for it felt safer to do this, and to become invisible – so that others would leave me alone. I also explored strategies that were not helpful, for numbing my feelings, so I could detach myself and be removed from it all. This included me committing suicide on many occasions.

'For me, the pain of experiencing hurt and separation from that feeling of oneness, and what I loved, sometimes felt quite unbearable. Over and over, I tried to convince myself that I was not sensitive, and through denial, even concealed my gifts from myself. This is what I felt that I had to do, so I could survive being on the Earth with other people, many of whom appeared to be quite uncaring and disrespectful. In this state of detachment, I could be very lonely and isolated. However, this was a prison of my own making, and I could never be happy by rejecting my own nature.'

She continued. 'It has become very clear to me, that my soul path has been about finding courage in myself, to overcome my fears, to forgive those that have hurt me, and to stand in my own light, trusting that I am supported, and what needs to be, will be so. I have needed to open to Spirit, and develop my faith, so I know I can express my qualities, and I can openly be myself with others. Although I have faltered many times, for long ages, I have been on that journey to accomplish this, to stand up rather than hide, and I have a special interest now, to be able to help those others that feel weak with their sensitivity, to help them to find their power and conviction, and to lead by my own example.

'In the lifetime as Kendren, I could have withdrawn, when I found myself so alone, with the pain of my mother dying and my father absent, but my instinct was to connect with the Community and to feel part of the life around me, so I could live happily. Thankfully, I could choose that, living my life in partnership and cooperation with others. And when it finally came that I could meet my father, this was a great moment of healing for me, and it felt like acceptance and recognition for who I truly am. I felt as if some important component of my core Self had returned to me. My sense of identity existed, not only through my awareness of Self, but through my relationship with others, and this meeting gave me hope. At that point, I resolved that while another human existed on the Earth, I would continue with my path and do what I came to do. I would not give up either. Nor would I hide.'

As I listened to Aurielle, my own soul was reacting with varying streams of energy emitting from my core. I was close to Aurielle's soul and loved her very dearly. In many lifetimes, I had known her and interacted with her soul actively. There were lifetimes where I had also been very sensitive, and I knew those feelings that Aurielle was describing. However, I was also aware of times in my own soul history when I had not been kind to her and had been one of those responsible for engendering fear in her soul. I had acted selfishly. This process of self-examination was very humbling. In more recent lives, I had been working very hard to overcome these tendencies, so that I could be respectful towards all beings, and support her, by giving her space to express her true self. It was what I wanted – to support her, but I could see that the source of her strength would not come from me or anyone else; it would be an energy that she drew into herself from her core, and that inner connection she maintained with the loving source of all creation.

Astoris now wanted to address us with issues that Aurielle had raised.

'On the Earth now, there are many, many, souls that hide themselves through fear, and because of this, they do not express their light and they block the Spiritual impulses that we could channel through them. The energy field of the Earth is much darker than it could be. If even most of the sensitive souls on your world, could open themselves, and feel safe to do so, the Spiritual transformation of the Earth would occur so much more easily. This darkness resulting from issues around sensitivity is prevalent amongst women, excluded minorities, those under dictatorships and totalitarian regimes, people suffering under restrictions imposed by religious doctrines, and so many other situations of oppression.

'All of this matters. It is important for us to realise that it is not just the suppressors that need to change but those that feel that they have been suppressed. For those ones need to emerge from their shadows and find their voice and express who they are. We all have great gifts that need to be shared. Education is needed so people will be willing to believe in themselves.

'If those sensitive souls continue to prefer to exist, hidden in their own fear – fearing that conditions are not safe, and passively condoning abuses around them, rather than standing up for their rights to be who they are, then the inner thoughts of suffering, will perpetuate those conditions of oppression. And this produces darkness in the energy of the Earth. You can help each other. If enough people on Earth can stand in their light and joyfully be together, your world will be such a happier place than it is now.

That is what we wish.

'You can accomplish very little through fighting each other or by trying to contain or outdo each other. The way of Spirit is gentle and nurturing, appreciative and tolerant, balanced and harmonious. In a Spiritually based society, the sensitive ones will have pride of place, and be honoured. For they will channel what is most intrinsically precious for all to share, and through their presence, life will be worthwhile.

'The ambience of the new Earth is a place where it is not conflict, power plays and oppression that are central to your existence, but love and the knowing of interconnectedness. Sensitive souls are only too aware that this is what they want, and they need to reach out to claim this – if it is to come to pass.

'Thank you for shining your light with us and speaking your truth, Aurielle. You honour yourself by asserting yourself with all of us.'

Aurielle was glowing, and so pure in her energy. The depth of her being extended to sources beyond what I could see. It was with wonder that we could all observe her and what she brought to us. She had positioned herself next to Oiva, and the two of them were like soul sisters and they smiled together.

During her incarnations on Earth, Aurielle had embraced the feminine side of existence far more than the masculine, and now she had had to learn to bring those masculine qualities of strength and assertiveness into her being and express those so she could be more balanced and brave. On Earth, the masculine and feminine energies had become quite split and the male had tended to rule over the female. But these qualities were two branches of the same tree, and we needed to express both qualities equally, and with love, to be able to experience our wholeness.

Once more, we were silent, and the wonderful Spiritual vibrations around us held us, as we all went through our own reflections and healing. We were building the fabric of love between us, and it was becoming deeply clearer why each member had been chosen to be part of the group. The dynamics within our membership brought balance and the possibility, where we could all learn from each other.

PROTECTING LIFE ON EARTH

It was later. We had completed some further stages of our training together, and now, we were being granted some time away from the group, to rest, and attend to other matters. The group process had been very intense and I was ready for a break from it.

As was typical for me, when I had free space, I felt drawn to visit a nature area, where I could be with the energy formations of very beautiful, and majestic trees. Here, I enjoyed so much to experience the peace that emanated from these marvellous beings, and, I was glad that I could, for a while, enjoy being by myself. There was one tree, which I was very fond of, that I wanted to visit. I went straight to him and lay down at his base. The name of this tree was Cidell.

Trees were important to me, and I adored them. When I was by a tree, I could go deep within myself. I loved to feel the texture of their trunks, the curling contours of their roots and the wonderful sounds of rustling in their leaves, that accompanied a soft breeze. In the Spiritual world, the reality of this was so animated and concentrated. I just wanted to curl up as close to Cidell as I could, and revel in those feelings to the full.

The experience of being on the bleak world, where nearly all the trees had died, had been immensely distressing for me. I could recall from my journeys with Kendren and Zelda, just how being around the stumps of trees, when they no longer had any life force flowing through them, how empty and miserable that had felt. It was like something unreal and unnatural, something that should never happen.

As I sat, leaning against Cidell's spacious trunk, I could appreciate not only him, but all his relatives that grew on Earth. These were wonderful beings. Trees grew on Earth for a reason. They were teachers for us, and companions. The way they put their roots deep into the soil and reached up to the sky, providing shelter and oxygen for our world, and food for many animals and other life forms – they were very important on the Earth, and deserved to be honoured.

Being in this environment, I became quiet. I was aware of the subtle aura of loving Spiritual creation all around me, like an unceasing vibration. It was so awe inspiring and amazing, I felt humble before it.

As I sat there, I felt moved to pray and release my heart wishes to the loving divine creator. In this silence, I wanted to call upon inner help for the success of our mission, and asked and pleaded for the strength so that I could play my part responsibly and well. My thoughts were also with the others, and I prayed for them too, and their efforts. After dwelling on this, I extended my prayer, and asked for help for our precious Earth and humanity. While I did this, I could feel my heart expanding, and higher beings descending closer, listening, and responding to my pleas.

The energy of Cidell was very comforting. I sensed that his roots had moved slightly to accommodate me, and to encourage me, while I meditated and prayed, and I cherished that. Now, I opened myself to guidance. As I listened inwardly, I could hear Cidell whispering to me, in his deep well-formed rumble.

Cidell was not a projection, but a living soul-being, that was linked to the physical world of the Earth, and trees that were there. Every living being on Earth, whether that be human, animal, plant or mineral, had a corresponding energy form which existed in the Spiritual Realms, an eternal form that was lovingly whole and exquisite. Many of these beautiful Spiritual beings, corresponding to life forms on Earth, were situated in the Earth Dome. But some, like Cidell, chose to live more independently, in places where they wanted to be.

Now, as I listened to Cidell, he was thanking me for my intentions to help the transformation of the Earth. He reminded me how trees are sacred beings that cared for humans and wanted to nourish them. As humans, we had a duty to look after our brothers and sisters, the trees, as well as all other life forms, and they in turn would look after us. If people on Earth could only open their eyes and hearts, they would not want to do anything else with trees, but to love them, and to offer gratitude for all that they gave.

I could certainly feel with what Cidell was telling me, but there was something else, too, that he wanted to convey. Slowly my mind opened, as I linked in with Cidell, and I began to experience the condition of the collective state of all trees on Earth. I could sense that what I was about to see, would not be very pleasant. There was a part of me that wanted to look away, but I couldn't.

Our friends, the trees, were not in a healthy state on Earth. They were struggling, and many of them had been decimated. As I tuned in with Cidell, I could hear their agonised cries and suffering. Even in the Spirit World, where there was so much understanding and love pervading everything, the feeling associated with what was happening to the trees, was incredibly disturbing. How could human beings allow these beautiful and precious beings to die and be ruthlessly cut down? I wanted to stop people doing this – immediately.

And as I thought of the trees, my thoughts began to widen to other life forms on Earth. There was a thread where my focus awakened and I began to tune in, not only to the trees, but also the animals, the plants and minerals. All these life forms mattered. I had to study them and find out how they were doing on Earth now? What needed to be done to help them?

When I thought about the mission to Earth that I was about to undertake, I wondered where my attention should be, so that I could make the maximum difference? From my gentle reverie, I was becoming more alert now, and actively seeking knowledge of these topics.

All at once, I was not snuggled up by Cidell's roots anymore – I found myself in the Earth Dome. And I was exploring expanses of the Dome where I had not been before.

Within the Earth Dome, there were spiritual libraries, where records of all forms of life that had ever been on Earth, were preserved. The essence of life forms could be experienced here, including the spiritual forms of all animals, plant life, and minerals that existed on Earth, now.

It was strange to me, how I suddenly came to be in these libraries, for I had not set out the intention to be here. However, being in this location, connected to my thoughts, and I was eager to proceed.

Now, as I explored the possibilities in my mind, I felt very drawn to the realm of the animal kingdoms. It was as though I was being pulled there. In the space of some short moments, I had gone from a place of restful and tranquil comfort next to the trunk of a delightful tree, to being in a very compelling chamber within the Earth Dome. I wondered if other forces were directing me here.

The reality of the immense chamber opened as I entered, and there were corridors stretching out in front of me, with the Spirits of so many animal forms, everywhere. The energy, strengths and characteristics of all the animals were evident, and even the sense of how they related to other forms of life on Earth.

I marvelled at all the animals that I saw. There were even dinosaurs, with their colourful feathers. And some of them were huge. I wanted to reach out to touch them, and I knew that I could, here in the Spiritual Realm, and the animals would never hurt me. I was safe here. It was a wondrous place to explore. Wherever I put my attention, there was more. And I could go as deeply into the experience of each animal consciousness that I chose.

As I moved on, the patterns of these wonderful animal representations, extended through immeasurable epochs of history. When I directed my perception to specific questions, this would bring forth further streams of knowledge. It was fascinating, and there was so much that I could learn with this. If I wasn't careful, I could easily become completely absorbed in all the details of animal forms stretching in numerous directions of history.

However, I had a specific aim, and it was not the past that I wanted to explore, but the present. I wanted to be situated in present time, and be with the Spiritual forms of those animals, still alive in the world today. And by stating this intention clearly in my mind, I zoomed ahead.

In a moment, I was there, viewing enormous vistas, that revealed the animals of the present epoch to me. All around me, there were the recognisable expressions of so many million forms of animals. I could feel the distinctive essence of love that each of these animals expressed, and the sacred contribution, which they were all seeking, in their own ways, to make upon our planet. They all had unique qualities, and they danced together in a movement of wholeness. There were also emotions with these animals. Some of them wanted to speak to me, and I felt as though many of them wanted to communicate with me, all at once. And because of this, I could hardly distinguish their individual thought forms. I told them to be quiet. They would need to elect one or two animals to speak for all. At this moment, I stopped, to centre myself, and tune in

There was a stirring of the animals, and they asked me to look deeply to a selection of them, to discern what was happening to them on Earth. So, I did that. However, I felt some anxiety about doing this, so I took some moments to centre myself and to be ready.

With each of the animal beings, it was possible to observe their potential destiny, and the Spiritual plan of how their evolution may be expected to unfold, going into the future. But this was where all was not well. And this is what the animals had been clamouring to tell me. There was a huge deviation between what had been meant to happen, and what was taking place. And so many of these animals were having their destinies cut short, by the actions of humans.

As I gazed in more depth at this, I could perceive numerous animal species that appeared faded and withdrawn in their energy output. These were ones that were struggling for survival on our present-day Earth, and they were not supposed to be struggling. Hardly any of the animals were flourishing. And when I opened my heart to this, I noticed how the animals were reacting. They were not happy. The emotion that I could feel from these animals was one of despair and sadness. For all the animals had a lot to give and contribute to our planet Earth, and they were not being respected or being given the chance to express themselves. Humans had killed so many of them, and taken away the grounds where they could live, that it gave those members of the animal kingdom little chance. All these animals had the potential to be able to peacefully co-exist with humans, if humans would respect them, and if they would be prepared to support the existence of the animals. It was a precious opportunity that was being cruelly lost.

The animals were all magnificent sacred beings. They had beautiful qualities about them that could gladden the human heart, if only people would appreciate them.

As I listened, it was like a cacophony of sound that sang out in protest. They did not want people to kill them – we had to change this way of relating to our animal friends. It was not right for the animals to lose their place of life on the Earth. This could not go on.

When I considered this, and widened my interest to the other kingdoms, the stones and minerals, and the plant kingdoms, the air beings, and the subtler nature Spirits, there were parallels of distress for all the kingdoms of life. They were all suffering. There was not enough respect given by humans, to any of these kingdoms.

I could feel in my heart, the sorrow of the animals, the plants and the minerals. It was a pain, that was heavy inside me. They did not want to hurt people, or be vindictive in any manner. All they wished, was for people to care for them. As the members of the Nature kingdoms communicated to me now, it was as if they were speaking to all humans, not just me. It was not my wish to hurt the kingdoms of nature, in any way.

As I was before them, I paused, and I asked the question of what I could do. In response, I was shown a map, with areas of the Earth highlighted, where activities were persisting that went acutely contrary to the Earth's highest good. I considered these, and then more and more areas showed themselves to me. It did not stop. And then, then as I concentrated further, the number of places requiring support multiplied. There were so many areas upon the Earth, where the nature kingdoms needed help. They were all impressing themselves upon me, coming at me faster and faster.

It was like a crying need. I could not take it all in. So, so much needed to be done. I had to slow this down. Slowly, I stepped back. I had to have space, to come, again, into myself.

Thoughts came into my mind, with ideas, of contributions that I could make, how I could help bring Earth life back into balance. There were many, many options, and I started to go through these. I wanted to consider the possibilities that had been given to me from the maps, and so, I persevered with my analysis of this. It was necessary for me to be away from the Earth Dome, for me to do this. I needed my own peace, where I could consider all this, with clear thought. In a moment, then, I was in a small meditation chamber filled with quiet blue light. That was perfect.

It was important for me to get started, make my plans, work out what I would do on Earth. These kingdoms of Nature, needed so much help. I had to find my way with this. Using my spiritual mind, I could place myself in numerous possible Earth situations, simultaneously. Hence, I projected my soul inwardly to many of the Earth places, that had featured on the maps, so I could imagine how I would react and what I would do.

I had my own capabilities, which needed a good 'fit,' so that I could be useful and successful with my aims. It took much work and concentration, to go through all the places and scenarios that had been given to me. I explored each option in my heart, tested them, and at the end of it all, I was still not convinced that I had found the right one.

Then I sighed. I could not do this on my own. It was necessary to combine my energies and concerns with those of the other members of my Spiritual working group. I would have to present these possibilities to them. That is how I had to do it. We were a team. Our path was to act together.

All at once, from behind me, I sensed the familiar, loving presence of someone approaching me, and it was my beloved guide, Astoris. At first, I did not want to give my focus to him, for I was still occupied with what I had been doing. But the power of his energy field gradually drew my attention, until I turned around. And I was delighted to see him.

Astoris was pleased with me, with what I was studying, and all my efforts. He also praised my commitment. It was necessary to plan for the mission very carefully. Now was the space to put our energy into this, and for the group to become set to act. There was an emergence taking place for all members of the training group, where specific preparations for the actual mission could begin. The others had been studying too. All of them were also beginning to get ready.

It occurred to me to ask Astoris if the urge to do this study within the Libraries of the Earth Dome, whether this had been implanted in me by him, or other higher beings? My teacher smiled wistfully, and he confirmed that this was so. Similar thoughts had been placed in the minds of all the others from the group, and they had found their own places to consider the mission.

I knew then, how we were never completely alone with our thoughts, and could be so easily influenced. However, Astoris assured me that these thought implantations were not intended to coerce us. The prompting and direction I had been given, and the others too, was only what was already in the depths of our souls, anyway. The Higher beings wanted us to study and begin our preparation. We were needed, and the Earth needed us, very soon, to embark on our mission.

The Higher beings were working with us, and I valued their loving support.

I wondered how much of our mission would be framed by higher beings, rather than our own thoughts and visions? Astoris could perceive what I was thinking. He smiled, and reminded me how the reality of our perception had many multidimensional elements to it, and that we were all interconnected. So, if we tuned in correctly, what we would be choosing to do together in our mission, would be bringing many forces and higher designs into manifestation, from numerous levels of consciousness. It just needed for us to come together with love, and for the right reasons, and for the highest good of humanity, and our beloved planet, Earth.

Astoris informed me that we may not know all that our mission would entail, before we went into it. Mainly, it would be the beginning elements that we would need to plan, and how we would come together. Like the experience of the Bleak world, it would work best for us and all those around us if we would open to the surprise of what unfolded, just giving our heart, and all we could, to every experience that manifested. The variabilities of life on Earth were very volatile, and could not be fixed too precisely. But we would need to discuss all this, and gather as a group, and the occasion for us to do that was forming now.

PREPARING FOR OUR MISSION

In many ways, our preparations for incarnation for our 'mission' life was like other spiritual planning sessions, that those of us from Earth, had been through before. We had to consider options as to where we would be best placed in terms of location, the conditions of our birth, our parents and genetic influences, and how our young lives were likely to be formed. We would need to plan this individually, but also in consultation with the others in the group, and those higher beings watching over us. This was all a process that I had been through many times before, and was quite familiar to me. However, there were important differences, and Astoris wanted to explain about those.

He started. 'Normally when souls charted their forthcoming incarnations, much was set up beforehand. Meetings with other souls, potential learning situations and karmic conditions – all this established a likely pathway for that soul to follow. The soul had free will to determine how he or she reacted to circumstances that were present. However, much was mapped out in Spirit, to help the soul stay within parameters that are appropriate to that soul's development.

'With your mission, there will be another focus. What we will do is to help you to set up signals and recognition tools so you can sub-consciously recognise each other, and maybe a small number of other souls that could be instrumental in your work. However, there will be no preset plan for you. All you will have, is the inner knowing of your mission, and the inclinations to connect with each other. All else will be up to you. It will help you to remain as inwardly open to Spirit as you can. We will work out some possibilities with you, of where your work may be most effective, and you can follow into one or more of these pathways, when the timing for this arises. But you will not be on Earth to undergo any course of soul learning, for your soul agenda will be about service to the Earth and humanity, and that alone. There will be no karmic restrictions placed upon you. Your mission will be to help as many people as you can, to awaken their consciousness, and to heal places on the Earth that need it. We will be encouraging you to work together. Even when you are away from the others, there will still be work for you to do, and one of your tests will be, to act with strength on your own, as well as when you are united together.

'With the general population, how others you meet react to you, all this will be up to them. You will have no special protection. And you will need to use your wits and intuition to care for yourselves. By having signals of recognition between you set up, you will know each other, and be drawn to each other. Collective action will be your best chance of success, for then, you will be setting examples to other people, by being models – through your interconnectedness – for others on Earth to follow. To elaborate on this, those you meet will also be free to interact with you as they please, so it is possible that they could awaken their consciousness to love others and the living Earth through meeting you, they could be indifferent, or they could also become hostile if they do not want to change their ways. You can only be true to your hearts, serve others, and seek help with each other and from Spirit. While you remain open, then your lights will shine brightly, and other souls on Earth will notice that, even if they are not consciously aware of it. Spirit will be at hand to bring you home here if conditions become too traumatic for you. If you are faltering and need our peace and love, then call on us.

'What you must remember is that you will be part of a mass movement that is urging humanity to waken up and experience the love and truth existing in its heart. Anything you can do towards that, as catalysts for that to take place, will be helpful.

'One important thing that you need to be aware of, is that every soul on Earth is carrying that seed of potential awakening to Spiritual awareness and knowing the interconnectedness of life. It is in the programming of human souls, now, to have that seed within. So, whatever the pathway, souls have chosen for their lives on Earth, there is that possibility of transformation, that could occur, and radically alter how that soul will relate to the world. Whether a soul is young or old, that awakening could manifest. All those seeds are there, and they need nurturing and nourishing to grow, rather than remaining dormant and unused.

'Once you get on track, you could be amazed at the support and help that you will receive. Trust in this and proceed with your passion. The Earth is ready for the kind of transformation you want to bring about. You only need to activate it, and facilitate conditions, so that resistances to it can be overcome.

'You are going to be Earth Warriors, and voices for Spirit, on Earth, fighting for the Earth's survival and its future peace. You can still decide now, if you have any doubts about doing this? Let me know and you can withdraw. Check in your hearts now and tell me'.

We all did what Astoris asked. He checked with us one by one. In my own heart, as he put this to me, I felt a bubbling of joy and determination. There was absolutely no doubt in my heart; I felt ready and wanted to proceed. As he went around the circle, all the others felt similarly. We were united in our dedication. Soon we would be ready to go.

'Good then,' Astoris retorted. 'Let us do it.'

SETTING UP

It did not take us long to begin our actual tasks of preparation for incarnation, although the kind of procedures we needed to undergo were quite intricate. As we started to consider the home environments that would be most suitable for us, and the families that we would be born into, we had many debates about what would be most appropriate. We wanted to be careful too, with the genetic traits that we would inherit from the body we chose, and the society that would be around us in our formative years. All this needed to be very carefully thought through, and agreed collectively. We were determined to get this part of our journey right, and to ensure that the conditions of our upbringing would propel us in the best way for us to move forward and to meet up later, and not impede us in any way.

Although I had been through these kinds of processes many times previously, this time *did* feel different, and I noticed that I was much more meticulous than I had ever been previously. Now I was taking a high degree of responsibility for the choices I made, for I had motives that went beyond me.

After such a build-up, I felt rather nervous, but at the same time, resolute, and I did not want to make any mistakes. It was good to have the others there, and the High Beings, assisting our decision making.

What I liked in this spiritual preparation chamber, was the atmosphere of reverence and sanctity that over-arched all that we did. With the presence of the very high beings that were amongst us, although their energy was so subtle that I could not see them, I could feel their vibrations in my heart. Their energy filled me with wonder and reminded me that I was doing God's work, and I needed to be true to that, in all my actions and planning.

It was so useful that we had had that projection experience in the bleak world together, for referring to that, formed a base, which in many ways, we could work from, especially in planning the potential relationships that we could share with each other. Those relationships could develop more strongly now, in the incarnations that we would be soon entering. The patterns of our relationships together would have some similarities with what we had in the Bleak world, but there would be some important differences too.

I went through what Astoris had told us, to process it. In terms of our intentions, our basic motivations would much the same as they were in the bleak world – we wanted to act together, and help. This time though, it was for real – the contour of what we would meet in our lives together, were not set out for us, as our efforts in the bleak world experience had been. I looked around at the others. They were all busy. I loved them all. 'We can do this,' I urged to myself. And then I refocussed on what I was doing.

While we all worked, Astoris busied himself going from one to the other of us, and sometimes addressing all of us collectively. At times, I noticed that he was absent, and he informed us of this, that his work consisted also, of coordinating with other groups of souls that were also in a state of preparation for missions. He had to ensure that there would be no duplication, and that plans for the many that were about to embark on Earth missions, would be complementary.

There were three pairs in our group, Oiva and Deli, Santi and Ormond, plus Aurielle and myself. Each pair was given an inner task in relation to the other one of that pair, so we would work in pairs to support and care for each other, as well as looking out for each other within the whole group. The individuals in each pair were quite harmonising with each other, and this was thought to be a means of adding stability to our group. I was delighted to be working with Aurielle on this. We had meetings about how we could combine our energies, and at what age we would meet, in the lifetimes we were choosing. From there, we also needed to plan how we would meet with the others. It was quite complex and we needed to attune carefully to arrive at workable solutions.

I was choosing a family structure where I did not know any of the souls within it, so that my attachment to them would be minimal. Then, I would be able to move on easily to my work when the time was right. My challenge would be to keep my heart open, and find what would inspire me, independently, from an early age. I had to keep my senses and awareness alive, and be careful that I would not withdraw too much from others. My aim, was that I wanted to be a model for people, to be able to develop heartfelt independence of thought and action, a sense of inner freedom.

For Aurielle, in contrast, she wanted to be with gentle souls as parents – souls that she did know well. From this base, she could receive emotional sustenance in her youth, to help her to be able to commune sensitively and warmly with others. Then she could expand this with others outside her family, when the time came to do that. Her challenge was for her not to become too cosy within her family structure, because of the uncertainties that existed around her, but for her to be willing to move beyond this, when it was right to do this. For her, what was important, was to help others to find within them, the capacity to awaken to the reality of our interconnectedness, and feel higher love, and to be brave enough to admit this. We were like opposites, but both sides of what we wanted to express could combine in a wholeness.

The process of planning what we wanted to do, and how we would do it, and how it could fit together – working through so many options, possibilities and complex scenarios – this took many conversations and negotiations amongst us, and we did not always agree, initially. It was a very involved task that had so numerous different aspects to it. Gradually, we could place pieces together. And it was a great relief, when, at last, we found a balance that was settled, and we all felt a measure of peace.

At this point, we prayed, and we were still, together. The time of departure for us, to go forth, from the Spirit World, was approaching now. We had prepared as much as we could.

THE FINAL CIRCLE

Once everything had been arranged and set, I went with the others to the Earth Dome. We all wanted to tap into those Spiritual energies supporting the Earth, once more, before we went on our mission. The love in my heart expanded as I saw the Earth Dome again, and it was as if we opened our collective being, to feel one with this magnificent manifestation. So many souls were here working and helping. It was such a mammoth project. And now, I was so fortunate to be able to fulfil my dream, and work directly, on the physical plane, and be one of those ones, striving to make a positive contribution, towards protecting and preserving our beloved Earth. Being here was just the start. We had our plan. Now, we were ready to put that into action.

Our willingness to help, was about to be tested on the physical Earth, and it would only be, once my incarnation was finished, that I would be able to feel, if I really had done all that I set out to do – or not. But this was not just about me. My concerns went beyond the personal, for I knew that I would only feel completely at peace, when I knew that the Earth was safe, and through her Spiritual transition – and that was far from certain at this stage.

As I gazed around me, I could witness the joy and expectancy on the faces of my companions – we were all on the brink of such an important opportunity. Astoris was with us as always, but he stood back, to allow us a sense of group unity, to nurture our togetherness, and to nourish our Spiritual connection with our Earth being. It was soon going to be our time to depart from the Spiritual Realms.

Before this though, we would come together in our usual meeting place, and gather for one last time, in advance of our descent to the material plane. By now, we had been thoroughly briefed about the latest conditions of the planet, and what we could be best expected to do, to help. Everyone was committed, although there was some uncertainty and excitement among us. How could we be tranquil in a moment like this?

For Oiva and Deli, this would be their very first incarnations upon the Earth. Oiva was not used to the density of vibrations, which she would find on Earth, or the rough and tumble of how people there would relate to each other. She had chosen a mild, protected upbringing scenario, to hopefully shield her from excesses, that could damage her. And Deli would be close by. The anxiety in her was palpable. But she had a very important role, and she knew it. Her reasons for attending this mission were not just about Earth, but the many other worlds that would be affected by how humanity on the Earth progressed. She was with us because she cared. Her vital gift was the fine and sensitive love in her energy field, – a love that extended to worlds and beings, far beyond us. When she was on the physical plane, it was her intention to help ground these vibrations on Earth.

For the rest of us, the atmosphere around the circle was also intense, with a strong feeling of unity and love. We would be there to support each other, but also acting alone. Our task was to be like mediators, to help build that bridge of Spirituality for humanity to awaken. None of us would forget the Spiritual place from where we had come, and our intuitions would guide us to be where we needed to be. I prayed fervently that those souls on Earth which we met, would listen to us.

With our human emotions, we would not be immune from feeling acute sadness and despair, if others rejected us. But that must not distract us. The responsibility that bound us and motivated us each, individually, in our pairs, and in our larger group, was simply, to serve. I could feel that we were all thrilled to be finally starting our mission. As I turned to Aurielle, I wanted us, as a pair, to do our job well. Our thoughts were in unison, and we both smiled.

Soon we would begin our downward journey, and our energy would contract, as we prepared for our entries into those physical bodies that we had chosen. I did feel a ping of trepidation, but was eager to proceed. Before we left each other, we opened ourselves to a beautiful, collective, loving, energetic hug. I felt this to be very calming for us all.

Astoris had some closing words to reinforce what we had been doing in our preparations.

'At the outset,' he told us, 'your souls will be entering into the physical body of a foetus. You will be combining with the genetic imprints of that foetus, and this will give you attributes and inclinations that will bond you with the family ancestry of those with whom you will become part. You must remember who you are as souls. Use the attributes from the genetic coding to give you strength and a foundation from which you can build. But do not let it determine you. We will support you to an extent with impulses and thoughts that we can project your way, but you must assert your own Self in these conditions, so that you can attune to your mission. Some of you have been through incarnations, many times before, on Earth, but this time, it is imperative that you do not get caught up in smaller concerns that are not 'you'. The first step, as you grow, will be for you to disentangle yourself from any family traits that do not serve you, so, more and more, inwardly, you can connect with your soul. As you do this, your appreciation and passion for your task on Earth, will strengthen. Be confident, and work with each other as well as you can. For all of you, there are events that we have programd with you, to help you get started. However, once you have reached those points, there will be no more clues or footsteps that we have set in advance. The path ahead of you then, will be of your own making, and you must be alert to the signs that we in Spirit, will give you, to assist you. May Divine light and love guide you and nourish you every step of your way. May you serve the highest good for both our beloved Earth being, and all life forms associated with it.'

We could all feel the power of the advice Astoris was giving us, and the invocation that he voiced for our mission. The light of Spirit streamed down at us. For some moments, we were there in silence together. But not too long.

There was no chance to linger, and hardly any opportunity to actively do any more together, for suddenly, we were being ushered to those energetic cubicles that would propel us towards physical incarnation. I felt startled, hardly able to believe that this moment had come. And I guess that there was a part of me, wanting to hang on, when I needed to let go, but there was no turning back now, so for the last time, I swung around and wished all my companions success and well-being. Then, I faced the direction of my travel and braced myself.

My thoughts went to our guide and teacher, Astoris. Although he had given us this final advice, he had not joined us in our group hug, and he stayed a little detached from us, or so it seemed. Why had he chosen to remain in the background? It was odd, and I felt also uneasy that he had not said goodbye to us in a manner that I would have expected – his last address was so formal. After everything that we had shared with him, I rather wished that he would be coming too. But he had given no indications of that. In my heart, I felt sadness.

As these feelings developed, I felt how precious Astoris had been for me, and all of us. He had given himself, wholeheartedly, to helping our group bond, and for us to be able to learn together. With my own personal journey, I could never thank him enough for all that he had done for me, not only now, but over so many lifetimes.

I recalled how he had been helping with all our preparations, and liaising with others, that were supporting us. But I did not see him make any preparations, in any way, to join us. This made me think that he would not be coming. So, I wondered, with some disappointment, what he would be doing, while we were engaged in our mission. I would miss him.

And as my thoughts continued to dwell upon him, I could feel his presence. In an instant, he was there with me, and checking that I was completely ready. He was reassuring as always. It was so matter of fact though, focusing on the practical side of things. Of course, he could pick up my thoughts. So, in the next moments, he gave me a full loving embrace, like I would have wished from him. The embrace of his energy was very comforting – but somehow, this still left me unsatisfied.

I could not help it, but I had to ask him. 'What will you do?'

Astoris paused, and gave me a knowing smile. 'You better keep your eyes open,' he told me. What could he have meant by that? He continued to check that all my energy systems were in place, and he went through with me again, some procedural tasks that I would have to do, while integrating with the physical body I had chosen. It was all sorted out in my mind, but it was good to check everything thoroughly, and make sure. Then suddenly, I felt his attention fully with me.

His huge energy body was hovering over me. I would soon be going; this seemed too late, but his Sprit eyes were penetrating mine, and it was, as if he could perceive every element of my being. I trusted him, and welcomed him to be so close with me, but part of me was on edge.

Then, in an instant he smiled, and it was like, he gave me a wink of encouragement, and affection. I felt that my heart was melting at that. It was a relief, and I relaxed a little. My channels to him were opening right up. That was when he spoke to my mind.

'I will see you there,' he told me simply. Then he was gone.

Part 4

The Mission

FORMATIVE YEARS

The name I had been given was David. I lived in a small house, in a satellite town, on the edge of the city, with my mother, father and my younger sister, Emma. We lived a simple life, perhaps a bit too simple in some ways, for my taste. There was something in me, from as early as I could remember, that wanted something different, than what I could experience in my home environment.

Now, as a teenager, I was staring out of the window of our living room, kneeling forwards on our old settee, so I could get the best view that I could. It was a position that I had adopted so many times during my growing up years. I always liked to know what was going on outside. There was not much to see, but doing this connected me with memories, and I wanted to be reminded of those former times.

When I was a young boy, I had been able to look out of that window, into open fields. I loved the beauty of the nature. On the opposite side of the road, there had been a line of trees, tall trees with thick layers of leaves that used to rustle in the wind. And I remembered how I could open the window, and hear an abundance of birdsong. Such a lot of birds descended upon those trees. In the early mornings and before sunset, they had made such a racket. I enjoyed it, and the sound of their noise, was comforting, somehow.

When my mother went out with the dog, I would go with her across the road, and we would wind our way along the track, to the meandering river, that flowed past the gate, at the end of the pasture. It was a wonderful walk. Our dog, Peter, would always go in the water, and then, as much as I tried to avoid it, he would come over right next to me to shake himself dry, when he came out. There were lots of places where he could shake himself, and I tried to persuade him to go somewhere else. However, he seemed to prefer nothing better than to shake his fur right next to me. I suppose it was a sign of his devotion. So, that was the way how Peter got dry, and I got wet.

It was one of those things that I thought would never change. And I smiled to think about it. Peter was such an affectionate dog, and he used to lick me, and wag his tail when he saw me. I loved to pat him, and tickle him under his chin. Whenever I did that, he nudged me, and he wanted more and more, until I finally lost patience, and moved my hand away.

We sometimes had picnics by the river, and I would throw stones in the water. I always felt peaceful when I was there, and the sound of the water, washing over the rocks, was incredibly restful. There was such a lot of wildlife, which we would see, not only birds, but animals, that would scurry between the riverbank trees, and tadpoles and insects that moved by the shallows of the water. The place was teeming with life, and I took great interest in everything that I could see. I enjoyed being there very much.

In those early days, Emma, would be with us, in the pram. Sometimes, my mother was kind, and she would let me direct the pram. Those were fun times, and I would not ever forget them.

Then one day, it all changed. I wish it hadn't, but it did.

I was still in bed, and my mother came in, looking at me very sadly. She told me that the government had decided to upgrade the road outside our place, and build offices on the other side of the road. I did not know what she meant. She couldn't be talking about our road? I questioned her. But the more she explained, the more it became clear that she did mean our road. That couldn't be right. Who was this government? And I tried to dismiss what she told me. But she insisted that she was telling me the truth. I didn't want to believe her. However, whatever I wanted, the reality was different. Like it or not, our peaceful times were over.

It was only a few days later, and there were machines and diggers and road work signs arriving. That was when all the construction work and development began. At first, I had been interested in all the machinery and curious about what would happen, but I felt apprehensive, and fearful as well.

I watched through the window, for hours on end. My concern was strongest around the roadside trees. The men were clearing all the vegetation around the trees, and marking their trunks with paint. Those poor trees. They seemed increasingly isolated and desolate. somehow. I feared for their safety.

When I went to bed that night, I prayed that they would be alright. I believed in prayer. Surely, nothing could happen to them. They were like friends to me, such precious trees. However, they were not alright. I didn't know it yet, but they had been condemned.

It was a couple of days later, and I will never forget that morning, I woke up with a start, to a tremendous screeching sound of a chain saw. The shock of it went right through me, like a tremor. I got straight up, and went to the window. Outside, I could see that they were cutting down the trees. I was certain that the trees were in pain, and the sound of the chain saws was so irritating and loud They had a very cruel sound.

I put my hands to my ears, and wanted to scream at the machinery to stop. Where would the birds go? I could hardly bear to watch. And I could see some of the birds flying around in confusion, as their perches were dismantled. I felt helpless to be able to do anything. I called for my mum in desperation, and she came in and cuddled me.

During that day, I cried many, many tears, and I pleaded with my mum to go and speak to those workers. All she did, was to look despairingly at the wall. She didn't do anything – she didn't think that she could do anything. For in her mind, she felt powerless. Because it was what the government wanted. And the more she tried to argue that with me, the more I started to dislike the government and wish that they would just go away. I did not understand.

Surely having beautiful trees was better than a wider road. What was this government trying to do? I felt like I wanted to protest to them and tell them what I thought. I kept on asking my mum, until she got cross with me. And I felt let down by my mother, for I wanted, more than anything else, to help the trees. I tried to go outside, and walk across the road to the men, so I could talk to them, but my mother stood in front of the door, and she wouldn't let me out, even when I struggled to squeeze past her.

The next day, when I looked out, there was just stumps. Without the trees, the ground on the other side of the road looked forsaken, wounded and barren. The birds must have gone to find some other trees, for there was no sign of them anymore, and I missed their lively songs terribly. Instead, there was the horrible smell of tar, and the constant noise of the diggers. The workers were laying the new road. And the traffic dribbled along outside our place, in one lane. We couldn't even go out to the river anymore, for there was no place where we could cross the road, and the track that we used, was fenced off. Instead, we had to take Peter along the streets and houses behind us for his daily exercise, and that was not nearly as nice.

And so, the construction and development went on, and more and more, the beautiful fields that I used to admire, were covered over with buildings, concrete and roads – and the nature that I loved, retreated further and further away. I kept watching, but I did not like what I saw.

It hadn't been that long after they built the road, when Peter had got sick, and he stopped eating his food. He was just lying in the corner, raising his head a little, but not doing anything else. I had tried to get him up, but he wouldn't move. He was an old dog. However, I couldn't imagine my life without him. So, my parents took him to the Vets, and they tried to give him some medicines. I patted Peter and asked my angels to help him.

I still believed in my angels, even though they didn't stop the workers across the road, for I felt peace when I thought of them, and I knew they were with me. They did help with Peter too, because I could feel the heat in my hands that the Angels gave me. When I touched Peter with my hands, it gave him energy, for a little while.

I thought that Peter might be giving up, because his world had been taken away. And if Peter was like that, what would have happened to all the other birds and animals? During those days, I resisted to go to school, and argued with my mum, for I wanted to be by Peter's side, but my mother insisted that I go.

One day, after I got home, Peter lifted his head and looked straight at me, with his soulful eyes. In my mind, I could hear Peter talking to me and telling me that he was still there. I did not want him to die. But I couldn't stop it.

The next day, the thing that I most feared, happened. When I arrived from school, Peter wasn't anywhere to be seen. He had been taken to the Vets and put to sleep. I howled when I realised what had happened. I banged at the wall in frustration, until my dad made me stop.

Later that week, we buried Peter's body in our back yard. We had a little ceremony, and we were all very sad. Even my sister, Emma cried. I felt that Peter's Spirit was there watching us, but that was little consolation. The loss of him in my life, was like a big hole in my heart, and after that, my life felt much emptier.

Without Peter, and the wonderful nature that I had known, the fun had gone out of my life. As I got older, when I looked out of the window, what I could see was a big row of office blocks on the other side of the street, and the road was much wider, and full of vehicles. The buildings were all smart and tidy, but they felt 'dead' somehow. Behind the office blocks, there were rows of houses, and I couldn't even see the river anymore.

When I opened the window, all I could hear, was the noisy whining of Lorries, as they piled along the road, with never ending congestion. The diesel fumes from their exhaust pipes made me cough. I could not avoid them though, for I had to go out in the street, amid those fumes, every week day. That was the way I had to go, to walk to school and back, at the end of the day.

Before the Lorries came along, I didn't have asthma, but afterwards, I needed inhalers, and at times, I struggled to breathe. Every time a lorry would drive past me, I felt tense, for I knew that I was being poisoned by those fumes, and I didn't like it, and could not understand why it had to be like that. Inwardly, I continued to protest, and I blamed this government for what they had done.

SCHOOL

I was told that the reason we went to school was to learn, but I did not agree with everything we had to learn at school. It did not all seem right, somehow.

There was one teacher we had, Mrs Bilych, and she taught us about building roads and communities, like what had happened in our town. She explained about the Government and praised what they were doing. Building roads and houses was called 'development,' and it was what our society needed. The more development we had, the more our society would progress and all this would lead to economic prosperity. Our government wanted to build a stronger nation.

I was not convinced. Listening to her talk, I felt a pain in my heart. To me, all this development seemed very destructive, not at all like progress. I could just feel the suffering of the trees and animals, who had lost their homes. It was not fair. I wanted to find a better way.

Once, I dared to ask my teacher why they had to cut down the trees? Couldn't the roads find somewhere else to go? My teacher must have seen the tears in my eyes, but she dismissed it, and just replied that all the roads were necessary, for the cars and Lorries to drive on. How would we get around if we didn't have roads? Without good roads, our economy would no longer grow. And that was what mattered to her. But not to me. I felt very isolated with my thoughts.

At home, I liked to go on my computer, and I was learning how to use the Internet. I started doing some research about these Lorries. I came across some sites that were about renewable energy. There were energy sources, which could run those Lorries – with no pollution – much better for the environment. Why were the Lorries that were passing through our town, not using those technologies? Surely, this was a healthier way, so I wouldn't have to breathe those fumes? Even the office blocks could have been set up in different positions – they did not have to be set up where the trees had been, and taking away the lovely walk to the river. Why did the government prefer for us to have Lorries that poisoned the air, and made such loud noises? I did not understand. I did not feel that my life was better because of having a big road outside – for me it was much worse.

When I went to school, we had to obey our teachers and do what they told us to do. We were taught basic skills and it was prescribed what we had to learn and how we would learn it. I did not like to have to do what I was told.

There was just one teacher, Mr Piper, that was different. He taught us literature. Mr Piper did not seem so much to follow the rules, and he encouraged us to think for ourselves. He was a bit of an eccentric, with wild hair and elongated limbs. He wore colourful clothes, while the other teachers wore outfits that looked so drab and uninteresting. I used to love going to his classes. I used to put my hand up and ask him lots of questions, and he winked at me, and he always tried to answer honestly. The other children were not kind to him though, and used to tease him and talk over him. But I always felt happier when I had been with him. Then one day, I woke up feeling sad, and I did not know why. When I went to school that day, there was no sign of Mr Piper, anywhere. I never saw Mr Piper again, and nobody told us the reason that he stopped teaching us.

The other teachers just followed their curriculum and they all told us, like robots, that we had to learn, and do what they told us, because it was expected of us. We had to follow the system and the rules, because that was the Law. Then, if we completed all our exams, we may then get a good job, earn money, and contribute to society.

Who wanted to help build society in the way they described it? Not me. They didn't make life sound very exciting, and I didn't wish to live a life that was so grey, like them. I wondered if their plan was for us to reach the point, where we could help with developments, like what had happened outside our house. They would never force me to do that.

I was a bit of a loner with the other children at school. While I was sitting on my own, they would be in their groups or cliques, chatting away. What I noticed was that they seemed mainly occupied with their appearance, fashion, what programs were on television, the latest computer games, going out in the town. These kinds of things were of no interest to me. They wanted to be accepted by each other, and feel part of a group, but they would not dare to do things that would bring ridicule to themselves. Basically, they wanted to conform, and they were too afraid to step out of that. They would intimidate other children that did not follow in their ways. In effect, they were being just as controlling as the teachers, and they were modelling the teachers in the way they behaved with other children.

The children I knew in the school, did not quite seem alive to me – merely fitting in with what was going on around them. Most of the time, I watched them all, from a distance, and stayed out of their way. Nobody really knew what I thought, but inside, I felt like a rebel, for I did not want to live like anyone else there.

STEFAN

One day, I noticed another boy of around my age. He, also chose to be a little bit apart from the others, but he was watching what was going on. We caught each other's eye and started a conversation. His name was Stefan. He was glad to have some company. Stefan was a thinker, and I was very interested in what he had to say. He thought that people were becoming like machines, just doing what the Governments and big companies wanted. And what they wanted was to make big profits, and they did not care about people at all.

In Stefan's view, our education system was merely making people compliant and less free, so we were slaves to what the governments and big companies decreed. He didn't want to listen to these teachers any more than he had to do. His attitude was that if we were going to be free, then we had to stay outside of the teachings of the school, so we would not become victims of the system.

Stefan was a little shorter than me, with glasses. Over time, we became close friends, and in our break times, we stayed together. He was not in my class, but I wished he would be. Sometimes, when I was listening to our teacher droning on, I wanted only to get away. I forced myself to learn some things, but I did not wish to be conditioned.

I was very influenced by Stefan and his ideas. Nobody had spoken to me like he did. I admired him. Listening to him, I felt inspired to investigate through the Internet and find out more, what was really happening in the world. I did not feel satisfied with what our teachers told us. At school, when we went on the computers, we were restricted and very limited in what we could explore. It was quite frustrating, and our teachers were insistent upon us learning only what they had been instructed to teach us.

I went through the motions of what I was told to do at school, but saved my study of what interested me, until I got home, and then I could go online with nobody watching me. I enjoyed to do my own research. Stefan told me some sites where I could go on, but I soon branched out further, to what I wanted to explore. There was a whole world of knowledge on the Internet.

Topics that I wanted to explore, included the natural world, politics, sociology, religion and history. What I could gain from school did not go nearly far enough.

When we studied history, for instance, it all seemed to be about wars, and how one side was superior to the other, but this distressed me. In my opinion, what was important was not about how one nation could defeat another, and be the great victor. Nations were not better because they won a war. Often, the side that won all the wars, did terrible things to the people who had lost. Why should we glorify in that?

I was much more impressed to learn about people that had stood up for other people's rights, and been true to their values, great people that contributed positively to making the world a better place. Those people were like shining lights.

Rather than war, we needed to learn to embrace each other's differences and work together cooperatively, not in competition with one trying to outdo the other. We had to get beyond models of society, where most people were oppressed by authorities, who were selfish and greedy. Instead, we all needed to feel empowered and free, and able to look after our world together. I hardly knew where some of my ideas came from. However, I had to follow through with them, and research articles with those values. It was like a compulsion erupting from inside me – and I could feel that my angels were encouraging me.

As time went on, I gave less and less attention to my school curriculum, and spent my primary energy upon research, that I did on my own.

I tried to speak with my parents, and gauge their opinions about the situation in the world, but they did not have the same interest as me. Their view was that nothing could change, and we just had to get on with our lives. They had no ambition or aspiration. All they wanted to do was what they were supposed to do, and live their daily life, in a way that did not cause any trouble. They thought just like the teachers at school.

It did not seem to bother them anymore, about the office blocks that had been built. Their attitude was that we could not stop progress. I felt that they had resigned themselves to a world that did not serve them.

I also attempted to engage my sister, with conversation about the world, but she was too young to understand. All she wanted to do was to play. My father tried to persuade me to go to sports events with him, and watch television with him. But I did not want to do that. I felt as if I did not belong with these people. The only one that I had, was Stefan – he had been so helpful.

Stefan and I often had discussions about how we could change the people around us, and make them more open to our way of thinking. We had lots of ideas, but never did anything. I suppose that the rebellion we both felt, was mainly in our minds. The lack of action though, fed restlessness that I felt within me. I was yearning to move into an environment where I could express myself more freely and openly. I did not want to stay in this area, where I had grown up.

A NEW LIFE

When I reached the time of my final exams, I tried hard, so that I could qualify for going to University. I did not know how I would feel, being there, but I thought that it could be a ticket to a new life. Surely, there would be opportunities.

I had important decisions to make about what I would do. My father wanted me to become an accountant. He thought that, because I was good at mathematics, that this would be a secure job for me, where I could earn well, and buy a house and car, and be a good citizen. I could think of nothing worse. But without my father's support, I would not be able to go to University. I had to negotiate somehow.

At this stage, my thoughts about wanting to change the world, were quite vague. I did not know how I could possibly put my ideas into practice.

My life had been quite insular, and I felt cut off from being able to express who I truly was. I was not strong enough, or clear enough yet, to know my own mind. My angels urged me to be steadfast.

I argued with my father about the accountancy, and proposed to him that he support me to do an Arts degree, with many subjects, so it would give me a chance to find out what I really wanted to do in life. I put to him, that I would not like doing a job where I would be stuck in an office all day and dealing with figures, as I would be, as a trainee accountant. I would not be happy. My father disagreed. For him, there was nothing more important than getting a good job, and buying a home, and he told me this, repeatedly. Sometimes, we needed to put our own happiness second, so we could do the right thing.

I felt exasperated. For me, personal happiness was paramount, and had to come first. I was not going to give in. Eventually, my father agreed to support me, reluctantly, and I appreciated him for that.

When the day arrived, it felt strange leaving the family home – it was a chapter of my life that was over. Somehow, I knew that I would not look back. My family mattered to me, but they were different to me. The main person I would miss was my friend, Stefan.

I guessed that Stefan was more radical than me. He did not want to stay in the system any longer. Stefan had decided, that he was not going to University, and he told me that he wanted to travel, so he was going to look for some casual work, to be able to save up, and then head overseas. I felt that we were now going our separate ways, but I accepted that, and I could acknowledge our friendship and the support we had given each other, with affection.

UNIVERSITY

Arriving in the big City and entering academic life, was quite bewildering for me at first. I was used to a very quiet, safe life, and here, there was so much going on, and people were everywhere. I had to keep telling myself that I would manage, for I felt almost overwhelmed by it all, and on my own.

I was given a small room where I could sleep, in a college, with hundreds of other students. For our meals, there was a large banqueting hall, with benches so we could all eat together. I did not know where to start, around meeting these people, and I felt embarrassingly shy.

Before classes started, there was a week for the new students – Fresher's Week. In the main Square, there were bunches of students with their own stalls, representing groups and societies and social opportunities, that the new students could join in. I was quite amazed by the range of activities that were possible. It was like a huge market, and such a lot of vibrancy.

As I walked along, it came to me, that there was no one telling me what to do, and I could direct myself wherever I wanted. Where would I start? What could I do with my freedom?

I wandered from stall to stall, reading literature, and talking to a few people that I met. Some of the students were noisy, and they shouted out their wares over megaphones. I did not like that, and stayed clear of those – the noise did not appeal to me. There were many other students browsing, just like me, some in small groups, and others on their own. I did not know anyone else from my town coming to this University, and I needed time to orientate.

For most of that day, I continued to look around, and in the middle of the day, I sat down just a little distance away from where all the stalls were situated. I must have passed each stall at least two or three times, while I decided what interested me. In the end, there were two clubs that I signed up to.

The first was a Spiritual Awareness group, which offered meditation and talks on Spiritual subjects. I had felt a strong urge to join this group as soon as I saw it. Because I had felt the presence of what I called, my 'angels' for the duration of my life, I had faith that there was some greater spiritual power at work, than me, and I wanted to learn about this. Joining this group gave me a warm feeling in my chest.

With the second club, I felt a passionate pull within me to be part of a particular organisation. The ideals and aspirations it had, were in tune with what I believed. But at the same time, I also felt fear, and my instinct told me that being part of this group could expose me to danger, and situations where I would feel quite vulnerable. This was a society devoted to environmental activism. For nearly the whole day, I hesitated about this, but just before the stalls were about to pack up, I found the courage, made my decision, and gave my details to the people there.

SPIRITUAL AWAKENING

It was a few days later. I woke up feeling excited. Today, there was to be a meeting, arranged by the Spiritual group, with an introductory meditation, and talk on reincarnation. I had decided to go. During my school years, I had studied about religions on the Internet, and learnt about reincarnation from that. I knew that there were different shades of thought connected to this subject, but in my heart, something about it felt right to me, and I was so glad to have the chance to hear someone talk about it in person.

I arrived at the talk early. There were rows of chairs laid out, and I found a place about half way back, and to the side. Because it was my first time, I did not want to attract attention to myself. Therefore, I avoided placing myself too close to the front. I waited and watched, while people came in. In the end, there were about 30 people present, and many of the chairs were not filled.

The person giving the talk was an Asian Holy Man. He entered, with a large smile, and sat down very still, on some mats, at the front of the room. For some moments, he sat there, without speaking, while gazing around the room, and looking deeply at each one of us, in turn. His watchful manner was not intrusive, just allowing us some moments to attune together. There was a great aura of peace about this man. It encouraged me to feel very quiet inside. He asked if those of us on the edges could move so we would be more together in the middle.

I got up, and moved to a more central position, and closer to the front. The Holy Man had a very soft voice, and I wanted to hear him. It was like a meditation, listening to him, and at times, as he spoke to us, I struggled to keep my eyes open. His presence was serene and engaging, in his subtle gentle manner. However, as much as I wanted to take notice of everything he said, my attention was also pulled towards the other side of the room.

There was a girl sitting there. I had noticed her when the Holy Man was looking around the room. She was about my age, and she wore a simple, light blue dress. Her dark brown hair went down to her shoulders, and she had eyes, which were soft and caring. She was also on her own. It was strange, but I kept being drawn to want to look at her. Then at one point, she was gazing in my direction, and our eyes met. She smiled, and so did I. But then, immediately, I looked away, so my attention was with the Holy Man again. I wanted to save myself from any discomfiture. But every time I thought of that girl, I felt tingles of excitement rising along my back. I did not understand why I would feel like this. And I turned to look at her, many times.

The Holy Man spoke about the evolution of the soul, and about the purpose we had for living our lives. A lot of what he said made sense to me, and I found myself agreeing with his words. He suggested that from the stillness of our inner consciousness, truth could be revealed. And his words led gracefully towards the meditation practice that he wanted to introduce to us.

He suggested for us to close our eyes, and to focus on that space in the middle of our forehead, the third eye, and then to imagine it slowly opening. I could do that easily, and I listened for his further instructions. But then, it all came unexpectedly. Suddenly, my consciousness was flooded with light, brilliant shades of light, which came with immense love. My angels were close; I know they were. It was not possible for me to stop this, and I felt as though I was not in a physical body anymore, but that I was an energy form, and I was stretching higher and higher, while streams of energy passed through me, and out of my feet, and into the Earth below. It was such a wonderful feeling, that I had not experienced, and I just wanted it to go on and on. The light was so bright, but it was also peaceful, incredibly peaceful. I felt my attention go upwards, and then, all at once, I could hear a voice, and it kept repeating, many times, 'Remember, remember,' and I did not know what that meant, but it felt to be of great importance to me somehow. I could not hear the words of the Holy Man anymore, for I was so immersed in my experience. But then, all at once, I heard him tell us to slowly come back and open our eyes. It took me a while to be able to do that, and I felt stunned, not quite knowing how to react.

The Holy Man asked people to give feedback, about what they had experienced, and he offered to make comments to help everyone. Quite a few people spoke, and there was a lovely atmosphere in the room. However, while they spoke, I was still finding my way fully into my physical body again, so I could hardly discern what they said. I felt astonished by what had happened, and could hardly believe it. I could not speak, and it was like being in a state of shock, for I was struggling to understand it all.

Shortly after that, the meeting broke up. However, while the others left the room, I continued to sit there, staring into space. The young woman that I had noticed earlier, then came, and sat next to me. Surprisingly, she rested her arm very lightly next to mine so I could feel the contact with her skin. She waited until she was sure that I accepted her, and then she spoke to me.

'I was told to come to you,' she told me firmly, and it was like her words cut right through me. What did that mean? Energy was flowing through my body and in my heart. There was a huge love for her, even though we had never met. How could this happen? For a while, we sat in silence, and she moved away slightly to give me space. I asked her if she enjoyed the talk and meditation, and she told me that she did. It was like there was an unspoken communication of electricity between us, and I could not find words.

Eventually, we exchanged some of our details with each other and I found out her name. She was called Sarah, and she lived in the College next to mine. We gave each other our room and phone numbers. It felt natural to do that with her.

This was a very important day for me, and it felt as though some vital aspect of me had started to wake up. Meeting Sarah was no accident, and somewhere inside, there was a clear knowing in me, that she and I would be around each other, for a long time to come. We did not make any arrangements, but separated after that. I trusted implicitly, that when the time was right, that we would meet again.

REFLECTIONS

In the days following the meditation, I noticed a difference in my perception. When I was with the other students around the College, I felt more relaxed, as if I could 'see' more clearly. It was as though that light that I had experienced, was everywhere. The Holy Man had spoken of how we were all really energy, light and love, and that we were all connected, whether we were conscious of it or not. I could sense truth in these teachings, and with the awareness of the light, which almost overwhelmed me, during my meditation, this affected how I related to everyone, and everything, that I encountered. I felt calmer.

When I spoke with people, it was as if, intuitively, I could perceive the inner person, including fears and insecurities that they carried, but also their positive qualities. And I could appreciate these more. I was eager now, to interact with lots of people, to learn about them, so I would feel better able to communicate.

As I considered my life, the way it had been until now, I could acknowledge how reactive I had been with others during my younger years. I had tended to focus on people's faults and limitations and judged them for this, while at the same time, removing myself from them, to protect myself. I had regarded myself as different from others, somehow, and maybe even, better. But this was not true. And all I had been doing, really, was to put up internal barriers. When I considered how I had been with my parents, I could sense how this pattern had played out with them. I felt like I didn't need to defend myself anymore. Now, after that meditation class, I felt able to view my parents more sympathetically, and with love. I was glad that I could do that.

WORKSHOP

Over the next weeks, I settled into my new life at University, attending classes for my course, making a few acquaintances among the students that were there, and gradually familiarizing myself with all that was going on in the Campus. I wondered how Sarah was getting on. Until now, I had made no attempt to contact her, nor her with me.

One morning, I woke up, having very strong thoughts about the need to care for our environment. From this, I wondered when I would hear from the activist group that I joined. Then, when I opened my computer and checked my Inbox, there was an email notification, detailing a 5-day environmental activism workshop starting soon. It was as though some part of me already knew that this email was on its way. As soon as I read about the workshop, I was inwardly making plans to attend. The hesitation I had felt before signing up to join this group, had gone. I did want to help the environment. This was something that really did matter to me. I would miss a few classes over those days, but this felt important to do.

The workshop was to be held outside the city, in natural bush land. Equipment I needed included a tent and sleeping bag, eating utensils, and simple clothes. Attending such a workshop was something that I had never done before. Transport was being organised to take everyone there. I felt excited.

There were about 50 students and four group leaders in our gathering. We were shuffled into old mini buses quite quickly, and soon into the countryside. When we got out of the bus, I looked around at the trees, and heard the birdsong. Our camp was in a clearing. Nearby, I was aware of the sound of running water. It was a beautiful setting, and I felt at home with it. I did not mind being exposed to the elements of the bush. In fact, I welcomed it.

After setting up our tents, we were called to come together. I looked around to explore if I knew anyone there. I could feel tingles on my spine. On the far side of the group, I saw Sarah.

We were given a tour of the property, where we were staying, and shown the trees, the plants and the wildlife. There were so many animals hidden away, and we were told about their habitats, and how they lived. I could feel my heart opening. It was so precious to be in a place, unspoiled by human civilisation. The nature here reminded me of what it was like when I was a child, having those picnics by the river. For a few moments, I felt sad, looking back, but then happy to be here now. I did not have to be convinced about the need to protect the environment.

At the end of the tour, we were led to a corner of the property where there had been some chemical pollution. Containers had been dumped there many years ago, and dangerous chemicals had seeped out. It was pointed out to us how there was no plant life in this area. The soil still contained toxins that would take a long time to clear. This whole area felt inert and desecrated, compared to the abundance of life in the rest of the property. We were told about how many poisonous ingredients made by people, could do tremendous harm to the environment. These included genetically modified organisms, pesticides, and many forms of chemical agents.

'Why would anyone use these poisons?' a young woman asked. It was a fair question. I did not understand it. Much discussion ensued, and people shouted out their views. This was a group that did not like what was happening in our society. Some of them were very angry, and swore about all the corruption and exploitation. Some were indignant about how corporate greed and desire for profits appeared to rule over all other concerns. Others spoke of their dismay with the total disregard and lack of care people showed for our natural world and environment. It was a volatile conversation and many of the comments were loudly expressed. Here I could tell that people were passionate about their cause.

At one point, our main course leader, Jake, intervened, and stood on a large rock, where we could see him. Jake put his arms out so we would be quiet. He agreed with much of what had been spoken, and he added to it

'You can see it all around us,' he started. 'Our world is being progressively destroyed, and degraded by humans. Every year, there is less forest, fewer animals, more pollution, increasing human population, and vast areas of land and sea made uninhabitable. The situation in our world becomes worse and worse. And those that want to destroy our environment, are protected by the law, because they have money and influence. If we do not stand up, and do whatever we can to help, then there will be nothing left for our children and grandchildren. And we will have some responsibility in this, because we ignored to make efforts, to act about what we knew was right. But we also need to learn how we can act effectively, so we can really make a difference, and that is what we want to encourage in you and teach you to the best of our ability, during this week'.

I looked over at Jake, and although he spoke in a calm and measured manner, there was fire in his eyes, and agitation. Jake was of medium height with long straggly hair, and he wore a tee-shirt and jeans, a man in his late twenties. His upper body was well-built, with evidence of strong muscles. He was someone, who could defend himself against attacks. But I sensed something else from within him. Somewhere, in the privacy of his own thoughts and emotions, he had been hurt by all that was happening in the world. For him, this drive to be an activist was personal, and he was utterly dedicated to it. I wondered, how many others in our group, had also suffered personal pain, through witnessing destruction of our natural world?

I knew in my own case how much the development of the road and office blocks, from when I was a child, had affected me. But this act of wonton destruction had also stimulated my urge to speak up, and do something. It was as if, that boy I had been, the small child wanting to go through the door and speak to those workers and tell them to stop cutting down the trees, this child consciousness was still there. The child in me wanted to act.

I glanced across at Sarah, and she was also staring intently at Jake. What was her story and reason for coming here? I could not tell what was going on inside her. She was listening, and yet, her inner being was hidden from me.

Later, when we had our dinner, I sat next to Sarah. By now, the sun had gone down and had been replaced by the night sky. We were sitting around, on logs of dead wood, watching a fire that had been set up to keep us warm. It was quite hypnotic, to gaze at the flames, and every now and again, the wood would crackle as it burned, and I would need to shield my eyes, when flares of flame shot up. In the distance, I could hear the intermittent sound of cicadas, and the occasional croaking of the night birds. There were a few insects around, but the fire helped to keep them at bay. I felt a quiet contentment being here. Sarah and I did not say much, just some casual conversation, but I felt very happy that she was with me.

We had an introductory presentation given to us by Jake and his colleague, Lydia, and they outlined topics that we would cover during the week. There was an exercise we did, where we had to go into small groups, to share about what we loved in the natural environment, and how we wanted our world to be. We all had to take turns to speak, and I found it quite a liberating thing to do. It helped my heart to open with other group members.

When I spoke, I talked about how much I loved trees, and that I wished for a simpler way of living, where we could cooperate and honour all living beings, the animals, trees, plants and the mineral kingdom, and people too. Human beings did not need to be dominant. But as humans, we could help look after the fabric of life on our planet and be a presence to facilitate harmony.

It was amazing listening to all the different perspectives that everyone brought. There was a lot to take in. Gradually, as the fire burned down, I felt tired and I was ready for my first night sleeping in my tent. The group disbanded for the night and I said goodnight to Sarah.

As I positioned myself in the tent, it took me a while to get my body comfortable. But it felt good to be so close in proximity, with the physical Earth. And I was aware of how much in our modern society, with living in cities and towns, we separated ourselves from the natural world, through all the artificial structures that we made. After a while, I settled, and I could feel a very faint but comforting vibration that was coming from under me. The Earth felt alive, and I smiled inside.

I must have drifted to sleep, for in the next moment, I was aware of the warmth and brightness of the morning sun, shining through the entrance, to my tent. It was time for the new day.

The way our workshop was structured meant that we were given presentations, with discussion, as well as small group sharing, so there was lots of individual participation. There were practical sessions too, about how to plant trees, and make yurts. We were given instruction about how we could be sensitive to the wildlife when we were in bush land, and how to survive if we became lost there.

Gradually, the focus of our work, moved to activism, and what was happening in the local area where we lived, and what we could do about it. We were taught about the media, and how manipulative and unfriendly it could be. If we spoke to the media, we needed to present a clear and simple message, that could not be misinterpreted. We were given coaching about what we could say, and how to present ourselves.

When we became aware of something happening in our area, which was very destructive, we may feel indignant about it. In response, we could alert the authorities, but in many cases, they would not do anything about it. For us to make a difference, we had to bring matters that we knew were important, to people's attention, as well as informing the authorities. We had to arouse people's caring and compassion, and arouse public opinion for our causes. When the Authorities knew that a lot of people were concerned about a given matter, then they would be more inclined to listen. Therefore, we needed forms of publicity to inform people.

Too often, the media, were not interested in environmental matters, and would rather give coverage to a murder or act of violence and instil fear in people, rather than give any mention to a situation that was harming the planet.

Fortunately, we now had the Internet, word of mouth, and people power that we could utilise. In many cases, if we could get the backing of thousands of people, all seeking some positive action about a cause that needed attention, then this could influence politicians and public figures – people in positions of power, so that they would act. Most politicians and public figures were primarily concerned about their image. If they could perform some action that they felt, would be popular with the people, then, many of them would do that. The thing they didn't like, was negative publicity.

The biggest problem, was that not enough people cared, and apathy played into the hands of companies and governments that wanted to be destructive for the sake of some extra profits. These organisations tended to be secretive about what they were doing, and if people did not seek to know about their plans to damage the environment, then they would take advantage of this. We had to be aware that there was a lot of corruption in our world, and just because we believed in what we were doing, and endeavoured to be honest, it did not imply that others were like us, in that way. We needed support networks, for solidarity, and to alert the people. Otherwise, our aspirations would be disregarded.

It was not an easy job to be an activist. Sometimes, activists could be judged and meet with hostility, even hurt. At times, it felt like there was a war going on, against the environment, and the Activists were at the front line, to defend it. And others that were less brave, would stand back and not help. But without the activists, the world would be in a much worse state, and the powerful people and organizations that wanted to manipulate society and abuse the Earth for their own purposes, would not have any opposition.

During that evening, Jake and Lydia spoke to us and they shared about some of the causes that they had been involved in. Both were veterans in this work, and they emphasised that they did not always win. The forces opposing them were often just too strong. They told us that we mustn't be downhearted by this, and we had to be ready to stand again, when we lost a cause, so that when we did have a victory, we could celebrate, and know that we were helping to preserve the Earth and acting to improve the lives for all of us on the planet.

One of the stories Jake told us was of an occasion when he chained himself high up in a tall well-branched tree, to try to prevent loggers from felling a magnificent forest full of old growth native trees. For six days, they could not reach him, and the risks of bringing him down were deemed too much. The loggers were frustrated. Finally, on the seventh day, after he had run out of supplies, he let himself down with a rope to the cheers of the other activists there. By then, there were other protesters camped in trees, and this made it very difficult for the loggers to proceed. However, eventually, the forest was cut down, and it was a big loss for the environment, but not before a lot of publicity had been given to what the loggers were doing. And consequently, other forests were saved.

Lydia explained how she too, had chained herself to machinery on many occasions, to stop companies from polluting and destroying habitat. These were useful delaying tactics but served a purpose, so the company would recognise the strength of community opposition, to what they were doing.

The authorities did not always treat the protesters well, and Lydia shared how she had had two ribs broken on one occasion when the police assaulted her. Another time, she had suffered concussion. Jake also showed us some of the scars that he had gained over the years. With assaults that occurred, if there were not independent witnesses, then nothing could be done about this. Jake warned us that the kind of activism they did, could be highly dangerous, and we should think carefully, before we decided to join in. It was our responsibility to decide. We could also engage in leafleting and street protests, which were safer options, if we wanted to help in other ways.

Jake emphasised, that with police and authorities, we must not be violent. What we wanted in the world was peace, and we had to act from a place of peace to be true to a path where we could achieve that. People opposing us could be very aggressive and they may not want us to interfere in their plans at all. However, if we reacted by being aggressive back to them, then this would be likely to fuel their belligerence further, and would not aid our cause. So, if we were attacked, we could speak our message and stand up for ourselves, but we must not attack back. We needed to be positive examples for those around us, even if we felt, that the way that those opposing us behaved towards us, was unfair. If we were going to be activists in this world, then we needed to be very dedicated and clear about our intentions.

MAKING A STAND

On the final day of the workshop, Jake and Lydia informed us about a situation which had arisen, that needed confronting. They were asking for our help.

Nearby, there was a high-conservation value forest that was under threat. A coal company had obtained the rights to that land, and they were planning to begin a mining operation there, from this coming weekend. They had been given permission to do this by the Government, even though no proper environmental impact study had been sought. As a first step in their operation, they were going to clear fell the forest, and many rare species of wild life would lose their homes.

As Jake spoke about this, I could feel the pounding of my heart in my chest. This was outrageous. I knew of that forest; it had some beautiful walks in it, and was a stunning place. How could this happen? The situation so much reminded me of what the road construction company and developers did in the area around my family home, when I was little. I could not do anything then, but I could now. In my mind, I kept repeating that thought, affirming that I could do something to help. I wanted to be one of those volunteers that would act to stop this. Nothing would get in my way this time. I did not like nature being destroyed. Coal should be kept in the ground. With all the changes in climate, we needed to look after our world, and not burn more coal. This was so unnecessary.

Jake explained what we would be doing, and he told us that they wanted to have as large a demonstration as possible, with banners and leaflets. Their plan was that they would gather by the gate at the entrance to the site, and do what they could, to obstruct the movement of machinery, to protect the forest. Members of the media had agreed to come, including a reporter from the local radio station, and another one from the regional newspaper. Having members of the media there, would offer protection to all of us there. This operation to fell the trees, had to be stopped.

Jake called for volunteers from those in our group, asking us who would like to attend. He proposed that those interested, raise their hands. My hand went up immediately to show enthusiasm, and Jake smiled at me. Others put up their hands too. There was considerable interest. I looked across at Sarah. She was glaring at me with an expression of concern and uncertainty. Eventually, her hand went up, but she seemed more reluctant and cautious somehow, and the thought crossed my mind, wondering if she was agreeing to do this, more out of concern for me, rather than what she truly wanted to do, herself.

Later that day, the workshop ended, and those volunteering to help at the demonstration were asked to stay behind to prepare for the big event. Lydia coordinated this, and suggested various titles for banners that we could make. It was important that our banners communicate simple slogans that would get our message across. We were given some basic instructions about how we could make the banners. Also, she suggested to us what we could say to the media if they interviewed us, sentences that would be most effective. She emphasised that demonstrations like this could be unpredictable. If there was any sign of trouble, we should not become involved, but should scatter so we would not be hurt. Lydia insisted that she was only warning us of this possibility as a precaution, as there would be a police presence there, and members of the company's security guards. These people could be ruthless if they decided to be. We would be responsible for our own welfare. But she knew that we could support each other too. For a few moments, the group was quiet, but the mood did not stay subdued for long.

People were asking what the chances were that we could get a result, and stop the company. Lydia answered that what we needed most was publicity, to make people aware of what was going on, and to press the government to authorise an environmental impact report, to be completed before clearing could commence. It was a long shot because the machines were arriving on the day. Lydia told us how they had been making submissions to the government for months, without gaining any kind of response at all. With this kind of operation, the attitude of the government tended to be, to lay low, and hope that nobody would notice. It was a sad indictment of our society, about how much the government was in cahoots with the mining companies, at the expense of local communities. If we could cause the government some embarrassment through our demonstration, it may give them a push to act differently and do something to save the forest. We could but try. It was just important to keep our protest peaceful, so the kind of publicity we attracted would be more positive, and the media would not be able to put any blame upon us.

BANNER

When the meeting finished, I went over to Sarah and asked her if she would like to meet up and make a banner together, one we could share. I had never made a banner like this before, and it felt something nice that we could do together. She smiled and was happy to agree, and so, we arranged when we could meet.

Afterwards, I felt quite excited. For the next few days, my thoughts continually returned to the demonstration being planned.

The day arrived when I would meet Sarah. I felt grateful to be able to see her again. We met in my room at the College, to do the banner. I had obtained some paper and wood and staples. Sarah brought some paint and an easel. The words that we thought to write were simply, 'Save our Forest'. As we started to discuss how we would design it, Sarah asked if she could do the painting. I agreed, and sat back and watched her. Soon, I was very surprised. She was an artist, and first, she outlined the words of our slogan, so that they were prominent, and could be easily seen. However, around this, she used greens, browns, blues and oranges, to weave in some exquisite scenes, of nature and trees. It was quite a revelation for me to witness her skill. The pictures of trees came alive through her brush, and I was astonished by the beauty of what she composed. She hardly paused in her work, and it was as if there was some inner knowing or inspiration guiding her.

When she finished, I was full of appreciation for her efforts. If anything could touch the hearts of the people in that company and the officials, that would be there, surely Sarah's art work would do so. I felt proud of her. She was not someone that spoke very much, but there was a depth to her. For my part, I placed the wooden poles around the edges of the picture to construct the banner, but it was basically Sarah's work. I gave her a hug to express my appreciation.

She wanted me to keep the banner, ahead of when we would meet again, and I was pleased to do that.

DEMONSTRATION

Now, it was the day for the demonstration to take place. I was surprised how well I had slept, and I woke up feeling strong and resolute. It did not take long to put on some clothes, grab some water and some food. Carefully, I picked up the banner, and then I was out of the door. The sky was still in semi-darkness, with a growing reddish glow to the east. I needed to find my way to the centre of the town where the mini-bus would collect us. Our plan was to go to the site very early, to join Jake and the others, who had already been camped out there overnight.

It was a cool morning. Sarah was already waiting in the City centre when I got there. I came over to her to greet her. It was good to see her again, and I was proud to hold up and show off the lovely banner we had prepared, with her exquisite artwork. Several others were also in attendance, but not quite as many people as I had anticipated. There was an old rickety bus waiting to take us, and I smiled when I looked at it. Hopefully, it would not break down during the journey.

Sarah and I sat together, as the bus bumped along. The suspension was somewhat lacking, and Sarah held onto me to steady herself. There had been an early morning edition of the daily newspaper on the seat where we sat down. When the bus stopped for a traffic light, I had a quick look at it. At the bottom of the front page, there was an article quoting a government minister, and citing an imminent police crackdown on protesters and disruptive elements in our society. This was addressed at us. No wonder there were not so many activists in attendance. What did they have in store for us? I felt a little uneasy.

I showed Sarah the article and the expression on her face was quite worried. Her fingers clutched at me a little tighter. I tried to reassure her, and remembered the uncertainty she had expressed before volunteering to come along. Being part of such a demonstration was another new experience for me.

All I knew was that I wanted to be part of it. This company had no right to destroy a pristine and precious forest in its greedy pursuit of coal. Such vandalism had to be stopped, and if we didn't stand up, then the forest would be gone. I cared about preserving nature and our beautiful environment. It was imperative for our voices to be heard.

Jake was there, waiting to meet us when we arrived. There was already a dozen or so people gathered by the gate to the forest. I did not recognise any of the others, apart from Lydia, who was being chained to the gate and fence, to act as a barrier to stop the company going further. A few of the others, also had chained themselves in strategic positions, and beyond the gate the road had been dug up in another effort to make it more difficult for the company.

Near the gate, a small camp fire had been made, and it was refreshing to feel the warmth of the flames. Jake invited all of us to make some tea to warm us up. He then gave us another pep talk, and he mentioned the article in the newspaper. His concern was very much for those of us that were here as activists for the first time, and he did not want any of us to be caught up in any violence. He repeated, and emphasised that at the first sign of any trouble, then we should scatter and get out of here. The bus could collect us later, but we needed to get ourselves safe.

Jake was still hopeful that the protest would be peaceful. For this to be the case, he was counting on those media representatives to be present. Jake had spoken to them both overnight, and they had confirmed that they would be coming. He knew that their presence would act as a civilising influence upon the police and security guards. All we needed to do now was to wait.

While we drank our tea, Jake was on his phone talking to people. He was chasing people up, questioning why more activists had not come to the protest. There was something in the tone of his voice that was less calm than I had heard from him previously, and I began to feel a small knot of fear in my stomach, as I nervously sipped at my tea.

About half an hour later, I could hear the rumble of vehicles in the distance, and soon we could see them on the track. There was a security car and police car, followed by three enormous trucks with tree cutting and earth-moving equipment. Three other police vehicles were further back. Their approach felt ominous, but they stopped about one hundred metres from us and did not come further. The police vehicle and security car were adjacent to each other, while the trucks were lined up single file behind them.

Two police officers at the front, got out of their car, and began to survey the scene. One of them had a camera, and soon was taking numerous shots of all the protesters, and what we were doing. I did not like this. Sarah quickly turned away; she did not want to be seen, and she put an arm over her face. Reaching into her bag she got out a scarf to put on, and sunglasses. I felt more defiant, and I stared at the officer taking photos. A few moments later, I went over to the gate, and unfurled our banner to show them that. Sarah did not want to join me, but I held it up anyway, so they could see what we were here for. Others did the same with their banners. This did not discourage the police officer, who kept clicking on his camera for a considerable time. The other officer was on his police radio, and must have been talking to colleagues. I could not make out what he was saying. They were acting in a quiet, but deliberate manner.

Jake was looking around in agitation, unhappy with the awkward standoff that ensued. I could hear him mutter continually about the media. Why had they not come yet?

The sun had risen now and bright streaks of light shone through the trees. I turned around and marvelled at the sheer size and majesty of these wonderful specimens of nature. Now, at last, Sarah joined me. With her scarf and sun glasses, I hardly recognised her, but we each held one side of the banner and I was glad to have her with me. Several of the group now had their banners open, and it raised our spirits to do this together. I smiled at Sarah, but she continued to look down. I knew that she was a shy and very private person, but this was something else – for she appeared to be hiding herself. As she stood next to me, she was slightly crouching, and she seemed quite small and almost fragile. She was nervous about those police officers. I felt an urge to protect her, and I made a promise to myself then, not to expose her to danger.

We waited. Finally, we could hear a further vehicle. Jake jumped up, moved forward, and stared into the distance. He looked mightily relieved when a car pulled up alongside of the police car. It was the reporters. They had come together. Soon, they were out of their car, and starting to walk towards us. Jake was waving at them, in a friendly gesture. But then, as they approached, they were intercepted by one of the police officers, and for several minutes, they spoke earnestly. Soon, the other police officer came and joined them. The man from the radio station raised his voice. He obviously wasn't happy. But the police officers were insistent. We strained to hear, but from the security car, suddenly, loud music was spewed out, and it was clear that this was put on calculatingly so we wouldn't hear the conversation. Jake moved forward towards them, but one of the police officers raised his hand in warning, to tell him to stay back.

The reporters were then escorted back to their car. The radio reporter shrugged his shoulders, as if in resignation. The other reporter looked back at us with a concerned expression on her face. They were being forced to drive away, and one of the police officers was going in his car to accompany them.

Jake looked around at us, and I could see fear in his eyes. As the two cars receded into the distance, it was as if hope was draining out of him. Now the two security guards got out of their car and came up next to the other remaining police officer. The other three police cars moved forward. The presence of the guards was quite threatening, for they were large muscular men, and they had, on them, offensive crowd control apparatus, that did not look friendly. They all stood now, in front of their vehicles, and glared at us. They appeared stern and tense, as if they were waiting. Somehow, I felt that we were trapped, and I swallowed hard.

CONFRONTATION

Why were they not doing anything? I could see Jake prancing around, very unsettled. He did not like it. He had a phone call from one of his friends. There was a group of them wanting to come in, and join us. But they were not allowed. They had been blocked by a police presence at the other end of the track. The police must be planning something.

I had another cup of tea with Sarah. We warmed our hands by the fire. Neither of us were saying very much. I kept glancing at the security guards and police officers. Except for the leading officer, they were leaning against their cars now, motionless, but they continued to stare at us, watching our every move. Sarah just looked at me with trepidation and anxiety.

I could hear birds singing in the trees behind me. This was a beautiful area. Somehow, I felt that I had something to prove today – something to prove to myself. Whatever those police officers did, I wanted to stand up for this forest, even without the reporters. I was determined not to be forced to back down. To look after the environment was what I believed in, and I had to be true to my beliefs. My will was ready to match itself with theirs. I did not expect Sarah to stand with me. This was what I had to do. I wanted her to be safe, but she had to be responsible for herself. Looking across at her, I sensed that she supported me. We spoke together. I urged her, if there was trouble, to do what Jake said, and for her to withdraw, and she nodded. For a few moments, we sat together, gazing into the fire, while the water boiled in the billy. I felt close to her in those moments.

But then suddenly, the sensitive atmosphere between us was broken. The situation changed.

All at once, we could hear more vehicles approaching from the distance. There was not only one vehicle, but several, and as they came closer, I could feel the cold sweat on my brow. I could only hope that this would be some of Jake's friends, and that they had been let through, but I was very doubtful that this would be the case.

Watching the main police officer, he was now very alert, speaking on his radio to his colleagues and busying himself – this all told another story. Jake told us all to stand up, and to spread out. Not many people responded. Jake, himself, was positioning himself closer to the gate. He wasn't going anywhere. I didn't want to be weak in this situation, so I picked up the banner that Sarah and I had made so carefully, and I moved once more, and carried it to be next to Jake, directly in front of the gate. I told Sarah now, to go away and find a place of safety. She looked at me with a mixture of puzzlement and fear.

Others acted like I had done, and we gathered closer to the gate, as a group, guarding the gate somehow, and coming together out of a sense of security. This is what we had come here to do, and now was our moment. I looked behind me at the tall trees in the forest. Their branches were swaying with the wind that had picked up.

And Sarah, she appeared torn somehow, for she had edged away, and now she stood forlornly beyond the fireplace. It was the last time I saw her there. I could not look at her now, for my attention was in front of me. They were coming, a whole host of police and security cars and three police vans. When they stopped, they were positioned in an arc around us, with their cars, and soon they were bundling out of their vehicles, facing us.

The police came together in a central point. There were so many of them, and they outnumbered us, easily. One of the officers was pointing towards us at the gate, and along different sections of the fence along behind us. They were assembling their tactics. I did not like what I saw, for they appeared to be carrying weapons and riot gear. Surely, they would not hurt us?

By now, some of our group were starting to move away, cautiously edging along the fence, and some climbing over it. The police were watching them closely. It was clear that they did not want anyone to escape.

Jake moved forward towards the police. He was holding out his arms and looking around anxiously, appealing to the police officers for restraint. The closer he came to them, the more edgy he became, for they were ignoring him. They had their own agenda, and nothing was going to stop them. He looked rather helpless, and awkward, as he stood there.

What was going to happen? Should I run and try to escape? What about the beautiful trees behind us? If we didn't stand by the gate, what would happen to them? It may well happen anyway. They may be doomed, just like the trees by the roadside that I loved as a child. But I was determined not to give up. This time, I was going to express my feelings and let them know. With our banner opened, I started chanting 'Save the forest, save the forest,' and others in the group joined in with me. It gave us comfort to repeat this, and we shouted this mantra louder and louder. But for the police officers, it seemed to infuriate them.

Suddenly, they were rushing at us, all of them together. Some were more covering the wings, and moving outwards. They had their instructions. I felt rising panic. A group of them headed straight for Jake. One of them had a weapon, it might have been a Taser, and even though Jake's hands were in the air, they shot him with it, and he collapsed to the ground, with his body writhing. I was shocked, and wanted to help him. But my feet would not move.

They were on to him immediately, four of them, pulling his hands behind his back and handcuffing him brutally. He had no chance. They were then pulling him along the rough ground, and hoisting him into one of the police vans. I heard him groan, and one of the police officers punched him in the head to stop his noise. They were pitiless. Was there any way that we could stop them? I felt bewildered. How could this be happening?

I did not know what to do. The banner I held was so flimsy, but it had a beautiful message. I had to stay with that, so I held it up boldly. Most of the police officers were running towards the gate now. There was an atmosphere of confusion. Members of our group were panicking, going in all directions. A few more of the protesters were attempting to climb over so they could retreat to the forest. I noticed Lydia, with the chains she had tied around her, and her eyes were full of alarm and dread.

There were three police officers now running directly towards me. They were so unyielding, and there was menace in their eyes. Part of me wanted to look away, but the stronger part of me resisted doing that, and stared back at them. One of the protesters had taken out his phone and was trying to take pictures. A policeman grabbed his phone and smashed it, and knocked him to the ground. There was no mercy. I could hear screams and shouts of pain, as the policemen reached their targets.

The three policemen were almost onto me now. I took one last deep breath. Before I could take stock, one of them had grabbed the banner out of my hands, and started ripping it and breaking it. I wanted to cry, after all the love that had been put into that. I tried to reach out, but I could do nothing. The picture was in shreds now, and one of the officers was stomping on its remains.

They pushed me, and cut my legs away from me, so I fell to the ground. Then I felt a sharp searing pain in my side. One of them had kicked me. I felt a tremendous agony and weight on my back, as another of them clambered on top of me. Then they were pulling my head back. My hands were pushed together, and I could feel the cold metallic vice of the handcuffs, as they were forced onto me. Next my head was pushed down, forcefully, onto the ground, right onto my nose. I could sense the liquid sensation of the blood, as it dribbled out of me. I could do nothing, for my hands were cuffed. They jerked me to my feet, and pushed me along. I was terrified.

In a quick glance, I could see that the remaining protesters, that had tried to retreat towards the forest, were being rounded up, and bolt cutters were being used to release Lydia, and incarcerate her. She was swearing at her captives, and they slapped her across the face. There was still screaming going on, roundabout me, and I prayed that some of the group had got away.

I struggled to walk, and they shoved me and pushed me repeatedly, to hurry me along. The pain in my side was excruciating, and I wondered if one of my organs had been damaged. Blood was still streaming from my nose, and I just had to let it splatter cross my clothes. I had never experienced anything like this. As they thrust me into the police van, I had one last look backwards. Where was Sarah? There was no sign of her. I hoped they had not treated her badly. I felt guilty. She may have not even come to this demonstration if I had not volunteered. Maybe she sensed what could happen? I had not watched out for her – merely telling her to go. I desperately wanted to know that she was safe.

The door slammed in my face, and I had to sit down and steady myself. Four others from the group were there with me, and they all looked in a sorry state. There was no internal covering in this van – it was hard metal with thick bars crossing the darkened windows. It was all designed to make our experience as uncomfortable as possible.

Just before we left, I could hear that the trucks were moving forward now. No doubt they were going to start cutting down the trees. All that we had intended to do, was lost, and in my throat, I could feel a big lump of despair. At least my nose was bleeding less, for I did not feel like I was swallowing so much blood. My body ached. As I looked around me, all I could see was fear and upset on the faces of my companions. This is not what we had anticipated. We had wanted to do good. Most of us were idealistic students, wanting to make a positive difference in the world, and protect the environment that we loved. Now it was all for nothing. We had been shoved together in this van, like hunted animals. What would happen next?

INTERROGATION

I had always felt uneasy about the prospect of being in a confined space, and stuck there. Nobody was speaking, and I could feel my body becoming clammy with fear. We were being knocked around by the rough roads. The only light came from a viewing point to the front. I didn't want to look there though, because one of the policemen kept peered back at us, through it, monitoring our every move. Every time the van went over a bump, I felt a slither of pain in my side and my back. My body was suffering. I just wished that it would be over.

Finally, the van stopped. We must have reached the police station. The door opened, and we were pulled out. I struggled to walk, but was nudged repeatedly to keep up with the others. We were herded into a small, plain, confined room with a glass window. They searched us. All the belongings that we had, were taken from us. We were ordered to stand there in silence, and then we had to wait for an interminable period. I thought that I was going to faint. It felt very uncomfortable, and I was yearning to sit down. But if we moved, they motioned us to be still.

I did not know how much longer I could continue to stand up. It was a miserable situation, and the pains I felt in my back and side pulsed unendingly. The discomfort in my side was worse, and I worried about how seriously injured I may be. I could hardly look at my companions. The police officers did not seem to care, and they peered at us through the glass window, from time to time. There were four of them there, nonchalantly eating their sandwiches, while we were on display. They had taken away our dignity. I did not like the expressions on their faces.

One of the others did faint, and they dragged him out of the room. Then, one by one, they told us that we would be going with them for interview.

When it was my turn, I was taken out into the corridor, where they took off the handcuffs. My wrists felt numb from the tightness of the metal from the cuffs, and I wanted to rub them to get the circulation flowing again. But they wouldn't let me.

The two officers with me, shoved me forward, and took me into a larger room to be fingerprinted, and samples were taken from my mouth for a DNA profile. Then I was placed against the wall to be photographed. It was all very intrusive, and although it was explained to me as standard procedure, it made me feel like a criminal. Once this was done, they put the handcuffs on me again, this time with my hands in front of me, and directed to another tiny room, that was quite dark and gloomy.

The two police officers here, were not ones that I had encountered until now. I had to sit opposite one of them, and a spotlight was directed on my face, so I could not see very well. Part of me wanted to push my way out of there. I did not like it, and I did not feel that I deserved to be there. On the breath of the officer opposite me, I could smell coffee, and it reminded me of how dry my throat felt. I swallowed uncomfortably, and asked for a glass of water. But they wouldn't give me any.

The officer in front of me turned on a recording device, and told me, that with this being an official police interview, anything that I said could be used against me in Court. He read out charges that were being made against me. There were three charges. The first was illegal trespass onto crown land, and civil disobedience. The second charge was assault against a police officer, and the third was incitement to violence. I was shocked; these charges were not true. I tried to protest, but I was shouted down by the officer standing next to me, and told to keep quiet. The officer in front of me was calm and clinical, with a very cold manner. I could feel his eyes were fixed on me and disapproving. For a few moments, I raised my arms to try to shield my eyes from the spotlight, so I could see him more clearly, but they told me to put my arms down again.

The officer conducting the interview read out a written statement, which had been prepared, outlining what they purported, had happened, and what I allegedly had done. I was given a pen to sign it. They wanted me to sign it immediately. I felt flabbergasted. Surely, they could not force me to do that. I insisted on reading the document, even though they had spoken what was in it, and as I did, I became more and more angry.

The version of events written in the document was full of inaccuracies, distortions and many outright lies. It was being portrayed that we had been the aggressors, not the police. I read through it, slowly, two or three times. The police officer in front of me was becoming impatient. He put to me that the statement was a true account of the events, and pressed me to sign it. When I did so, he could then organise bail. This man was attempting to induce me to incriminate myself. I did not know the law, but this was wrong, and I was not going to do it. They persevered, but I resisted them. I could sense that both men were becoming irritable. The policeman opposite me turned off the voice recorder.

The two officers shouted at me, and tried to coerce me, saying that they would go much easier on me, if I went along with it. The one standing up threatened to slap me across the face, but was prevented by his companion. It was a very frightening situation.

I tried to remember what Jake had said to us. All he had told us, was that if we ever were arrested, then we had the right to legal representation.

He had not elaborated. I guess he had not expected this outcome. And I recalled seeing the fear in his eyes, just in those moments before he was shot by the Taser. I felt pity for Jake.

The police officer then began going through the statement again, sentence by sentence, emphasizing to me that what was written was what had happened, bullying me to admit events that had not ensued. My body was still feeling very uncomfortable. I felt intimidated, and the other police officer, standing, was leaning over me, as if he could strike me at any moment.

The interviewing officer tried to persuade me of the advantages I could gain, if I signed the document, but I just shook my head. There were no advantages. Somehow, I knew that I had to refuse to give in to this. He tried many times. And as my resolve remained, the two officers became more and more exasperated. They went through it again and again, and they clearly wanted to break me down. I was both hungry and thirsty, but they refused to get me anything when I asked, again, for a drink. The handcuffs were rubbing on my wrists again, but they wouldn't remove them. They would not let them off, until I agreed to sign.

In the end, I raised my head up, and said that I wanted a lawyer in attendance. I looked in the eyes of the interviewing officer, with as much courage as I could, and repeated my request. At this, the police officer in front of me stood up, and slammed the papers onto the desk. The other police officer forced me to my feet. They weren't going to speak to me anymore. Soon after this, I was taken away.

THE CELL

I didn't know what would be the impact of me asking for a Lawyer; I felt that I had to do it. They seemed angry by me doing it, but I sensed that it was within my rights. Would they bring a lawyer? I just had to have faith. There was little I could do, for I was completely in their control. Now that I was out of that room, I felt the pressure on me eased.

Two other policemen were with me now. They were taking me away, and they wanted me to move quickly, but I couldn't do that. These officers were also rough. They kept pushing me, and I fell down a couple of times. I was taken down some stairs, and led along a corridor, where there was a row of metal doors on either side. These must be the cells. Soon, I was made to halt next to one of these, and it was opened for me to go inside. One of the officers grabbed my hands and took off the hand cuffs. After this was done, they thrust me in, and the door was slammed shut behind me.

I was breathing heavily. There had been so many ordeals. The cell was just a small narrow room with an immovable wooden bench where I could sit, a wash basin and basic toilet. The first thing that I did, was to turn the tap on, and gulp down some water. I was so thirsty.

Then I surveyed the room, more fully. Lighting came from a glaring barred fluorescent light placed on the ceiling. There was also a CCTV camera watching over me. I noticed a small air vent up next to the ceiling, so at least I would get fresh air. It was such a sterile environment. The walls and floor were made of some hard, unyielding, artificial material. There was no window, no link with the outside world. What could I do? I was imprisoned here, and I was at the mercy of the policemen that had put me here.

Although it was somewhat unsettling to be confined in this cell, on my own, it was also a relief, after all I had been through. I wanted to orientate myself to what I could do, so the situation I was in could be more tolerable.

I went to the wash basin and made efforts to clean myself up a bit. It felt good to wipe my face clean from all the blood. That felt better. I drank some more. But then, what next?

I sat down on the bench, and looked at the bare, blank walls. They gave nothing back to me. I had no watch to tell the time, no means to communicate with the outside world, no nature that I could tap into. I was all alone here. How long would I have to stay here?

For a while, those thoughts caused agitation inside me, but then I remembered the meditation class that I attended, and I decided to try to calm myself down. I took some deep breaths at first, and it felt as if my body did not want to relax. Everywhere, I could feel tension, and my body was tight. I must have been holding so much in. But, as I observed this and just allowed myself to 'be' with it, slowly the tension began to give way. As this happened, my body started to twitch, and to shiver and then shake. I could not control this. My body was doing this by itself. I had been through a lot of trauma today. It was a startling reaction, and I had to quell my tendency to panic. What was my body doing?

I searched in my mind, and as I did so, I remembered the Holy Man telling us that when we started to meditate, it could bring to the surface, emotions and psychic blocks, that we carried inside, so by letting our emotions express themselves, we could release this, and clear the inner passages to peace. If this was true, then the shivering and shaking was probably my body releasing the feelings and fear from what I had experienced today, and I wanted to let it go. That would make sense, and the very thought of releasing all that tension, carried with it, a huge wave of relief, that travelled through me. Inwardly, I chose to cooperate with my body, and quietly acquiesced for all the tension that I had gathered to come out from me.

My body continued to shake, and I wanted to laugh, because the more I shook, the better I began to feel. I had discovered my body's own self-healing mechanism. It was interesting. Associated with this release, there were thoughts, and I started to replay in my mind, all the stages of what I had experienced with this protest. I went through it many times, and it was quite emotional to do so, and I perceived different layers of perspective, every time that I did it. There were also memories of when I was little and I saw, in my mind again, the trees across the road being chopped down. It all came to me in flashes, and I chose to welcome every thought and memory that wanted to present itself. With these memories, there were also tears, and I let myself cry.

One of the most poignant moments of reflection that repeated itself, was inwardly seeing the expression on Jake's face when he saw the reporters being shepherded away and then afterwards, when the police came at us. He looked so despairing and hurt, as if he had also let all of us down, and destroyed our hopes. Inside his heart, he felt responsible. This was tremendously hard for him. I had to remind myself, that this was not my burden, even though I felt compassion for Jake. And with this, my body shook some more.

I also was puzzled about Sarah. I hoped that somehow, she had escaped, and that she had not been bundled into one of the police vans without me seeing. I did not want her to have gone through anything like what I suffered. She was innocent. That would be too much, if they got her too. We were all innocent. But I prayed for her, and felt warmth in my heart for her.

It was so pointless and destructive for those officers to destroy her beautiful banner. I remembered seeing the shreds of it on the ground, and even glimpsing out of the corner of my eye, one of those officers deliberately stomping on the remains of the banner – all this while they were kicking me and forcing me to the ground. Could not these police officers respect beauty? They were very harsh.

Then I thought about the trees. How many of them would be cut down now? I could feel the despair, how all our efforts seemed wasted, and it was so debilitating. I sobbed and sobbed.

After a long while, I opened my eyes from this process of release. The shaking and shivering had settled now, and I felt still. As I continued to sit there, I just stared at the bare wall in front of me, searching with my eyes, noticing a few faint cracks of imperfection in the otherwise completely bland surface.

Gradually, as I sat there, I became more attentive to the other discomforts that had been bothering me. I could feel the pain in my side where I had been kicked. This felt very tender, and it was still throbbing. My back was also aching and I could tell that it was severely bruised, for I could not bend or stretch myself very easily. There was no better thing for me to do, but to rest. I had not received any medical attention for my injuries since arriving at the police station. Ultimately, they had left me to cope on my own.

Gently, I placed my hand upon my side, the area where I had been kicked, and I attempted to comfort myself, by keeping my hand there, while I sat quietly.

My thoughts returned to the teachings of the Holy Man. He had taught us that we were connected to what he termed the universal loving consciousness. We could call on that universal consciousness to help us when we were in a time of need, for it was a force that was everywhere.

I opened myself to test the teachings he had given us. It felt like a good opportunity to try out those principles, so I sent a directed prayer asking that the universal consciousness could help me. For some moments, I sat there still, and I waited for something to happen. I did not want to confine my attention to myself, so I also included within my prayer, a request for inner help to be given to the other activists, and especially, Jake. This seemed to shift the energy.

I noticed in the quietness that I soon became more peaceful and my hand was heating up. There was some transference of energy going on between my hand and my side. The heat in my hands created a tingling sensation. Gradually the sensation of heat spread through my body, and it almost reached the point where it felt overwhelming. What was remarkable, was that the pain that I had been feeling in my side, was lessening. I kept my hand there for quite a long time, until the throbbing was almost gone. As I finished doing this, I sent out a thought of gratitude to the Holy Man. His teachings had really helped me.

I started to think more about my situation. The cell where I had been put must be a holding cell. It was not the place where regular prisoners would be kept, for there was no bed, just the plain bench, and they did not keep people permanently imprisoned in police stations. Therefore, I would not be here forever. I needed to be patient, and wait. In this moment, I felt very still, and able to do that.

Now, in my mind, I had the chance to be able to contemplate, and attempt to understand more fully what had happened. I had to remind myself that, whatever the policemen told me, that I was not a bad person, and I had not done anything deliberately that was 'wrong'. All of us that had come to protest at the gate in the morning, wanted to protect the trees and help the environment. There were one or two, like Lydia, who were setting out to obstruct the authorities by chaining themselves to the gate. However, even with them, their motives were not malicious, for they had no intention to harm. They were coming from a place of seeking to be noticed, of wishing to plead with the authorities to listen, and act differently. None of us were inclined to be violent. The violence had come from the police side. Fundamentally, we were people that cared. And we wanted others to care too, in the hope of making a positive difference.

As I affirmed all this to myself, I could feel a warm flow of energy in my heart. This was all true.

Next, I turned my attention to those men that had attacked us. What was their agenda? I felt that that they deliberately wanted to torment us, and to hurt us, and to engender fear in us. They had created circumstances where we would be isolated from the outside world. No one then would hear our voices, and there would be no independent witnesses to their behaviour, and actions towards us. It was classic bullying tactics.

Why would they want to be violent to us, when we were innocent? We were obviously a threat to their operations, because we objected to what they were doing. Our wish was to stop what they wanted to do. If we could communicate to others how much the forest mattered, then others would object to them clearing away all those beautiful trees too. The company did not want any objections, so they used the police, to set out and weaken us, by making us feel afraid. If we didn't stand up, then who else would do it?

They wanted to eliminate our risk to them, and squash our passion for wanting to protect the environment. What would be left then? Fear bred indifference and ignorance as to what was going on. Once the protestors were suppressed, the company could carry on with its operations, unimpeded.

Who instructed the police officers to arrest us? It could have been the Company, the Government, or the police, themselves. It was difficult to know whose hand was in this, but from what had been announced in the morning press about the prospect of an imminent crackdown, it did appear to be coordinated, and part of a wider strategy – as if the action of the police to suppress our protest had already been prefigured. It was a nasty business, and quite ruthless.

Ultimately the outcome of all this meant, that this beautiful forest, a significant home for many creatures and wildlife, and a peaceful refuge for people, was being cut down and destroyed. In its place, there was to be a mine that would be erected, desecrating the land, and producing material that would pollute the air, and make money for some rich people, who would claim ownership of the mine. In the meanwhile, the habitat in the local area there, would be left barren, and our Earth would be further scarred. The people that stood up against this development would have nothing, but a sense of failure in their hearts.

Our Western society was going along the wrong track. When people decided to be activists, like I had done, this was a brave step, with the intention to point out to others, that we did not want imbalances, and that we were willing to stand up for fairness and justice, and for a better world. We should be ones that were honoured in our society for our efforts, not put in prison.

However, I did not hate the men that had done this to me and my companions. My only wish was that they could find their humanity. Whatever they did to me, I needed to remain true to my path in life and be ready to step forward. I was not going to be deterred from being an activist. If anything, this experience and imprisonment for some baseless offences only served to strengthen my resolve. Through the Spiritual practices, that I had observed, and my contemplation, my energy had been renewed. I felt peace.

Now, that I was calmer, I asked for my Angels to be with me. I felt that they were present, and encouraging me, and telling me that it would be alright. I closed my eyes, and asked for the light, and I could sense this, not like when I was in the meditation class, but enough for it to comfort me.

It was a strange sense of timelessness in this prison cell. There were no outer distractions or anything to amuse me. I did not even know whether it was daytime or night time. The fluorescent lighting above me gave a slight buzzing noise, but apart from that, there were no sounds, only the occasional clunk of cell doors being opened and closed, and footsteps in the corridors.

For what felt like a long time, I could endure being in the cell, just by being quiet, but I could not sustain this indefinitely. No one came to my cell. I waited, and waited, and continued to wait. As much as I had worked things out in my mind, I could only remain with my inner thoughts for so long. I was yearning for some activity.

There was no pillow, so I took off my fleece and used that to rest my head, and tried to lie on the bench so I could rest, or even sleep. I didn't manage very well to be comfortable, for the side of me that had been kicked, was still tender, even after the healing, and my back was delicate. I shuffled about restlessly. And there was nothing else that I could do. I was tired and hungry, and could feel myself becoming irritable. It was a form of torture, being in this cell.

After I had laid down for a while, I then shifted, stood up and sat down again, paced along the length of the room. And when I finished that, I tried once more to rest. I struggled to occupy myself. This process was something that I repeated several times.

Then, when I wanted a break from that, I looked around at the various aspects of the room. I must have got to know every corner and detail of that room. And I kept looking, and sometimes touching the surfaces, not because it interested me, but as something to do.

Eventually, I made myself lie down and stay down, and I started to feel myself drifting off to sleep. I had to do something to break the monotony. But also, I was just so exhausted.

RELEASE

I must have been quite deeply asleep, for I was suddenly being jolted to wakefulness. There was a sudden noise, and the bolts on the door of my cell were being unclasped, with several loud clangs. The door opened, and two police officers strode into the room.

I was struggling to regain my normal consciousness, when one of the officers made his way, forcefully, onto the end of the bench where I was lying, and he shoved my body along, so he could sit next to me. My body jerked into action, and my back ached, as it was so unexpectedly, forced to bend, and contract. I felt crunched up and violated.

The policeman was pushing up against me. I could hear his laboured breathing. His hand was motioning at me menacingly, and so I stayed very still. The other Officer stood over me in a very threatening manner. They were both intruding into my space, and I felt shocked by their proximity. I did not recognise these two, but they appeared to know all about me. The one on the bench demanded eye contact. They were intimidating me, and I felt forced to appease him. I was bewildered, but had to be present with my attention.

'You might think that you are fortunate when you get out of here today, scum,' the officer told me disdainfully. 'But we have you on our files now. We will be watching you, watching your every move. You just need to attend one environmental meeting, or be at some march or protest, and we will know it. We will pick you out, and have you. And the next time you come in here, it will not be for a short visit, it will be for a long time. And you will not get any mercy or help. Do I make myself clear?' He glared into my face, and I nodded slightly.

Then he pushed himself right up against me and pulled my shirt up to my throat. 'Do I make myself clear?' he repeated, and I found myself freezing inside, with renewed fear.

I forced myself to speak. 'Yes sir, I hear you,' I croaked. And he pushed me back against the wall.

'Get up now,' he ordered. 'Get up.' And he physically pulled me to my feet, and jerked me forward. His colleague forced my hands together, and put handcuffs on me again. 'You come with us.'

I did not understand why these men appeared to hate me so much. They did not know me. It was more that they wanted me to be afraid, and I could not help myself from reacting. They would know that I was gentle, and not at all violent. This was so alien to me.

We went along the corridor and up the stairs. As we went further, my hopes rose that we could be going to the entrance. They stopped me before I reached there, and took off the handcuffs. Then they directed me to tidy myself up, and led me into a small bathroom. I did what I could, and they watched over me, keeping the door open. Who did they need to impress?

It appeared as if they were preparing to let me go. Why would they be doing that? It did not make sense to me. They gave no explanation.

'You keep yourself away from these events,' the rough Officer reminded me, while he once more, squeezed the top of my shirt together, right next to my throat, and he held his hands there, staring at me. He did make me feel scared, and vulnerable. My neck felt sore from the pressure he applied. I found it hard to breathe.

Finally, he let me go and thrust me in the back, to get me to move. Then we went around the corner, to the desk, next to the entrance. The policeman, who had done the initial interview, with me was there, and he looked up at me, blankly.

'You have been released without charge, *this time,*' he spoke firmly, emphasizing 'this time'. 'Here is your phone and keys. Sign this, to confirm that they have been safely returned. You can go.'

There was a click as I turned the handle of the door in front of me. Slowly, I opened it. I gave a big sigh. With timid footsteps, I moved forward. I felt a huge relief.

FREEDOM AGAIN

Now I was in the public entrance area. There was light streaming through the window, natural sunlight. It was so bright, that I squinted and my eyes needed time to adjust, but it was so welcome, somehow. There were two people who had been sitting down, that now stood, as soon as I appeared. One of them was a young woman, whom I knew, and the other, a man that I did not recognise.

The young woman had tears in her eyes. She was half running towards me, and I felt a sudden warm feeling in my chest. Of course, I knew who this was. It was Sarah. – Sarah. I could hardly believe it She hugged me so tightly, that my back started to hurt again. When she noticed me wince, she pulled back a little, and was concerned.

'Are you alright?' she asked imploringly, scanning me up and down. I nodded to reassure her, even though many places in my body still ached.

By now, the man who had been with her, had stepped forward, to be by her side. Sarah introduced her companion, with a smile. The man with Sarah was smartly dressed. He had a twinkle in his eye, and Sarah was very much at ease with him. This was her father. He told me, that I could call him Simon.

For some moments, I stared. How had they come to be here? Simon motioned with his finger against his mouth, for us to be quiet, for it was not the time yet, for proper introductions. He directed us both to the front door. Simon tried to hurry us, but I could only hobble. Sarah put her arm around me to support me. Coming out into the fresh air, I was so glad to be away from that police station. Simon's invitation to come with them, was like heaven.

DEBRIEFING

There was a car waiting for us. Sarah sat next to me as the car travelled along. She held my hand and was very affectionate towards me. We did not speak very much. I just found myself daydreaming and trying to orientate myself. I didn't know what to say. Even after all the healing that I had done on myself, I felt that I needed some space to recover. We were in the leafy suburbs now. I wondered where we were headed.

I had always assumed that Sarah must have come from a similar background to me, and I was surprised to learn, now, that this was not the case. As we entered the driveway of Sarah's family home, I was quite astonished by how extensive it all was. There were lush grounds and gardens, with lots of trees, especially at the back. Her family were not short of money.

I realised now how little I knew about Sarah. We had not talked about our lives; it had been that more unspoken connection that had drawn me to her. Seeing her family home made me question her identity. I needed to know more.

When we went inside, I was introduced to Sarah's mother, Eve. She was quite an upright woman, softly spoken, dressed in elegant clothes, and her eyes were sparkling and kind. She greeted me with a simple hand shake, and I noticed that her hands were warm. Eve told me that she was a Doctor, among other things. She was aware of the ordeal, which I had been through, and she asked me respectfully, if she could check my body for injuries.

Eve was someone with whom I could feel safe, very easily, so I agreed to her request without hesitation, and was grateful for her attention. We went into another room for that, and after examining all my injuries, Eve was satisfied that there were no broken bones. She also photographed the bruising on my back and side, to have a record of what had happened to me, and then applied a soothing ointment, to hasten the healing process.

I found Eve to be very reassuring, and knowing that Sarah was safe, was a big relief. However, I did not understand how all of this had come about. One moment, I had been locked in that horrendous cell, and the next moment, the police officers had let me go. I felt very confused.

Eve gently ushered me to go with her into their living room, where Sarah and Simon were sitting and waiting. They wanted to talk with me. It was Simon that began.

'Welcome to our home, David,' he began. 'Let me introduce myself properly. My name is Simon Davies and I am an Environmental Lawyer. My wife, Eve, here, as well as being a trained medical doctor, is also a human rights advocate, who does a lot of work with the UN. Our daughter, Sarah, you have met, and I believe that you are both very fond of each other.' I looked away slightly in embarrassment, and noticed Sarah smiling awkwardly.

'We want to tell you about how it is that we have been able to help you, but also about our interests.' Simon paused for a moment. I looked up at him and noticed the deep, intense expression in his eyes. He smiled at me momentarily, and then went on.

'Our overriding, principal concern is about the state of the planet, Earth, and the degradation that is occurring. We are people that are wanting to help. All our efforts are ultimately about that. My wife and I have different spheres of interest, but they come together, and we often work in conjunction with each other. Sarah, too, is very interested in our work, and we are fortunate that this is so.

'For some months, we have been concerned with developments, around the proposed coal mine, in the forest, where you held your protest. The Nature Reserve in that vicinity contains many rare species of vegetation and wildlife, and it would be a great loss, for that to be destroyed. In addition, we are also concerned for the CO_2 emissions that could come from the coal extraction, and its use. It is our belief that this project is irresponsible and a bad idea in all ways. The government has bypassed all the usual channels of checks and planning regulations, so they could get this coal mine up and running. There have been secret, corrupt dealings going on. For a long while, we have struggled to know what we could do about it. Our intention has been to stop the mine. So far, with the company, government and other agencies all conspiring together, we have had no chance to influence what they did, at all.

'We have known about the Activist group you joined, and the protest that they wanted to launch, against the mine. It was a chance for us to become involved, so we sent Sarah along with a task, where we hoped that she would give us the breakthrough that we sought. We knew that the coal company was all set to start their clearing of the forest, and they had their equipment prepared for that. The information that we received, indicated that the authorities would not tolerate any opposition. So, there was a confrontation brewing. But we did not know how it would pan out.

'We instructed Sarah about what we wanted her to do, and we apologise that she could not tell you. I insisted that she keep her operation completely secret, so there would be no possibility of divulgences.

'Sarah carried with her in her bag, a small high resolution video camera. What we wanted was clear, unambiguous evidence of what the company and government were doing – anything that could bolster our case for stopping the coal mine. We were concerned about Sarah's safety, because we knew that if she attended the protest, it could be a very volatile situation, and one that could ignite into violence. And she was rightly concerned about you.

'To give our plan the best chance, a couple of days before the demonstration, we went with Sarah, to the site, and worked out three or four positions, under bushes and in ditches, where she could conceal herself, to be able to film. We examined what would be the best pathways, of how she could go to get to these places – ones that would be least conspicuous for any onlookers. We rehearsed it all, with her, as meticulously as we could. And we are sorry to say, that we were very firm with our instructions. We insisted, that, on the day of the protest, for her to leave you to your own devices, and not involve you at all. Otherwise, all our efforts might fail. We had to explain this thoroughly to Sarah, for she found this most difficult.

'You might have noticed that when some of the protesters tried to film what was happening, the authorities stamped on these phones and broke them. They did not want any part of their activities filmed or recorded. They had their own narrative that they wanted to play out in the world, and needed to be careful, that there would be nothing of any substance, to contradict that.

'Sarah did very well. When the police started taking photographs of the protesters, she put on her sunglasses and scarf, so she would not be identified. Again, I had prohibited her from making any suggestion like that to you. She had to keep her own integrity from the authorities, and had even given a false surname to Jake, so that the police would not be able to trace her identity. Sarah had her association with you, but we had to just trust that this would not give her away.

'There were a few bushes in a ditch quite close to the fireplace, and this is where she felt that she could go, to be hidden, and as close as possible to the action. Then, when the other police cars were arriving, and all the attention was upon what was happening at the gate, she slipped away and hid herself there. She did not want to leave you, and she feared for your safety, but she was strong, and did what we asked of her.

'Sarah was busy filming from the start, and she got some very incriminating videos, including when the police officers fired their Taser gun at Jake and dragged him away. She also managed to video all the assault that the officers made upon you, including how they tore up the banner, and she got several other clips of the incidents that occurred. She kept filming, right up to when the police vans drove away. It was a remarkable effort.

'Of course, Sarah was very upset about you. And she wanted to go and help you, but she was sensible, and, as we had coached her, she knew that the best approach for her was to stay put. This is what she did, and she waited underneath the bush, until all the police officers had left. Then, all that remained were the company trucks and workers, and a couple of security guards. They did not even notice her when she left.

'Sarah had to walk a considerable distance to reach another road, off-site, where we could meet her, but we had planned that too, and she knew the direction in which she needed to go, and we were there waiting for her, when she arrived. She had done her job very well.

Soon we could process her camera work and upload it to our computer. I made several copies of the video, including one, that would be kept completely secure. Then I sent copies of the video to the police, the company headquarters and the Government, all with an accompanying message.

'I simply demanded that the company stop work on the mine, immediately, and that all protesters be released forthwith, without charges. In addition, I insisted that a thorough, independent, open, national environmental impact study be made with regards any mining works to be done in that area, the announcement of which had to be made within 24 hours, with no further work being done on the mine while this is in process. I put to these authorities, that these conditions were non-negotiable. If they were not met promptly, in full, I promised that I would release copies of the video to all sections of the media, including social media, without delay.

'It was game up for them. How could they refuse me? Even with all the control and influence that the authorities had, there were enough media outlets that were not in the Government's pocket, for the potential exposure of this to be explosive.

'They had to trust me, that I would keep my word, but they knew my reputation, and that I was a person of integrity. I am sure that the minister was very angry. They don't like anyone getting in their way. But I didn't hear of it. All my demands were agreed upon, without any fuss. The Environmental Impact assessment has just been announced, and all work on the mine has stopped, and will not proceed until the assessment is completed, and the subsequent report assessed.

'We are confident that, as a outcome of this, work on the mine will either be halted completely, or delayed indefinitely, by legal challenges stemming from the environmental impact report. Only a small number of trees have been felled. It is a great victory for the environment.'

Simon looked delighted. Eve was holding his hand. Only Sarah looked a little uncertain, and I guess she was not sure how I would react.

But I felt delighted, and full of admiration. This had been so clever, and I had not suspected, at all, what Sarah was doing. Somehow, now, even though I had received a few injuries, the whole process seemed to have been worthwhile. I was very pleased for the forest, and happy that none of the protesters would be held in prison. This was all remarkable. I could certainly see Sarah in a new light now. Her actions had been a revelation.

There was something else though. I liked this family. They were closely bonded, and united, and they were acting together to try and make a positive difference in the world. This is what I had wished from my own family, but I had never experienced that with them. Here with this family, I felt like I was coming home; they felt familiar somehow. And what's more, they were welcoming me to be with them.

DISCUSSIONS AND WAYS FORWARD

I told them about what had happened to me in the Police Station, the false statement they had put to me, and the threats they made. Simon made notes while I spoke, and later composed my story into a legal statement, that he encouraged me to sign. He would also approach the other protesters, and get statements from them as well. The more documentation we had, the stronger our case would be. With the existence of the video, in combination with the statements, which the police did not need to see, Simon was basically going to tell them to leave us alone, and give them some of their own medicine.

It occurred to me that Simon may be placing himself in great danger, by making all these stands, to help people and the environment. When I put this to him, Simon smiled and told me, that, with all the documents and evidence which he had accumulated over the years, if anything were to happen to him, or his family, there were people that would release those documents into the public domain immediately. It was as much protection as he could give himself, and until now, it had done the job.

Simon was a remarkable man. I admired his courage and his passion. When I considered Eve, his wife, I sensed that she expressed similar qualities in the work that she did, but she was a little less vocal about it. And Sarah had gifts and strength that she was developing too. They were a good team. I wished that I could work with them, for I wanted to join them, and there was a very powerful impulse from deep inside of me, which was prompting me to address this. And it was strange, but I had never wanted anything as much, in my life. I could feel it in my heart, like a pulling sensation.

That evening, I found the words, and the nerve, to ask if I could assist them with their projects. I put this to Simon, with the others there too, and looked at him, directly in the eyes, as I spoke. His gaze back at me never wavered. For some long moments, there was silence in the room, and it was as if there was a crackling of psychic energy. Simon then laughed, and with his laughter, the energy released itself. He said simply, 'Of course you can be with us!' It was as if it were the most natural thing in the world.

That was the beginning of it all. From then on, I became a regular visitor to their house. I was very curious to know about other projects that they had been involved in, and they told me, and there were many amazing stories to be shared. Both Simon and Eve had their own ventures, as well as ones they did jointly. Eve sometimes travelled to Geneva for her work with the United Nations. And Simon travelled too. They were both involved in activity, which extended far beyond this country, and they had support networks around the world, in which they were involved, and active. The common thread in relation to all these groups, with which they were involved, was that the people in these groups wanted to help the Earth and the people on the Earth, with the aim that our world could become a better, and more peaceful place.

As I learnt more about their activities, I was astounded that so many of these groups existed. It was like an underground network. Simon told me that it was imperative for all such people to liaise as closely with each other as possible. The onset of the Internet had made this achievable, and helped like-minded people with similar aspirations and ideals to come together, in a way that had never existed previously.

I was fascinated to know what the various people associated with Simon and Eve were doing. It felt important to me, to learn as much as possible, about the seeds of activity that they were involved in. I felt enthralled. But Simon wanted to assure me that it was not all an easy ride.

The forces of oppression were very strong, and the darkness of greed and corruption and fear in our world, was so ruthless, and so destructive to our planet, that it would take an almighty mass group effort to overcome it. Simon told me, that in his heart, he did not know if the destructive forces could be overcome, but for him, there was but one choice, and that was to challenge it.

Sarah was already engaged with helping her parents in many of the projects where they had an interest, and I asked if I could help in a similar fashion. I particularly wanted to help Simon, for I also was very interested, not only in matters concerning the environment, but also politics, and structures of power in the world. There was so much that I wanted to learn.

Simon was agreeable to this. However, he wanted me to consider very carefully, what I would do with my university work. For a moment, I paused, and then told him, that I could do both. But it was clear, in my heart, which way my passion was directing me.

In the days and weeks that followed, I became like a young apprentice to Simon, and doing this, filled me with delight. He gave me simple tasks to begin, but I found it all, very interesting.

For so much of my life, I had had thoughts where I wanted to change the world, but I had no idea how I could do it. I made what steps I could, like talking to Stefan, coming to University, and the groups I had joined, but in honesty, I did not know where any of that would lead. However, with what had happened, as I was now beginning to work with Simon and his family, the change was remarkable. I was beginning to believe, that transformation in the world, was not just a remote idea, but that it was possible. And I could be part of it. This was what I had always wanted, and I felt very enthusiastic. I felt full of appreciation that Simon and Eve, could dedicate their lives to this, and it was what I wished to do, too.

SARAH

In truth, it was not merely being around Simon and Eve that made me happy. I felt enormous gratitude to be able to work with Sarah. She was the one that touched my heart more than any other. But since she had met me at the police station, she had been very quiet around me. I could tell that she was carrying feelings inside, which she was not sharing, but I did not know exactly, what they were.

One day, we were alone together, and I prayed that she would find the courage to tell me. We were having a break from our work, and siting alongside of each other. Sarah looked up at me, and her lip was quivering. I listened and waited. Then she began.

Sarah explained to me how difficult it had been, for her to do that task, with the filming, for her father. When she saw that I was being kicked and hurt, she wanted to rush out and protect me. It had been so hard for her to crouch silently, in between the bushes, and continue to film, while that was going on. She told me, when she filmed all the violence, that the tears were rolling down her cheeks and she had to hold her breath so she wouldn't sob. It was as though she was betraying me, by not attempting to do something to help. And she could see me wincing and gasping in pain from my injuries.

But she also knew that if she had come out, that she would also have been bundled into the police van, the camera would have been destroyed, and she wouldn't have been able to do anything to help get us out.

I reached out to her and held her hand gently, and she started to sob then. It was as if all the emotion had been held inside her, now could burst free. I spoke softly, to tell her that she did the right thing, and that I accepted her. Finally, her sobbing subsided, and when she unclasped me, she gazed into my eyes, and there was such a lot of love there, and I could feel the tears welling up in my eyes too.

It was necessary for me to confide in her, how I felt that I had neglected her too. I had become so caught up in the drama of confronting the police officers, that I had not even noticed where she had gone. I had not honoured my promise to her to look after her.

She stroked my hair, and smiled at me. This was not an issue for her, but she appreciated me telling her.

Now, we were close again, and able to enjoy each other's companionship. After then, we were largely inseparable. We met regularly at the University to share meals and to talk. She became my best friend, and we learnt so much about each other. But it was not the kind of relationship, where we went out on dates or got dressed up in fancy clothes. What bonded us was this work in helping the Earth. She had very similar interests to me, and it was like we had been waiting for an outlet where we could be together, and do this work. Somehow, the academic life of the university felt rather empty for what we wanted to do. While it was good for us to develop our minds, we wanted to engage physically with people and the environment, and wished to make a difference. Even though we had lived out such different backgrounds from each other, it was as though our inner purpose in being alive was linked together.

This realisation was something that Sarah thought as well as me, and it made us both feel very happy to consider it.

CAMPUS

When we were at the University, we sought out Jake and Lydia to find out what they were doing, but we could not find them. There was a leaflet hanging up on one of the notice walls, informing people, that the environmental activist group was now disbanded. We felt very sad about that.

Simon had spoken to Jake on the phone, when he endeavoured to gather statements from all the protesters. Jake told him that he had decided that the group was not viable anymore. He could not forgive himself for bringing other young people into danger, as he saw it, and preferred now to act on his own rather than having that responsibility. Neither Sarah or I felt that it was Jake's fault for what happened. We missed not being able to attend that group.

However, although we did not have the Activist group, we still had the Meditation meetings with the Holy Man. Once a week, we would go to the inter-faith sanctuary room at the University, and he would teach us meditation and inspire us, with his wise words about how we could develop our inner life. There was only a dozen or so other students that usually attended the group, and he got to know us, with us being so regular. He would smile when we entered.

I enjoyed the meditations very much, and found that when I did them, I became very still inside, and it was as though, my inner world opened to me, and it was so light and expansive; I wanted to stay there. It was also interesting to do this with Sarah, for I felt linked with her somehow, when we did this, as if our souls were very close. Sarah had similar experiences to me, but with her, she felt as if there was some reality inside her that she was not quite accessing, and that it was waiting for some moment to reveal itself. She felt anticipation without quite knowing what it was about.

Always, after the meditation group, we both felt more peaceful and in tune with our true self. While other students were rushing about, or behaving in a crazy fashion, we were very calm. I also felt sensitive after these sessions, and I could discern other people's moods and inner states without them saying. The Holy Man had told us to expect this, and to let it be. This was all an expression of the Oneness of inner reality. Often, his words would reverberate in my mind for days afterwards, as if they were refining my consciousness and helping me to open. This was a very important part of our week together.

AN EXCITING EVENT

One day, when we were at the meditation group, our teacher announced that on the following week, he would have two friends offering a presentation about their work with Channelling and helping the Earth.

This man and woman travelled extensively, and were attempting to raise the consciousness of people, and to help the planet. He rated them very highly, and would be pleased if we could inform others, to help publicise the event.

Suddenly, as the Holy Man began to mention these guest speakers, I felt a tingling sensation in my spine, and Sarah clutched my arm. There was something about these two people, and we both knew it. I wanted to tell Simon and Eve, for I felt that they should attend with us, and Sarah felt the same. We were excited.

I wanted to help the environment so it would not be so damaged, and, I wished for people to be more aware of what they were doing. However, I also felt that people needed to be spiritually awakened on our planet, so they would care. I believed that Spiritual awareness needed to be combined with environmentalism, for the transformation of our world, and I had a strong intuition that these two people that were coming to address our group, could hold the key to that.

Later that week, we spoke with Eve and Simon about these two visitors to the meditation group, and they struggled to restrain our enthusiasm. We told them our thoughts and shared our feelings, and our sense of 'rightness' that we should all be there. Eve looked in her diary, and to her amazement, there had been a cancellation of a long existing appointment during that time frame, so the space was clear. Simon was also able to rearrange his schedule too, so both decided to come.

Sarah and I offered our services to the Holy Man, and spent hours putting up posters handing out leaflets all over the campus. People took the leaflets, but we had no idea how many would be truly interested. There was something very familiar about working with Sarah and seeking to engage people in a more Spiritual outlook to life. We both felt exhausted after the days when we devoted ourselves to this, but happy also.

On the night before the presentation, I struggled to sleep, and I had to recite the meditation mantra we had been given, many times, to help me settle. Finally, I did drift off, but my inner world was very active that night. In my dreams, it was as though the sun was rising over the horizon, and I felt very optimistic.

KURT AND JULIA

Sarah and I had agreed to be doorkeepers, to usher people in for the meeting, and to welcome them. I had expected lots of people, for we had handed out so many leaflets, and it seemed to me to be such a great opportunity for people. But not many appeared, only a trickle. And most of those chose to sit up near the back. I kept looking out through the door, hoping that there would be more, but it was not to be. It was disappointing. I did not understand why more people would not be interested in this.

Eve and Simon eased into the room, and I was pleased that they went straight to the front row of seats. A few more came, and we waited until the last moment to close the door, and then we joined Simon and Eve.

Our teacher, the Holy Man, brought our two guests in from the side door. They walked in together; a man and a woman, and they seemed close. The man had quite a striking appearance. His disposition was very open, and he had a high forehead. Although he had a young face, he had long and straggly silvery hair. He had the appearance of being somewhat eccentric, and I liked that. As I looked at him, his gaze also went outward into the room. Our eyes met, and he gave a small but embracing smile.

With the woman, her demeanour was much quieter and more mysterious. She had long dark hair, and eyes that kept facing downwards so they would not reveal themselves. Her movements were slow and deliberate. It was as if she wanted to keep an aspect of herself hidden, something that was very fine and sensitive. She sat down, while he continued to stand, giving space for him to be at the forefront. He was clearly the more assertive one.

Now he called for our attention. He introduced himself as Kurt, and told us that his companion was called Julia. Kurt prompted Julia to stand, and they both said a few words of acknowledgment, but then Julia gave way to Kurt as the spokesperson, and as soon as the formalities were over, Kurt began his presentation.

Kurt's voice was clear, and projected easily to the back of the room. The tone of his voice was soft and reassuring, a little bit like Eve, in his manner of speaking, and he made gentle eye contact with everyone in the room. He stood and moved his arms in a flowing manner as he spoke, and I felt more and more drawn into his words.

He began by giving thanks, and offered a simple meditation, intended to help us connect with the stillness and love inside us. Kurt affirmed that we were all valued and precious souls, and encouraged us to open to that within our hearts. From there, he told us to reach out inwardly, so we could experience the others in the room, also as precious valued souls, and gradually extending that to include all people at the University, the local community and then beyond. In our essence, he told us that we were all love, and worthy beings. He paused while we contemplated that.

Then he went further, encouraging us to open our consciousness, to the trees, animals and plants, even the Earth itself. These were precious valued beings, as we were. They were love, just like we were love. And we were all connected.

It was a beautiful simple meditation, and I could feel my heart opening, and a gentle warm atmosphere developing in the room. The silence grew. Then he concluded with a chant, the sound of it penetrating deep within me. Finally, we opened our eyes. I looked along at Sarah and her parents, and could sense the stillness in them too.

Kurt next began his lecture. He spoke forthrightly, in a way that at first felt very strange, but as he went on, the themes in his speech became increasingly familiar.

'My colleague, Julia and I are here as emissaries to teach you,' he started. 'Our teachings are from higher realms – knowledge that has been given to us through meditation, over many years – knowledge that was within us, before we were born into this world.

'Our main intention is to enable you to connect with the Spirit of the Earth. We live human lives like you, but our souls are from other worlds, and we are here to help. Your humanity is going through a great transition of consciousness. You need to embrace this with your love so that we can all evolve together, and we want to share our understandings and wisdom to help you.

'Your Quantum Physics teaches you that particles and wave motion are interchangeable, and that implies that all physical objects could also be regarded as energy. Consequently, this means that all of us, as people, are basically energy beings. The ground under our feet is energy – all that we see is energy, even if it seems to be solid and material. And it is just the limitations and prejudices of our awareness that mean that we do not perceive our environment and each other, more openly.

'So, if we could perceive the energy of the Earth, for instance, instead of seeing it in solid form, what would it be like?'

He paused for some moments, inviting members of the gathering to offer their thoughts. Somehow, I felt my heart was expanding. My instinct told me that the energy of the Earth was profoundly beautiful, but I could not find words to say what I felt. It was good to consider this. Nobody spoke. Kurt looked at us all, in turn, with deep compassion, and then went on.

'I would put to you that the energy of the Earth is a marvellously intricate and majestic being, and exceedingly precious. It is the energy of the Earth that supports life on your world. If you could only perceive the energy of the Earth, you would not want to harm her, you would be grateful to her, and you would do all you could to be in harmony with her, and open to the connection you share. Your Earth is sacred.

'I call the energy of the Earth, "her". In your traditions, she has been called "Mother Earth", the "Goddess", "Gaia", and many other names. In some of your more ancient cultures, people perceived the Energy of the Earth truly, and they have been cultures that lived peacefully.

'People who have been in genuine communion with the energy being of the Earth, have never engaged in battles, but preferred to cooperate with each other. Battles have only taken place between those that had their eyes closed to the true nature of the Earth. For, with the true Spirit of the Earth, there is only love.

'I am here to teach you and help you learn how you can open your perception to the Earth Spirit, and to the energy of all beings around you. For, in your essential energies, you are souls, and you come from a realm apart from the Earth. However, when you incarnate, you combine your soul energies with that of the Earth Spirit, to form your so called 'physical body'. If you are to love yourself, which is the only healthy way to live, then it follows that you must love the Earth, for your body is made from the substance of the Earth. So, if you hurt the Earth, you are, in effect, hurting yourself.'

Kurt went on to speak extensively of the damage that we were doing to our Earth, not just on the physical level, but with the energy of our planetary being, far more than we realised. And then he began to speak of Julia and their relationship together.

'Julia and I were born three houses away from each other. We met when we were very young children, and from the moment we saw each other, we knew that our path in life was to walk together, and that we had Spiritual work to do. As we grew older, our Spiritual awareness grew stronger and clearer. When she was twelve years old, Julia channelled the Earth Spirit for the first time, and I knew exactly what I needed to do, to support her with that. In the conversations that we had together, we had shared visions of the work we needed to do, and clear memories of the worlds where we had come from.

'For you, as people on Earth, you need to learn about who you are as souls, and the true purpose that you have in being here. Julia and I had to do that, and now we are living our path of service to your world.

'We are not the only ones here to help on your world just now, but we want to assist to awaken as many souls as we can. When you are awakened, you will be sensitive to life around you, and know what you need to do to help save your beloved planet.

'You see, there is that inner reality where you can experience light and love. With the guided meditation that we did, you may have already started to feel it. Perhaps in your experiences with our friend here,' and he pointed to our teacher, the Holy Man, 'you have been able to go even deeper. However, you must understand that this light and love is the true reality, and the more that you experience it, then you will also notice in your everyday life, that people, animals, plants and minerals, in fact, all the Earth, has a living vibration. All that is around us is alive. And we are connected to that. So, what we experience as separate from us is essentially illusion. But it is not just a matter of perception, it is to do with our hearts.

'When we feel that we are lovingly connected, say, to a tree that is in the courtyard outside, how could we then chop this tree down when we know that the tree is feeling pain when we do that, and is giving us not only air that we can breathe, but also peace that will still our soul. As you feel this connectedness, you will want to cooperate with the kingdoms of life around you, and want to look after all this, so you can enhance the love in your world. You will certainly not wish to disregard or recklessly destroy all that is good in your planet.

'The Earth itself is awakening its Spirit to share all its gifts with you, and there is much that you can learn and open within your Spiritual nature, now. However, if you destroy what is sensitive and beautiful in your world, and if you manipulate elements to poison and distort this world, then this will affect your perception, and limit what the Spirit of the Earth can give you. Your consciousness will not open to the extent that it could, and much that has been planned for your humanity on this wonderful planet, may not occur.

'There has been so much destruction in your world now, so that the evolution that could have taken place to transform the Earth – is now in doubt. The materialistic culture that is so prevalent in your societies, it is like an opaque screen, and the dullness that this emits, is like a shadow, that interferes and inhibits you, from perceiving the true reality that exists within.

'Julia has come from a world where all life forms live in wonderful harmony with each other. The inhabitants of her world share profound love with each other, and are dedicated to serving and supporting other beings, including the life on your world. The consciousness, that her people have attained, has been achieved through their own efforts.

'It may surprise you to learn, that in contrast to Julia, I have experienced a world that ultimately destroyed itself, because the humanoid people there, did not pay attention to their Spiritual core. I have suffered greatly because of the destruction of my home world. It is my dedication to prevent that type of situation from occurring on other worlds such as your Earth. I do not want you to suffer as I did'.

Kurt then paused and motioned for Julia to once again stand up.

'What we are going to do today – is for Julia to channel the Spirit of the Earth and to lead you into a meditation where you can open to this connection yourselves. From your familiarity with meditation, just allow the energy of the Earth Spirit to support you with this. Let's come together.'

PURPOSE REVEALING ITSELF

There was a mat that was laid down for Julia to lie on. People in the room were invited to come closer and gather around. Inside my mind, there was something about this that was so familiar. I felt perplexed by it all, and excited at the same time. Kurt instructed us to sit quietly, and to give our love and attention together to all that Julia was doing. She closed her eyes, and appeared to go into a deep trance. Her body was very still, and her breathing slowed right down. As I observed what she was doing, I felt that I was relaxing and going inward as well, and there was a lovely atmosphere of peace enveloping the room.

Julia swallowed and cleared her throat. Her body was moving slightly, but her energy felt different. There was an unfathomable calm around her. We were all watching, transfixed. When she began to utter sounds, her voice was much deeper than it had been when she briefly introduced herself. It was as though it was not her that was present, but another Spiritual being, much more powerful and enigmatic. At first, whoever it was that was attempting to use her voice, was struggling to attune to it. Julia's head came forward slightly, and she swallowed a few times, while adjustments were going on. Gradually, the connection was made, and she prepared to be that channel and to speak for us. There was a hush in the room, and the energy was electric.

'I am the Spirit of the Earth. I greet you with love. You are my children sharing this world together. You must stop harming me, for you are destroying me. In your hearts, you are here to love and cherish your world, and for me to help you. We need to work together. If you open yourself to respect and be kind to all beings, then this world can be a wonderful place, for all of you, and for all life forms, with whom you share this place. This is your path, to help each other, and to care. This is what you are here to do. If you do not start to listen soon, then it may be too late, and I will not be able to function anymore to support you. You must help me, and help each other.

'With your free will, you take and you manipulate and you damage me, far more than you realise. I am alive; I am not some inert material that you can use. The life that is me – is the life that is you. We are one and connected. We have different functions and different consciousness. But the love that could unite us, has the potential to transform so much. That is what we need to do – transform this world with love. If we do not act upon this, then we may not have a world anymore.'

At that point, the energy started to fade, and Julia's head fell back on the cushion, which supported her, and she became lifeless again. It was only a brief channelling, but very strong.

Kurt asked us to close our eyes, and he led us in meditation, and encouraged us to imagine, going down, through our feet, into the earth, to a place deep within, where the Earth Spirit was waiting for us, where she would speak to each one of us individually.

I could feel my body trembling, as my consciousness expanded into a realm of deep and wondrous love. I sensed that I was approaching the heart of the Earth being, and it felt such a privilege to be allowed to be there. In my mind, I heard words, imparted with the same tone that had spoken through Julia. It was the Earth Spirit, communicating with me. I was told to be brave, and join with my group. The inspiring presence that was with me offered gratitude that I was meeting her, and I felt warm tingling at both the crown of my head and the base of my feet. It was as though I was being blessed and there was a tremendous flow of loving energy in my body. At this juncture, I must have gone away somewhere deep inside me, for when I became aware again of the seat where my body was resting, it felt as if I had emerged from a long sleep.

Julia was sitting up now, and I could hear Kurt's words, as he brought us out of the meditation. We then had a discussion, and Kurt informed us, how, when Julia did this work, her own consciousness moved completely to one side, so that the Spirit of the Earth could address everybody. She did not remember anything of it when she came back. It was a selfless act of service, and yet, at the same time, it opened her to spiritual communion with this profound being, and brought her closer to the Earth Spirit, every time that she did it.

Julia and Kurt, both, received daily instruction from the Earth Spirit in their private meditations. This guidance had been evolving as a spiritual vision of work that they could do together, to serve the people of the Earth.

Kurt wanted to tell us about this. He shared how he and Julia had the ambition to open an international school, where children from many countries could learn about the values of the Sacred Earth, and respect the links that existed between all life, an education based on meditation and shared love, the rights of all people and other life forms to co-exist in harmony, and for the children to learn work that could be done to transform the world.

This school could be part of a multi-faceted community, which also facilitated personal development courses for adults to help them connect with the Spirit of the Earth, and gain skills for actual environmental work, to help restore the Earth to its abundant pristine state. Kurt told us that they wished to manifest this Community, and bring it from being a dream, into reality. They did not know yet where this place would be, but had complete faith that it would emerge. Kurt and Julia wanted to be involved in the construction of this place, and Julia had seen visions of them doing that.

I could feel an energy rush, flowing through my body. Immediately, I knew that I *had* to join this project, that this was what my life was all about. I wanted to help manifest this Community too. Nothing else mattered as much as me being part of this. I glanced across at Sarah, and there was a light in her eyes. She squeezed my hand, and I knew that she felt the same. Simon and Eve were looking at each other, and she nodded to him. Then Simon stood up, and spoke aloud to confirm that he and Eve wanted to join with Kurt and Julia in this venture. Sarah and I stood up to make sure that we were included too. We were all 'in'. It was like a 'coming home'. Kurt looked at us with appreciation.

When everyone else had gone, the six of us remained. We had much to talk about. Simon invited everyone to come to their place, and we did that. And the discussions and sharing went on until the early hours of the morning.

A MEETING OF SOULS

Eve and Simon were very inspired by the vision set forward by Kurt and Julia. They were practical people and were used to making ideas come alive and be manifested.

In her work with the United Nations, Eve had contact with many agencies that were working in Third World countries with children. There was a huge need for young people in these countries to receive worthwhile education – especially girls. What would be even better would be a more spiritually based education, designed to help the Earth. For Eve, such a concept had been at the back of her mind for a long time. She wanted to explore how it would be possible to arrange sponsorship campaigns, and select young people, with sensitive qualities, and the potential for leadership, to receive tuition at this school. She could see it happening. Even children from more affluent Western countries could benefit, because the spiritual outlook of caring for the Earth, was so much lacking in mainstream Western systems of education.

In Eve's mind, it was a meeting of Western and Third World cultures that was needed, putting children on an equal footing with each other. The community base of this project could be a model for how our world needed to be transformed. Eve felt that she could do a lot towards facilitating the international outreach of the project.

Simon, also, was enthusiastic, and felt that he could have a role in the legal side of establishing legitimacy for the project. In terms of raising finance, Simon had much experience with various forms of Crowd-funding organisations that were utilised online, and he had many connections and contacts that could help. He was confident that once a place was found and the financial needs of the place could be formulated, then many people would be prepared to contribute to this. It needed a keynote that would appeal to people. Once that was established, Simon knew how to engage in publicity campaigns to energise financial support. It would be a joy for him to be engaged with a project where he felt so much passion.

It was as though Julia and Kurt were the spiritual visionaries, while Eve and Simon were the more Earth-based ones, with expertise that could ground the vision. Sarah and I were not so sure how we were to fit in, but we were happy and content to sit there and listen.

From talking about the project, the conversation shifted. As the evening went on, there was space for more personal sharing, and Simon had the idea for us each to share about our backgrounds, and important experiences that we all had – experiences which had motivated us for what we wanted to achieve now.

Eve became teary when she started talking about her early life. She had been one of a large family, and when she was growing up, Eve was very close to her younger sister, Cindy. One evening, Cindy had been walking home when she had been set upon by a group of youths, who had taunted her and then dragged her down an alley, and raped her. Eve had heard the commotion from the window of her house and rushed out. She desperately tried to intervene and stop them physically, but they pushed her away violently and she fell against a stone wall and was knocked unconscious. The last thing she remembered hearing was the frantic screams of her beloved sister. Eve was taken to hospital and recovered, but two days later, Cindy's body was found in bushes some distance away. She had been killed by these youths.

After this, there was never peace in her family, and her mother and father quarrelled continually. Those youths were never brought to justice, so it was not possible to find resolution. The trauma of this event split the family apart, and it never recovered. Her parents divorced and stopped speaking to each other. Neither of them wanted to be reminded of the pain they felt, and they preferred to try to start completely new lives, away from each other.

Eve had nobody, but she was fortunate enough to receive counselling that eventually helped her to come to terms with her sister's murder, and she had several visitations from Cindy's soul to reassure her that she was safe in Spirit.

After years of therapy, Eve decided that she wanted to spend her life helping those that most needed it – especially families. She wanted to uphold people's rights, and to help others that were likely to suffer abuse. It was this experience that propelled her to doing the work that she was doing now.

Simon had his story too. As a boy, his family were poor, and a lot of the time, he barely had enough to eat. His father had a walking disability which made it difficult for him to work, but he knew that he had to work, to support the family. Because of his commitment, his father found work in an office, and worked long hours to provide enough income to keep everyone well. They rented the property where they lived.

Sadly, the Landlord, who owned the property, was a cruel and greedy man. He continued to raise the amount charged for rent, even though Simon's father appealed in vain to keep the amount affordable. Thus, Simon's father worked longer and longer hours, and Simon very rarely saw him. Finally, his father's health gave way, and he could not work any longer. He had to go to hospital, and the Landlord evicted them for not paying their rent. Consequently, they all ended up homeless. Eventually, they found their way to a homeless shelter, and Simon was placed in Care. His father died in hospital.

It could have been a terrible situation for Simon, except that the people who looked after him, were very kind and loving. And they lived on a farm. This was where Simon awakened to his love of nature, and his wish to preserve it, for his foster parents were both environmentalists. The experiences with his father made it very clear to him about the adverse effect that greed and corruption could have upon people, who were being impacted unfairly. Simon wanted to help people, who were vulnerable in this way.

When Simon and Eve had come together, not only did they love each other, but being with each other helped them both to recover a sense of family that they had lost when they were young.

We also heard from Kurt and Julia and more about their background. They had known each other from a very young age, and felt from the moment they met, that being with each other was a necessity. It was an inner knowing. So, everyone else, including family, receded in importance, and they were together all the time. They tried to be friendly with other children so they would not draw attention to themselves. But somehow, they felt different, and saved all their important talks for when they were with each other. They both had open minds, and were gradually able to discern a clear sense of their Spiritual purpose together. In their everyday life, they were inseparable, and Kurt was the protective one, always watching out for Julia.

They completed their schooling, and then followed their inner guidance about what they needed to do next. In their early adult lives, they visited many sacred sites where the energy had been damaged and together, they did Spiritual repair work. But they, knew ultimately, that their work was to be with people. Kurt wrote a book about channelling Julia had made from the Earth Spirit, and this helped to establish their reputation, so they could go on the Speaker's circuit, to various parts of the world.

They found, that when they told their story, to groups of people, that the best approach, was for them to be truthful, and open. It would then be up to people whether they accepted them or not. Happily, many people were open, and ready to receive their ideas, and Spiritual channelling. This made their work gratifying.

Not many people had come to the gathering organised at the University, but there was a special reason for that. Often, they did manage to speak with large groups of people at various events that they attended. However, both had felt inner signs, that this evening at the University, would mark a new phase of their work, which would expand greatly the scope of what they were doing. They both felt, that meeting us, signified the beginning of this, and had been meant to be. We all felt similarly.

It was a wonderful evening, and there was such a lot of warmth and happiness through being together. It felt so natural, as though we joined as a family of souls together somehow, and we pledged a commitment to support each other. Even though Sarah and I were the young ones in physical age, we still felt that we had our place. I did not feel overawed by the others. We all wished to work with Spirit and fulfil the vision of this project – it was a grandiose vision, but if we worked together, then maybe, just maybe, we could do it.

At the completion of the evening, we had a meditation together in which we allowed ourselves to spiritually unite and invoke Spirit to guide us, so we could fulfil our tasks together, for the Highest good, and for all beings on the Earth. It was a powerful meditation, and we all spoke about what we wanted to bring to the group. I volunteered to bring my strength and determination, while Sarah offered her love and gentleness. There was a great feeling of peace in the room when we had finished.

BEGINNING THE PROJECT

Simon and Eve invited Kurt and Julia to stay in their spare room as their guests. Meanwhile, Sarah invited me to share her room when we were at the house, so I wouldn't have to go back to the University. I was delighted. This way, we could all have time to be at the house, talk and work out our plans.

We were fortunate that Simon and Eve had a large house, for there was also a room that we could use to meditate together.

It was to be an intense period of activity between us, and we all adjusted our schedules, so that we could be as much together as possible.

Within days, Julia began to channel guidance about the location of the property where we needed to found the project, and gave suggestions about how we needed to set it up. We recorded these sessions, so that we could listen to them closely, and amazingly, we all accepted the truth of what she channelled, without question.

Simon was soon scouring the Internet to investigate sites that may coincide with the guidance received. He wrote down all the information for Sarah and me, too, so we enthusiastically joined in the search.

We had the name of the country, and the fact that it was a large expanse of land, which had been formerly rainforest. The Earth Spirit told us that it was a hilly landscape, and that one of those hills was a particularly strong power point for the Earth, one that needed to be reactivated. It was not a huge amount to go on, especially knowing how much of that country had been deforested in recent years.

Simon suggested that we look at properties for sale in the first instance. We were fortunate that this country allowed people from English speaking countries to purchase their property to a limited degree, so there were surveys of various land pockets that we were available. Julia could check with what we found, and none of them were right. We searched far and wide until we began to wonder if we were looking in the right places.

But then Eve had the hunch, to suggest for us to explore possible disused land, owned by the government of that Country, so we searched records, to discover what that would yield. It took a while to gain any information about this, for many of these sites were classified. However, there were a few that were open to public viewing. Sarah was the one who found it. Suddenly she stopped what she had been doing and told me to look. When she saw the description of this place, she had experienced tingles all the way through her body.

I trawled through the information on the computer, and the more that I read of it, the faster my heart was beating. Just as the guidance had stipulated, it was a very large expanse of land, and the terrain was hilly. The property was formerly rainforest, but had been cleared for cattle farming, and, as was typical with this type of clearing, much of the fertility of the area had then been lost. The cattle farmers were ready to move on, and claim further swathes of land, when uranium was found on one of the hills. A big mining company had subsequently purchased the property to obtain the uranium. However, after several years the seam of uranium that they had been exploiting, was exhausted and the mine was closed. Nobody wanted to buy it, and the government took the land because of the delicate nature of what had been mined there. From that time, the property had fallen into disuse. The rainforest had not grown back, and the land had become fallow with some piles of low-radioactive waste placed near the mine, which no one wanted to go near.

We had a meeting about it, and everyone was excited. It was concerning about the radioactive waste, but Simon had investigated about this, and as far as he could determine, the instances of this were confined to a few areas in the property, and he sensed that it need not interfere with what we wanted to do. Simon and Eve were in earnest conversation, exploring possibilities. It was hard to stop them. They already formulating their plan for action.

Simon suggested that their best chance for success may be to request to obtain a very long term lease of the land from the government – and to set it up as a Charitable Trust. We would need to present a proposal to the government of that country – a proposal that would be attractive enough, so it would find favour with the ministers concerned.

Sarah had discovered that the overall size of the land of the property was around 100,000 hectares, which was a huge amount to manage, but if part of the project aimed to replant the rainforest, while at the same time, using some of the land for propagating new systems of renewable energy, then these initiatives could have the potential of becoming an asset to the country. The government may gain much helpful publicity, through its support of this, and there could be economic benefits for the country too.

If, in addition to this, there could be a school established on the property, for children of various countries, for them to be educated and gain awareness of the needs of the planet. And if adults, especially from the local community, could be taught skills for sustainable living, that they could then, return and use, in the places where they had lived, then how could the government refuse? The sections of the property, with raised radiation levels could be fenced off. The ideas were flowing thick and fast.

Eve was the more sensible one, and she was already formulating ideas of a detailed plan to present to the government. This would have to emphasise the environmental and education aspects of the project, rather than the Spiritual side of our work, only so that it could gain acceptance within the Government circles. Then we would need lobbyists to put our proposals forward to the relevant ministers. Eve made clear, that we would have to set up a formulation for our Charitable Trust that would give a legal basis for our work, something that could also be examined by the ministry.

If we did all this well, Eve was confident that the proposal would have appeal. It would not cost their Government anything, and could give them international recognition, and credibility, that would be very beneficial to them.

But then, we would have to fund the project. How would we do that? That was another matter, an important matter, but for Eve, to have contracts for obtaining the lease was what was most crucial.

This was where Simon stepped in. He was confident that we could do it, even the funding. He and Eve had a network of people that would be interested in this project. They could impress them, to harness their support and their skills. There would be much to do. Simon was ready to activate this.

With Simon, his thought processes were so rapid, it was as if the whole project was already in motion, and Eve was not far behind him. Together, they were a formidable team. But even as they were in full flight with all their ideas, Simon paused for a moment, so we could catch up, and reflected with a sigh, turning towards Eve in acknowledgement.

Simon agreed with Eve, that in dealing with governments and competing interests, which may be calling on the attention of governments – getting them to grant permission to implement projects could be a very complex process, one that was hardly ever as straight forward as it should be.

'Then we need to pray,' spoke Julia. 'We need to pray and invoke Spiritual help every day, and we need to envision our project flowering and manifesting to its full extent and being a positive vehicle for healing your beloved Earth. This needs to be a project, not from our personal wills, but in tune with the greater good, and with higher purpose of what is meant for our work to be, in service to the Earth Spirit and humanity, and all life forms on your world, and beyond.'

'I can also help,' added Kurt. 'During our travels, we have met with some extraordinary people with gifts that could be employed most usefully on our project. Some of them are teachers, and others are inventors, scientists and technicians with skills in the field of renewable technology, and further ones we know, that are interested in the restoration of the environment. This will be a project for the many, not the few.' It was all coming together.

Later, Kurt led us in a meditation, to link together, and to invoke Spiritual help for the manifestation of our project. It took a while for my mind to become quiet, for it was buzzing with ideas, but eventually, it did so. Then I could hear the deep sombre sounds of Julia's voice, channelling the Earth Spirit. From that very quiet place within, I listened intently.

'You have been brought here together because you want to help. We, in the world of Spirit, cannot affect the free will of people. How others respond to you is up to them. However, this is a time of need. Every act of kindness and love you make in your world, will make a difference. Remember that in what you do. I speak as the Spirit of this Earth. You have many Spiritual brothers and sisters acting with you all over the globe. If we can but succeed, it will mean that I can shed this old worn body of limited consciousness that has affected your perception. This act on my part, as the Spiritual being of the Earth, will enable you all to open to a much more expansive awareness of great light and love and connectedness. I will be renewed, and all life in this world, will be liberated, to a wondrous state of joy and peace. This is what I am here to do. I am grateful therefore, and offer my support, for all you can do to assist this transformation.'

AN APPRENTICESHIP

The next days, weeks and months were frantic. I decided to quit my university course. My parents argued against it, and my father threatened to withdraw all support for me if I left my studies. But I did it anyway, without hesitation, and they stopped all contact with me, and support. I did not feel happy about this, and knew that at some point, I would need to resolve it with them, but I would have to do it later.

Sarah stopped her university course as well, and we lived permanently together, in her room at the family home. Julia and Kurt stayed for a while, but then went on their travels, so that they could continue their public engagements and summon interest for our project. From that moment, it left four of us in the house to administrate our next steps.

Sarah and I worked with Simon and Eve. We became like Personal Assistants. They explained what they were doing, and we had to learn, so we could help them and supplement their efforts. It was quite a change of life. Sometimes, I was with Eve, and other times, with Simon. The work never stopped. There were letters to be drafted, emails sent, legal statements prepared, networking publicity arranged. A lot of the work was computer based, and it was a big learning curve for me. But I enjoyed it – we all enjoyed it. And each day, we would set up our plans and objectives, and go about achieving all those.

Sarah and I travelled with Eve, to a meeting at the United Nations. Eve was speaking to workers, from Agencies, that may be able to supply young students to learn and be educated at our Centre. She also attended another meeting aimed at fund raising. Sarah and I had to be dressed up. I wore a suit and tie; I had never worn anything like it. We had to meet with representatives from these different countries, and offer positive words and affirmation about what we would be doing. It was a new world, but one in which Eve and Simon wanted us both to be familiar.

We were also able to accompany Simon when he arranged meetings. Julia had channelled information about the design of our Centre and what that could look like and the materials to be used. Simon needed, to then meet with a team of architects, to explore if the vision of those designs would be feasible, and how the centre could actually be built. Sarah, with her artistic nature, could add input to this, and she helped the architects compose drawings that would be representative of what had been channelled. I noticed how sensitive Sarah was becoming to the channelling of the Earth Spirit, and her connection with this energy was becoming ever more confident and assured. We needed these sketches of our vision for the Centre and outbuildings, as part of our presentation, to the ministries of the Government in the country where our project was to be.

We also had to meet with environmentalists, and begin to assemble a team that could take responsibility for planting trees and restoring the rainforest. This was a field where I had interest, and it did not take long before a group of volunteers were ready and willing to be involved with this.

There were a couple of diplomatic functions where the four of us were invited. For the first time, I mingled with politicians and their representatives. Simon instructed us to be polite and positive, praising the achievements of the host country of our project, and the efforts of its government, and answering questions about our project, simply and honestly.

I did not find it easy, at first, to be able to speak, and some of the luminaries' present did not speak a lot of English. Therefore, I smiled a lot, and stayed quite close to Sarah. Many of the dignitaries gathered around Simon, and he was busy explaining various aspects of the project. Eve, too, attracted interest with her position, but the country where we wanted to found the project, was not a country where women tended to be considered so important. For Eve, this enlivened her determination, in making the case for investing in education, and bringing youth together, more vital.

We did not always go with Eve and Simon, when they went away, and sometimes just one of us would be asked to go. But the work did not stop, and we would have assignments to complete on the computer, when Sarah's parents were not with us.

At the end of each day, we made it a ritual, to meditate, and to connect with the Earth Spirit and to ask Spirit to assist us in the manifestation of the project. This helped to bring about an emotional bond between us, but we wanted to nourish the Spiritual bond with the Earth Spirit, which we felt, already existed.

From the moment, I met Sarah, Simon and Eve, I felt a sense of belonging with them, but the longer that I stayed with them, the more this bond deepened for me. It was like, the genetic family I had had, faded into the background. They did not contact me, but also, I did not miss them. My father had paid a considerable amount of money towards me going to university, and I felt that I needed to pay him back. I spoke to Simon about this, and he gave me an allowance for my work with him, to enable me to do that. I did not need a salary, for I was doing this work for the love of it, and Simon and Eve were committed to care for my basic needs, to honour the contribution that I made. However, I was grateful for Simon being willing to support me with this, around my father.

My world was taken up with the project, and all those involved. I could think of nothing else that mattered to me. I felt happy and at peace with it all. With Sarah, also, we were becoming ever closer. We shared a bed, and we often talked until long into the night, sharing our hopes and dreams. I found it so easy to be with her, and she seemed to be very relaxed with me as well.

VISIT

A few weeks later, Simon received an email, and we had an invitation to visit the land of the property, which we wanted to lease. It was still not certain whether the government would grant us permission, but it was encouraging that we were to be given a tour of the site and the opportunity to outline our plans, to officials from the government.

We had to plan our trip carefully, and in our party, we informed the Government representatives, that we wished to include our chief architect and environmentalist, plus two representatives of disadvantaged groups coming from the United Nations, a few competent translators, as well as an economist friend of Simon. Julia and Kurt would be with us too.

Before we left, we had a long meeting, where we were all briefed, so we would have common positions on issues, which we would be likely to discuss. Our Spirits were high.

A delegation of officials was waiting for us at the airport, and after resting that night at the airport hotel, we were then driven three hours on a dirt track until we reached the gate at the entrance to the property. All around the property, there had been a high wire fence erected, with signs prohibiting access. The site itself appeared to be in ruins. Not many trees remained. There were a few rainforest remnants at the far end of the property, scattered rotting logs, and other trees standing in isolation. The ground was waterlogged in many places, and not much general plant life was growing there anymore. Piles of rubble and abandoned machinery were littered here and there. It was quite a desolate scene, and it went on and on – such a vast area of land. In my imagination, I could project what it may have been like before the cattle farmers cleared all the forest, and I felt a lump in my throat, and intense sadness.

There was a specific place within the property where Julia wanted us to go, and Kurt asked the officials, on her behalf, if Julia could direct us. The Government people were curious, knowing that we were all there for the first time, but acquiesced to Kurt's request. We drove on through the wasteland, until Julia pointed to a mound just ahead of us.

When we got out of the jeeps we had been travelling in, Julia's face was beaming. She touched the ground with her hand and kissed the Earth. There was something quite unusual about this mound. Sarah reached over and held my hand. She must be feeling it too. Underneath my feet, I could sense a faint vibration that brought tingles of energy through my body. The Earth Spirit was strong here. It must be the place, which Julia wanted to find.

Nearby, there were two trees standing together. They looked quite alone. One of them appeared withered and quite droopy, as if it had suffered in silence. But the other one appeared to have life for two, and was much more vibrant and tall, with a thick trunk and a bountiful canopy of leaves. I was so grateful that these trees had been spared from being cut down. Julia whispered to us, that they were the Guardian trees.

For a few minutes, we conferred with Julia. She was full of enthusiasm and certainty. This was to be the position, where our centre would be built. This was the power point for the Earth, that she had spoken about.

In this moment, Simon went into action with his team, and soon they were busy engaging the officials in all sorts of plans and proposals. There was much hand pointing and nodding of heads, while the practical vision of the project was discussed in detail and presented knowledgably. Trust had to be built with these officials, and we needed to listen to them, as well as put forward our own ideas for the project. The officials were busy taking notes, and recording what we were purporting to do. I could hear Hugh, our chief environmentalist, explaining techniques he would use to rejuvenate the forest. It was quite exciting, to listen to him speak. Sarah took an interest in the talks, that Eve and her colleagues gave about the schools and the adult education. As well as classrooms and outbuildings, Simon had come up with a proposal to build a conference centre, that would host delegates attending international seminars and workshops. All these people would need to be housed, so the infrastructure for that needed to be considered as well.

Underpinning the project, was an ethos, where we wanted to establish a culture of sustainable living, including renewable energy – solar power with battery storage, extensive rainwater tanks, living organic sewage plants. We wished to set up sizable permaculture gardens, with organic food growing – a way of life in tune with the Earth. It was a very, very ambitious scheme, which would need lots of backing, and many people to be involved. Ultimately, we were looking to create a small village here, rather than a single Centre.

The officials were concerned about how much local involvement there would be, and Simon had to assure him that we would be employing local teachers, and that many of the children attending classes would come from surrounding villages and townships. It would be an international centre where English would be spoken, but the native language here, would also be encouraged, and used as a second language. It was hoped that students that graduated from the school could bring their knowledge into local communities to help them. He emphasised that most of the workers, within the Project, would also be hired from the local area, and classes would be given, so they could learn principles of sustainable living. These skills could be transferred, by our workers, to other outlaying settlements, away from the property, to enable prosperity and self-sufficiency within village communities in the country, so they could become more embedded.

Over on the mound, while all the talking was going on, Julia was lying down and meditating, and Kurt was next to her. Sarah went over to join them, but I wanted to continue to listen, so I stayed with the officials and our group.

By the end of the day, there was a happy atmosphere among everyone. The Officials escorted us back to the airport, and told us that a decision would be made shortly. As we flew in the plane back to our own country, there was a strong feeling of optimism that what we wanted, would be granted to us. The government was basically supportive. Julia told us that the Earth was with us with her love. This was the right place, and those loving beings of Spirit would guide us.

FUND RAISING

It was only a few days afterwards. On this morning, Simon switched on his computer, and there was an official letter attached to an email from the consulate, about the property. He shouted for us all to come, and we gathered around, barely able to contain our excitement. As he opened the attachment, we all peered over Simon's shoulders, to read it together.

We were to be granted a 99-year lease for the property, subject to conditions. Reading through, the main condition, stipulated that we had six months to demonstrate, and produce, a certain baseline level of financial support for the project, with written detailed plans, commensurate with that. Without that financial backing and detailed infrastructure projections, which met with the local building regulations, the offer of the lease would then lapse.

There was silence in the group. This was the first step, and a hugely significant moment. We had been granted conditional permission for the lease. But this was only the very beginning.

Simon was thoughtful. The government was being supportive and flexible. He felt that they wanted us to succeed. But the amount of money, which we would need to raise in this short time – was massive. And there were so many other preparations we would need to make too.

Where to start? There was no faltering in our resolve. We all had roles that would be needed in this. Sarah and I both felt, that we would need to continue to work under the guidance of Eve and Simon. We would need a much bigger organisation. It was so daunting, but very exciting.

Julia and Kurt left us once more, to continue their speaking and workshop tour. They could, at last, ask for donations and general support from people, for now there was an actual place that gave substance to the vision that had been given to them. Our two Spiritual friends were determined to fulfil the work they had to do with as much energy as they could muster. We were in daily contact with them and meditated at the same time with them, so inwardly our efforts would also be attuned together.

Simon was our coordinator, and he would manage the overall work we had to do. He wanted to delegate tasks, so we could be both efficient and productive.

Simon suggested that the most productive means of gaining funding, could be through general Crowd-funding. Sarah would oversee this. The needs of the project would be placed in various categories, for we had to raise money for the School, for the Conference Centre, for the Sanctuary, the Renewable Energy Project, the Forest restoration environmental management scheme, as well as money to construct housing and general infrastructure that would be needed. We had to seek funding for each of these individually, for there would be different groups of people with specific interest in aspects of the work, that we planned to do. Therefore, Sarah had to focus not only on the whole project, but she needed to find outlets for all these facets of our work, and seek this support from many countries, because of the international interest that this would attract. The rest of us would assist her with the details.

I was to help Simon with social media publicity, writing and contacting organisations and philanthropists, fielding much of the correspondence, that came our way. Simon himself, wanted to orientate himself, not only to the raising of funds, but also to the practical particulars, how we could construct the project and get it running, once we had the funds. He and Eve, would also liaise with government personnel, and organise visas, and all that sensitive detail, which was required.

Eve was not with us very much, for she was travelling and raising consciousness about our project, with all the agencies, which she knew, from within the United Nations and beyond. She was primarily interested in the establishment of the school, and wanted to investigate how children could be selected to attend the school, and devise the curriculum, which the school would offer. Eve promised that she would also promote other facets of our work with the people she met.

The scope of our project was mammoth, and we could not manage it on our own. We were fortunate that Simon had so much experience at managing large scale enterprises. He told us what we would need to do.

We would need highly skilled people, with the abilities to help us organise all the various facets of the project. It was necessary for us to proceed, as if we would have all the capital we required, and that all the branches of the project, could come into being. Much would be preparatory work in the beginning, but it was all needing to happen at once. We would need to delegate authority to these skilled workers, while maintaining an overview of holding the vision, while giving attention to those areas that most needed it.

Simon wanted to train Sarah and I so we could directly assist him, and support with the overall management. He and Eve were also willing to invest a substantial amount from their own capital and savings to help provide salaries and support in the beginning stages. Fortunately, both Simon and Eve had people that regularly worked with them – people with expert knowledge in their fields. Many of them, were willing to help us, and some of them became full-time workers in our fledgling organisation, working from their bases in other localities and connecting with us via their computers.

We set up our office spaces in Simon's and Eve's house, and soon it became a hive of activity. Simon was patient with us, and gave us as much time as he could, but often, we had to learn on the job, for Simon would be away, and we just had to do the best that we could.

We had volunteers that were drawn to us, some coming via Julia and Kurt, and we sought to find meaningful work for all those interested, to assist us in our project. For me, it was such a huge learning curve, and I often wondered how we could possibly do it all. There was a need for discipline, taking one step at a time, and working together with as much harmony and awareness as we could. With all those many people linking in with us, ultimately, we needed to be responsible, and ensure that we kept to the highest path of our vision.

Each day, we began early, with our joint meditation, and then a group Skype session to link up and to discuss issues and the needs of the day, to also share emotionally, how we were coping and progressing. Once a week, we had a more encompassing meeting, with some of us online, but we needed this meeting, to support each other, and to give gratitude for what we had achieved. There were times when we were more hopeful and other times when some of us doubted. We had to feel that we were there for each other, and during the rest of our time, to offer support to all those working with us, so that the sense of organism within our larger group, could grow, and flourish with love.

Every day was very intense and full. I was on the phone, and the computer, talking and communicating for many hours at a time. I had to speak with so many kinds of people, and groups from diverse cultural and personal backgrounds. It was necessary to be calm and know how best to deal with each one. In the beginning, I had a few fumbles and did not know what to say, but Simon coached me, and I learnt quickly. This was all totally new for me, but somewhere inside, it felt as if I had been waiting for this time, all my life. I felt joy.

HEALING AND PROGRESS

One day, Sarah and I made a trip to the university. It was a bit of a break for us, but we wanted to place some leaflets and information about our project around some of the departments, and meet faculty members, to discuss what we were doing. As we went along the central Walkway in the Campus, there were a couple of familiar people in front of us.

Sarah was holding my hand, and I felt her grip tighten. She had noticed them too. It was Jake and Lydia from the activist group. I had thought about them many times, and my heart jumped, when I saw them. Their eyes looked down, as if they wanted to avoid us. They must have still felt some shame about what happened. They didn't need to feel like that. I felt them as my friends.

Rather than just casually pass by them, I made a point of stopping. Sarah stood with me, and we looked them in the eye, to greet them openly. This appeared to help them accept us. For a few minutes, we spoke about the coal mine, and how that had all worked out, and it seemed to relax them, for us to be so open about it all. But then I started to inform them about our project and the plans we had. Sarah joined in. They both looked up at us, and their eyes lit up, and they were very interested. As we shared more, Jake stopped us, and he looked over at his partner, and she nodded. Then they smiled. It was like they could communicate with each other telepathically. Each knew what the other was thinking. It was as if they were another Spiritual pair like us.

They wanted to help us, and be part of what we were doing. After all that had happened, they wanted to do something now to make a positive difference and stop engaging all their efforts on fighting authority. What could they do? Their strongest interest, of course, was the environment, and the tree restoration, and I knew that our environmental expert, Hugh, needed some assistance. I felt ecstatic that they may become involved. When we spoke of the location, they were even more pleased, for they wanted a fresh start, and felt this would be perfect. They wanted to do it, and they were enthusiastic with our ideas. Simon could organise their visas for when we moved there.

We went to a nearby café to talk in more detail. They shared how after the demonstration, that they had been in a kind of limbo, not knowing how they could move forward. Jake became emotional, when he told us how difficult for him to accept what the police had done to everyone there. Lydia tried to comfort him. They really did need a worthwhile task, where they could put their energies.

Soon they were asking when they could start. I felt happy in my heart. It would be great to team up with them again. They were also happy to help with our fundraising. We all said 'yes' and agreed to it then and there. Meeting them was a big boost to our day.

Sarah and I were gaining more confidence, both with administration and with our contacts with people. Relating to others about the Project, when it meant such a lot to us, certainly made it easier. We also supported each other, and had to use our own initiatives to deal with the situations that we faced. Often, it was just the two of us together in the house, and we would sit near each other, as we were on the phone, or engaged with tasks.

We rarely saw our friends Kurt and Julia, but spoke to them regularly by Skype. They were attracting growing support. Julia and Kurt now inspired hundreds, if not thousands of people, especially through Julia's channelling of the Earth Spirit. When Julia channelled the Earth Spirit, it would have the impact of breaking through into people's inner consciousness. Some of the people attending their talks and seminars, had great and important aspirations and tasks to fulfil. When they opened their consciousness to the voice and presence of the Earth Spirit, they would realise their own mission to help the Earth. For many, it was a revelation that changed their lives. Among these, some felt drawn that they wanted to contribute, and be part of the Project we were initiating. Others had their own projects they could foresee, and they wanted to create that in conjunction with ours. And of course, there were people motivated spiritually to act towards an independent goal that did not interact with ours. It was inspiring to witness the work that Kurt and Julia were doing..

Each day, there would be people making enquiries, offering their services, asking questions. I tried to tune in with each person, to be as positive as I could be, and encourage them with the best way that they could help. Within myself, I knew that every person that made contact, was there for a reason, and it was important to honour them, rather than turn them away. Where it was necessary, I referred enquiries on to other channels. Simon and Eve had compiled a list of people and contacts, who could work with people in specific fields.

Simon had worked out the legal framework for our Project as an international Charitable Trust. We received many donations of various sizes. All these, we had to acknowledge, and offer gratitude. We had some wealthy benefactors that offered us some of their fortune, and others that had only a little, but offered it with their heart. All donations were valuable and important, irrespective of the amount, and we needed to accept them all, with love.

The crowd-funding opportunities gathered lots of financial pledges of support, and some of the schemes, and facets of the Project, raced towards their goal, for future manifestation. Simon also worked out some investment ideas, around the Conference Centre and Renewable Energy project. In the case of the Conference Centre, where groups and organisations had events that they wanted to showcase – and they needed to be activities in harmony with our ideals – then they could invest in the establishment of the Conference Centre, and its associated facilities, in exchange for future guaranteed usage of the Centre for their clients, at various times in the year. With the Renewable Energy, we wanted not only to be completely self-sustaining in energy with Solar power storage systems, but we wanted to offer research and development faculties, which could help these new technologies to have a space to be explored, and made viable. In this, we were looking for organisations, which would sponsor our work, in exchange for a share in the returns, from the future.

Eve was busy gathering agency and governmental support for our Project. There were many charities prepared to gather funds to sponsor children to attend our school. The means for this to happen, all had to be set up carefully, and in accordance with international agreements already in place. We wanted an international school, that not only would have a Spiritual base, with concern for the environment, but would also promote multiculturalism and education for diverse societies, and underprivileged groups that needed it. From our meditations, we knew that for people to open to a sense of interconnectedness, not only with each other, but with all living beings, it was vital for those people to be in environments where they could practice this. Children were open and receptive, and could learn this from a young age. Then, the principles and reality of inter-connectedness, would be embedded in their consciousness. Our school could be a model and example, and we hoped that other schools like it would follow.

There was a vibrant hub of activity where we worked together. I had never felt so much alive. It was so good to be engaged in something that could make a positive difference to our world, and more than anything, I wished for it to work and to be successful. Gradually, step by step, our planning advanced, and the financial baseline that we needed to be able to build, and start the construction of the Project, became nearer and closer to our grasp.

I was pleasantly surprised by the level of support that we were attracting. What I sensed, was that in many communities in the world, that there were people yearning to be able to act and make a positive difference. They needed something, that they could believe in – not ventures that were infiltrated by corruption and self-interest, or enterprises involved in activities, that were basically harming our planet. We all had the capacity to recognise what was good for the world, and people needed to acknowledge that and wake up. Our project was intended as a beacon of light to show what was possible, to give people hope, so our Earth could become a better place. Many people had these ideals, but we wanted this to be achievable, and to do it.

A BIG MOMENT

It was close. Only three days remained before the deadline, when we finally got the financial backing in place, that we needed. The tension had mounted in the days before this. It had taken some last minute substantial loans from a few of Simon's friends, to bridge the remaining gaps. But we were there.

Now we could make our submission to the Government that held the land for our Project. We were all nervous and rather excited, as we prepared this. Simon had drafted in lawyers and accountants to assist with the paper work. It was a substantial document.

We all stood around the computer with Simon, while he sent the document away. Then, we looked at each other, and asked Higher Beings to help us. Julia had told us to hold true to our faith. It was out of our hands now, and we would have to wait, while the Government scrutinised the documents and gave its response. So much work had gone into this, so many people offering support. Surely, our proposal would be accepted? This was a crucial moment.

Over the next nights, I did not sleep very well, and Sarah was restless too. We tossed and turned. In the mornings, we meditated together, but I didn't manage very well to still my mind. I was too occupied with my thoughts, and Sarah seemed to be reacting similarly. It was only Julia who appeared to be calm, when we spoke to her on Skype. She was always calm.

Then one night, I slept, and Sarah slept next to me. We both woke up with the clear feeling that this would be the day. So, it turned out to be. Sarah and I were having our breakfast in the sitting room, when Simon came in, grinning, broadly. He had an announcement. For a minute or two, he kept us in suspense, while we put our plates down, and stood up. Then he told us.

The government had approved the project to go ahead.

We went a bit crazy. I was shouting, Sarah too, and we were jumping up and down. Eve had been sleeping in after arriving from a late flight. She came out of her bedroom wondering what all the fuss was all about. Then she joined in our celebrations too. Simon opened Skype and connected with Kurt and Julia. They were delighted.

Simon told us the details. It had been decreed that we had sufficient financial backing and detailed planning in place, which they required. Now we could have the keys to the entrance of the property and start building. It was amazing!

Two days later, we all gathered together. Julia and Kurt had travelled to be with us. Kurt led us in a meditation, and Julia channelled the Earth Spirit. With our inner vision, we were directed to be standing at the base of the Guardian trees on the land where we would base our Centre. I could feel the energy of the trees, and there was a warm glowing energy rising, and emerging from deep below. The Earth Spirit was with us, and bringing us sustenance for what we wanted to create and manifest. It was a new dawn, and I felt very excited.

It was not long before we were on the plane to gain entrance to the property, as lease holders. I was so thrilled in anticipation for us put our feet on the ground there. We decided that before anything else happened, that the six of us would go to the Guardian trees alone, and conduct a ceremony of thanks and welcome.

In my own mind, although we had been working very hard, long hours each day, with a high level of commitment, and we had good people working with us, it still felt a major miracle, that we had achieved, and got this far. I just believed that there must have been inner forces working with us, and supporting us, so that it all would be possible, to enable our dream to be ready to be built. All the financial support, and the many people contributing towards achieving our goals – it had been incredible. I felt gratitude inside my heart, and tears of joy streamed down my cheeks.

Walking along that path towards the two Guardian trees, I stood next to Sarah. She held my hand, and then, turning to face me, she whispered to me. 'I am happy David'. I nodded and gazed at her, with a contented smile. We enjoyed walking together, with the soft damp earth, beneath our feet. There was a slight mist in the air with a slight breeze, and the temperature was warm.

I valued very much, Sarah's companionship. She was very gentle and quiet, a lot of the time, but she had tremendous strength and determination. When she spoke with people, she could be very firm and insistent, but she could be soft as well. We sometimes spoke about our hopes for the future. Our whole life together was wrapped around the Project and our dedication to that. She wanted to be a teacher for the children and to help Eve, but she was also very interested in Julia's work. Sarah felt great joy and ecstasy when connecting with the Earth Spirit, as if she was held and embraced by this Spirit, and it gave her a tremendous feeling of peace. For both of us, working together with the Project gave us a feeling of 'being at home,' and doing what we were supposed to do.

Julia and Kurt, plus Simon and Eve, were close by. We walked together and made a circle next to the Guardian tree. Together, we held hands, and Kurt led us in a blessing invocation, asking that we could be guided to work in harmony and love, and that our actions would be attuned to the Divine plan for this place. He invoked the help and support of the Earth Spirit, and all the other Spiritual beings working with us, with the aim of bringing the unfolding Earth Consciousness into the hearts and minds of humanity. We then stood in silence, and opened ourselves to the Earth Spirit and the land around us. It was a beautiful place to found our community, but it also needed a lot of healing and work, to clear the damage that had been left here, and to replenish it.

Julia started to hum, we listened, and joined with her sound. As we chanted together, she uttered sounds and words that I did not recognise, for it felt like a very ancient language. Julia was channelling the Earth Spirit and other Star beings. She could channel many different Spiritual beings. Julia was amazing, and I listened in awe.

My intuition told me that Julia was creating an inner link between the Earth and other worlds, and grounding that through her voice. I trusted her. It was a very poignant atmosphere, and one that held deep meaning to all that we were doing. As she continued, I opened my eyes, and looked up at her, and there was a strange but brilliant light that I could feel around her. And she was smiling, in a way that I had never seen from her before.

When she had finished, again we stood in silence, and then Kurt invited us to speak about our wishes for the Project, and what we each wanted to bring to it all. It was good to voice this, with all of us there, and to listen to each one, within the circle. We each had our own individual interests, but also common aspirations, which united us. I could sense a great many Spiritual beings joining us, and adding their presence to the occasion. As our sharing, continued, we all felt a great deal of closeness with each other. One at a time, we voiced our commitment to the work we would do, and I felt wonderful warmth in my heart as I spoke, and had my turn.

At the end of the ceremony, we released hands, and all was quiet. There was peace. We contemplated the wonders of this land.

What would we call our project? We began a discussion to determine a name for our Centre. It was Eve that came up with the name 'New Earth Community'. It did not seem especially original as a name, but it resonated with what we were doing. As we all attuned to this, there was agreement, and we smiled. It was good to have a name for it all.

After this, we discussed more practical matters. Simon had brought drawings of the site and proposals of where buildings would be situated. He showed us, by pointing out landmarks, how the drawings translated into actual locations for the various structures that would be built. We had been through this already at Simon's and Eve's home, but it was very different doing it here. Simon and his architects had had to rely on satellite imagery to envision where they could place things. Now, as we looked, there was general acquiescence for the plans. For Julia and Kurt, the most important building would be the Sanctuary. Simon went through this with them. He traced the position carefully with our two friends, and made some minor adjustments, until they were satisfied, and pleased. We discussed the positioning of the other buildings as well. The whole centre would be like a small village once it was constructed. It was an incredible operation, now about to commence its building phase.

COMPLETIONS AND NEW BEGINNINGS

Simon had amassed a formidable team of architects and planners, builders and project managers. There were so many logistical problems to be overcome. It was not the easiest of situations, when the only entrance to the property was a dirt track surrounded by muddy and rocky ground. We would have to clear some of that, widen the road, and take down fences that no longer served any purpose.

There were basic requirements such as water that needed to be supplied. The property was in a tropical region, so there was a plentiful quantity of rainfall. To solve this problem, we had decided to install numerous large rainwater tanks, and a reservoir.

As much as possible, we wanted to be self-sufficient and sustainable in all aspects of our life together.

There were also plans for large spaces, where we could grow vegetables, and other areas for orchards with various fruit. Then there was housing, and play areas for the children. So many details needed to be considered. However, even with all the building and infrastructure, this would be utilizing only a small portion of the land that we had been given. Much of it remained for the forest and land regeneration.

At the end of the day, we left the property to go, where we had come from. As I sat in the plane next to Sarah, my mind was full of ideas and visions. It was a strange feeling to arrive at Simon's and Eve's house, knowing that soon we would be leaving and moving to be permanently on site with our Project. Simon was going to sell the house, so that the proceeds from that could be used to help with the costs of the Project. It was time for completion, and there was one important task that I still had to do. I had been thinking about it for some time.

My important task, was to visit my family, and to return the money to my father. It did not feel easy. And it was not the money, but the feeling that I had let my parents down.

When I spoke with Sarah about this, she could see the pain in my eyes. I had not fulfilled what they wanted me to do, and I had moved outside their circle. Since starting all the work on the Project, I had not had contact with them. Part of me felt like I was abandoning them, but I knew that I had to do what was right for me. Sarah offered to come with me, but I felt that this was a journey that I needed to make on my own, and to stand in my own strength.

I took a deep breath as I came up their drive way. Knocking on the front door, I felt some trepidation, unsure whether they would even want to see me. My mother answered, and she invited me in. My father was in the living room, and I reached out to him, with the envelope of money, and he took it appreciatively. We sat down, and they offered me a hot drink. I tried to explain to them about what I was doing, and the aim of our group, to help the Earth. They listened patiently for a while, but then changed the subject, and they talked about the people they knew in the town, and the football games they had attended. Neither them nor I were more than half-interested in what the other had to say.

My sister came in, and I gave her a brief hug. She sat silently next to her mother and snuggled up next to her. I looked around awkwardly. The conversation faltered, and did not go on very long. At one point, I realised that all that we could say to each other, had been said. I stood up, and I made my excuses to leave. They came over to the door with me. Our partings were cordial, and I looked in their eyes, each of them. Our paths were going in different ways. As I went down the driveway, I felt emotion and sadness in my chest. I was glad to have made the effort. The further I went away, the more it felt like a weight had been lifted from my shoulders. And I let them go.

Later that day, I was with the work of the Project again. I was happy to surrender to that. There was much activity.

The day soon came when I left Simon's and Eve's place for the final time. I glanced back at their house with gratitude. We were all leaving together. As I travelled on the plane, with my suitcase and the few belongings that I had, on board, I felt genuinely eager and happy. Sarah was sitting next to me, as was natural with us. It felt great to be doing this together.

FIRST DAYS IN A NEW LAND

For the first nights in our New Earth Community home, we slept in tents, while we waited for workers and volunteers to join us. As I woke up in the mornings, and looked out, there was early gentle mist lingering around the contours of the land. When I stood up, and went outside, I could feel a soft vibration of the Earth Spirit under my feet.

Before long, our builders were busy. A temporary administration building was constructed, with solar power and satellite technology erected. This enabled us to access the Internet and to continue our office work. Each day, we continued our rhythm of early morning meetings and meditation, and then further meetings with the building staff and all our support workers, followed by hours of physical work. There was a lot of movement and much to be achieved.

I spent a lot of time with Hugh, our chief environmental co-ordinator. This was the aspect of our Community life, where I felt most drawn. I wanted to plant trees. However, before any planting could begin, a toxicology report needed to be prepared, so areas with residual radioactivity from the mining could to be cordoned off. Then people would be protected from any risks posed by this.

As much as possible, Hugh wanted to manifest a rich variety of biodiversity, which would match what had previously existed on the land, before all the land clearances. He had been researching about this ahead of us all arriving.

With the environmental work, and in other areas, we were employing local people to help us. There were people in the nearby villages, who engaged in shamanic practices, and prepared medicines from plants, that grew in the rainforest. These people were experts in the natural cultivation of the land. We needed them to help us and Hugh was gathering a group of them to work with us.

There was a large vacant area close to where the main buildings would be. This was where Hugh wanted to construct a nursery, which could propagate lots of indigenous plant and tree species. These fledgling plants and trees needed a nurturing space to begin their life journeys and our local friends were advising and helping us to create this.

In one of our makeshift shelters, we had classes each day, to learn about the culture and history of the native people that lived in this land. In addition, we were offered tuition from local teachers, to learn the language of our friends from neighbouring villages, so we could communicate. Not everyone attended these, but for Sarah and I, we regarded this as being very important, and we both applied ourselves to learn as much as we could.

At the end of each day, we all lay on rugs, as a community, while Julia channelled the Earth Spirit. This gave our wider group, a structured daily opportunity to meditate. I felt a lot of joy on these occasions, and could feel that the Earth around us was welcoming us to be here. This was what we needed to bring all our efforts together, so that we felt connected, and that all that we were doing came with the Spirit of love, and a common sense of purpose.

Eve and Simon were not with us all the time. They both had international business obligations, that they needed to fulfil. But the rest of us stayed on site. If anything, the office work was even more concentrated now, and we had a larger team helping us. The members of our staff were kept very busy.

Now that we were building, we needed to continue to accrue funding, rapidly, for the initial costs of setting up the project were enormous, and we had to be very alert to seek outlets where donations and support could find their way to us. On the other side, we had to work out priorities for how the money that we had, could be most usefully spent. A couple of our office workers were engaged, providing ongoing online reports of our progress, to keep our supporters informed, so we could remain linked, through information, with our network around the world.

With the scope of what we were doing, I sometimes wondered how it could possibly be working. However, it was not so much the efforts of any one individual that kept us going, but the actions of all of us together, a united effort, which brought in further support from Spirit. This was the pathway for our new Earth – group endeavours, where people could consciously attune together and work together so that the focus would become about being of one mind and one action, and doing what was right, and for the highest good. It involved conscious individual choice for people to act together, in harmony with others, and with all life, including the Earth Spirit, and what was beyond. Once our intention was set, and aligned with Spirit, then so much could be achieved. Our aim was to be a model and inspiration for the world of how this could be done.

It was not all clear sailing, for we each had our weaknesses, and prejudices, and we had to work with these. Sometimes, we had arguments and disagreements, but always, when we brought matters back to considering what would be best, and for the highest good, then there would be a solution and a way forward. The people that we had with us, had been selected or volunteered, because they cared about the Earth and were driven by a desire for our Earth to be a better and happier place, where we would be living in harmony with all life forms around us.

In those early stages, it was hard to imagine, that all the structures, which were in our plans, would be erected. It was an enormous undertaking. All the foundations and infrastructure had to be placed first, and building materials brought in. It was part of our philosophy that we did not want to use artificial building materials, but where possible, for all to be constructed in the most natural way we could. This required a great deal of ingenuity, so we could be true to this.

Simon had many discussions with his architects and project managers to explore how close we could act to achieve this objective. It was not always easy. For a couple of months, it rained very heavily, and this slowed the building work rate. We could be appreciative that the Earth Spirit was cleansing the land and giving us water for our rain water tanks, but the sodden conditions did not help the building tasks to make progress. We had to accept this, and give thanks for all that happened to us.

For me, just to be in this environment of building and manifesting, was exhilarating. On the grey rainy days, when not much physical work was possible, we could get together in other ways, meditate, make plans, and have fun in the rain. Even the days that appeared to hold set-backs, held gifts for us.

CLASSES BEGIN

Our construction workers were very busy. We all helped them as much as we could. They built several temporary structures, while the main building work was going on. There was a pressing need for us to provide shelter for our food; our first power generators, all the equipment we had, and our personal belongings. Setting up a dry, protected space for these items had to be done quickly and urgently.

Once, our builders had these storage rooms up, our local friends showed us how they built their simple huts in their villages, using stones and discarded branches from the trees. We built a few of these huts, and were pleasantly surprised how sturdy they proved to be. In those early days, once they were erected, we all slept together in that group of the huts, the workers as well. It was very cosy, but it also brought us closer together.

I noticed how Julia and Kurt did not use a mattress. They had only a blanket between them and the bare Earth, with another blanket covering them. They did not need more. I tried this for myself and made a slight hollow in the ground where my body could fit, and although it was uncomfortable at first, I got used to it and slept surprisingly well.

Sometimes, I lay awake at night, and I could hear everyone's breathing around me. My body felt relaxed, and I could feel a great sense of peace, knowing that I was supported by Mother Earth beneath me. I liked to go outside in the middle of the night, and gaze in wonder, at the stars in the clear skies, and listen to the wildlife around me. I understood that the amount of wildlife had been reduced tremendously by all the land clearances, but I could still hear lots of animal, insect and bird sounds. Listening to it all, I could only marvel at the miracle of Nature, and I was yearning to begin the process of planting trees to bring all this land to its full vitality again.

One evening while the others were sleeping, and I was outside, sitting and listening, Sarah came and joined me. For a long while, we sat there together in silence, with our arms around each other, appreciating our surroundings, and the opportunity that had been given to us, that we could be here. This was indeed a precious place and we would have to do our utmost to protect and nurture it.

Sarah was proving to be very adept at learning languages and was making a sturdy effort to be able to communicate directly with the locals. She was at the forefront of initiatives, to establish a prototype for the school. There were a couple of women from the outlying villages. They were going to assist us, and help us with the local children. Sarah spent many hours talking with them, learning about their customs, practicing pronunciation with their words, consulting with them about a potential curriculum. She was eager for the school to commence, and was determined to be involved with the teaching.

Although the school was intended, in the medium term, to have an international base, with children from many countries, we could not begin accepting them, until the building work was well-advanced. Those children from other countries would need to be satisfactorily accommodated. In the meantime, Sarah was very keen to make a start with the children living closer to us.

We had to share with the government about our curriculum for the school. They wanted to be assured about what we would be teaching. But this was a delicate process, because we also did not want them to interfere with what we were doing. One matter that they insisted upon, was that we include some references in our teaching, to the good work of the governing party in the land. We were prepared to do that, with the older children, as part of our work, in helping the children learn, about social organisation in the world. And this satisfied them.

Although there was some schooling in the local villages, what was available, was limited, especially for girls. Our aim was to improve upon this, and give girls, as well as boys, the chance to be educated. We wanted to teach basic skills, including language and self-expression. Also, the emphasis of our work with the children would have many practical elements, including weaving, basket making and cooking. We wanted the children to value and honour the best of their local traditions and culture, but also learn about other cultural possibilities. They could do some work in our vegetable gardens and take some produce for their families.

In addition, it was our plan that the education we offered would have a Spiritual aspect. Each day, the children would meditate and learn to commune with the Earth Spirit. We wanted to teach them through stories and guidance about the new Earth consciousness and how we were all connected, together, with love.

It was important for them also to learn about technology and renewable energy – practices that they could later bring to their communities. There was so much that we wanted to include. Sarah talked a lot of all these matters, with me, for she wanted my opinion, and feedback.

While a large hut was constructed to be our first school building, Sarah went out with her two teaching colleagues, to various villages and settlements within reach, and spoke with representatives of those places, to inform and invite interest for the beginning of the school. On some of these trips, I went with Sarah.

It was not easy, because many of those tribesmen and leaders of the local communities, were quite set in their ways, and did not want to change. Sarah had to be very patient, and explain many times, the purpose of what we were doing. Gradually, she won some of them over, and children were signed up to attend. Sarah had to make it clear to families that she met, that our classes were not just for boys, and we wanted to encourage the girls to learn too, so they could become leaders in their communities too. Not all of this was acceptable to the local leaders, and we could not force people to forego practices that were established in their way of life.

It was good that Sarah was becoming increasingly competent, to speak the language of the locals. This impressed them in their deliberations, and they respected her for it. Through all this, Sarah was gaining confidence. It was agreed, even though she did not have any prior experience of teaching, that she would be one of the founding teachers in the school. Somehow, she seemed to have a natural affinity with children, and she related to them, with grace and ease.

The day came when the school opened. A large hut, built in the local traditional style, had been erected. For the children, being in a physical structure like this, felt safe and familiar to them.

To honour the beginning of classes in the school, we held a brief ceremony of thanksgiving and blessing inside the building, with Julia and Kurt, where we all held hands. There were fourteen children of all ages in our first intake. The two women, who had been with Sarah from the beginning, were going to work alongside her, and Sarah had been nominated to be the coordinator.

On that first day, Sarah asked me if I could be present with her, to give her some support and witness this important day with her. I was happy to do that. There was much enthusiasm.

Not everything went to plan, but at the end of the day, the children were happy. This was just the beginning. We knew that the numbers in the school would grow.

EXPANSION

While the school was establishing itself, there were developments in other parts of the community, where considerable work was also being done.

By now, Jake and Lydia had arrived, and there were many other workers joining in, to help with the reforestation project. Hugh had been researching about the various varieties of fauna that existed in the area. He wanted to establish what plants and trees would be most compatible and support each other, and the terrain that would be suitable for different species to grow in. With the help of satellite technology, Hugh had prepared maps of the whole property. Plans were needed as to how the whole effort of reforestation could best proceed. He proposed, because of the size of the property, that our efforts could be divided into sections. Some tracks had to be laid throughout the property, with outposts constructed within these various sections. Then, work could proceed efficiently, and our equipment would have various places where it could be stored. We would need to delegate teams for different areas within the property to maximise the scale of the propagation of trees, while ensuring that in any given area, what we planted was appropriate.

It was a huge operation, and Hugh needed to know that his willing workers were also capable. Because the conservation effort was close to my heart in terms of my own interests, I joined in with this work whenever I could.

Initially, a big task was for workers to travel outside the property and gather seeds. A massive seed collecting process was needed, and this had to be carefully calibrated. In conjunction with that, not just one, but a series of nurseries, were being constructed so all those innumerable seedlings could grow.

While the main sanctuary was still being built, Julia and Kurt led meditations outside next to the Guardian trees. This was regarded as a sacred space within the community, an area where the power and love of the Earth Spirit was very strong.

We arranged classes for the local adults, as well as the children, so they could learn to meditate and commune with the Earth Spirit. In addition to this, with all the many practical tasks around the community, interest in assisting us, grew, and we enlisted many volunteers. We welcomed our friends from neighbouring villages, to join us. Many of these people had skills that were useful for use, so they could help us, and we them. Being with the local people certainly also encouraged me to learn their language, so I could communicate. Gradually, I did that.

We arranged for a series of Community planting days, so we could place the trees and plants in positions around the property, and they could establish themselves. More and more people became involved. We needed millions of trees to fill that now empty land. But we had to start somewhere. And it was a task that the children also enjoyed to participate in.

These were joyous days. Many of the locals were skilled builders and they taught us some of their traditional methods of utilising materials. Simon directed his architects to be flexible, study the practices of the local people and work with them, so our plans could incorporate their ways.

Some of our builders also began to learn the language of the local people and they were learning to speak our language. A very useful interchange of knowledge was taking place.

There were people supporting us, both local and international, that were innovative experts in many forms of sustainable living. We had a team of workers making our living sewage unit – where plants, rather than chemicals would filter and purify our waste products. The big rainwater tanks and reservoir were already supplying us with water that we needed. All the food leftovers went to contribute to compost heaps, for use in the gardens. Further, we had experts in permaculture and biodynamic gardening helping to build our vegetable gardens. Our aim was to become as self-sufficient in food as feasible.

With any food that we had to purchase from outside, we wanted to safeguard that this was organically sourced. Most of us were vegetarian, and for those that needed it, meat was one of the items we had to purchase externally. Wherever possible, we wanted our community to function without chemicals, or any harmful ingredients, so that the way we lived, could be in harmony with our wish, to support and nurture Mother Earth.

Our electricity was generated by Solar Power. We had battery storage so our power needs could be met completely independently of the main electricity grid. Building these units started right at the beginning of our construction work, and we had experts that Simon had brought in, to do this for us. We needed power for all our facilities to operate, but also, we wanted lay foundations for our goal with this, which was to house a research Centre into renewable energy. For us, it was fundamental with our outlook, to promote the benefits of more natural forms of energy generation.

It was suggested in one of the Channelling sessions that Julia had done with the Earth Spirit – that in the future, in addition to the power of the sun, that we may learn to be able to harness the Spiritual energies of our Mother Earth directly, without any physical exploitation, through an exchange of giving and receiving, and that this would go a long way towards meeting our power needs. In our consciousness, as humanity, we would have to be further evolved, for us to be able to do that. It was a very interesting thought.

While we were working on the ground of the property, Eve was travelling and networking, setting up mechanisms to prepare for the school to accept its first intake of international students. She spent her time meeting delegates from various countries, explaining our philosophy and what we intended to achieve, obtaining funding so all our enterprises could continue. Her work was less visible to the rest of us staying on the property, but so important.

Simon was most concerned with the establishment of the Conference Centre and ongoing legal issues that required his full attention. He was also away for some of the time, meeting and soothing the way with government officials, but his main job was as overall manager for the Project.

We were so fortunate that Simon was building a constructive relationship with the President of the country. They had already had several meetings. Simon had invited the President to be our special guest, for the ceremonial opening of the Community, to be held once the main buildings were erected. The President had agreed to do this, and he had also granted a special status for workers coming in from other countries, so they could stay here indefinitely. This was so helpful.

Julia and Kurt had gained a large, and diverse following of people, interested in their work, from all over the world. Kurt had written a book called simply 'Earth Spirit,' where he outlined about their work together, and its potential for humanity. There were many sales of this book, and Kurt had bequeathed that all the proceeds be given for the development of our Centre, and for the costs of building the Sanctuary. He and Julia had decided to base themselves fully at our Community now, rather than travelling. They addressed their followers through social media, and invited people to help what we were doing.

Many of our volunteers and workers came to us as a direct result of being exposed to Julia's channelling of the Earth Spirit and Kurt's teaching. Their presence was a very central asset to all that we were doing.

When we were not engaged in our other interests, Sarah and I were very busy answering inquiries in our temporary office. So many people came to us because they were disillusioned with the corruption and destructiveness expressed in the societies where they lived. They wanted to put their energy into activity that would inspire their dreams, and give them hope. We did not wish to turn anyone away, and we wanted to give, people who found their way to us, every encouragement.

We had to delegate many aspects of our office work, and over time, we acquired many secretaries, and management assistants, to help us

My happiest working times, were when I could be with the reforestation group. Through being with them, I came to know very well, the layout of the land of our property.

In the next valley from where our Centre was being built, there was a place that I loved. It was one of the first places where we engaged in tree planting. Here, a small river meandered downwards, surrounded by the gentle slopes. The gushing sound of the water, flowing over rounded stones here, was so refreshing. It was a spot where I liked to go often, for it reminded me of the river, where I went when I was a child. Sarah used to come with me, and we would sit down by the water's edge and watch the sun go down. We would snuggle up together, and I could feel the warmth coming from Sarah's hand and her body beside me. Inside, I had a feeling of deep contentment in my heart, reassuring me, that all was well.

THE FULFILMENT OF A DREAM

And so, it came to pass. The Conference Centre was completed, the Sanctuary built and utilised, the International School was established and opened, accommodation and kitchen facilities were set out – it all happened as had been envisioned. Young trees and plants filled the landscape and wildlife had returned; the Renewable Energy research centre was flourishing. Our goals for sustainability were in process of being met, and the vegetable and herb gardens were extensively used, while left over produce was distributed to nearby villages.

Many thousands of people visited our New Earth Centre – for a variety of purposes. Some stayed and worked at the Centre; others visited for a short time and left again. So many were inspired – whether it was by connecting with the Earth Spirit through meditation, or by witnessing and taking in, the structure of how we had set out our community, or by working in loving cooperation, with us.

One of our happiest days had been the official opening of the Centre. The President had been there, with a host of officials from his government, and representatives from other international organisations as well. All of them were dressed in their finery. We gave our guests a grand tour of all our facilities, and showed them the forest, that was beginning to grow. It was a sunny day, and the beauty of the Community was evident for all to see. Julia and Kurt conducted a brief meditation outside, by the Guardian trees, and then we adjourned to the Conference Centre for some speeches. Simon gave a special tribute to the President for his support, and a plaque was revealed in his honour. The President spoke graciously in reply.

And, as I looked over at the President, after the speeches, I could acknowledge how vital his patronage had been, for the establishment of our Centre. I knew then, that while ever he was in power, our work would be protected, and could keep expanding. I remembered hoping, that he would remain in power for a very long time to come.

There was a lot of media attention for this event. News of the President's speech at the official opening of our Centre spread around the world, and helped us to gain a measure of global recognition. It was all good, and how

I wished it to be.

Later, after the officials had gone, we celebrated, until well into the night. It was a great occasion.

The Conference Centre hosted many important gatherings. Topics included international cooperation, education, conservation, renewable energy, the future of humanity, Spiritual development. All these assemblies of people gathered together for one fundamental purpose. Whatever topics were being discussed, the sharing between people would weave around aspects of a central theme, relating to generating a 'new Earth,' and facilitating a transformation in the consciousness of humanity, so we could feel more spiritually connected with each other, and acting in harmony with all forms of life on the planet. This is what we were here to do.

The initial Conference Centre had been increased in size, so now thousands of people could be accommodated. People of high international standing had been invited to come and give keynote speeches, and groups advocating similar ideas as us, could hire the facilities for their members, so the Conference centre was well used.

The pride and joy of Julia and Kurt, was the Sanctuary. Although they still had some meditations outside, the Sanctuary itself, held a wonderful energy. It was circular in construction, with much wood and stone. Light shone in through the windows, and many plant species grew there on the ground, and brought the lushness of nature into the sacred space. The base of the Sanctuary was rich soil, and when she channelled the Earth Spirit, Julia lay on a blanket in the middle of this, while there was seating on cushions and rugs, for everyone else, that would participate. There was much natural beauty in the Sanctuary, and it was tended with a great deal of love and care.

So many people experienced connection with the Earth Spirit through Julia's channelling. Julia was now teaching others to channel, and had started her own School of Spiritual development to facilitate this. One of her first pupils had been Sarah, who now conducted the channellings as times, when Julia was not available.

Our renewable energy centre had not risen to the heights of some of our other work, but we had all the power that we needed through natural sources. There were many other companies already developing renewable energy technology throughout the world, but we were happy to embrace it, as part of what we were building together.

Altogether, our Community did create a model of how we could live together on the Earth, and many of the people visiting us took their perception of our ideas back to their homelands, to create or help other communities, to adopt Earth friendly practices, and assist the consciousness of the people there.

Not everyone endorsed what we were doing. We once had a sceptical journalist that proceeded to interview people and then write a very disparaging article, claiming that all the teaching about the Earth Spirit was a hoax. Other religious groups with strict doctrines, dismissed our practices as blasphemy. A lot of the media, that was not interested in our ideas, ignored us. But we coped with all of that, and people kept coming to us, wanting to be inspired.

We all felt very satisfied. All our hard work had been rewarded, and to see the smiles on the faces of people that visited our New Earth Community, was enough to give us determination and strength to keep going. With the six of us that had started the project, we were all still part of it – ten years on. We had all grown into our responsibilities.

As well as channelling with Julia, Sarah continued to have a major role in teaching within the school, and she did some administration. She was well-loved by everyone in the Community.

Julia was regarded with reverence for her channelling. She had opened her human side, and ventured to share with the children about her experiences as a channel. She had grown in confidence, as the years had gone on, and felt more comfortable to be around people.

Kurt had contented himself to be master of ceremonies and taking care of the Sanctuary. He felt that this was his place, and where he wanted to stay.

By now, Kurt had written several books, and his teachings continued to generate interest worldwide. Videos of Julia channelling the Earth Spirit were very popular. Even Simon had written a book about how our Community had been created. It was a heartfelt book that had been very well-received.

Meanwhile, Eve kept her focus upon liaising with the external world and networking our project, with the many spiritual communities that were taking root in other parts of the world. This was her role, and she enjoyed doing it immensely.

Simon continued as the overall manager of the Centre, and he was the public face for our Community with outside bodies that sought contact with us.

For myself, I was happy to remain in the background, and continue to gain skills. Now, I was at the centre of much of the administration work. I kept my finger on the pulse of all that took place around the Centre. I felt at 'home' and at peace. That was what mattered to me.

We still had our meetings, but not so frequently anymore. It was a time when we felt we could rest a little after all the hard work in initiating and establishing the Centre. There was now a firm foundation to all that we were doing, and the momentum of all our activities carried us forward. There were some moments when it felt like we would go on like this forever – that is what I wished, what we all dearly wanted. And it was like bliss when we looked around at all that we had achieved.

However, there were hidden shadows – we did not know it – but these shadows were approaching rapidly.

THE TURNING

On occasions, I went travelling with Eve. While she was at meetings, I got to explore cities and places where we visited. Life in the world outside our

Community was very different from the way that we were living it. So many people struggled. I could see it in the expression of their eyes.

In big Western cities, people were stressed, and not relating to each other. They were locked in their own worlds. When we visited third world countries, there was evidence of extreme poverty, and people begging for scraps of food, and clean water to drink. And wherever we went, there were too many homeless people, living on the streets. Our world shouldn't be like that. These experiences affected me. At times, living in our New Earth Community, I lost sight of how challenging life in the world outside of our land, could be.

There was still rife corruption and greed operating in so many places on our Earth. Also, there was overpopulation, inequality and millions of people suffering. Other problems included unchecked pollution and wars, governments that suppressed the rights of their people, rising temperatures, destruction of the environment. It was a very troubled world that we lived in. And even with a few sparks of light here and there, a lot of darkness still permeated our planet.

Our work in the Community could only reach so far. To achieve a global transformation of consciousness was another matter, and for so many people, thoughts of survival were as much as they could manage.

Sometimes, it felt to me as if our Community was like a bubble of light, which was insulated from the rest of the world, separated from the suffering and difficulties so many people had to face in their everyday life. It was amazing to me that we had been so protected, as if 'God' had put a ring or light shield of energy around our Centre, so that the troubles of the world could not enter, or be near us. This did not seem right somehow.

We wanted for our Community to connect with the world, and for the many strands of transformation that we were nurturing, to grow, while we embraced our Earth – not for us to be separated. I wondered if we were fully serving our purpose while we were so insulated. These doubts unsettled me somehow.

When I shared this with Sarah, she tried to comfort me, and retort about how much our work was respected in the world, and that our Community had influenced many groups and organisations all over the world to adjust their outlook, and adopt more harmonious practices in the way they went about things. We were not a protected bubble, but pioneers and leaders. Even in the local communities, villages and townships, in areas around our Centre, people looked to us and joined with us, and we went to their markets and taught their children. We had to keep going and become even stronger.

I appreciated her perspective, and her commitment. When I looked in her eyes, I saw a deep affection and conviction. I did not want to drag her into the realm of my doubts

Then one day, I had a vision that affected me very much; it startled me, and I felt very occupied about what it would portend.

It was a normal day. I was doing my daily meditation in the Sanctuary, and I could hear Julia's deep resonant tones, as she channelled the Earth

Spirit. While she spoke, I went along the familiar inner route of my consciousness, which took me to a place deep down, where I could fill my being with light, and the unique Spiritual energy of our Earth being. I always felt peace, and a sense of certainty, and connectedness, when I journeyed here.

However, on this day, without warning, I felt an energy come through my body that pushed me out of there. I tried to resist it, but I could not do so. Instead, I found myself standing in a huge beautiful blue/green crystal. It seemed familiar and safe, and I could wander around in it, quite freely. While I took this in, the crystal glistened with energy that radiated outwards, and I sensed, as I stood within it, that there were many with me. The feeling of this crystal was quite magical, and the energy that it emitted was that of the Earth Spirit. Light streams spread into surrounding regions, creating sparkles and love in many different places. But beside these light places, there was much dark, and no matter how much energy the crystal gave out, the darkness remained, and as I considered the darkness, it appeared not quite impenetrable, but very gloomy.

As I watched, there was a dreadful moment, when that darkness started to leak into the crystal. There did not seem to be any reason to explain why it did that, but it did, and it was a horrible sticky substance, which felt repulsive. In a panic, I desperately tried to stop the sticky darkness from entering, but the more I tried to prevent it, the greater the volume of that dark substance came in. The number of leaks increased, and the crystal was struggling. I so much did not want anything terrible to happen to the crystal, but I could not prevent it. The inundation of darkness continued to penetrate. There came a point where that wonderful crystal could no longer hold itself together, and it appeared to collapse under the strain of the infiltration. This was frightening. I felt helpless, and I pushed myself against the wall of the crystal, to brace myself against what was happening. The dark substance poured in like a deluge, and nothing felt as if it was the same anymore. I began to feel very upset, and I thought that all good would be lost. But I could still breathe, and then I noticed something important.

All that dark matter, which had come into the crystal was not sticky anymore. Somehow, it had been transformed, and was different somehow. The surrounding area was not so dark either, but varying shades of grey. It felt as if the crystal had sacrificed itself, in its efforts to transform the dark. There was not much left of the magnificent crystal, for it had largely disintegrated, and the light that had radiated from it was all but gone. What remained were just some sad embers of green/blue light. There was slight comfort that at least these were not extinguished. But I felt devastated, and desperately afraid.

I came out of this meditation with a start. People were looking at me; I must have shouted out. My body was shaking and it wouldn't stop. Frantically, I wrapped my blanket around me tightly, for I was freezing cold. Sarah sat next to me, and she placed her arm around me. But she could not help me.

All I knew then, with absolute certainty, was that the protection that our community had enjoyed from outside elements over such a lengthy period, was not going to last much longer. The crystal was a symbol of our beautiful community. I felt so afraid.

CHANGES

As I reflected about this meditation afterwards, I wondered why this vision had been shown to me. I had shared it with the others, but none of them had had it. Yes, it had occurred during a group meditation with the Earth Spirit, and this made me speculate, if the revelations of the vision, had been passed onto me from Spiritual sources. If this was so, was it a warning, or to prepare me for some dramatic changes? It had to mean something. I could not dismiss it.

Over the next days and weeks, there were no disruptions, and all within our project continued to run smoothly. I began to wonder if the vision I had had, was simply a subconscious outpouring of the confusion that I had felt about our project being insulated from the world. On the one hand, I did not want the activity of our project to be curtailed in any way, but on the other side, it was important for me to have faith in my inner visions. So, I waited and watched, keeping my own counsel. Thankfully, life appeared to continue as usual.

Over the duration of our project, we had done a lot to help people in villages and townships throughout the land. We had helped to raise standards of education, given impetus for the people become more self-sufficient economically, supported communities to live in harmony with their environment, and begun various initiatives to further the rights of women. Many of our staff and workers were from local areas, and some of them had become very good friends to the Project. There was a continual interchange between what we were doing, and life in the surrounding communities. We were pleased that there were now other reforestation projects occurring in various parts of the country, and several villages with whom we had contact, were now obtaining their energy needs independently through solar power systems. Things were progressing well.

The President of the Country had been quietly supporting us all the way through. He had been ruler for many years, and we could be very grateful that he allowed us the space for our Community to function. We were aware that he was getting quite old now, and we did not know for how much longer, he would retain his position of power.

One day, I was fortunate enough to go on a trip to the Capital with Eve and Simon, and we met with the President in person. This was the first time that I had seen him since the official opening ceremony for our Community, and I noticed that he had aged quite considerably, in the intervening years. Talking to him, I was impressed with his kindness and quiet dignity. He complimented me about how well I could speak the native language, and I thanked him for all that he had done for us.

The President then said something quite unexpected. He retorted that nobody really owned the land – and that it belonged to the Earth. The

Earth needed help, and we were trying to assist her. He looked at me in the eyes, and I knew then that he understood our philosophy and condoned it. My heart warmed that we had a friend, in such a high and respected position. He had been like a protector for us.

Our conversation with him continued. However, just before we left him, he looked up at us, very intently, and spoke to us in English.

'We live in a very uncertain world you know.' Then he paused. 'Whatever changes occur, you must be strong, have faith, and continue the good work you are doing. The world needs you.'

He did not explain any more, but indicated, gently, that our time with him was over. We shook hands with him, and left through the door to his office. I turned around, and he smiled to us, and waved.

Inside, I was shaking. Simon and Eve seemed unperturbed, but I felt disturbed. Memories of the vision that had revealed itself to me, flooded my consciousness. The President's last words felt like a sign to me, and it felt like he was saying goodbye.

I did not feel as if there was anyone with whom I could share my anxieties, even Sarah, so I stayed quiet. When I could, I took time out, to pray and contemplate about the inner turmoil that I was feeling.

It was only a few weeks later, when I was in the Office, that there was a sudden important news flash. I felt disconcerted, and I could feel my body reacting again. The President was broadcasting his intention to step down from his high Office, and retire, with immediate effect. It was a shock announcement, one that nobody had anticipated. He was giving thanks for the wonderful opportunity he had been given, to serve his country for so long. The President assured everyone that he had been under no pressure to retire, and he was doing this only so he could have a rest, from all the years of responsibility, that he had carried. In conclusion, the President announced that he had nominated his long-standing deputy to be his successor.

I watched the news, almost in disbelief, and now the new President-to-be was speaking, vowing to continue all the policies of his predecessor, and operate a seamless transition.

My own inner senses told me that it would not be that way at all, but I tried to maintain a sense of calm, for the others. It was a sad occasion for all of us.

We met as a Community, to honour the President and to remember how much he had assisted us. Meanwhile, Eve went to the Capital to meet representatives of the government, to express our appreciation for the old President, and to pledge our cooperation and support, for his successor.

Over the next months, I followed news of the new administration, and how it was operating. From what I could tell, the new president was quite erratic and did not have the same sure touch with the people. He was more of an administrator, than someone who had any skills as an orator, and he did not appear to cope well, when people contradicted him. He had no contact with us, and he seemed to remove himself more and more from what was going on around him. Because of this, over time his popularity dipped, and people began questioning if he was the best person to lead the country. We also noticed, that he was someone who liked riches, and showing off the trappings of power. This set him apart from the people, who resented him for it. He made the decision to raise taxes, and the people revolted, and started to openly oppose his policies.

That was when I started to become worried. There was a restless and angry mood beginning to develop in the country, and protests occurred outside the presidential palace. For some time, this unease persisted, and it showed no sign of going away. Arrests were made and this inflamed the tensions even further. Instead of being conciliatory, the new President threatened the people with further security action, unless the protests stopped. Of course, they didn't. One fateful day, a protester threw a petrol bomb at the gates of the Presidential Palace, and he was shot by police. The protesters rioted, and more people were killed.

The following night, there was a military coup, and it was announced that the new President had been relieved of his duties. The leader of the Coup announced over state television, that because of social disorder, the military had been left with no choice, but to assert their authority to re-establish law and order in the country, through Martial Law. The General, who was leader of the coup, promised elections in the coming months, to choose another president, once the situation in the country, was calm again.

In the meantime, the army was setting up security checkpoints, along key road links, all around the Capital, and in provincial cities. A Curfew was to be enforced. Many media services were to be temporarily curtailed, so only broadcasts from the military leaders would be televised.

The people in the streets were stunned. That morning, when I woke up, I had a feeling of dread in my stomach, and in our Sanctuary meditation, the room was filled with anxious people from the Community. We prayed. However, the Earth Spirit spoke nothing about the situation, when she channelled through Julia. Instead, she simply offered love to all of us.

Over the next weeks, the Military consolidated its hold on power. From what I could perceive, the moves made by the Military, had not been spontaneous and without foresight, but had all the appearance of having been carefully planned, and even premeditated. When protesters dared to come out onto the streets in the Capital, many of them were summarily taken away and imprisoned. Human Rights campaigners objected, and they were also arrested, so they would be silenced.

There was international outcry to this. But the new Military rulers countered this by giving assurances that they were doing all that they had to do, to maintain Law and order.

People were forced to obey, and do what they were told, and the implementation of Martial law persisted. Basically, this was a peace-loving country, and the inhabitants did not want trouble. People did not like their freedoms being taken away, but there was no possibility for anyone to object. If someone raised their head to speak, they were imprisoned forthwith.

The old President was quiet, and made a recluse in his own country. He was refused permission to give any interviews. It was a very tense situation, that showed no signs of ending. Talk of early elections receded into the background, and instead, the Military Government propagated extreme stories, about security concerns, so they could maintain their stranglehold on power.

We had no contact from the Military rulers. Our official position was to refrain from taking a position, relative to the political turmoil in the country, even though this was difficult for us. We felt torn because of Human Rights violations that were occurring. Eve sought help from her colleagues at the United Nations, so that diplomatic efforts could be made to speak up for those imprisoned. But we did not wish to do anything to antagonise the Military rulers, for our existence was in their hands. Simon and I had many talks about this, and the only thing that we felt we could do for now, was to sit tight.

In our activities around the Community, we did all that we could, to carry on as normal. However, there were many hushed conversations, and an atmosphere of unease. I spoke with my friends from the surrounding villages. No one liked what had been happening and many people were afraid.

Julia and Kurt persevered with meditations in our Sanctuary, and the benevolence of the Earth Spirit was a tranquil presence, which encouraged all of us to be expectant, that the upheavals around us would settle, somehow, and that we would be looked after. I prayed, but was not very hopeful that this would be so.

HOPE AND FEAR

There was a viewpoint not far from the building area at our Centre. I had to climb a rather steep hill to get there. It was quite rocky, but I enjoyed the exercise. From the top, I could see over much of the great expanse of land, which had become our home. I could remember, from the earliest days, what it had looked like, when we had first come here. It had been a huge desolate wasteland, with some ragged tufts of vegetation here and there, some piles of sludge left over from the mines, and hardly anything growing. The cattle had long gone, and the miners had abandoned their search for uranium; all had been left deserted before we arrived. But now – what a difference!! The results of all our planting was marvellous to behold.

We lived in land where there was both warmth and rainfall, so when the conditions were right, vegetation could grow very quickly and profusely, and that is what had happened. The trees we had planted were still young and growing, and the density of the new forest was patchy, because there were some areas where our planting teams had not reached yet. However, the vibrancy of greens and beauty of the colours in the areas where planting had occurred, was remarkable. Some of the plants had rich aromas that were delightful to smell, and I could hear birds and other wildlife enjoying the environment, as it was unfolding. The whole place was returning to life.

From all the meditation, which I had done with the Earth Spirit, my sensitivity had grown, and I could perceive the energies of the young trees, with all the growth in them, bursting forth. As I breathed in the fresh air, I could sense that the Earth Spirit was smiling with joy and pleasure, at what we had achieved. And there was still so much more to do.

When I turned around towards the Conference Hall and the Sanctuary, I could view the extensive vegetable gardens and orchards. These, too, had been carefully laid out and planned, with vast rows of different forms of fruit and vegetables. We were quite close to having enough food, now, for all our needs. There were some items like grains, that we still had to import, but with the food we did produce, we had an excess, compared with what we required, and could go to local markets, to sell or give away what we had grown, and even export some of our exotic fruit to other countries.

With all the income that we now received, from our conferences, our food production, renewable energy, and other merchandise that we made, we did not need outside donations anymore. Apart from the school, which still required external support, we had reached our goal of self-sufficiency.

We could not pay our workers huge sums of money, but we could supply accommodation and look after their basic needs. Within our outlook for the New Earth consciousness, we advocated a collective barter system of exchange, ensuring that all work would be regarded as worthwhile and no one would go without. We did not feel that the present monetary system of capitalism was appropriate anymore. Too much greed and abuse had come because of it. We advocated a barter system that was more compassionate and promoted equality, and a sense of connectedness amongst everyone.

As I breathed in the environment of our New Earth Community, I felt enormous pride in what we had achieved, and yet, I also sensed how fragile the status of our project appeared to be. When I turned my attention to the Military Dictatorship, which was now in power, I felt acute unease. It had been some months now, since they took over control of the government, and so far, they had given no indication of how they regarded us. But I did not know for how long that would continue.

The leader of this new regime was a hard and cruel man. He did not tolerate any dissent. Many hundreds of people had been imprisoned for speaking out, or having views in opposition to his Government. A lot of those people arrested, had been placed in solitary confinement. Media publications had now been shut down permanently, and press freedoms revoked. The people did not have a voice anymore.

We had to be very careful in our communications with the outside world, so we not bring wrath onto us, from the Military. There were a lot of tensions, in the local communities. We hoped, because of our international focus, that we would be safe. But we couldn't be sure.

The policies and dictates of the new government were also distressing, and I felt vehemently, that they were wrong, and causing harm. Multinational companies were being encouraged to invest in the country, and rights for workers had been withdrawn, so these businesses could make more profits. Among the companies being given licences, were several big logging companies, whose only concern was to clear as much of the rainforest as possible. Budgets for social care and education, even for hospitals, had been cut, and military expenditure had been sharply increased. There was talk of compulsory conscription for young men, even though the country was not at war.

This government did not care about the people. They only wanted power. Many felt disquiet, but they could do nothing about it. A mood of resignation and suffering was spreading through communities. We also felt powerless, to be able to make any difference to it all.

People asked Kurt and Julia, if the Earth Spirit could do anything to help. The Earth Spirit spoke through Julia of her sadness, but she could only continue to offer love, and had no defence against the will of human beings. The Earth was a nurturing being and had a consciousness of peace. When we attuned to that, we kept affirming the possibility of love, and harmony for all. But people could use their free will, and follow their own interests, at the expense of others. The Earth Spirit would not intervene.

But our role as humans was different to the Earth Spirit. We could act, and it was our place to act. Maybe we would need to fight for what we believed in.

It was a time where our spirits were dampened, and levels of activity in our Community dropped. We were waiting. On several occasions, we had Community meetings, within the Centre, with all the workers. During these, we considered options, of what action we could take, but rather than react as some wanted to do, we chose to remain true to our mission with the Centre, and stay out of the politics of the land.

We had regular meditations, where we joined together to envision peace, both in our Centre and the country where we lived. It was important for us to spread this thought, in trust, so that it would take root where it could.

Diplomats from other countries had voiced their concern about the human rights violations and some governments had applied economic sanctions. We did feel increasingly cut off, within our Community. The Military Dictatorship in the country where we lived was establishing itself ever more firmly, and we had no idea what they would do next. We could only maintain our work for a New Earth Consciousness, one day at a time – and be open.

URANIUM

One morning, a military jeep arrived outside the main office of our Community. The Officer in the jeep had an official letter for Simon. A group of us came out of the office to see what was happening. Simon stepped forward, and he called me over to read the letter with him. When I saw the contents of the page Simon was holding, I was filled with trepidation. I did not know how Simon was really feeling, but he kept his expression impassive, while I felt a surge of emotions within me. My instinct was to step back, but I took the letter, and forced myself to read the details. Then I passed it on to others.

Basically, the letter was an announcement, that beginning in two days' time, representatives from the state mining corporation, were going to carry out exploratory drilling on site, in search of uranium. At this stage, the drilling was purely exploratory, and was not intended to interrupt the functioning of our Community. There were no rights for us, as to whether we would agree to this or not. The letter was merely an information document. What Simon had to do was to sign it, in acknowledgment that he had read and understood its contents. That was all. He did this, without comment, and the jeep drove away.

As soon as people knew, pandemonium broke out. We held another community wide meeting in the Conference Hall. People were panicking and some were shouting, while others were in tears. What the military were doing felt like a violation. What would they do if they found Uranium? How much disruption would they cause? Where would this lead? Simon found it difficult to control the meeting. There were members of the Community wanting to protest, some even wanting to prevent the mining vehicles from having access. Simon tried to assure people that Eve was already on her way to make direct representations to the Government, but we all knew how much impact that was likely to have. Was there anything we could do to stop this?

For many interest groups in the world, the work of our Community was very precious, a beacon of hope for how our world could be. Some of the workers in the meeting expressed outrage that our work could face this interference. What if the company did find deposits of Uranium, with viable potential for them to be able to mine it? Where would that leave us?

The military leadership of the new government wanted to build up their power as a nation, and generate a formidable supply of weapons. What could be more useful to them than freshly extracted uranium? Our thought about this government was that they cared much more about having total control of their situation, belief in their defence capabilities, and having a huge stockpile of weapons, than anything else. It was deeply worrying.

People in the Conference Hall were very much aware of the motives of the Government. There was chaos, with no consensus about what we should do. Simon pleaded with everyone, to take a non-violent approach, and not to interfere with the mining company. They were coming, only to take samples, and test for any rich veins of uranium ore. With the contract that we had signed when we first took on the lease, it was written that the Government did have the right to do mineral exploration on our site. But for them to embark on a full-scale mining operation, that would be another matter. We had to keep our nerve, and take one step at a time. That was what Simon counselled. But for many in the room, what the government was doing, was already taking things much too far.

At the end of the meeting, Kurt suggested a meditation with prayers and for Julia to channel the Earth Spirit. But some walked out before we could do that. They felt too unsettled. It was decided that the meditation could take place, not in the Hall, but in the Sanctuary, afterwards, for those that wanted to attend.

As the Hall emptied, I sat on my own, thinking. If we were going to fight with this government, then we had to find an effective way of doing it, which did not compromise our principles. We felt rage, because they would be encroaching on our space. If we tried to sabotage these mining vehicles, or deny them entry, we could be enflaming the situation. We would be using our will to assert our power in a similar way to how they would be doing, and that would not be true to our values.

Our values were about the consciousness that we were developing. They involved opening to that sense of interconnection and mutual belonging that existed between all of us, and all life forms. Within our community, people were feeling that, more and more, especially the children. There was such a wonderful happy energy that permeated, with all that we did together. To sense that interconnectedness, was not just an ideal for us, but an experience, which we could share. This is what we wanted to spread out, so that increasing numbers of people in the world would embrace this open form of consciousness as reality. Then the transformation of consciousness on our Earth could really take root.

Now with this mining company, people in the Community felt agitated. We had to remember our core values, even though we were being threatened. It was important that we remain true to what we believed and live from that. Whatever would happen to all of us, we must not compromise our ideals.

We knew that when those individuals from the state mining company arrived, then they would bring their own consciousness, and it may feel dissonant to our own. But perhaps if we were strong, we could influence them positively, rather than allow our fears to override us, so we felt intimidated by their presence. This was a test for us, and we needed to stand firm.

TESTS AND DRILLING

So, the day came, and the government company brought their trucks, drills, Lorries and other equipment, just as had been outlined in the letter. They were very noisy, and showed very little care. We had some beautiful flower beds on the edges of the tracks leading through our grounds, and their trucks drove over these. They also broke the branches of saplings, which had been lovingly planted, and haphazardly made their way through the property, with no regard for what we were doing, focussed only on their task of extracting mineral samples.

Their spokesperson had another paper for Simon to sign. Simon read it carefully, and although he hesitated, he eventually did sign it. Basically, it was legal agreement giving permission for the Company to do its work on the land, as they wished, but it gave us no rights to stop them.

Each of the trucks had an army officer with a rifle. None of us liked to see guns. But, when Simon challenged them about this, we were told that the officers with guns, were there to protect the equipment, and to ensure that the workers could keep working, without impediment. They promised that they would not use their weapons, except in a case of severe disruption.

It was not easy to have this type of energy around us.

Some of the workers had scientific expertise. They had their Geiger counters, and various forms of metal detectors to test for levels of subterranean radioactivity. From tests that we had done, we knew that levels of radioactivity on the surface of the ground, apart from a few areas far from our main Centre, were quite negligible. We had investigated that thoroughly before we started to build our dwellings, so we could be sure that the area was safe for people.

Our pleading about this did not deter the Company, for it was what was beneath the surface that mattered to them. We were told that they would be setting up several sites for testing. And one of the prime sites that they decided upon, to drill, was on the hill, just behind the Sanctuary.

It took them a while to set up their equipment, but once they did, the sound of drilling was relentless, and the trucks going backward and forward were so disruptive. The fumes from the vehicles were not pleasant, and we were not used to this form of contamination anymore. Right through the day, until dusk, their work persisted. They had vehicles for each drilling site, and I wondered when it would ever stop.

Kurt insisted upon the meditations continuing, even with the noise, but it made me feel upset, that we had to endure such conditions. However, the calmness of Spirit, when we joined together for meditation, was still present. Kurt counselled us to be in our world and do our work, and leave them to be in theirs. We could not stop their choice of activity, but we would not let them stop ours.

One day, with his silver locks flowing behind him in the breeze, Kurt was brave enough to approach the workers on the site behind the Sanctuary, and he invited them to join us for one of our meditation sessions. The workers looked embarrassed, and some were dismissive. However, at the end of that day, a few of them did come along. Kurt welcomed them warmly, and after he had shown them what to do, they enjoyed the meditation, and they began to open to us. From then on, at the end of their day, those workers continued to join the meditation, and more of them tried it.

I attempted to engage one or two of the workers in conversation. Could they not appreciate the worth of our community and the life we lived together? They told me that they had a job to do and it was in their contract to follow the directions of the company. They had to do what they were told, or they would not have a job anymore.

For several weeks, they continued to drill on the property, and as we became used to the noise, we could begin to tolerate it, and adapt to it. I asked if the company representatives and their workers would be careful around the young trees, not to damage them, and a few of them were sensitive to this, but some were not.

It was a great relief then, when the day came, and they packed their gear, preparing to leave. But we could not be certain of what they found. In my mind, I needed to know if they had discovered any uranium ore deposits, or not. I tried to question a few of them, to implore them to tell us. However, it was one of their instructions, for them not to talk with anyone about that. Their standard answer was, that samples would be sent away for analysis, and further to that, they would not comment.

One of the workers, who had been to our meditations, had tears in his eyes. He noticed me observing him. Carefully, I approached him, and asked if he wanted to come to the Sanctuary for a last look. I said this as a pretext, so we would have space to talk. Once away from the others, I then whispered to him, urging him to tell me if they had found any uranium? With the tears flowing down his face, he looked at me, momentarily, and nodded his head. Then he shoved himself past me, and quickly hurried away, before I could ask any more.

Suddenly, I felt a big lump in my chest, and my body felt cold. Our troubles were going to get worse.

FOREBODING

It was quiet without the drillers present anymore – almost eerily still. The workers had largely tidied up where they could, but many piles of rubble were strewn around many areas of the property. Energetically, all the drilling had created disturbances to our Mother Earth, and groups of us went to the places most disrupted in the property to physically repair the ground, and to ask for healing from Spirit. We endeavoured to mend the matrix of energy lines for those sites.

I told our core group what the worker had indicated to me. They were all quiet. There was nothing that we could do. Simon urged us to refrain from telling everyone else in the Community, and continue doing our work as we always did. I did not agree with Simon, and we argued. People in the Community had to know. We could not exclude them. Eventually, Simon relented, and I was glad he did. But Simon urged calm. We must not become hysterical. Nothing was certain yet.

Eve would engage in her diplomatic missions, and she would seek advice and help from outside sources, as much as was possible.

During those days, I found it very difficult to concentrate, and always I felt like I was carrying an underlying feeling of unease. I spoke to Sarah about it and she felt very similar. At night, when we were together, she held me very tightly. There was a strange feeling of foreboding, which we could both feel, and we were waiting with resignation, for the next moves from the government.

On the State run media, there were repeated broadcasts and interviews, about possible aggressive attacks from neighbouring countries and the threat of terrorism. It was all propaganda, to justify huge increases in military expenditure. The suggestion was implanted repeatedly, that what the country needed was an active and well-trained extensive Security

Service, and a credible Military deterrent, so we would be invulnerable to attacks.

They showed videos of their fighting aircraft, and their spokesmen talked about the type of advanced weapons, the country needed to develop and acquire. They were preparing the population, for actions, that they had already decided to do.

The local people did not like these new military leaders. They were changing the country, and it was not a good change, for people were becoming fearful and reclusive. Many of the locals turned to us, and asked if we could help, but they did not realise how much threat we faced to our very existence.

Simon called a core group meeting for the six of us and posed the question for us all to consider, about what we would do if the government decreed that we had to close the Community, so they could mine Uranium.

At first there was silence, but Kurt spoke up, and Julia agreed with him. They were adamant that this was the place where they were meant to be, to do their work. There was nowhere else for them to go. Under no circumstances would they go, even if it resulted in their deaths. Their response was passionate and defiant. Slowly the rest of us agreed, and I felt a sinking feeling in my chest, that we might all die.

It was a huge test for our faith. Sarah was crying.

Simon sent a letter to the Military leadership, asking for reassurance about our future, but there was no answer. Eve made several trips to the United Nations, and to governing bodies around the world, to bolster support for our existence. Many were sympathetic, and pledged that they would make representations to the government, but it all seemed rather futile.

Sarah and I had many long talks, often going deep into the night. She was scared, but determined to go on. She loved the school, and had developed, to become an expert in channelling, under Julia's guidance. Sarah was utterly devoted to our 'New Earth' project, and for her, it was our home, and always would be.

I took time on my own, and trekked through the young woodland and forest that we had planted. There were special glades where I liked to go, and small waterways, with larger stones, where I could sit. Here I would listen to the wonderful sounds of the nature and touch the glistening dew on vines and shrubs, while I watched the insects and birds move about. I had some favourite trees, none of course to compare with the two guardian trees outside our Sanctuary. But there were some trees that I had planted, and I continued to keep a watchful eye over their progress. Often, I would hug their slender trunks, and give them my love.

While sitting on the stones by the water, I closed my eyes, and with the bubbling of the water, I slipped into that deeper inner state. I wanted to return to meditation I had had with the giant crystal to explore if there had been any change. Soon, I was there, and the vision was continuing, from where I had left it.

There was still much darkness around me, and I found myself standing in the crystal with its light, as it was breaking apart. With the breaking of the crystal, its light could not shine anymore. Again, I felt very distressed, but I could hear an inner voice, urging me to look closer. What I saw, was that the crystal was, in fact, moving itself apart, so that the dark could come in. It was the most extraordinary sight. The dark was being invited in, even though its substance was slimy and sticky, and the most repulsive matter that I could imagine. I wanted to cling onto the crystal and force it closed again. But I was inwardly directed to let this desire go, and stand firm. And I was surprised, that I could do this, and I endeavoured to steady myself, so I could watch more fully. Beneath me, there was glowing energy, which I had not noticed before.

All at once the vision faded and I did not know what happened next. What I was left with, was a feeling of some transformation, which was taking place, a changing situation that went beyond my comprehension. And it was not something that I liked, in the slightest bit.

ULTIMATUM

The next morning, the moment that we had been dreading, arrived. Another letter was delivered, addressed to Simon, as General Manager of the Centre. It was brought by Military Courier, as the others had been. Once more, it was a document that Simon only needed to sign, indicating that he had received, read its contents, and understood. Several of us gathered around him as he opened it, and there were gasps of horror as people began to read it.

We were being instructed, that the Community would be closed within seven days. The lease that we had obtained with the old President was now revoked. The Government had need of this land for National Security operations. Reasons for this was classified information, and the details would not be disclosed. There would be no possibility for any appeal. The decision of this closure was final.

All foreign Nationals, outside the core group, that were either visiting or working at the Community, would be required to leave the Country within 72 hours, and would receive a military escort to the airport. The Core group personnel had a further four day's grace to complete their business, but then, they would be required to leave also.

Simon made sure that all of us there, read the document, before he signed it. That took a while. At the end, he took the clipboard that was provided, and placed his signature at the bottom of the page, and gave it to the Official. Then, without comment, the Courier got in his vehicle, and was gone as quickly as he had arrived.

Even though we had expected it, the content of the document was utterly shocking. How dare they do this! News of the letter spread rapidly through the Community, and there were people wailing, suffering huge distress.

For many, the Community was more than home. We had put so much work into this. People did not want to leave; they certainly could not countenance for the Community to be closed. It was agonising. We were all stunned, and did not know what to say or do.

Simon was standing on the driveway; his body was stiff with tension and shock. He stared blankly into the air. His expression was filled with defeat and despair. He did not see a solution. Otherwise, he would have been motivating us towards it.

Part of me wanted to shake him. We must not surrender. I was not prepared to accept this dictate. Somehow, we had to fight, for our Community to continue to exist. We had to do it.

Later that day, we all met at the Conference Hall. People were crying and comforting each other. Simon stood in the middle of the Hall, shouting, and informing everybody, that all the Foreign Nationals would have to go, as directed. We could not put anyone's safety at risk. People did not agree with Simon. Some were angry. It was quite chaotic.

There were reporters in the room, from the international media. I welcomed them. They had converged on us from other parts of the country. We needed the publicity, and, through my own initiative, I had made sure, that we sent out press releases, soon after we received the news. The world had to be informed. Maybe they could help us. I desperately hoped so.

The local press was not allowed to give this any coverage. But I encouraged our workers from the outlying villages, to spread the word, far and wide. People in the country could learn, by word of mouth, via social media and from satellite TV. They had to know. For this situation to be imposed upon us, was outrageous.

Cameras were zooming into pictures of the distress, which our workers were feeling, and many interviews with individuals were being conducted. Simon refused to speak to the media, but I did. Nothing would stop me from talking to the press, and I endeavoured to remain as composed as I could, and give out information that we knew, factually. When other workers from our Community checked with me about offering interviews, I told them to do it. What did we have to lose? I was pleased that our state of affairs was attracting media attention. There needed to be more of it, much more of it, and pressure had to be put on this disgraceful government.

In general, there was tremendous disgust with this new regime, and the way it was repressing the people in the country. Many of those who had been arrested, had not been seen again, and nobody could account for them. This was a country, that been a happy place, with a gentle humanitarian government. Now, all the people could feel, was fear and terror and suppressed outrage. And the military ruled with an iron fist. What sort of society was that?

We had been issued with a heartless ultimatum. It was a shocking decision. We could protest to the media, and scream and shout, but otherwise, what could we do about it? The regime wanted to mine uranium – and build up its weapons base. It was a battle between war and peace, and how could the side of peace stop military might?

Simon must have found some resolve. It could have been the reporters. He stepped up to the stage, and waited for people to quieten down. He wanted to speak to everyone. There was a hush in the Hall. For some moments, he stood by the microphone, and looked around at everyone. His eyes were defiant, and I was happy that he had found his strength. There were cameras clicking, and every word would be recorded.

Simon started his speech. He made it clear that this decision to close the Centre was made completely against the will of the custodians of the Community, and without any consultation. The actions of the Military Government, while legally within their rights, was wrong. What they were proposing to do, was without compassion, and strongly at variance with the intentions of the lease that we had signed, and the vision that we had shared with the previous government. He instructed everyone that we must follow all the orders that were given to us, so that we would not break the Law.

He urged non-violent protest as a response to this. This government must learn the strength of opposition that existed to this decision. To close the Community would impact on the lives of thousands of people – more than could be known. The work we were doing, through all the activities in the Centre, and its outreach, was undeniably precious. What we were doing, did not hurt anybody, it was self-sustaining, and it helped to make a lot of people's lives better. The New Earth Community had a right to exist, and for us to continue to do our work. He asked everyone to contrast the work that we were doing on the land, to improve it, and promote peace, with the prospect of using the land to mine uranium, and make bombs. Which path forward did we all want? Which way into the future was right? He pleaded with any members of the Government, who would learn of his speech, to reverse this decision. It was not too late.

I was so happy that Simon's speech was being broadcast. People were moved by his passion, and he was saying the words that we all felt.

At the end of his speech, there was spontaneous standing applause. His words gave us hope. We had to cling on to what we believed. Simon gave way to Kurt, and we finished the gathering with a communal prayer. Then there was silence in the room. The residents of our community slowly eased out of the building.

In the meantime, Simon was mobbed by journalists who had innumerable questions. Now he was prepared to speak. We all stood back, and for a long time, he patiently addressed the issues raised, as well as he could, until he reached a point where he felt it was enough, and he left by the side door.

There were reporters continuing to talk to various people in the Community. It seemed a good opportunity for the world to bear witness to what we had been doing.

I invited a few of the reporters to come with me, and I showed them 'before and after' photographs of the landscape of our land within the reforestation project. I also went outside with those reporters, and climbed up to the viewpoint with them. Then I pointed out the damage that had been caused by the recent drilling and the movement of the trucks through the property. There was clicking from cameras. It was not the kind of publicity that the regime would want, but we had to express our truth.

I gave the reporters information of all aspects of our work, and shared details, with stories, of how our community had grown, and our aspirations to help our world, in areas such as education, the environment, renewable energy, and as emissaries of peace. I talked until I could find no more to say, and the reporters listened patiently, recording my words, and taking notes.

We were engaged in a test of Will with the Military. It was necessary for us to stand up for what we believed in, but we had to do it by adhering to our values, and not descending into any form of brutality. Some workers had spoken to me about the possibility of constructing some form of blockade, but we would not do that; it would not stop them. We could not know the outcome of this, but we had to be steadfast, and pray, and ask Spirit to support us.

TENSIONS RISING

The situation of our Community prompted reaction throughout the country. There were protests again in the Capital and other provincial cities, and more people were arrested and detained. The security forces used tear gas to disperse crowds, and injured many people with batons and stun guns. Ambulance sirens rang out across the city and soon the hospitals were full with the injured. There was a great restlessness building among the people in the country. We could tell that they were reaching a point where they had had enough.

The Government reinstated a curfew over the entire country, and this appeared to quieten the situation a bit. They used the state run media to accuse the protesters of being terrorists, and to assure citizens that they would take all steps necessary to strengthen national security, so people would be safe. They insisted, that their instructions had to be followed. Anyone involved in any kind of protest would be punished severely.

There was an announcement of a clampdown on the international press, and reporters now risked detention, if they issued any news items, that did not have prior approval of the regime.

Nobody would believe the Military's version of events. People protesting were certainly not terrorists. There was no mention on the official media about our Community closing. They were completely ignoring it, with all their pronouncements. People did not like these sorts of tactics being employed by the government.

There were rumours starting to circulate, that segments of the Military were not happy with how the regime was administering its power. However, there was no sign of this dissent in the streets. Armed security personnel were deployed in all townships, and protesters were told that the Military would be using live ammunition for anyone else coming out on the streets to cause trouble. People then stayed out of the way, to protect themselves. But behind closed doors, people were seething. The government may have been able to stop the press from reporting, but they could not halt social media.

In the meantime, there was international condemnation. Meetings were called in the United Nations. Economic sanctions were strengthened. Huge petitions were gathered from interest groups in many countries, and presented to the Military Government. Diplomatic delegations met officials from the Dictatorship to express their dismay.

We were aware that the underlying protests from other Nations were not about our Community. They did not want another country with an unstable regime to have a nuclear capability. That is what they were concerned about. But I did not believe that the Military government would be swayed by international opinion, in the slightest.

I kept hoping that there would be a change of heart, on the part of the regime. However, as much as we could tell, all the reaction, which had been brought to bear, was only making this military government more determined. They were not the sort of people that would let others tell them what to do.

Then came another shock. After many years without it, the Government announced the return of the death penalty for those caught undermining the Rule of the State. Prisoners convicted, would face Death by Firing Squad. And many of those already arrested were in line for this outcome. We could hardly believe how far down a violent track, the situation in the country had gone. The Military Government were becoming more draconian by the day.

There was no sign whatsoever, of any reversal in terms of the decisions concerning our Community. It seemed that our fate was sealed.

As the clock ticked on, we all followed on the Internet, what was happening in the country around us, but the mood of our members, was one of despair and submission. Our workers had been packing, and gathering their belongings. The time for our foreign nationals to leave, was imminent, and as they prepared themselves, buses came to the property to ferry them all to the airport, complete with the promised military escorts.

Lists had been drawn up by the Military, with records of everyone that needed to be on the buses. Soldiers stood by in their jeeps, ensuring that all our members would comply.

There were many tearful goodbyes, especially amongst the children. None of them wanted to go, and some of them shouted out to us, to keep the Centre open. It was so sad, when the buses drove away. I had never felt so desolate. After they had all gone, the place felt very empty and deserted. Some of the local workers wanted to remain, but Simon urged many of them to return home. Only a skeleton staff remained, and we only had a few days, until we would have to go as well.

FACING THE INEVITABLE

Nobody said very much. Julia and Kurt spent their time in the Sanctuary meditating, and in prayer. Sarah chose to be with them. Eve was away, doing her diplomacy, frantically trying anything she could, to help us.

Simon was on his computer in the office, so I joined him there.

'What if we do have to hand everything over to the Military?' I asked. 'What has it all been for? All these years we have been building this – all the effort, and the ideals we have had about helping our world. Even the trees – many of them will be cut down or trampled without any care. The energy of love we have gathered here will be broken – all in the name of power and greed. How can it happen like this? It isn't fair.' I could feel the tears in my eyes and my voice was breaking.

Simon stopped what he was doing and looked over at me thoughtfully.

'I understand your feeling upset,' he started slowly, 'for I feel it too. We will all be struggling to cope with this. But you must admit,' he continued, 'we have had an amazing run. There has been support for us in so many directions, all the way along. It has been incredible. And what is happening to us now, is symptomatic of what is taking place across the whole globe. Those of us that care about each other, and the Earth, are striving in every way, that we can, to make the world a better place. We can feel in our hearts, that a more loving world is possible, almost within reach, but for us to be able to embrace this, there needs to be a certain threshold of acceptance for that, among the population of humanity, for it to be manifested. And we are not there yet. It is sad, but true.

'If those that are power hungry, self-interested and greedy, decide to assert themselves, to squash and suppress those that oppose them, with little regard for the consequences, and its impact on the planet, then there is very little we can do to combat it. We are not the violent ones, and we choose not to be. All we can do is to appeal to these people's compassion, show them what they may be losing, what we all are losing.

'Life on Earth is precious and needs to be honoured and respected in all its aspects. Some of those officers may wake up to this, and most of them may not. If enough of us band together as a mass consciousness and action as a collective, this may help. And this is what is happening now around our project. But whether it will be enough – at this stage, it seems not.

'You see, we cannot fight those people that want to destroy, because it is not in our nature to do that, for we are peaceful people, and peace is what we want, so we have to uphold that in what we do. However, what we can do, and what we must do, is to continue our efforts, in all the ways that we can, and not give up.

'If our Centre is closed, there will be other cells of activities taking root in our world, other people making efforts to establish similar projects, to what we have been doing. The motivation to achieve love and liberation for our planet and its people, so that we can live together in peace – the impulses for this are very strong, and come from the deep core of our being. That is why meditation is so important, and why Kurt, Julia and Sarah meditate even now. Through meditation, we do link together, we channel light and love, and we do become aware of what is truly important.'

I listened to Simon in appreciation. With him, I sensed that whatever the outcome of the trial that we now faced, that he would feel peace, and know that the good work that he has done, will have supported the establishment of a more peaceful world. For myself, I did not feel so satisfied, for I felt that we had much more to do. I could not just resign myself to passively let go of our project just now.

That night, when I went to bed, Sarah and I talked for hours. She was also very upset, and wanted our work to continue. Sarah could sense the good that our work did to help people, especially in the school, and she had witnessed enough joy and healing and transformation in so many people's outlook, during her time at our Community, that she could not accept that it would be all over so soon. During that day, she had meditated, and spent time with Julia and Kurt. Julia channelled the Earth Spirit, and Sarah also connected with that, but there were no answers, no remedies to our situation, and no guidance to tell us that our Community would continue in its work. Sarah could sense that Kurt and Julia were also reconciled to what would happen, feeling peace about that, just like Simon. We appeared to be the only ones that could not accept that.

CLOSING DAY

It was our last full day for us within our beautiful Community. On the following morning, we would have to hand over our keys and rights, to the Military. This was the day before we had to leave.

There were still local Staff members that had insisted upon staying with us, but it was the five of us that chose to meet by the Guardian tree. Eve was not with us.

As we gathered, there was a slight warming breeze, rustling the leaves a little, and we stood together, holding hands. I could feel an electric pulse vibrating between us, and around our Circle. We had certainly built some very warm and lasting bonds of friendship between us, over these years that we had been working together. I opened my eyes, and looked at each of our group, in turn, feeling great appreciation and respect for each one, and all the contributions and service that had been expressed.

I turned my head around, and could see the curved dome of the wonderful meditation Sanctuary behind us. Over the years, there had been so many thousands of people meditating in there, listening to Julia channel the Earth Spirit, the souls of people finding their own inner peace and guidance. People's lives had been touched and transformed by having this Sanctuary here.

And then there was the School, now greatly expanded with many classrooms and workshops – a wonderful hub of activity, where the children could learn, on so many levels. It had been such a brilliant venture, bringing together children from such a lot of nations of the world, teaching tolerance and understanding, helping those children gain skills and inner awareness, caring for the Earth and each other, with the hope, that many of them would become leaders in their own communities, and bring greater understanding to our humanity.

And on the other side of the sanctuary, was the magnificent Conference

Hall, with its wooden structures and eco-friendly designs. There had been some great assemblies in that building, with groups from all over the world. This had been a space for adults, exploring fantastic possibilities of how we could better live on this planet Earth. So many people had developed friendships and networking links here, finding inspiration with others, who believed like we did, and wanted our planetary life together to succeed, and for our Earth to be a happy place. This was Simon's baby, and he had done a brilliant job at managing the Conferences. I felt proud of him.

Of course, there were also the massive vegetable gardens, the Renewable Energy centre, and all the accommodation blocks. Such a lot of building and construction had been achieved in a short space of time. And now those accommodation blocks and office buildings were deserted, like the rest of the property, and it felt like desecration, that this would be so. Over the years, our community had become like a complex intertwining village, a place for people to gain inner sustenance and strength, for their Spiritual path.

My favourite part of our project was the forest, and there was nothing that gave me more pleasure than the replenishment of the nature here, and the returning wildlife. Our Earth needed to display its natural beauty, and not be filled with human concrete monstrosities and wasteland, formed through human abuse of the land. To have been able to help with this reforestation, gave me unfathomable joy. But now, with my friends, Hugh, Lydia and Jake, and all our teams dispersed, and sent away, suddenly, I could feel a sharp pain in my heart, and a restlessness that was not prepared to agree to this.

The others were now looking around too. They would all have their own thoughts.

Simon broke the silence, and told us that Eve was in the Capital, and she wanted to go in person, to meet the Military Commander. She wished to make one last appeal for the closure of our Community to be halted. She had letters and affidavits from interested groups, and political leaders from around the world. For her, it was important for the leaders of the Military government to be made aware of this. If only they would reconsider?

Simon turned to me, and asked if I would be willing to go there, to meet her, and video her going into the building, so that if there was any problem, and she was detained, then we would have the evidence of her going into the building, and the time that this occurred. I thought about what Simon requested. I wanted to do it, and it felt right inside.

Simon waited, and I finally nodded to confirm that I would go. However, I also felt anxiety, and turned to Sarah. 'Will you come with me?' I asked her softly.

It was not that I needed her support, but I wanted to know that she was safe. I did not know what would occur here in our Community, in the coming hours. It was difficult for me to be separated from her now.

For a few moments, Sarah looked at me hesitantly, but then her eyes firmed in their intensity. Sarah was quite adamant. 'I am not going to leave here,' she told me. 'This is my place, and I am going to stay.' I saw Simon look over at his daughter with concern, and I felt a shiver go through my body.

I tried again, and pleaded with Sarah, reassuring her that we would come straight back, but she was not going to change her mind. Instead, she encouraged me to go, so that I could support her mother.

As I worked it out in my mind, I did not imagine that the military vans and trucks would come until the following morning. Therefore, I had time to travel to the capital and return before then. It was feasible to make the trip. I agreed to go.

Somehow, it felt very sad to say 'Goodbye' to everyone. There were tears in my eyes, and I needed some moments to steady myself. Sarah came over and hugged me, and told me that she loved me. It was not just her that I was sad about. I just hoped that everyone would be alright in my absence.

Simon showed me the cameras to use, and gave me two, one that would be the best one to record videos and the other for snap shots. He explained how I could zoom in, to obtain clear long distance photographs, and gave me instruction about uploading them onto a computer afterwards, and where the photos and videos could be sent.

I needed reassurance. We all had our phones, so we could stay in contact throughout my journey.

The Capital was about three hours' drive away. If I was going to go, I wanted to leave soon, so I could be back before nightfall.

Simon continued to discuss the journey with me. He suggested that I take one of our four-wheel drive vehicles, and go along the unmarked track, on the other side of the hill, behind the sanctuary. This would take me through to the closest local village, and keep me away from any military vehicles. He did not feel that it would be wise to go out via the main road into the Centre. There may be soldiers monitoring it. This made sense to me.

Over the years, we had dismantled many of the fences, which had been erected around the Community. We had made tracks, for access to the local villages, and others that linked different segments of the property. We never advertised these, but they were very useful, with our transport needs.

I could tell what Simon was thinking, and he wanted to take precautions. He did not want me to be detained, and he did not trust these military people. Simon gave me sunglasses, and a cap to wear, so I would not be so easily recognised. I was happy to agree to his suggestions.

As I left the Centre in the four-wheel drive, I felt pleased to be doing something useful, for I did not like to wait and to be passive. I prayed that Eve may have some communications, and papers, that could make a difference. Somehow, I doubted it, but we had to try.

Once I got in the four-wheel drive vehicle, I put on the scarf and sunglasses that Simon had given me. From the village, after I had exited from the grounds of the Community, I drove along the road, which crossed the intersection, with the driveway that headed back into the Centre. As I looked, there were two Military vehicles parked at this intersection. There were armed guards monitoring traffic, and blocking the route into our

Community. I felt afraid, and although I nodded, and smiled pleasantly to the guards, as soon as I was out of sight, I put my foot on the accelerator and sped as fast as I could. I wanted to be finished with what Eve was doing as soon as possible, and to return. I phoned Simon to inform him of what I had seen, and then raced ahead.

DISTURBING DEVELOPMENTS

It was a mighty relief to meet Eve, and she was glad to see me. She had not been around for the whole week, and she wanted to know directly how things had been going. We went through the details rapidly. She was concerned about the morale of all of us that remained. But I wanted to know about her work.

I pressed her to tell me about her efforts, and she told me how there was a great deal of diplomatic pressure being applied behind the scenes, lots of appeals to the Military Government, in all the ways that were possible. However, the regime was not shifting, and they claimed the right to make use of their sovereign land, in whatever way they saw fit.

When neighbouring states had made threats to them, they just became more intransigent in their response, and argued, that they were entirely justified in their actions. Eve confirmed the rumours that we had heard, that not all elements of the Military Junta agreed with the direction of decision making. But the leadership were maintaining control, without any obvious wavering. The options, which we had now, were very limited, and for her to present the papers she had collected, were virtually the last throw of the dice.

We found a quiet place, and I filmed Eve, speaking about all the papers that she had, and her intention to present this in person to the Junta. All I had to do would be to video and photograph her as she entered the Government building, and save that onto a computer.

Eve was very nervous about going to do this, for she felt that there was a high chance that they would detain her. But she was still willing to do it. She gave me her phone, and showed me another new phone, which she would take with her. This phone had no history or contacts on it, and would be unhelpful to the regime, if they took it from her. She could phone me, when she was safe, but I could not phone her. Eve wanted me to have copies of all the papers she would be sharing with the Junta, so I could share these with the world, if necessary. She put those down next to me.

Suddenly, she held my hands tightly, and implored me to stay safe, and to report to Simon immediately, making it internationally known, if she did not return. She was shaking, and I could sense the tension in her. It was not just about her safety. As with all the rest of us, she cared enormously about the Project, and she could not bear that anything would happen to it. I looked in her eyes, and saw her longing. Eve had been like a mother to me, and I did not want anything to happen to her either.

The Capital was not an easy place to get around anymore. There were armed patrols continually travelling along the streets, and guards posted next to important buildings. I just found it hard to believe the change that had occurred from the peace-loving country I had known. We could see people with their heads down, walking along the streets. Nobody wanted to be seen anymore. People were afraid. We had to park a considerable distance from the City centre, as to not attract attention. Eve and I did not walk together, but within sight of each other.

There was a hotel opposite the Government building. This is where I needed to go. Eve nodded to me, and I entered and headed for the restaurant on the first floor. No one stopped me, and I just smiled at the people that passed me. Now, as I was on the first floor, I found the window Eve had told me about, overlooking the Government building. There was a curtain there, and I could hide in the folds of that, and see outwards. I gave Eve a signal, as she glanced up at me from the corner, where she was waiting for me to be ready.

I took the cameras out of their bags and positioned the camera on its tripod, to be directly facing the entrance to the Government building, and held the button in my hand, so I could take as many single image shots, as I could. In my other hand, I held the video camera ready. Eve gave me a few minutes, to get settled in my position, but then I saw her crossing the road. Immediately, I started to film her. She walked up the steps of the grand Parliament building, resolutely, with her brief case, and hand bag. As she approached the front door, two armed guards came, and took her belongings, and directed her inside. I zoomed in with the still camera, and took as many pictures as I could. Just for a slight moment, she looked around, deliberately, and I could photograph her face. The guards were wary, and one of them immediately turned his attention outward, looking and checking, but then, they nudged her forward. That was the last I saw of her.

As the door to the building closed, I felt a horrible feeling of loss, but there was no time to feel that; I had to move, pack the cameras and get out of there.

I had the camera equipment in a simple brown bag. There was a far entrance to the Hotel, away from the main street. I had to head for that. Soon I was going down the stairs. When I reached ground level and came out of the building, I looked up towards the main street, and there were two guards standing on the corner there. Fortunately, they were looking the other way.

Now, I had to find a way back to my vehicle without attracting attention. Putting on my sunglasses and cap, I asked for Spirit help, that I may be protected. As calmly as I could, I joined the road, that went away from the Government Building, and I walked slowly and evenly along the path, looking in at the shops, so that I would appear normal. I passed several soldiers on the way, but none of them stopped me.

It was a great relief when I could climb into the four-wheel drive, and be away from the centre of the town. Now I had to wait.

Eve had arranged that as soon as she was finished, that she would phone me, and if I had not heard from her within an hour, then I should raise the alarm with Simon. I looked at the time on my phone, and took some deep breaths to attempt to calm myself.

As the minutes ticked by, I started to feel very restless. An hour passed, and there was no call from Eve. I decided to give her another twenty minutes, just in case the Authorities had taken her phone, and to give her extra time to reach me. I could feel the perspiration forming droplets on my forehead. I was becoming increasingly anxious. I had parked the car in a quiet side street. There were a few teenage local boys passing by, pausing and making comments about my car. I could not stay there very long. Inside, I pleaded that those boys would let me be.

Finally, I lifted my phone to ring Simon. What would they all be doing? The phone rang on, and on. There was no answer. He must be out of the office. I tried his mobile – it went straight onto answer machine, as if it was switched off. That was odd. I looked through my contact numbers, and rang Sarah's phone next. No answer with her either. Now I was getting worried. Where were they? Maybe I could get Kurt or Julia. Same response. No one was there. What was happening? I rang some of the numbers again, and then tried the Staff phone and the kitchen, going through all the numbers that I had. They were all blank, going straight onto answer machine. I next rang one of my friends in the neighbouring village. He answered, but he knew nothing that could be going on. They had not spoken to him.

I had to go. Something was not right. I was three hours away, but I had to get there sooner. Eve could manage, if she came out of the Government building. I had to get to the Community. Maybe the Military had come in early. They mustn't hurt my friends. I had to be careful – not to just sacrifice myself. There was no means for me to take on the Military, for I had no weapons, and I wouldn't want any. I had time to think; I needed to go into myself, and not panic.

GROWING ANXIETY

It was as if I was being looked after; all through my drive, I had no stoppages; the journey out from the City was smooth, cars moved to the side for me, people waved me through. My mind was so full of thoughts. I wanted the journey of traversing that distance to go quickly, and to get there. Inside, I was struggling, and I kept trying their phones. The more they failed to answer, the more heightened my anxiety became.

I approached the corner, which, when I went around it, would lead to that intersection at the entrance to the Centre. Something made me stop. Would those military vehicles still be there?

Many years earlier, Sarah had taught me the value of taking photographs and gathering evidence. I remembered the environmental protest rally and how she had retreated to take photographs and record what had happened. It was her pictures that had saved me, and saved all of us, on that day. Now it was my turn. I had to do the same, and be like her. The thought had come to me while I was driving, and I was determined to do it, and gather evidence.

I walked forward to a position near where I would have sight of the intersection, and I clambered behind some bushes so I would be hidden. Then I got out my camera. I took a few deep breaths to steady my feelings, and proceeded to do my work.

With the zoom lens, I could obtain a clear close-up view of what was happening. It looked quite busy. There were now several military vehicles and soldiers gathered at the intersection. As I adjusted the lens, and looked even closer, I could see that there was a motorcade slowly disappearing along the road into the Centre. It must be someone important, for they had armed escorts. I clicked as many photographs as I could, and added a short video where I gave a simple commentary, of where I was situated, and what was happening.

With all this military action, I felt very alarmed. The regime was not waiting till the morning. I just hoped that my friends were safe. Suddenly, I felt another shiver through my body, and I was not sure at all. There had still been no word from Eve. I knew what I had to do next.

Turning my vehicle around, I then went the long way to get to the village where I had come out from the Centre in the morning. Going this way, I could bypass that intersection. It was now late afternoon. I did not want to be seen by those guards, and it certainly did not feel safe to pass all those military vehicles. The roads in the area here were familiar to me. Again, I travelled as fast as I could. The whole situation appeared urgent, and incredibly dangerous.

On the outskirts of the village, I stopped by briefly to see my friend Tomas. I told him what had happened, and he was very concerned. Tomas had worked on the reforestation project with me, and now he was helping at the local village. He asked if he could come with me, and I was very tempted to invite him, but somehow it felt better if he stayed away from the Community, so he could be a resource, if help was needed later. I did not want him in danger. As horrible as it may be, I felt that I had to go on my own.

He suggested a route for me, which would keep me some distance from all the buildings, and end up at the back of the hill, behind the Sanctuary. It was important for me to remain concealed, and to find a vantage point from where I could observe and photograph the events that were taking place as close as possible. The hill behind the sanctuary would be ideal. At the top of that hill, was my favourite viewpoint.

Once I was ready, we hugged, and I left to go into the grounds of our Community.

Slowly I ventured forward, and tried to move very steadily with my vehicle, through the terrain. My body was shaking, but I felt compelled to go on. I did not want to attract the attention of the Military, and prayed that they would not see or hear me.

I had not gone far when, for the first time, I saw the smoke. At first, it was just a few faint wisps, but then it became stronger and thicker. It was coming from the direction of the Conference Centre. There was a rising panic inside me. I had to hurry. What were they doing?

From having been already quite restless, my heart began to beat quite violently; I could feel it pounding in my chest. Even though I still had to go carefully, part of me could not wait. I felt torn inside, but I made myself concentrate, so I would continue to avoid the dips in the road.

What could that smoke be all about? They must be burning something. My attention would not go there. I must keep looking at the road in front of me. All I could do, sensibly, was to proceed safely, and reach my destination. I had a job to do, and I had to get there to do it, and soon.

I was very grateful to have this four-wheel drive vehicle. The directions that Tomas had given me were good. My car served me so well, for it was an electric car, with a very quiet motor. I found a place to park, under the covers of some trees. Without hesitation, I jumped out and got my equipment. Soon I was clambering up the hill.

By now, I could hear the crackling of burning and the smell of fire. I hoped and hoped so much that the military may be burning some extraneous items from the buildings, and not hurting my friends. But inside, from the knot in my stomach, I feared that it was worse than that. I knew.

HORROR

As I climbed closer to the top of the hill, I reminisced about being a small boy, when the developers and road builders came to cut down the trees that were opposite my house, and how flats and buildings were erected in the beautiful field, which had been the precious world, that I loved then. I remembered how I had been determined, and wanted to stop those developers, but my mum had prevented me going out to them. I had vowed then, that I would always fight for justice, and what I felt was right.

Whatever I was going to see when I reached the top of the hill, I had to remain true to my vow. Now was my test. I sensed that this would be the time for me to be very strong.

In my mind, I had several flashes of memory, where I could imagine my dear companions, and all the efforts which we had made to build this Community. We had been blessed. For a few moments, I saw Sarah's face in my mind, and tears were flowing down my cheeks. I had to reach the top now. I had to see what was there, and what I could do. I had to do this, whether I liked it or not.

Now, as I approached the crest of the hill, I noticed a pile of rubble left by the drillers. It was a perfect place for me to hide, and to set up the tripod for my camera. I did all that without looking down, because I did not want to look down, not yet. I had to position the cameras properly, and check all the aspects of the apparatus, and I did those things I had to do. Then, when I had done that, I paused, and took some more deep breaths.

Now, there was no more reason to avoid it. The point had been reached, where I could not stop myself from looking down anymore. I had to do it. And when I did that, nothing could prepare me for what I saw – nothing!

Somehow, I had imagined that the soldiers would have made a bonfire, and were burning loose items of furniture. But it was not a pile of extraneous items that they were burning; it was the Sanctuary and the Conference Centre. Both were alight and ablaze, and soldiers were pouring petrol on the walls of the school to burn that as well. It was terrifying, and unbelievable. There were lots of soldiers scattered about, all engaged in the act of destroying the buildings of our wonderful Centre. The flames were hot, and I was breathing hard.

I wanted to go down there and dowse those flames, and shout and scream at those Military officers, and tell them how cruel they were, how terrible they were, with their actions. I wished to hit them, and punch them, and push sense into them, until they stopped. It was so unfair, so mindless, so destructive. And there was some important military person down there, giving orders, watching passively from his jeep, a safe distance away.

And as I began taking pictures, and videos, and zooming in, I could see that the man in the Jeep, was the leader of the Junta, himself – here to oversee our Project being destroyed. And as I looked closely through the lens, he appeared to be smiling – a malevolent grin, with no compassion or care, only the urge for power and asserting his domination over others. How could he be enjoying this? His heart was cold.

I could feel my body jerking and shaking, because I really did want to go down there, to fight them, and I had to stop myself, and force myself to take in everything I could see, to film it, and record it as fully as I could. I had to do this job. So, I clicked away and turned on the video camera for it to survey the scene.

But then, I saw something even worse, something that my mind did not want to accept, like my worst fears coming true. I so much wanted to look away, and pretend I had not seen it, anything but that, for in the shadows near the buildings, there were bodies. I noticed three of them at first. And as much as I wanted to break down, and rush towards them, somewhere inside me, I remembered my commitment, and I turned the lens towards the bodies, and began to film.

When I zoomed in, to the maximum magnification of my camera, I could recognise the bodies, as they were lit up by the flickering flames. It couldn't be, but it was. The first one that I saw was Simon. I so much didn't want him to be dead, but there was a pool of blood around him, and I recognised his clothes and physique. And then I could identify the flowing silver hair of Kurt, and next to him, Julia. They were all there, in a group. And none of them was moving, and they seemed to be dead. There were residues of blood next to all of them. I adjusted the lens, and looked at them very closely through the camera. Somehow, their faces were peaceful.

My body wanted to go into convulsions, and for a few moments, I put my head down, so I could compose myself. And then I forced myself to go on filming.

There were other bodies further away, and I recognised them, as members of the staff that remained. And soldiers were standing by them, pointing guns. This was an atrocity. How could they do this? But where was Sarah? I could not see her body? I surveyed all the grounds in front of me, and there was no sign of her. I searched again, and again. Could she still be alive?

With the sound recorder on my video camera amplifying the sounds below me, I could hear through my earphones, as the leader of the Junta barked an order. Then I noticed a group of the soldiers performing an act, which horrified me even more. One at a time, they were throwing the bodies of my friends and the staff into the flames, so they would burn, and be unrecognisable. I took my video camera, and filmed it all. They kept going, until all the bodies were immersed in flame, and then the soldiers were pouring some liquid over the ground where the bodies had been laid out and they burnt that too.

The soldiers were destroying what they pleased. No doubt, they would have a story for this, some vaguely plausible account, which would completely absolve them of any responsibility, for what they had been doing. I had to keep going with this. They were lighting up further buildings now – the Renewable Energy Centre was in flames. I was feeling a mixture of acute distress, and huge rage at these people. They had no right to do this!!

The President of the Junta was now seated in his jeep, and preparing to leave. His soldiers had their orders and knew what to do. I kept filming, everything that I could, but then I found a creeping restlessness growing in me.

Part of me just wanted to sleep, and my body felt so heavy. It was too much for me. But I couldn't do that. I had to think, and work out what to do. I had to make myself do that, somehow.

I had to find Sarah. If she was not with the others, where was she? What was I going to do with all the evidence I had collated? How could I upload it onto the Internet? I checked with my phone – still no word from Eve. There was no signal here. I needed a computer. That's what I had to find. The Satellite system and communications equipment from the Centre, was all gone in the flames. We were in a remote area. I had to think. Where could I find a computer? For some moments, I tried to get my mind to focus. And then I knew. There was one.

We had constructed huts as part of the reforestation project, placed in various locations around the property. The nearest one had solar power, a computer and satellite equipment. It was the one that Jake and Lydia had used. I had been there many times. There was a small office with it.

I could not delay; I had to go there. These pictures had to be uploaded and sent out. I preferred to go to the hut, rather than attempt to drive my car to the village, for the soldiers might notice my car. I did not want to go away from the area, until I knew what had happened to Sarah. My fear was that the soldiers had got to the hut before me, but there had been no smoke from that direction. I needed faith.

The sky was darkening. That was a relief. I would feel safer with the night sky. Now I had to put my camera equipment away – I had to run.

Where was Sarah? I was missing her – I could not accept to be without her. She had to be alive. I could not think very far, just what I had to do next – that was all that I could manage.

I thought through other options again. Better to go here to this office, rather than for me to risk going to the village of my friend. I would be safer on foot. Who knows, by now, the soldiers may have closed the village off too? And the four-wheel drive – I would leave that, where I had hidden it, under the foliage at the base of the hill on the other side to all the burning. I had to remember the way. The terrain was quite dense with trees on the way to that hut. I did not want to damage any of the trees. At least, they had not been touched until now.

Climbing down the slope of the hill, the physical exertion of moving competed with a terrible uncontrollable energy of grief, that was flowing through me. I had to keep going. Somewhere inside, I was being helped to move. One step at a time; I did not look around, but kept running and pushing through the undergrowth. I knew the direction approximately, where I was going, and I kept on rushing and stumbling now, using the starlight to help see. Once or twice, I slipped, but got to my feet again.

In one moment, I saw another vision of Sarah's face in my mind and she was smiling. I just hoped that this was not a sign that she had passed over. From my experience of her, I knew that if Sarah had been in my position and seeing all the fire – that she would have done exactly what I was doing. She would have filmed it too.

I had to get these pictures and videos out to the world. It was not clear to me, if it would make the slightest bit of difference, but I had to get it out into the public domain. The world must know what this junta was doing!!

The last section before I could reach the hut meant that I needed to climb this quite steep slope, and although I wanted to get up there quickly, I was struggling for breath now, from having over extended myself. My body was just about exhausted, and all I wanted to do was to rest. But I had to get there; I could not stop now.

Finally, as I reached the top of the slope, and scrambled through one last clump of undergrowth, I reached the door of the hut. I had found it. What a relief! And it was still standing there, untouched. But it was locked, for it had not been used for several days, and I did not have the key. This would not stop me. I had to get in there. I was just so determined, so completely absorbed in this task; I slammed my shoulder against the door, over and over. It was a well-built hut and it did not want to give. But I was not going to let that prevent me. Finally, I felt the door moved a little, and then after a few more shoves, it creaked, and there were more sounds, that the hold of the hinges was weakening. It was going to give way, so I kept pushing, repeatedly, until the hinges disengaged, and it collapsed inwards.

It was so good achieve that, and get inside, and pushing a door open like that, was something I had never done before. But there was much more I had to do. I had to power up the system, engage the solar power storage, the Satellite link, and open the Computer. I was familiar with this equipment, but it seemed to take so long to be ready. I was waiting and waiting, and I felt the energy draining out of me. As soon as I stopped being active, I could feel my exhaustion. I had to keep going. From fear, I kept looking out of the door, in case there were soldiers after me. I did not feel safe, not at all safe.

The Solar power still held some storage power. Now the Computer was connecting. Thank God. The satellite system was working, and it was coming together. Not long now. I connected the files from the cameras to start uploading them. I had a list from Eve of people and groups who needed to be informed about her. I could use them. Also, I had lists on my phone, of friends of the Community, media outlets, and contact email addresses, with local groups that supported us. They all had to receive these files, every one of them, and more.

For the next while, I worked furiously, going from one to another, sending files collectively, and then individually, leaving nothing to chance, making sure on every occasion, that the files were sent, and sent again. I kept on going through every list of contacts, which I could find, transferring all the photos and video recordings I had. The world had to be informed.

On some emails, I wrote an explanation or used a voice recording to give further information. I did everything I could to sort it out, so others would know, and I acted as quickly as I could. Once sent, I had to release what I passed on to them. Now I would have to leave it to them.

And as I reached towards the end of my task, the energy drained further out of me. I felt utterly spent. And I still did not know what happened to Sarah.

When I had checked and double checked what I had done, I finally closed the computer, and the power source, and then, with only the sounds of wildlife outside, and the light of the stars and moon, so I could see, a little, I felt terrifyingly alone. What was I going to do now?

All at once, my body started to sob. I was very thirsty; it was several hours since I had drunk anything. My mouth was dry, and my heart was aching. And in that space, it began, just a little bit, to sink in to me what had happened. My body wanted to collapse. So much, I wanted some love and support. But I also wanted to be alone. This was the worst day of my life.

I remembered seeing Simon's eyes as I left the Centre. He had looked deep inside of me. It was as if somewhere inside of him, he knew. I felt that now. And the others – somehow, they were also at peace, that they had done their jobs. But I did not feel that I had done mine. I did not feel finished at all.

As the tears, and my wailing voice continued to express itself in the loneliness of this isolated hut, I felt prompted to look up at the window, in front of me. And there, as I looked again, and for a third time, there were two big eyes, looking in at me. Who was that? I was startled at first, but they were friendly eyes. Who was looking at me? I had no strength left to move. My first hope was that it would be Sarah, and I felt my heart sink when I realised that it was not.

Those eyes belonged to a young teenage local girl. She was one of our students. I could see now, and I waited now for what she would do. One part of me felt embarrassed, that she would see me in such a state of utter distress, but I did not feel that she was judging me. I felt warmth in her eyes, and because of that, I relaxed a little. Never had I felt so relieved to see someone in my whole life.

DISCOVERY

I leaned back, and the tears were streaming down my face. It did not matter what would happen to me now. I had done what I could. The girl came in, and put her hands on my back. She did it without asking, but I just accepted it. I had no vitality anymore to resist. All my fight had gone, and in my mind's eye, I could see our beautiful Sanctuary and Conference centre burning, turning to ashes, and I could hardly believe it. After a while, I was only a little aware anymore, that this girl was with me, and memories of lots of times my companions and I had spent, with the buildings of our community, all these memories moved through my consciousness.

I did not know how my life would be now. All my most close companions – it appeared that they were all gone now. Maybe they were all dead, and the Project destroyed. Where did that leave me with my life? What had it all been for? The tears continued to pour out of me.

For a few moments, the girl stopped what she was doing and gave me a flask with some drink. I was so grateful for that, and I gulped it down. She was helping me. Soon she placed her hands again, on my back, and I could feel the heat from them, and the energy that was pouring in from her hands was spreading. I started to feel calmer. How did she find me, this girl? She was a healer, just when I so desperately needed someone. My body was relaxing now. But she did not want me to sleep.

Soon she was shaking me on the shoulders. I felt so tired, and all I wanted to do was rest, but she kept on shaking me, until I started to rouse myself.

'We must go,' she was urging me. 'Come with me. We must hurry.' She was speaking in English. It seemed like she did not know many words, but she meant what she said. I had to trust her. She did not want to explain anymore, but she helped while I struggled to be able to stand up, and leave the hut.

'Follow me,' she ordered. And we started walking down the slope. She wanted me to go more quickly, and there was an urgency in her manner. We were headed back towards the buildings of the Centre, what was left of them. I could still smell the smoke, and there was a glow in the distance, which told me that they continued to burn.

She wanted me to run with her, and I did not understand, because we were headed straight back towards where the soldiers would be. Would that not be dangerous? When I hesitated, she pulled at me, and she didn't want me to stop. We had to keep going, and when I asked her where we were going, she would not tell me, but she looked in my eyes, and was insistent that I do what she directed. Swiftly, we kept walking, and I found that I had renewed energy in my legs. She really had helped me, and my system was somewhat replenished.

As we got closer to the Centre, I could see the flames of the fire, now more over towards the accommodation blocks. They were going to leave nothing, this Junta, and I could hear the distant shouts of some of the soldiers. Every now and again, one of them would bark out a command. And they didn't do it quietly. They seemed to be enthusiastic about what they were doing, like they were being driven by adrenaline.

Now, we were only a few hundred metres from what was left of the Conference Centre. The girl directed me around behind the cover of bushes and rocks, so we would not be seen, and urged me to be quiet. Then, I slipped on a loose piece of soil, and we both froze, and crouched down. My heart was beating so fast, I hoped so much, that they had not heard us. We waited for a long while, until we were sure that they had not noticed us, and then, I breathed a big sigh of relief as we stepped on further. I still did not know where we were going. And we were getting very near to the soldiers now. I could hear their voices and the crackling of the flames. What was she doing? I tried to stop her, and question, where she was taking us, but she frowned at me, and urged me to be quiet, and go forward.

At the last moment, before the soldiers would have gained sight of us, we veered off to the left. We were going over near the sanctuary. I couldn't look at what remained of it. It caused me too much distress. But there was a hollow, which we were approaching, with a few small trees growing within it. I knew this hollow. It was a place where people could feel the peace of the Earth. I felt it as one of the sacred places. And I looked down into it, and with the light of the stars, I noticed movement. There were two other children, and they looked up at us, at first with uncertainty, but then with happiness.

As I started to clamber down, I saw that it was not only the two children. There was someone else with them, someone lying very still, someone bigger than them. I did not even know if this third person was alive. The children were holding a pad, from the leaves of plants, against this person's shoulder. Yes, it was an adult. They were trying to reduce the bleeding. The person seemed to stir a little, as we came down into the hollow, to join them, but the girl who had led me, put her hands to her mouth, urgently, for us to be quiet.

At first, I could not see clearly the adult who was lying there, being attended by the children. But as I came closer, I could notice long brown hair – flowing hair that was somehow, very familiar. And I started to hope, against hope. Could it be? I had to see. I motioned myself downwards and crouched, so I had a clear view. And then, my view of this person became more distinct. It was a woman, and not just any woman. This woman was breathing, but her breathing was shallow. I could tell that she was in a bad way, desperately needing medical help, and soon. But she was alive. And I felt such joy. It was Sarah. It was Sarah!!

ESCAPING DANGER

We had to do it very carefully, to protect her shoulder as much as we could, and I lifted her up to carry her, and the children helped me, and showed me the best route to go, so we could reach my vehicle. Sarah needed to see a Doctor, and get treatment urgently. Her body was limp and pale in the moonlight, and I sensed that she had lost a lot of blood. Each step we trod took us away from those soldiers. The children were scurrying along next to us. This was such a miracle. I do not know where I found the strength to carry her all that distance, but I did, and I did not falter once. I was so glad to see Sarah, and feel her in my arms. I thought she was dead, but I knew that her ordeal was not over yet. She was unconscious and I could feel that she was getting weaker. Her body was so listless, that I started to worry. Surely, I would not lose her now.

We got to the car, and the children nursed Sarah in the back seat while I prepared to drive. I now understood why the girl wanted me to come, and why she had been so insistent; she wanted me to help Sarah.

My eyes were adjusted to the dark, so when I started the car, I kept the lights off and went forward steadily. I knew the land. But I still needed to be careful. There were shouts from the soldiers. They must have heard something, and they were spraying lights around the countryside. But we were at the back of the hill, where their lights could not reach. When I came out from behind the hill, I quickly went behind the cover of the trees. They directed lights in arcs around the area to try to find us, but they didn't manage. There were two gun shots, and I don't know how close they were to us, but I kept driving, and did not look back. Only when the main area of the Centre buildings was completely out of sight, did I turn on our lights, and then I moved quickly, to locate the track going out of the property, to the village where we had to go.

The children directed me to a large hut near the centre of the village. One of them went running, and soon there were people coming out. One man pushed forward and told me that he was a Doctor, and there were some other people with him, to assist him. I went with them into the hut. They had animated voices, and they lay Sarah down. For a long time, they were working with her, extracting the bullet from her shoulder, dressing the wound, giving her fluids intravenously. Meanwhile, I sat there in the room, watching, and waiting.

At last, the doctor came over to me, and placed his arm on my shoulder.

'We must watch her,' he told me. 'She will stay here.' And I knew that if she was staying here, then I would stay too, and would watch over her, for as long as it took.

STORIES TO TELL

For the next days, I remained in the room. For long hours, I sat next to her, holding her hand, and praying for her. The Doctor and other nursing staff, monitored her progress, and supported her as well as they could. She looked very peaceful lying there, but I was longing for her to open her eyes.

They made up a bed for me next to her, and I must have slept a long time too. Whatever was going on in the outside world, I was quite oblivious to it. I only wanted to be with Sarah.

At last, she did open her eyes, and looked at me, and gave a small smile. She seemed quite weak. I wanted to hug her and speak with her, but instead, all I could do was to squeeze her hand. The Doctor told me, that she must not over-exert herself, until she was much stronger, and able to sit up, and eat and drink by herself. So, I had to wait for that.

No one else was allowed into the room with us except for the medical staff, but their attention to Sarah's needs was exemplary. They were very kind. When I asked if I could do anything, or how things were going outside, they just reassured me, and encouraged me to be quiet, and to stay with Sarah, while she recovered.

Finally, the Doctor gave permission for us to talk. By now, Sarah was much brighter, and even able to sit up, with some assistance. I could give her a gentle hug now, but I had to take care, not to aggravate her wound.

For a while, we did not say very much, but then I suggested that we needed to share about what happened to us. It wasn't easy. Sarah began to get upset, even thinking about it. But we had to talk. I told my side first, and then I waited for her. She asked me to hold her hand and keep myself still, until she could say it all. She could only tell me, bit by bit, and I did not interrupt, except sometimes, to get her to repeat some detail, or understand better what she meant, but gradually I was able to piece together what she had experienced.

This is how her story came together.

'The soldiers had come in the early afternoon; they rounded us up together and took all our communication equipment. We told them to leave, and asserted that they had no right to be here, until the following morning, but the soldiers ignored us. What they wanted, was to make a broadcast of Simon, willingly handing over the lease of the land to the Military, and showing agreement, that they could mine the uranium. They were looking for some publicity that would give validity to what they were doing. Simon was given a script on the monitor that he could recite. This would express his praise for the Military government as he handed back the lease. Of course, Simon refused to do it, and we all refused.

'The Officer speaking there offered some inducements, and told us, about another piece of land that we could have to rebuild the Project – land that would not set up conflict, with the rights of the government, to mine a valuable resource. The Government was willing to give funds to help with that.

'Simon replied that the land where we were standing, was the place that we chose for the Project, and that he had been given every assurance by the previous government, that we would be able to stay on this land and have use of the land indefinitely. He showed the military Officer the contract he had signed, and pointed out the relevant clauses, so that the Officer would be in no doubt as to the legality of our being here. The officer was not impressed.

'He tried to extend the offer he had made, including, that all the people sent out of the country could return if we left and went to that other land. He even offered a permanent right of occupancy for that land, which we could sign, and which the Government would countersign. But Simon would not agree, and none of the rest of us wanted to say 'yes' either. We all stood together, intransigent.

'The Officer pleaded with us, citing our welfare, and that what he was proposing, was a way out, where both sides could have what they wanted. We discussed this, and we were shown on the map, the location of this other land. However, it did not feel right, for any of us. This was the place where we needed to base our work, not there. There was no other place that would do. The officer became frustrated and started shouting at us, until after some time, he was withdrawn, and another officer was summoned in his place.

'This second officer was much more threatening. He made it clear to us, that if we did not do the broadcast and agree to all their demands, then all the property would be burnt down, and we would each be imprisoned in isolation, until we were old and people had forgotten about us. He stared at Simon, but he did not budge.'

Sarah started to cry at this point. She told me that she felt proud of her father; he was so strong, and these military men were extremely cruel. Then she continued.

'They hit him, and then assaulted and hit Kurt until he was bleeding, and they were going to hit Julia. But Simon shouted out to stop them. Simon could not accept violence, and so he indicated that he would consider what was being offered, but insisted that he must speak with the leader of the Military Junta in person. The second officer informed us that he was already on his way.

'This was strategy on Simon's part, to buy a little time. We could talk a little, while guns remained trained on us. He communicated to us, that in his opinion, unless we did as they asked, then we would be killed, and we might be killed anyway. Having gone this far, there would be no other option for them. We all sensed that Simon was right about this, and Simon put to us the question, whether we wanted him to make the broadcast or not. We were unanimous in our opposition to it. Consequently, Simon suggested, that while he spoke with the leader of the Junta, we needed to slowly move apart from each other to give ourselves a chance, and at his signal, we must run, and try to make an escape.

'He put to us, with tears in his eyes, that we might not all make it, but it was our only chance. I sensed that my father was sacrificing himself, and there was nothing I could do about it. We shared a beautiful group hug, and I felt such a lot of love for all of them. We knew that this could be the last time that we were together.

'When the Military Leader arrived, Simon started arguing with him, telling him how despicable his actions were, making it clear how wrong he was, to be doing what he was doing. Simon blasted him, with his own opinion about how miserable he was making the country. While Simon spoke, we used this as our opportunity to spread out. But Kurt and Julia didn't go far; they stood together, not too far from Simon. With them doing this, I hesitated, but decided to follow my father's direction, and so I edged myself down the slope towards the Sanctuary door. And the staff members went further around the side of the building, past me, just slowly, trying not to attract attention.

'There reached a moment when Simon became very animated and waving his arms. He walked towards the jeep carrying the Military leader, shouting at him, and accusing him of all sorts of things. Suddenly, the Military leader became aware of what was going on around him, with the rest of us, and was looking at what was happening. He turned to the officers near him. Simon continued shouting at the Military leader, demanding that he answer what he was saying. It was getting very tense.

'Then, before the Military leader could react, Simon shouted "Run", and without turning around at all, I ran as fast as I could. Shots rang out and a couple of half screams. I did not look back, for I was so determined to reach the Sanctuary door, and I almost made it, I nearly did, when I felt a tremendous pain in my right shoulder, and I knew that I had been hit.

'In desperation, I struggled on those last few steps and collapsed just inside the entrance door, and pretended to be dead. I thought that was the best thing I could do.

'After that, I could hear hurried footsteps, a few further shots, and the soldiers dialoguing with their leader, while he barked out instructions. I tried to be as still as I could. But then I could hear them dowsing the building with petrol. They were going to burn it, and I thought I was going to be burnt alive. They put some petrol on me too.

'But then, I became aware of the children. They must have come in the back way. They told me to be quiet and pulled me backwards. One of them was leading. And they tried to carry me. It was hard for them, and very painful for me. I tried to stand up with them and managed to stagger out the back door. The soldiers mustn't have noticed, and by the time we got out, the Sanctuary was already burning. So then, we went a bit further, until we came into the hollow. I remember falling then, and I felt very weak. That must have been as far as I could go. I have vague memories of someone pressing a pad into my shoulder, and some warmth in my back. But then, the next thing I saw, was your eyes here looking down at me.'

Now I could understand what she had gone through, and it was so good that we could speak with each other. Sarah was very anxious and concerned about her mother, and very upset about her father and Julia and Simon. But at least, we could comfort each other, and it gave me some hope now that I knew that Sarah was recovering and alive.

SOME SURPRISES

Later that day, we had a visitor, and the girl who had taken me from the hut, came in to see us. I asked for her name, and she told me that she was 'Shara'. It was an unusual name, and she told us that her parents were from different countries and it was her mother who had chosen her name. Her father had been the Doctor, who attended Sarah.

We were full of gratitude for Shara. She told us how she and her friends did not want the Community to close. They all loved the school, and Miss Sarah was their favourite teacher. They had walked from the village to be there and to watch. Shara said that they did not like the soldiers, and decided to stay hidden. When they saw Sarah falling from the gunshot, they thought that going through the Sanctuary to reach her, would be the best way. Shara had been looking around, and she saw me in the four-wheel drive, when I came, and after they got Sarah in the best position that they could, she had followed me. Shara knew from her father, what plants and herbs she could best use to help her teacher's wounds, and she told her friends to press the pad so the bleeding might slow.

As I listened to Shara, I felt some joy growing in my heart. There was something, very, very familiar about her. Shara was quite remarkable, and I kept on being drawn to look in her eyes, but there was another name that kept coming into my consciousness. The name I could hear was 'Astoris'. This was an even stranger name, and I didn't know where this came from, but as I focussed on this name, I could feel a wonderful peace inside. Did Shara have another name – 'Astoris'? There was something about this that reassured me, and gave an important answer to a question, which I had never quite asked.

Being in the room, with the three of us together, this gave me another sign of hope, and I began to feel that maybe, just maybe, there was a way forward, out of this.

Later that day, my friend Tomas, from the outskirts of the village came to see us. He was glad that we were finally able to meet with him. He was a foreigner, like us, but because he lived and worked in the village, even though he had also helped us in the Community, he had been exempt from being expelled from the country, when the Military ordered it.

It gave me joy to see Tomas, and he seemed happy as well. He asked if we had heard the news, and I told him that we had not. Tomas's face lit up, and he told me to sit down, for I would be amazed. I sat at the edge of the bed, next to Sarah, and we eagerly awaited what he would say. Tomas began to tell us.

The videos and the pictures from the Centre burning and the bodies of Simon, Julia and Kurt, had gone viral on the Internet, and they had prompted outrage, both internationally, and locally. There had been riots on the streets of the Capital, and the military had not been able to contain it anymore. The burning of the Community had been a catalyst where the people resolved that they just were not going to be beaten down anymore. A statue of the Military leader had been brought down, and government buildings attacked. The Military came in heavily, and used tear gas and batons, but the riots did not stop. In fact, they grew in intensity, and demands were made for those arrested to be released. Orders were made for the soldiers to shoot upon the demonstrators, but there was hesitation, and although there were some soldiers that fired, many did not. And suddenly, the authority of the Military began to break down. It all happened quickly, and there was a counter coup. A group of generals came together to dispose of the Regime that had done so much damage, and the leader was arrested.

There was rejoicing in the streets, and the Generals announced that the old President would be brought back to lead the country in place of the Military, and the President had put forward a date, 18 months' from now, for there to be elections. Everyone was glad about it, for we knew that the old President would keep his word.

Tomas told us that the media had been speculating where Sarah and I would be, and indeed, if we were still alive. Nobody had known where to find us, and the people from the village had been all sworn to secrecy about us. There had been much discussion and mourning about the burning of the Community. Nobody though, except officials, had been in there. Tomas made clear to us, that as the only members of the core group of the Community, that remained, we would have to decide what to do.

Sarah and I looked at each other, and there were tears in our eyes. We had some decisions to make, some very important decisions.

BUILDING THE FUTURE

Over the next days, many developments took place. We sent out a news release to the media to tell of Sarah's wounds and recovery, and to request privacy while she found her strength again. In response to that, there were massive quantities of correspondence with well-wishers, offering their support and encouragement. There was far too much for us to answer, so we sent a second statement to the media, expressing our gratitude. We were so glad to have our own space in the village, away from the wider world for a while.

The charred bodies of Simon, Julia and Kurt and the three members of staff, were excavated from the ashes and remains of the Sanctuary and Conference Centre. The bodies were taken away for post mortems so they could be formally identified. Thankfully, we were very glad, to be spared the ordeal of having to see their remains, ourselves.

News came that the old President was releasing all prisoners that had been detained for political reasons, during the reign of the Military regime. The morning that this announcement was made, there was a call on my Mobile, and it was Eve. She was safe. Eve was safe. Sarah cried with joy, and arrangements were made so that she could come and join us.

There were many questions being asked in the media, about whether the New Earth project would continue, and resurrect itself in some form. There was an almost overwhelming desire, from people, all over the world, for us to build it again. But people understood the degree of loss we had suffered, too. It was the question, which was silently unspoken between us.

We even had an email from the old president, offering his condolences, and an official apology for all that had happened. He communicated that if we should decide to restore the Centre, then his Government would give us a substantial grant to help with our costs, as a form of compensation. It felt right, and we were touched by his kindness.

The day arrived when we had to make a move. Sarah was well enough now to travel a short distance in our vehicle, so we went with Eve, and with Shara and Tomas, on the track into the property of our beloved Community. It brought up a lot of emotion, as we approached the hill, next to where the buildings had previously stood. Then we got out, and walked around to survey what was there. Looking at the main buildings, there was very little left of them. All that remained was stone and iron pieces, scattered amongst ashes and rubble. When we could recall the majesty of the buildings that had stood here, it vibrated through us, as an intense loss. How could we ever restore that?

When I gazed towards the sites where the school had been, and the Renewable Energy Centre, the kitchen and dining areas – they were all decimated – and nearly the accommodation blocks were gone too. Just a couple of buildings on the edges of the Community, further away, remained.

But not all was lost. The huge expanse of the vegetable gardens and orchards were largely untouched. The walls around them were a little bit of fire damaged, but thankfully, the gardens themselves had been spared. And the tree planting Nurseries, they were also still intact. I felt relief at that. And the forest restoration – the beautiful expanse of growing trees, in front of us – they were still there.

We all had our own quiet reflections about it all. I considered about the skill and capacities of Simon, Kurt and Julia. How would we be able to replace them? Thoughts swayed backwards and forwards through my mind.

We gathered in our group. And there was one remarkable sight, that I had overlooked. The two Guardian trees – the old one that had only a few leaves now, and the younger one that was tall, delicate and beautiful with its crusty bark – they stood where they had always been. The bark on their trunks were slightly charred, but they were alive. It had to be a sign.

The five of us stood, and held hands, right next to the trees, where our original group had stood, many times before, and the energy between us was hot and electric. Sarah started to hum – as Julia had taught her – and we all joined in. And we summoned the Earth Spirit to join us. There was a sudden burst of birdsong, and we knew then, that the Earth Spirit was present.

What would we do? What was our way forward? We stood there together for a long time, and eventually opened our eyes and looked at one another. This was a beautiful place. Even with all the destruction, I still felt that I belonged here. Eve glanced upwards, and we all looked at the clouds in the sky. There was movement, with some of the clouds, and they created a pattern that looked like three figures, overlooking what we were doing. And it appeared just then, and we all had the same thought, that Simon, Kurt and Julia, were looking down at us, and blessing what we were doing.

Shara stared up at me with her big searching eyes. 'We have to rebuild,' she implored me. And I studied the expressions in the eyes of the others. Between us, we could hold the energy for some of the areas of the Project – Eve and Sarah with the School, Sarah with the Sanctuary; I could do some administration, and Tomas could help us with the forestry work. Shara would grow into her role, for sure. And we had so many supporters, and workers that would be willing to return. It was all new, and we were a new group. Could we do it? We would need some more expertise in our team, and lots of help. It would be a completely fresh phase of our Community, and may not be a replica of what we had before.

'Shall we do it? I asked everyone, and waited for everyone to respond.

Sarah's eyes lit up. She answered 'yes,' and her mother Eve joyfully added, 'I say "yes" too.' And then we all agreed and we all said 'yes,' and we hugged each other. We gazed around at the vast lands we had been given. The lands of our project were sacred, and they connected with other sacred regions around us. And those regions connected with nations and other countries, other lands and the seas, and the skies above. We lived on one Earth, and our world connected with other worlds, and underlying all these worlds was love, the love of 'being'. It was all joyful and all sacred.

We would begin and build on what had been before. We would put all our efforts into co-creating and helping to re-establish our Community, and manifest it anew. Our aim, as it had been, would be for our work to exist as a beacon and pathway, for peace and harmony, and the unfolding of the New Earth.

We could never be sure if our efforts were going to be successful – not yet anyway – for we lived in a volatile world, where many elements of human existence opposed what we were doing, and occupied themselves with more selfish alternatives. Our way was not to fight these people, but to shine our light, to expose what these other forces were really doing, and give space for people then to make their own choices. Given the chance, we knew that living in the consciousness of the New Earth was what people truly wanted, and this is what people would choose when their Spirit awakened. Our work was to help people find their Spirit.

It felt beautiful to be together as our group, even with the loss of our precious friends that had now passed on, and the destruction of the fantastic buildings that we had constructed, and had been so much loved and used. But these losses were not enough to entice us to give up. There was no way. Our commitment was steadfast. We felt strong. There could only be one positive way forward, for us to act upon, and that was to say 'Yes'. So then, I lifted my arms up, and the others joined me. And we shouted 'yes' together.

For a few moments, we could celebrate, and rejoice with the opportunities we were being given. And then the work would begin.

About the Author

Paul Williamson was born and brought up in Australia, spending time in Bathurst, Broken Hill and Sydney. From an early age, he was very attracted to alternative lifestyles, religion, and the need to protect our environment. In his twenties, Paul left Australia, travelled through Europe, and spent four and a half years living at NewBold House, within the Findhorn Foundation, in Scotland. In 1988, Paul trained in Past Life Therapy and Hypnotherapy, and has since studied with Dr Roger Woolger and the Newton Institute. Presently, Paul travels between the UK and Australia with his work. Paul is very concerned about our Earth, and the need for all that is precious in our beautiful world to be nurtured and protected for future generations. It has been this concern and his work with regression therapy that have formed the foundation for the writing of this book. This is Paul's seventh published book. Paul can be contacted via his website, www.soulhypnotherapy.com.

Also by the Author

Healing Journeys (Capall Bann Publishing)

Atlantis – The Dark Continent (co-authored with Lynda Braithwaite, Capall Bann Publishing))

Soul Pathways (Capall Bann Publishing)

A Seekers Guide to Past Lives (Capall Bann Publishing)

Marjorie (Inner Light Publishing)

Ilsa – Ancient Celtic Leader (Balboa Press)

Thoughts

Thoughts

Thoughts

Thoughts

Thoughts

Thoughts

Thoughts

Thoughts

Thoughts

Thoughts

Thoughts